Water Graves

New World Studies
Marlene L. Daut, Editor
Frank Moya Pons and
Sandra Pouchet Paquet,
Associate Editors

Water Graves

The Art of the Unritual in the Greater Caribbean

Valérie Loichot

University of Virginia Press
Charlottesville and London

University of Virginia Press

Printed in the United States of America on acid-free paper

First published 2020

9 8 7 6 5 4 3 2 1

Library of Congress Cataloging-in-Publication Data
Names: Loichot, Valérie, 1968– author.
Title: Water graves : the art of the unritual in the greater Caribbean / Valérie Loichot.
Description: Charlottesville : University of Virginia Press, 2020. | Includes bibliographical references and index.
Identifiers: LCCN 2019030994 (print) | LCCN 2019030995 (ebook) | ISBN 9780813943787 (hardcover) | ISBN 9780813943794 (paperback) | ISBN 9780813943800 (epub)
Subjects: LCSH: Caribbean literature—21st century—History and criticism. | Art, Caribbean—21st century. | Victims in literature. | Funeral rites and ceremonies in literature. | Mourning customs in literature.
Classification: LCC PN849.C3 L67 2020 (print) | LCC PN849.C3 (ebook) | DDC 809.8/9729—dc23
LC record available at https://lccn.loc.gov/2019030994
LC ebook record available at https://lccn.loc.gov/2019030995

Cover art: Jason deCaires Taylor, *Silent Evolution*, underwater sculpture, MUSA, Cancun Underwater Museum, Mexico, installation date 2009 (© Jason deCaires Taylor; all rights reserved, DACS/ARS 2019); school of fish underwater (Shutterstock/littlesam)

Contents

Acknowledgments

THIS BOOK is the convergence of transnational flows, breaking waves, and thought gyres; of currents regular, unplanned, horizontal, downwelling, and upwelling; of surfs carrying debris, plankton, or memory; of surface tides and unfathomable undercurrents that shall remain unseen. It is the encounter of the minds and acts of colleagues, students, friends, and family members. Those whom my memory fails to recall at this moment are nonetheless crucial. Édouard Glissant would have called those who remain unnamed "neutral relays": agents who act below the radar of the spectacular, who act in the continuous. I would like to thank my fellow *soukougnans* in work and spirit: Dominique Aurélia, Jacqueline Couti, Anny-Dominique Curtius, Gladys Francis, Ananya Jahanara Kabir, Fabienne Kanor, LénaBlou, and Myriam Moïse. Yes, they can fly. My Emory colleagues energized me and enriched me from their multiple disciplines: Allison Adams, Kadji Amin, Carol Anderson, Deepika Bahri, Munia Bhaumik, Stefan Boettcher, Jericho Brown, Justin Burton, Vincent Bruyère, Chad Córdova, Catherine Dana, Susan Gagliardi, Robert Goddard, Elizabeth Goodstein, Walter Kalaidjian, Melanie Kowalski, Elissa Marder, Sarah McKee, Sean Meighoo, Alexander Mendes, Claire Nouvet, José Quiroga, Deboleena Roy, Liv Stutz, Ben Reiss, Donna Troka, Subha Xavier, Nathan Suhr-Sytsma, Kimberly Wallace Sanders, Dianne M. Stewart, Allen Tullos, Deborah Elise White, Cynthia Willett, and Michelle Wright, are among many. Fellow researchers, some of them dear friends, enriched this projects with ideas, insights, and book recommendations: My thanks to Cécile Accilien, Axel Arthéron, Hugues Azérad, André Benhaïm, Géraldine Banaré, Michelle Bloom, Yarimar Bonilla, Keith Cartwright, Tom Conley, Huey Copeland, Kara Malika Daniels, Juliette Eloi-Blaise, Emmanuel Bruno Jean-François, Annalee Davis, Babacar Mbaye Diop, John Drabinski, Brahim el Gabli, Fanny Glissant, Sylvie Glissant, Virginie Greene, Yanique Hume, Kipton Jensen, Deborah

Jenson, Nicholas R. Jones, Eileen Julien, Lawrence Kritzman, Benaouda Lebdai, Alexandre Leupin, John Lowe, Anne Garland Mahler, Judith Misrahi-Barak, Emma Monroy, F. Nick Nesbitt, Manuel Norvat, Oana Panaïté, Adelaide Russo, Harilaos Stecopoulos, Wallis Tinnie, and Liran Razinsky. To my partner in laughter, travels, and words, Naïma Hachad, and to my rock in friendship, Carolette Norwood.

We critics would be naught but empty shells without artists, poets, fiction writers, and curators. They give meaning to our work. Giscard Bouchotte, Edwidge Danticat, Patricia Donatien, Édouard Duval Carrié, Jean-Joseph Céleur, Patrick Chamoiseau, Eugène Ebodé, Gwladys Gambie, Epaul Julien, Ricardo Ozier-Lafontaine, Atadja Lewa, Pascale Monnin, M. NourbeSe Philip, Vanessa Selk, Jil Servant, Candy Tate, Henri Tauliaut, Jason deCaires Taylor, Dinizulu Gene Tinnie, Carol Thompson, Natasha Trethewey, Eric Waters, Tiphanie Yanique, Frantz Zéphirin have offered conversations and insights either throughout the years or at one single yet crucial point. Martinican artist Victor Anicet holds an esteemed place in my heart. Édouard Glissant's teachings in the 1990s continue to live with me. The galleries and artistic spaces that welcomed me made this book more complete: in Haiti, the Atis Rezistans of the Grand Rue in Port-au-Prince, the metal artists of Croix-des-Bouquets, and the Galerie Monnin; in Martinique, the Fondation Clément, the Habitation Saint-Etienne and the Anse Caffard Memorial; in Guadeloupe, the Mémorial ACTe; in the United States, the High Museum of Art in Atlanta; the NSU Art Museum in Fort Lauderdale; the Wolfsonian-FIU and the Little Haiti Cultural Center in Miami; the Civil Rights Memorial in Montgomery, Alabama; and the Whitney Plantation on River Road, Louisiana. I am grateful to the Jack Shainman Gallery, the Sikkema Jenkins & Co. Gallery with the Collection of Marc and Lisa Mills; the Artists Rights Society (ARS); the NSU Art Museum; the High Museum; and Wesleyan University Press, who provided reproduction rights. With special thanks to archivists and collection managers Gabriela Gil, Laurie Kind, Monica Truong for their patience.

The undergraduate and doctoral students I taught while the book was in progress brought me invaluable feedback. Their backgrounds in literature, religion, philosophy, African American studies, women, gender, and sexuality studies, and environmental studies, among other fields, made this book interdisciplinarily rich. I particularly thank the members of the graduate seminars Water Graves I and Water Graves II, as well as Amanda Anderson, Franck Andrianarivo Rakotobe, Dr. Bronwyn Averett, Jane Battison, Brenton Boyd, Hugo Bujon, Natalie Catasús, Ben Davis, Rubén

Díaz Vásquez, Marcelitte Failla, Joseph Fritsch, Hannah Griggs, Lauren Highsmith, Tiara J., Haylee Harrell, Taryn Jordan, Yazan Kamalulddin, Dr. Souad Kherbi, Hannah Hjerpe-Shroeder, Dr. Ania Kowalik, Dr. Stephanie Iasiello, Stephanie Larson, Ra'Niqua Lee, Mike Lehman, Judith Levy, Francisco Lopez, Dr. Guirdex Massé, Alexis Mayfield, Christopher Moller, Brendan Moore, Dr. Nicole Morris, Manuela Ossa, Suzanne Persard, Gloria Pham, Dr. Nicolas Rémy, Alicia Rodriguez, Carlie Rodriguez, Dr. Dominick Rolle, Dr. Erika Serrato, Dr. Angelica So, Dr. Eric Solomon, Dr. Marlo Starr, Dr. Marion Tricoire, Ninon Vessier, and Dr. Blair Watson.

I was lucky to deliver portions of the manuscript in progress as lectures at many venues. I am particularly grateful to audiences at, in chronological order: the Center for Latin American and Caribbean Studies and the Department of French of Italian at Indiana University, Bloomington; the Department of Romance Languages at SUNY, Binghamton; the Department of French Studies at Louisiana State University; Harvard University's Department of Romance Languages and Literatures; the Twentieth/Twenty-First French and Francophone Studies International Colloquium; Emory's Psychoanalytic Studies Program; Emory's Global and Postcolonial Studies Program; the Forty-First Caribbean Studies Association Conference in Port-au-Prince, Haiti; the "Islands and Identities: Memory and Trauma in Comparative Perspectives" conference and workshop at Georgia State University and L'Institut des Amériques; the "Aesthetic Afterlives: Memory, Transfiguration and the Arts" conference presented by the Department of Comparative Literature at Princeton University; the Department of French and Italian at Princeton University; the Mémorial ACTe in Guadeloupe; the international colloquium "Edouard Glissant: L'Eclat et l'obscur" at the Université des Antilles, Martinique, co-organized by Louisiana State University; the Tout-Monde Festival in Miami, cosponsored by Florida Atlantic University and the Cultural Services of the French Embassy in the United States; and the Department of Romance Languages at the University of North Carolina at Chapel Hill.

I am grateful for the institutional support that Emory University has provided throughout the years. Dean of the College of Arts and Sciences Michael Elliott, Senior Associate Dean for Research Ronald Calabrese, Provost Dwight McBride, and Senior Associate Dean of the Faculty Carla Freeman, a fellow Caribbeanist, provided unflinching support. Uninterrupted writing on the manuscript was made possible by a University Research Committee (URC) grant. Emory enhanced the writing and publishing of *Water Graves* with a Scholarly Writing and Publishing Fund grant (Center for Faculty Development and Excellence) and a Scholarly

Writing Book Publishing Subvention (Emory College of Arts and Sciences and Laney Graduate School). In the Department of French and Italian, I was lucky to get the constant support of Leslie Church Hartness, who helped with daily logistical details, and of Amandine Ballart, who provided invaluable technical and brain support in the last stages of editing. Drs. Cynthia Blakeley and Eric Solomon made this manuscript more concise and eloquent thanks to their editing skills. My fabulous research assistants, Dr. Caroline Schwenz, Dr. Roselyne Gérazime, and Dr. Charly Verstraet, helped identify and locate crucial sources for the book. Alicia Rodríguez, who served as research assistant from book contract to book production, was creative, persistent, precise, and savvy in getting the book ready for copy editing, in contacting artists and galleries in French, English, and Spanish, in problem-solving, and in providing invaluable digital help for the illustrations.

An earlier segment of chapter 1 was published in *Callaloo* 36, no. 4, and another (in French) in *Contemporary French and Francophone Studies: Sites* 20, no. 4. I thank the Johns Hopkins University Press and *Contemporary French and Francophone Studies* for granting permission to reuse. Everyone at University of Virginia Press has been supportive, enthusiastic, and responsive. I thank particularly Eric Brandt, Helen Chandler, Morgan Myers, Ellen Satrom, freelance copy editor Emily Shelton, and the two anonymous reviewers whose advice made the book immensely better. New World Studies series editor J. Michael Dash passed as I was working on final revisions. He will remain an inspiration, as a critic and as a man, for me and for generations of Glissantian scholars.

To my father, Roger, whose body is gone but whose love for literature and music endures. To my mother, Françoise, who shows me love and courage. To my brother, David, for the help and care. To my cousin-aunt, Jeannette, and her unflinching passion for books and forests. To my daughter, Zoë, who brightens my days with musical theater tunes and swoons. To my son, Nathan, who astonishes my ear with piano riffs, syncopations, and silly improv. To Peter, my companion in life, who makes everything possible. May the ones with unmarked graves, of water and soil—in my family and in all families—find solace.

Water Graves

Introduction

A Twenty-First-Century Requiem

> There's no marker. We don't have the bones. We don't have the tombstones.
>
> —M. NourbeSe Philip, *Zong!*

> The dead do not die. They haunt the living. Both free and unfree, the undead still speak in the present landscape of terror and ruin. The dogs of hurricane Katrina, citizens turned refugees in the United States; prisoners . . . the rationales and rituals of terror proliferate. But perhaps we need to think more deeply about the dying and the dead.
>
> —Colin Dayan, *The Law Is a White Dog*

WATER DEATHS matter. *Water Graves* considers representations of lost lives in poetry, mixed-media art, and underwater sculptures produced since 2005. The book investigates how writers and artists create ways of mourning and remembering the dead when survivors are foreclosed from their basic human right of providing rituals. Its main zone of investigation is the Greater Caribbean, which includes parts of the Atlantic, the Caribbean Sea, and the Gulf of Mexico, waters that constitute both early *and* contemporary sites of loss for the enslaved, the migrant, the refugee, the destitute. Geographically scattered in coastal or below-sea-level Haiti, Martinique, Cancun, Florida, Louisiana, Martinique, Mississippi, Georgia, and Tobago, the artists and poets featured in *Water Graves* comprise an archipelago connected by a history of the slave trade and aquatic vulnerability. Above all, their art and literature provide, I argue, rituals to the desecrated drowned in the absence of, or in complement to, official wakes and memorials. Artists and poets fight the unritual, not in a vacuum from sacred practices and memorials, but in their prolongation. In addition to figuring death by drowning in the aftermath of slavery and natural and human-made catastrophes, their creations serve as memorials, dirges, tombstones, and even material supports for the regrowth of life underwater.

or "below water").[9] For Bachelard, "water, the substance of life, is also the substance of death for ambivalent reverie" (*Water and Dreams,* 72). The sea is a necessity, a sustainable resource for fishing communities, but also a threat in the form of rogue waves and floods. As performance and religious scholar Yanique Hume poetically writes, the sea "has been the unifying metaphor utilized to explore the passage of African religious grammars across the Americas" ("Death and the Construction of Social Space," 133). Water links the historically related events of the Middle Passage and Katrina to the ecological and social fragility of our twenty-first century. In *When the Levees Broke,* film director Spike Lee combines documentary footage from the Great Mississippi Flood of 1927, the Katrina toxic waters, precarious housing projects, and bird's-eye shots and maps of the vulnerable Gulf landscape. The predominantly African American survivors interviewed in Lee's film explicitly link contemporary racism with a past of slavery, as if the Mississippi and Gulf waters continued the work of Atlantic currents of the *Maafa* under a connected history of oppression through enslavement, capitalism, and socioeconomic and environmental racism.[10] This is what literary critic Christina Sharpe calls "the weather," where "antiblackness is pervasive as climate" (*Monstrous Intimacies,* 106), or what geographer Kathryn Yussof terms "black anthropocenes," an "inhuman proximity organized by historical geographies of extraction," which are "predicated on the presumed absorbent qualities of black and brown bodies to take up the body burdens of exposures to toxicities and to buffer the violence of the earth" (*A Billion Black Anthropocenes,* xii).

In water, the abject and the sacred sharply intersect. Grotesque are the deformed, grimacing, swollen, and discolored bodies resurfacing or washed up on shores. Gloomy are the bodies forever lost to the sea abyss or shark teeth: "Along the dreadful way, 1.8 million of them died, their bodies cast overboard to the sharks that followed the ship" (Rediker 2007, 5). Severe is the pain of the people mourning bodies of lost ones that cannot be retrieved, dug up, and given funerary rites such as interments, incineration, or embalming. But especially abject is the gesture, multiplied by millions, of throwing bodies overboard or the neglect of populations vulnerable to floods or mass exiles.

At the same time, religions and rites prevalent in the diasporic New World privilege water as a sacred site, a shared place between the unborn and the departed, a necessary vessel for the dead to travel safely to another shore, and for the living to send their beloved departed *home.* Our aesthetic corpus features recognizable religions such as Vaudou, Catholicism, or *Kongo* that stem from spontaneous relations between humans and nature through a shared vulnerability. All incorporate water as a sacred substance and site. The *Dikenga,* or Kongo cosmogram, omnipresent in the African diasporic Americas, also generously dwells in the poetry and arts featured in this book, such as Radcliffe Bailey's mixed-media creations and Philip's *Zong!*[11] The figure of the crossroads, with its vertical and horizontal axis, constitutes the most basic form of the *Dikenga* in the Americas. The horizontal axis or line of *kalunga* represents "a permeable boundary between the land of the living and that of the spirits" (Fennell, "Kongo," 230) or "the watery boundary dividing the worlds of the living and the dead in Kongo cosmology" (Stewart "Kumina," 611). The vertical axis as well as the central and external ellipses of the cosmogram add a cyclical movement, indicating that the world above and below the *kalunga* can communicate. As archeologist Christopher C. Fennell writes, "A principal metaphor for the *kalunga* line is the reflective surface of a body of water, showing a mirror world of the dead and spirits in relation to the realm of the living" ("Kumbina," 611). What is below the line, below water, or *anba dlo,* in the lingua of Haitian Vaudou ceremonies, is a prominent site in Beyoncé's visual album *Lemonade* and, really, in the production of all the artists featured in *Water Graves,* including Édouard Glissant, Edwidge Danticat, Radcliffe Bailey, Epaul Julien, Patricia Donatien, Jason deCaires Taylor, Édouard Duval Carrié, and Frantz Zéphirin, to name a few.

Water sites, and water sacred, unite the Greater Caribbean's continental shores, islands, and islets under analysis in *Water Graves.* I focus on the creolized zone of the Americas—namely, the greater and lesser Antilles—but also on New Orleans, which Louisiana poet Mona Lisa Saloy calls the "Caribbean North."[12] To this Caribbean North, we can add Florida, the US Gulf Coast, and the Sea Islands.[13] The Francophone and Anglophone Caribbean and US Gulf South are my primary foci. However, it is my hope that *Water Graves* will provide food for thought for scholars of Cuba, Puerto Rico, the Dominican Republic, and the Caribbean shores of Mexico, Venezuela, and Columbia, to continue the reflection on seas overcrowded by the many water deaths of enslaved Africans, European mariners, and Indigenous peoples along these shores.[14]

The creolized zones under analysis share a specific type of relationship to death and the sacred, and particularly, to cemeteries. To quote Glissant in *Philosophie de la Relation:* "The cemeteries of countries and cities of creolization, and, generally, of powerful hurricanes—Guadeloupe, Martinique, Haiti, New Orleans, Cartagena—grow in turn into glittering small towns like white beaches, whose avenues open onto fleeting illuminations rather than onto the mute space of a dull hereafter" (145).

The chapters that follow will explore fully the relation between creolization, hurricanes, and the glitter of death, but my hunch is that they are all marked by vulnerability: the vulnerability of humanity in the wake of slavery and colonization, the vulnerability of vernacular languages, and the vulnerability of exhausted land and ocean. In *Create Dangerously,* Danticat shares the common Haitian maxim "Ayiti se te glise": Haiti is slippery land. Haiti has slippery soil because centuries of deforestation by French and American colonizers and occupants have removed the roots that hold the land in place, rendering it more vulnerable to mudslides, earthquakes, hurricanes, and floods, which in turn lead to hunger, precarious living, and epidemics.[15] On a planetary scale, climate change, which was propelled by the logic of conquest, colonization, slavery, and imperialism, is precipitating the number of watery deaths and water graves.[16] Instead of receding, the memory of the drowned victims of the middle passage resurface at an alarming rate with the mass drownings of exiles and refugees. Artists, poets, and critics, when memorializing events such as the aftermath of Katrina, are then inevitably recalling more ancient victims.

While *Water Graves* is anchored in the Greater Caribbean, I aim to raise awareness of prevalent and barbarous (sometimes legally so) acts of desecrating the dead across time and space, myth and history, while highlighting the iridescent and fleeting illuminations that poetry and art can appose to what I call "the unritual." Art in the face of the unritual is not a matter of absolution, victorious redemption, or putting the dead and the living at peace. Saidiya Hartman, at the end of her West African journey along the slave route, confesses: "I could not be persuaded, despite wanting to believe otherwise, that angry slaves could be put to rest. . . . I would have preferred to imagine them resting in peace. Yet I didn't have faith in the serenity of dead slaves or trust that our offering could bring an end to their sorrow. I envisioned the dead raging and dispirited, like us, waiting for a future when all the slave marks would be gone (*Lose Your Mother,* 204). The immense and deep state of turmoil that Hartman evokes and the state of unritual that I describe in the following section point to the irremediable damage inflicted on the victims and the survivors. Art and poetry cannot, en masse, offer a remedy, a reparation, a cure, a rite. Instead, volatile substances such as glitter, evoked by Glissant and used profusely by Bailey in his mixed-media creations (chapter 2), as well as signs of the sacred in Vaudou, might begin the work of countering the unritual.[17] I mean glitter not for its prettifying and festive use, but rather for its assortment of minuscule, shiny, reflective particles, for its propensity to disseminate, for its uncountable angles, for its multiplying refractions and reflections in the millions. Martinican writer Patrick Chamoiseau puts it poetically in his *Frères migrants*—a manifesto, an homage, and an ethical declaration to migrants. Beyond walls and fences, he hopes for the proliferation of "a hundred times a hundred million of fireflies!" ("cent fois cent millions de lucioles")—one to keep hope at everyone's reach, the others to ensure the vastness of this beauty against contrary forces" (*Frères migrants,* in Article 16).

Unritual

Unritual is the privation of ritual. I understand "ritual" as the manifestation, performance, and structuring of the sacred, whether connected to an organized religion or to ad hoc solemn beliefs.[18] Since rituals are practiced by all societies, they are understood as a defining mark of humanity. *Water Graves* is concerned with rituals or rites of passage, healing, and remembrance, specifically those of the kind that help the departed, the living, and the interaction thereof, to transition into an afterward or a hereafter.[19] These rituals of crossing are sorely needed in the aftermath of the massive rupture between living humans, ancestral land, and tutelary Gods, and the demolition of family and social structures made by the Middle Passage. As Hume explains, speaking of Jamaica, "The commemorative rites refashioned over time and space placed ritual action at the center of a psychosocial imperative to be free" ("Death and Performance," 131). Art historian and religion scholar of the African diaspora Kyrah Malika Daniels argues that ritual is "a process of orchestration—an ordering of time and space, and in each instance, a manifestation of aesthetics" ("Ritual," 400). The constitution of ritual through aesthetic expression is central to this book as well.

Unritual is a state more absolute even than desecration or defilement, since the latter imply the existence of a previous sacred state or object—a temple, a grave, a ceremonial. Unritual, the steering concept of *Water Graves,* is the obstruction of the sacred in the first place. Anthropological paleontologists mark the first burials as the threshold of humanity. For instance, in *Things Hidden Since the Foundation of the World,* philosopher René Girard proposes that the tomb "is the starting point of the constitutive displacements of culture. Quite a number of fine minds think that this is literally true on the level of human history as a whole; funerary rituals could well . . . amount to the first actions of a strictly cultural type"

(164).[20] Following Girard's logic, the stripping of rituals is a fundamental attempt to uncouple humans from their humanity.

Through the prefix "un," referring to absence or undoing, I consciously link *un*ritual paradigmatically with the word *un*dead.[21] The unritual and the undead dwell in a state of limbo between life and death, where those gone without appropriate rituals persist in dwelling among and haunting the living. Victims of the unritual are akin to *zonbi* figures roaming in the texts and works featured in *Water Graves.* I use the Kreyol spelling instead of the Americanized "zombie," since the Haitian spelling conserves the liminal figure's state of dehumanization, of deontologization produced by enslavement. The Haitian—and Caribbean—*zonbi* figure has a body, a shell, a carcass, stripped from her or his soul and being. While mechanically in movement, the *zonbi* exemplifies Orlando Patterson's social dead with a shell of the body and a dead self.[22] In short, the slave is a zonbi.[23] Historian Laurent Dubois convincingly contrasts this understanding with the Hollywood creation: "By making zombies into generic horror-film monsters, such representations obscured the fact that in Haitian Folklore, the *zonbi* is a powerful symbol with a specific, haunting point of reference. It is a person devoid of all agency, under the complete control of a master, that is, a slave" (*The Aftershocks,* 298). While sufferers of the unritual resemble zonbis in that both are undead, they are similar in a chiasmic way. Indeed, whereas the zonbis' bodies are living (animated, haunting) and their souls dead, the victims of the unritual are corporeally dead but with living (animated, haunting) souls.[24] Yet the zonbi may be the physical manifestation of a departed victim deprived of community rituals who "haunts Haiti as the most powerful emblem of apathy, anonymity, and loss" (Dayan, *Haiti,* 37). As anthropologist Melville Herskovitz observes, the zonbis' deaths were "not real but resulted from the manipulations of sorcerers who made them appear as dead, and then, when buried, removed them from their grave and sold them into servitude in some faraway land" (quoted in Dayan, 36). The unritual dead and the zonbi are thus sometimes parallel, sometimes merging, figures whose mistreatment by rites or religions act as a powerful mask for the historical harm inflicted upon them by enslavements.

The casualties of the unritual are Dayan's "dead [that] do not die," introduced in this book's epigraph. They are Jacques Derrida's remnants, which we must "ontologize" to make present "in the first place by identifying the bodily remains and by localizing the dead" (Dayan, *The Law,* 9). This act of localizing (in space, in language, in philosophy) is inseparable, for Derrida, from the act of mourning, as he explains and pleads: "One has to know . . . one has to know who is buried where—and it is necessary (to know—to make certain) that in what remains of him, he remains there. Let him stay there and move no more!" In the same vein, albeit with a slightly different solution, these casualties of the unritual are the ones who have disappeared with only a water tomb in Philip's "Notanda": "Does it mean that unlike being interred, once you're underwater, there is no retrieval . . . the gravestone or tombstone marks the spot of interment, whether of ashes or of the body. What marks the subaquatic death?" (*Zong!,* 201). Although poet, critic, and lawyer Philip copiously cites Derrida in the "Notanda" of her book *Zong!,* her answer to what the poet, critic, and archivist should do is a bit more self-confident. It is precisely in not telling that we will put the dead at rest: "The ration at the heart of *Zong!,* however, is simply the story of be-ing which cannot, but must, be told. Through not telling" (200). The language of Philip's "Notanda" is itself, through its fragmentation of vocabulary and grammatical units, words, and sentences, an act of not telling, all the while telling: an ungrammatical language all the while present.

For Hartman, the archive works a bit like Philip's sea. It is a tomb for the enslaved, a hallowed place that needs to not be disturbed yet demands a gesture from the critic, who will insufflate long-gone remembrance into the dead without aspiring to the impossible feat of resuscitating them, without even giving them a voice through the form of a narrative performance: "The archive is, in this case, a death sentence, a tomb, a display of the violated body, an inventory of property, a medical treatise on gonorrhea, a few lines about a whore's life, an asterisk in the grand narrative of history" ("Venus," 2). The ethical gesture of the critic "reopening the casket" involves what Hartman calls a "critical fabulation," "straining against the limits of the archive to write a cultural history of the captive, and, at the same time, enacting the impossibility of representing the lives of the captives precisely through the process of narration" ("Venus," 11). This need to complement archival documents with a narrative, a *fabula,* with fiction and imagination, must be coupled with an awareness of its own limit and lack of definitive value. This is perhaps why, in *Lose Your Mother,* Hartman *fabulates* not once but seven times the tortured death of a girl on a slave ship ironically called *Recovery* (136–48). The girl, "suspended from the feet to the slaver's mast," "appeared as a tortured virgin, a pregnant woman, a syphilitic tart, and a budding saint" (136). The critic's narrative performance refuses to stop on one image or another, refuses to elect either the sacred ("saint") or the profane ("tart"). It is precisely this oscillation or recognition of doubt and opacity that offers into our present, as Karla Holloway compellingly explores in *Passed On:* "The anticipation of death and dying figured into the experiences of black folk so consistently" that their "literature and film, [their] visual arts and music (from early era spirituals to latter-day rap), and [their] lamentation and [their] contemporary street-corner memorials consistently called-up a passed-on narrative" (6). The exploitation in life and discard in death of black subjects extends from the plantation to the Civil War to our twenty-first century. Harriet Tubman bears witness to the discarded dead black soldiers of the 54th Massachusetts Volunteer Infantry: "And when we came to get in the crops, it was dead men that we reaped" (Tubman, quoted in Brannon, "*The Negro Woman,*" 3). Jesmyn Ward, in her 2013 literary requiem *Men We Reaped,* gives Tubman's words a shocking contemporary resonance with her evocation of the violent and premature death of five black young men she knew: "A brutal list," Ward writes, "in its immediacy and relentlessness," and "a list that silences people" (7).

In such states of legalized or common unritual, the border between the dead and the living is not properly sealed, and the angry and suffering dead, in the form of zonbis or ghosts, become unpredictable and threaten living humanity. Dayan, in *Haiti, History, and the Gods,* explains: "If the disposal of dead slaves was a careless deed that marked irrevocable humanity, funeral rites in independent Haiti became central to both the living and the dead . . . if not served, fed, or remembered, [the dead] can become evil and unpredictable" (264). This unritual is not just an affront to the dead but to the living as well. In her more recent *The Law is a White Dog,* Dayan calls gestures such as Article 14 of the Code Noir "ritual[s] of degrade," which "harken back to the Ibo, whose longed-for return to Africa was thwarted by white masters who desecrated the body so it could not travel."[31]

Though the main focal points of *Water Graves* are the descendants of the African diaspora, I am aware that one unritual often hides another. There is, indeed, a sedimentation of unrituals whereby new dead hide ancient ones. The flood of cemeteries in Louisiana, for instance, jumble new dead with old ones, mixes up the newly drowned with much older floating caskets.[32] A character in Ward's 2011 novel *Salvage the Bones* evokes a similar abject mixing of the old dead, the new dead, and the living in the aftermath of a hurricane: "She said the newly dead and the old dead littered the beaches, the streets, the woods. She said papa Joseph found a skeleton in the yard" (218). On a deeper temporal scale, the bodies of African American troops who fought in the Civil War and were left to die without rituals dwell on Native American land and burial grounds, themselves forsaken, desecrated, and covered with cities, highways, shopping malls, or pipelines. These overlapping sites mean that one unritual often barely covers another. Natasha Trethewey's *Native Guard,* featured in chapter 5, reveals and explains these neglected intersecting memories. For instance, the term "native," with respect to the colored troops of the Louisiana Native Guard, I argue, is the surface level of a palimpsest barely covering the narrative of Native Americans of the *Ol' Man River,* the Mississippi in *Misiziibi* or "Great River" in *Ojibwe.* In her extraordinary reflection on black lives, Christina Sharpe investigates the compelling metaphor and experience of the wake, which she understands in its multiple meanings of the disturbance in water left after the passage of a ship or body, the aftermath of an event, the act of keeping watch with the dead, and the state of awakening (*In the Wake,* 17–18). She qualifies "wake work" as a project of *longue durée* and full engagement: "Wakes are processes; through them, we think about the dead and about our relations to death; they are rituals through which to enact grief and memory" (21). It is work such as Sharpe's that counteract the state of unritual.

Whether forsaken swamp, sea abyss, or riverbed, unspecified places of dying or repose render all ground ambiguous: the dead are both nowhere to be found and potentially everywhere. This *unmarking* not only desecrates soil and water but also makes all ground possibly sacral. Thus the Western duality between profane and sacred places, objects and acts, fails. The unritual strikes back at the system responsible for it in the first place. Slavery's excessive and arbitrary segregation into categories, even in death, caused its very failure in the pollution of categorical thinking by the unritual it produced. This ultimate failure of segregating the enslaved from the free, the baptized from the unbaptized, the living from the dead, also paradoxically opens up a space for the sacred to dwell outside its defined ritualistic borders. Gestures that would belong to the realm of the profane in the logic of organized religions, as well as productions by secular artists mounted in museums, on the streets, or underwater, function as sacred objects. This manifestation of the sacred outside the boundaries of organized religions occupies my reflection on what I term "relational sacred" (chapter 1).[33]

The ubiquity of unritual in postslavery societies does not entail the absence of mortuary rituals. Quite the contrary. The number of dead in the millions of the Middle Passage, the omnipresence of the spectacle of death through lynching and legalized tortures in black codes, the outlawing of all non-Christian rites, and, generally, the "slave trade as commerce in death," as historian Vincent Brown eloquently put it, contributed to systematic attempts at dehumanization are not to be seen as competing subjects, as Michael Rothberg shows in *Multidirectional Memory.*[37] For instance, the enslaved raped woman simply named "allongée ouverte" (open recumbent) in Glissant's novel *La Case du Commandeur,* who offers her unbearably pregnant body to a multitude of men in the prison hell of the slave plantation, resembles the crouched living dead of Auschwitz, *der Muselmann,* the most extremely weakened prisoner of the camp, which Primo Levi evokes in *If This Is a Man* (*Se Questo è un Uomo*). Agamben qualifies him (and we will imagine *her* as well) as "a being from whom humiliation, horror, and fear had so taken away all consciousness and all personality as to make him [her] absolutely apathetic" (*Homo Sacer,* 184–85). The same goes for the "open recumbent" of Glissant's novel, with the exception that, under the guise of her utterly submitted body, a persistent consciousness remains. While Agamben scrutinizes the ability to mete out death within the law and away from ritual and the way this shapes society, I am concerned with the ability to legally deprive the dead of a marked burial, with the unritual as furthering the *homo sacer* into a stage of the *cadaver sacer.* Like Agamben's *homo sacer,* who can be killed away from ritual yet within the law, *cadaver sacer* can be stripped of the human rituals in the bestial fashion of the perpetrators, while the perpetrator's act remains legitimized by law.

Finally, there is the quotidian unritual of representation. As I open my daily newspaper or computer app over breakfast, I have to wonder whether I will see dismembered body parts, the bloodied face of a dead girl; the traumatized, dust-covered face of a boy; the sliced-open body of a she-wolf and her discarded, dark, unborn pups; or a four-year-old wearing a pretty pink and purple flowered dress as she lies dying on the concrete floor of a hospital in a pool of bodily fluids with her eyes and mouth wide open.[38] Again, the list is disorderly and incomplete. I have to wonder daily what to hide from my own growing children, who increasingly devour the news. I have to wonder, especially, about the mother of that little girl whose dying face was reproduced thousands of times on the front pages of newspapers and computer screens. As in the experience of unritual, not all subjects are created equal, and the death of some are more publishable, even palatable, than others: US citizens vs. non–US citizens; whites vs. nonwhites.[39] The epistemic violence of representing the unritual kills a second time, desecrates once more what has already been deprived of a veil of decency in the first place. These representations impound, once more, human beings' right to the sacred. As Hartman aptly puts it, "How does one revisit the scene of subjection without replicating the grammar of violence?" (*Venus,* 4). Is *Water Graves* complicit in this disturbing replication? I delve into such questions in chapters 2 and 3, which focus on the use and abuse of Katrina imagery. Spike Lee, Kara Walker, and Beyoncé Knowles walk a fine line between creating ceremonials in the wake of the unritual and extending that very unritual by exposing once again indecent images. Philosopher of aesthetics Fred Moten calls such gestures "terribly beautiful."[40] The critic who exposes such works yet another time also walks a fine line between reproducing the unritual and providing a critical aperture, a space to think, feel, mourn, and eventually act. I reflect on this working through as a critical and pedagogical project in chapter 3.

Living Graves

Oscillation best describes the aesthetic rituals at work in *Water Graves.* Historian Pierre Nora identifies two forms of remembering. The first, *lieux de mémoire,* sites of memory, consist of objects such as memorials, epitaphs, or temples: "a *templum:* something singled out within the continuum of the profane . . . a circle within which everything counts, everything is symbolic, everything is significant" (*Lieux,* 19–20). The second, in contrast, *milieux de mémoire,* realms of memory, define "settings in which memory is a real part of everyday experience" (1). While Nora argues that *lieux de mémoire* exist only because *milieux de mémoire* are no longer, I show that they exist simultaneously. A successful act of memory oscillates between the site of memory and the middle of memory, between the cold marble and the warmth of placing seashells on a grave, between the monument to the dead and the performance of the living. For instance, in New Orleans remembering the dead oscillates between a stiff mausoleum in the St. Louis cemetery and a twirling parasol of a second line parade. Joseph Roach qualifies performance in the Circum-Atlantic zone at stake in *Cities of the Dead* as the place "where time is sculpted as cogently" as it can be (*Cities,* 33). Some performances, such as a requiem, based on an established liturgical text and its live musical interpretation, incorporate both the fixed and the dynamic, the past and the present, the dead and the living, the sonorous, the bodily, the tactile, the visual, and everything in between. In our creolized Atlantic world, ways and shapes of mourning also inevitably oscillate between Kongo, Fon, Vaudou, Catholic, Hindu, Muslim, and spontaneous forms of ritual not necessarily inscribed in organized or namable religions. Accordingly, chapters 1, 2, and 4 feature examples of an ecological sacred, which I argue are spontaneous rituals of solidarity existing outside the frame of an organized religion. Finally, the borderline between the aesthetic and the sacred is blurred. Artistic creations pick up a sacred function, especially in cases in which religious rituals are missing. For instance, "Fugue," by Haitian American performance artist Gabrielle Civil, featuring the artist walking, mirror in hand, into the Atlantic Ocean in Ghana, is seen by local bystanders as a religious performance.[41] Underwater sculptor Jason deCaires Taylor, who initially installed his "Vicissitude" sculpture series in the ocean shallows without the intent of evoking the slave trade, saw his installation become a sacred monument, a cenotaph of sorts to the memory of the drowned, because of the sacredness of the underwater site.[42]

This fluid relational ensemble of sacred gestures does not prevent the manifestation of discrete objects, sites, or performances recognizable as such. We can list the monument, the cenotaph, the crypt, the cemetery, the mausoleum, the tombstone, the *nkisi,* the urn, the face vessel, the memory jar, the broken mirror, the mask, the cross, the anthropomorphic or zoomorphic grave sculpture, the epitaph, the conch shell, the blues, the requiem, the dirge, the elegy, the eulogy, the *tombeau poétique,* the lament, the ululation, the moan, the testimony and seeking of black churches, the New Orleans second line, the door of no return, the candle, the tree, the rock, the sea, the archive, the glitter, the silence, the gap, the absence.[43] The list is an open one and could also include quotidian and unpredictable objects, such as a stuffed teddy bear, to memorialize a very young life.[44]

Artists and critics explicitly present their aesthetic or theoretical creations as tombs or funeral performance. Trethewey and Philip see their *Native Guard* and *Zong!,* respectively, as a tombstone and song to the dead (chapter 5). Glissant conceives of his *poétrie* as an "ontological communion" (chapter 1). Eric Waters photographs clarinets ravaged by the toxic waters of Lake Pontchartrain and beautifies their disintegrating cases, evoking tomb decoration. With his 2006 "Katrina Quilt," a patchwork of his own photographs, Epaul Julien evokes the quotidian, political, and creolizing function of the quilt while performing a sacred gesture, since the blanket is commonly used as shroud in African American communities. Lee subtitles his Katrina documentary *A Requiem in Four Parts;* the soundtrack to Lee's film by New Orleans jazz trumpeter Terence Blanchard's *A Tale of God's Will* is dubbed *A Requiem to Katrina* (chapter 2); and critic Karla Holloway adds the term "A Memorial" on the book cover of her critical study entitled *Passed On: African American Mourning Stories.*

The relay is one of the key concepts and methods of this book. I intend the word in its daily sense of a supply of things, people, animals, or electric currents, which "afford relief from time to time."[45] I also envisage it within Glissant's framework of *Relation,* whose triple properties are to link, to relay, and to relate.[46] I emphasize the most prosaic, but also the most humanizing, of the three properties of Glissant's Relation. Relaying can be understood first as an act of solidarity between those touched by the unritual, such as humans and their hurt ecologies. It calls for disciplines like literary and artistic interpretation, history and science, to join forces where they meet the epistemological abyss of the unknown. It brings together multiple art forms (e.g., music, poetry, sculpture, ceramics, quilting, and carpentry) manifest in the many mixed-media creations featured in this book. These alliances across forms of expression build knowledge about unfathomable disasters more effectively than any single art form could. They are necessary to mourn and remember Afrodescendant forebears and contemporaries, in the face of the temporal, spatial, and criminal depth and scale of the unritual. This dissolving of genres and disciplines, and, hence, their reinforced proximity, establishes communication between a diverse set of Caribbean Basin artists who respond to catastrophe in a common effort. *Water Graves* creates a narrative out of the juxtaposition of multiple forms of literary and artistic productions, from which meaning, and hopefully healing, can emerge.

Hence the omnipresence of mixed-media creations in the book with sound relaying sight relaying the tactile; with poetry relaying painting, relaying sculpture, and back. Each and every one of the objects and performances offered to the dead warrants its own discussion, and I will discuss many of them—the quilt, the dirge, the second line, the elegy, the moan, the song, the cenotaph, the epitaph—at various moments throughout the book. But first I would like to turn to the subject of this book, the grave, and, eventually, on its avatar in the water grave.

The word *grave* and its French translation *tombe* (cognate of the English *tomb*) carry meanings of urgency, danger, loss, and solemnity. *Grave,* from the Icelandic *gröf* and traveling to modern English through the Anglo-Saxon *grafa,* refers to the act of both digging and carving. Thus it points at the same time to the hole in the earth, to covering, to oblivion, and to the gesture of decorating and remembering through an inscription of carving. Girard defines the grave precisely as what "marks and conceals" the dead.[47] Encountering in its etymological journey and merging with the Greek *grapho,* "to write," *grave* is once more reinforced as both interred in an excavation and inscribed on a surface. *Tomb,* from the French *tombe,* derives from the Greek *tymba* and defines "a mound." The travels of this word through time offer, on a superficial yet telling level, a history of the evolution of Western treatments of the dead, from forming a mound to interring in a hole. Derrida poetically reflects on the phonetic kinship between *tombe,* the grave, and *tomber,* to fall down. The two words have altogether distinct histories and meanings: *tomber* comes from the Old French *tumer,* or "to dance, to gambol, to tumble" (*Le nouveau Petit Robert*). Derrida plays with the verb *tomber* and its imperative form *tombe!* (fall!), linking it to its homonym noun *tombe, grave,* to create new meaning. The left-hand column of his *Glas,* dedicated to French poet, novelist, and playwright Jean Genet, contains the recurrent paradox of a simultaneous falling down and falling up movement through the graphic and phonic identity of *tombe* (grave) as the erection of a monument, and the imperative *tombe!* (fall!) as an abysmal descent. Each of the columns inhabiting the pages of Derrida's *Glas* (death knell), which juxtapose Hegel and Genet, relay each other, pull up the body of its companion when it stumbles: "One of them keeps things in check, keeps watch, assimilates, interiorizes, idealizes, rectifies the fall in the monument. The fall remains, embalms and mummifies, monu-memorializes, names itself—falls / grave [tombe]. Yet, thus, as it falls, becomes erect" (7). This movement of relay and companionship between the two columns, between the philosopher and the poet, refers to the helpful yet paradoxical gesture of solidarity in mourning. It also refers to the paradoxical nature of the grave (*tombe*), which situates mourning in the irremediable depth between the erection of a monument and the abyss of memory.

But what happens to the grave (*tombe*) when its site is water? When the only movement is down? When there is only a *tombe* (fall) without a *tombe* (grave)? Is there such a thing as a watery grave or liquid casket? The enigmatic figure of the "fish-room" ("poisson-chambre") in Glissant's novel *La Case du Commandeur,* told by the storyteller Ozonzo to the orphan girl Cinna Chimène, is precisely described as a "tomb sans tomb" (graveless grave, or graveless fall, 64). The fish-room, simultaneously Jonas-whale, plantation home, and slave ship, reveals the fragility of the grave when falling is its only movement: "Well then, the trap that you see below, it hurls you to the lowest depths" (*Case,* 64).[48]

Excavation and engraving are necessarily impossible in this graveless grave, grim without *grafa,* digging or inscription. Yet Romantic poet John Keats, who died at age twenty-five in 1821, wanted neither proper names nor dates to appear on his tombstone, merely this line: "Here lies one whose name was writ in water."[49] Young Keats understood that his name "writ on water" would be nowhere to be found, yet everywhere in water's fluidity and changeability. This brings us back to our earlier paradox: that water deaths are nowhere but also potentially everywhere.

Literary, poetic, and aesthetic objects act as replacement tombs or cenotaphs for missing water graves. While Keats's name wanders on water, Keats's phrase—"Here lies one whose name was writ in water"—is inscribed on his tombstone as epitaph and engraved as testament in his poetry. The literary or artistic object takes a charged, sacred meaning in such cases. There is a long tradition of *tombeaux poétiques* or "poetic tombs" in Greek and Latin antiquity and in French Renaissance in which collections of epitaphs are published in anthologies rather than engraved on the stone.[50] In the Hebrew tradition, books such as the Yizkor Bikher offer some of the most ancient symbolic tombstones for those departed without graves, as James Young discusses in *The Texture of Memory* (7). Trethewey, too, provides her mother and the Louisiana Native guards with a hardcover book grave where a stone tomb could not be had (chapter 5).

Frequently, artists and poets work from fragments of stones and seashells. In his Nobel lecture, St. Lucian poet Derek Walcott refers to the shards of Antillean history as "sacred vessels": "Antillean art is the restoration of our shattered histories, our shards of vocabulary, our archipelago becoming a synonym for pieces broken off the original continent" (*Twilight*, 69). Under the prosopopoeia of a crab, Barbadian poet Kamau Brathwaite observes,

pebbles became my continents of dreams
i was content w/ shallow water
here my feet dipped
fishing the circles of its pale fragmented mirrors. (*Black + Blues*, 66)

Even the proverbial mirror, reflecting limbo between the departed and the living, has lost its unity and glitter. Haitian novelist Émile Ollivier reflects on what is left in the wake of the overpowering sea of memory: "Immense and complex palimpsest of memory! Ebbing and flowing like the sea, you dig up the sand of a life and leave behind broken shells in which we hear again and again the sea. Is it naïve to think that we can remake the world, its scents and its music, from dead shells?" (*Mille Eaux*, 134). This state of generalized fragmentation will increase the task of the poet, artist, reader, and viewer not just as collectors of rocks, but as committed sculptors of meaning, monuments, and rituals.

Another lesson of *Water Graves* is that a grave itself is never enough. That the *lieu de mémoire*, the cold marble, needs to be activated by the living, or a *milieu de mémoire*. Such performances include gestures as simple

It examines productions dwelling in what Moten calls "terrible beauty." Haiti, Danticat writes in the immediate aftermath of the 2010 earthquake, carries on after disaster not only with survival and resilience but with the enduring and flourishing expression of beauty that affirms its humanity above unspeakable loss and unritual. It is "a stunningly beautiful chocolate angel with her face turned up towards an indigo sky as she floats over a pile of muddied corpses" (*Create,* 169).

Constellation is our antidote to disaster. Whether from the Greek *aster* or the Latin *stella,* disaster and constellation come from the star.[54] In sharp contrast with disaster, though, constellation highlights relation, collection, community, rather than separation or dysfunction: While it refers to a multitude of discrete objects within a known system, the units are named individually. At the same time, they resist being completely seized, comprehended in a system. Their meanings, as animals, mythological figures, or musical instruments, emerge from a reading of the shape they form in their spatial relations: Ursa Major the Great Bear, Aquila the Eagle, Cassiopeia the Queen, Lyra the Harp, and, in African astrology, the "Three Zebras," the "Male Wildebeest," or the "Flock of Birds."[55] While ancient and contemporary astronomers—western, eastern, northern, and southern—have settled stars in named asterisms and constellations, nothing prevents the viewer's imagination from reading them anew and spotting in them fresh objects, animals, or mythical creatures. This is the method I use, for instance, in chapter 2 to interpret Julien's "Katrina Quilt," which presents an unlimited aesthetic constellation through the vertical, horizontal, crosswise, and overlapping reading directions. Constellations are also fashioned out of shining objects and masses such as candles, mirrors, or glitter, which frequent our artists' creations.

Each chapter features a *constellation* of juxtaposed artists who provide new meanings and objects. I follow Glissant's relational principle as a guide for reading and interpretation, in which "repercussions of cultures, whether in symbiosis or in conflict" leave us to imagine "the position of each part within this whole" and "at the same time the urgent need to understand the hidden order of a whole—so as to wander there without becoming lost" ("pour y errer sans s'y perdre") (*Poetics; Poétique* 131, 145). The poem, the salvaged window frame, the jar, the fish, the coral, the wave, the seaweed, the couplets, the elegy, the legal proceeding, among many parts, relay one another in a fluid solidarity in order to form "the hidden order of a whole," to create meaning in the immense, and unsayable, state of unritual. They are necessary in their complementarity, in the compositeness they create through their juxtaposition, their attempt to control disaster. Meandering and wandering, all the while not becoming lost, *Water Graves* provides yet another intervention to shape this transient but meaningful whole.

As it has now become clear, my reading embraces a relational and creolizing methodology. Creolization, in Glissantian terms, evokes at once a cultural mode of mixing, opening onto "a broader ethnocultural realm, from the Antilles to the Indian Ocean" and an epistemology in which "an attempt to get at Being . . . would constitute a step backward in comparison with how creolizations can function" in the speed and movement they bring into Relation (*Poetics,* 89). My tools of interpretation are predictably creolizing, both in the cultural and philosophical sense. They are relational in shape and draw from Kongo and Vaudou cosmogony, ancient philosophy, and contemporary scholarship and poetry from this and the other side of the water.

The focus on water requires adapted methods. Philip, in her poem *Zong!,* privileges the verb *exaqua* over *excavate* to capture the gesture of salvaging the spirit, name, and voice of the drowned. With a similar objective, albeit with methods and tools other than the poetic imagination, the archeologists, historians, scuba divers, and museum curators of the Slave Wrecks Projects (in the George Washington University, Smithsonian, and Iziko Museums) recover artifacts from sunken ships.[56] In my analysis of aesthetic works, I apply methods of literary, artistic, and cultural criticism to help bring to the surface of consciousness the lives of drowned Africans. In his 1989 poem-essay "The Open Boat," Glissant reads the corroded weights attached to the sunken slaves as an underwater text "punctuating" the bottom of the sea. Similarly, "underwater" poetry, visual arts, and sculpture, I argue, exist in a continuous *relation* with historical artifacts such as the iron ballast brought back from the sea floor by maritime archeologists and oceanographers. Thus, humanities methods do not detract from archeology but *relay* it in a reciprocal relationship.

Such is the lesson of *Water Graves:* that in death, as much as in life, all humans deserve dignity. Aesthetic creation and the critical scholarship it fosters help to alleviate—not to forget, solve, or absolve—the unritual. *Requiem aeternam dona eis. Give them eternal rest.* Regardless of whether we imagine this plea in the context of liturgy, the jazz productions of Terence Blanchard and Branford Marsalis, the classical Western musical tradition of Mozart and Fauré, or the ecological sacred of Glissant and Taylor, the artists of *Water Graves* instill rest in the turmoil of water deaths, precisely through what they put into motion.

of repose, a little over a year after Glissant's death, rust, salt winds, and maritime moss have already altered the shallow gold inscriptions, making them hard to read. This rough deciphering of the object of Glissant's grave invites us to question the aesthetic, political, historical, and philosophical motif of the grave in Glissant's works. It also opens an avenue of reflection on his poetics of the sacred and provides a response to the unritual at the heart of this book.

Departing from the submarine grave of drowned Africans inhabiting Glissant's "Open Boat" in *Poetics of Relation,* this chapter then reflects on the grave in Glissant's last single-authored book, *Philosophie de la Relation,* published in 2009, two years before his death. Focusing on Glissant's late work will allow me to question his passage from obsession with the calamitous death of the enslaved Africans to the confrontation with the author's own death, which is inextricably linked to a collective and ecocritical consciousness. In *Philosophie de la Relation,* the recurring image of a "renfoncement de terre," or "hollowing out of earth," acts simultaneously as the site of the beginning and end of life; as the mother's birth and death; and as the refuge for what Glissant calls *le poème.* This questioning of the grave allows me to approach Glissant's notion of the sacred linked to the production of poetry and in relation with his late *pensée du tremblement,* or "thought of trembling." The sacred in the face of the unritual can only function with the ecological help of the *entour. Entour* signifies for Glissant the whole environment comprising the poem, human and nonhuman animals, vegetation, rocks, lavas, and "nature" and "culture." The latter terms lose meaning since they exist on a continuum, not in a system of opposition. While grounded in a specific reading of Glissant, this first chapter is meant to be generalized to the rest of *Water Graves,* where ecological solidarity, the relational sacred, and artistic compositeness consistently appear as the modes of healing and dealing with the unritual.

In accordance with this relational logic, my methodology is somewhat unusual, since it mixes tools of literary, cultural, and art criticism, a reflection on the sacred, a personal experience of the grave, and testimonies of Glissant's friends in Martinique. It is my hope that this open method will begin to explain the inscription on Glissant's grave—"Nothing is true, all is alive"—by not privileging one specific method of investigation, and by *relaying,* in the Glissantian sense of the term, the poem with its environment, and literary criticism with living testimony. This inaugural chapter's close-up shot on the Martinique, with a zoom-in on Glissant's actual grave, does not aim to restrict the book to a myopic vision of the local.

Indeed, as Glissant's critic and translator J. Michael Dash has compellingly demonstrated, the shimmering island rock just off the Martinican shore contains, for Glissant, the Whole-World, as the Whole-World contains a trace of the impenetrable basalt volcanic formation ("Martinique/ Mississippi," 97). The local and the global communicate in a reciprocal, often sacred, bond. Glissant's concept of the local closely resembles Michel Serres's notion of nature, not in isolation, but as a bonding tie. As scholar George Handley has it, Serres builds "a new ethics that connects the local to the global, what he calls a Natural Contract as opposed to Rousseau's Social Contract: 'Never forget the place from which you depart, but leave it behind and join the universal. Love the bond that united your plot of earth with the Earth, the bond that makes kin and stranger resemble each other'" (*Home Waters,* 15–16). Rather than a *locus solus,* then, Glissant's Martinique provides a base of kinship for *Water Graves,* which can be generalized to the places evoked in this book—New Orleans, Haiti, the Greater Caribbean, a suffering planet—and to the zones beyond its scope ok, yet necessarily present, such as the immense human rights catastrophe of drowned migrants in the Atlantic Ocean, the Indonesian seas, the Straits of Florida, or the Mediterranean graveyard.

Cemetery *Entour*

As is well known, Glissant in his *Caribbean Discourse* claims that Antillean history is memorialized through its landscapes: "Our landscape is its own monument: its meaning can only be traced on the underside. It is all history" (11). In the absence of erected monuments memorializing the tragic or glorious events the past, trees, beaches, and sea winds act as keepers of the past. This is a common function of landscape in Glissant's works and generally in postslavery cultures where trees and plants act as witness to a past with no written archive.[1] In his late work, Glissant increasingly replaces the word *paysage* (landscape) with the French word *entour,* which establishes a continuum between the natural environment and its historical surroundings. The two, in Glissant's mind, relay each other in comprehending the past and the cultural present. Literary critic Carrie Noland reflects on Glissant's poetics of the *entour* in her subtle analysis of the symbolic function of landscape in Glissant's poetry. She highlights the discontinuity between the symbolic mapping of landscape in Africa and the symbolic mapping that occurs in Martinique, which is disjointed from experience ("Edouard Glissant," 143). For Glissant, the symbolic mapping of landscape occurs in poetry, which in turn becomes part and parcel of the *entour. Entour* blurs and even annuls the division between cultural productions and landscape. For Noland, Glissant "is mobilizing an unremarkable, symbolically neutral word (as opposed to 'paysage,' 'nature,' or 'environment') and charging it with a new meaning and function within the economy of his own text" (163).

The location of the cemetery provides an ideal site to understand this concept of *entour* as a place of fluidity between the natural and the cultural, the philosophical and the mystic, the human and the vegetal, the dead and the living. As Rolle has elegantly demonstrated in his ethnographic work, cemeteries in Martinique have to be evaluated in their full context, in their *entour,* in order to make sense: "A care for method and respect for Martinican history can only consider the legacy of Martinican cemeteries through a global vision, which, more than an analysis of isolated graves, reveals the Martinican cemetery in its full complexity and in its Creole dimension" ("Les Cimetières," 2). One can ponder what Rolle means by "historical respect" and "Creole dimension." All places of mourning should naturally be places of respect for the departed and sanctuaries for individual and collective memories of the dead. The expected respect is increased, however, in a Martinican and Creole postslavery context, where the burying of the dead often associates narratives of individual fates with collective histories. In the aftermath of the calamity of slavery, where the dead were not always given proper or appropriate burial, it is particularly important to pay them respect, as Rolle highlights: "The claim to a decent site of burial emerged from the times of slavery" (4).[2] Mark Auslander, a historical anthropologist of African American ritual practices, echoes Rolle's views when he accentuates the importance of creating proper commemoration and burial for the formerly enslaved: "In these acts of witnessing let us honor the fact that in slavery and freedom many African Americans who were long excluded from these virtual enactments of the afterlife did not necessarily reject the premise that these spaces embodied" (*Accidental Slaveowner,* 149). Auslander's Georgia and Alabama cemeteries and Rolle's Martinican graves thus form part of a transnational network of monuments to the dead of the African diaspora and their descendants.

In his evocation of the Creole dimension, Rolle also has in mind the relationship between the living and the dead inherent to African-derived perceptions of death. Cemeteries illustrate "a Martinican conception of the dead entailing that an ill-buried human can return to the world of the living. The cemetery . . . is thus a place of separation that cannot be too abrupt. There again, a radical severance could potentially give the dead a reason to haunt those who have neglected them. Hence, a section of the cemetery always borders the habitat of the living" ("Les Cimetières," 2). In *Philosophie de la Relation,* Glissant indicates in a similar vein that "the cemeteries of lands and cities of creolization, and, generally, of powerful hurricanes—Guadeloupe, Martinique, Haiti, New Orleans, Cartagena—grow into glittering small towns . . . whose avenues open onto fleeting illuminations rather than onto the mute space of dull hereafter" (145).[3]

Thus, Martinican cemeteries, like the *Cimetière du Diamant,* are often in close proximity to the living, in the heart of town rather than in its margins.[4] The *Cimetière du Diamant,* with its modest walls and openings onto the sea, the street, and the parking lot where locals and tourists alike can enjoy sorbets exemplifies the fluidity between the world of the living and the dead, of daily trivial pleasure and mourning. Manuel Norvat, a Martinican friend of Glissant and the author of "Le Chant du divers: Introduction à la Philopoétique d'Édouard Glissant," recounted to me the testimony of the poet Henry Corbin: "Edouard feels right at home in the Diamant cemetery. All he needs to do is go around the cemetery walls and voilà! He enjoys his little sea bath every night."[5] This affectionate and humoristic testimony has repercussions that are greater than their anecdotal value. The case illustrates a separation of the living and the dead that is not too abrupt. As Anicet comments, Glissant wanted his body to be placed in a specific way: "His feet are oriented towards the sea and he is facing the sea. The horizon is a sign symbolizing the (acoma) tree and its branches embrace felicity" (Anicet, "De Martinique," n.p.).

Glissant's *entour* is simultaneously natural, cultural, poetic, historical, and political. The location of Glissant's grave in Le Diamant is significant on all these levels. Glissant elected to have his body buried in Martinique, not in Paris or New York, where he would also reside for parts of the year.[6] Poet and critic Hanétha Vété-Congolo insists on this Martinican specificity that allowed Glissant to communicate with the world: "Seizing the Martinican ethos and building the Martinican axiology in the World, in the worldly World, can only be achieved through the relationship with an intimate Place located in humanity's fundamental sphere, through the Relation with all the Places of the world" ("L'Acomat," n.p.).

The poet chose to be buried not on the Morne Bezaudin (where he was born), nor in the Commune du Lamentin (where he grew up), but in the Commune du Diamant, which he elected as his Martinican residence for the final decades of his life. Le Diamant, and particularly the Rocher du Diamant, or Diamond Rock, became the epicenter of Glissant's fiction, poetry, and philosophy. I will not revisit here the admirable work that

Dash has published on the meaning of Diamond Rock for the poet but will simply say that that, as Dash rightly states, Le Diamant constitutes the point of encounter between the extremely particular and the universal, between Glissant's conceptual philosophy of Relation, and his grounding in the particular place of Martinique.[7] Le Diamant, Glissant's poetic epicenter, is the elected place of his eternal rest.

The natural landscape of Le Diamant is also meaningful. Its beach is perhaps the part of the Martinican coast most brutalized by sea winds and rough waves. This surfer paradise swallows a few swimmers each year, unlike the child-friendly and peaceful waters of Sainte-Anne, just a few miles across the shore. The sand on the beach is black, as Glissant has pointed out in his writing, and volcanic.[8] It is a place where sea and volcano, the two forces that define the island itself, meet. Le Diamant also offers a striking contrast between the horizontal and the vertical. The dramatic abruptness of Diamond Rock, a formation of 175 meters, and the imposing Morne Larcher, a gigantic mount resembling the bust of a recumbent woman, break the horizontality of the longest beach in Martinique. The juxtaposition of these two opposites recalls the poetic taste for extremes Glissant has expressed, for instance, in *Poétique de la Relation*.[9]

The natural exceptionalness of Le Diamant is inextricable from its history, past and present. The town's lively politics of memorialization over the last decades have attenuated Glissant's claims that landscapes alone act as monuments. Indeed, Martinique and Guadeloupe have seen monuments commemorating slavery flourish in recent years.[10] A statue of the *Neg Marron* (the Black Maroon) realized by Hector Charpentier in 1998 marks the urban landscape of Le Diamant. The town officials have renamed streets according to a politics commemorating the Amerindian past of the island as well as its present connections with a transnational Africana consciousness (e.g., Rue des Arawaks, Rue Barack Obama). Also situated in the Commune du Diamant, at the foothill of Morne Larcher, the minuscule multicolored cabin of the sculptor Médard Aribot, a.k.a. *le Bagnard* (the Convict), still stands with Diamond Rock as its background. Aribot, who was sent to the penitential colony of French Guyana for having sculpted a satirical wooden effigy of Colonel Coppens, is a center figure of anthropologist Richard Price's *The Convict and the Colonel*, which focuses on a minor event in Martinican history to give a larger historical account of the country.

Equally poignant, a few miles from the Le Diamant lies the Anse Caffard, where the captives of a clandestine slave ship perished in 1830 in the hold of a sunken vessel.[11] In 1998, 150 years after the abolition of sign enwrapping Glissant's grave, could very well be the title of his next book, evoking a place-based consciousness at work in several other titles (*La Lézarde; La Terre le feu l'eau et les vents; La Cohée du Lamentin; Les Indes; Pays rêvé, Pays réel;* etc.). The title also places itself in continuity with the titles of the works of the poets he admired such as Saint-John Perse's *Vents, Anabase,* or *Exil;* Victor Segalen's *Stèles, Lettres de Chine,* or *Un grand fleuve;* Paul Claudel's *Connaissance de l'Est, Partage du midi, L'Ours et la lune;* and Aimé Césaire's *Cahier d'un retour au pays natal.* All of these poets located their poetry in stars, cardinal points, and natural elements. But what can be understood by the enigmatic "Presence of a Multiple East"? The expression radically breaks from a division of the world organized around the geometric model of four cardinal points. With a multiple East, the compass loses its West. Why evoke the presence of the East when the geographic *entour* of Glissant's burial is situated west of the West, according to the Eurocentric cutting of the world between East and West using the Ural Mountains as its border? In light of this geographical oddity, East might be more conceptual than geographic. In Glissant's poetry and essays, the notions of East and West are turned on their heads. In *Caribbean Discourse,* attempting to clarify what he means by the Occident or the West, Glissant indicates in a footnote that it is not geographic but teleological.[24] In the introduction to his anthology, Glissant states that "Rising Suns [les Levants] could equally be Setting Suns [des Couchants] for those who care only about the movements of the wind" (*La Terre,* 13). In a discussion with Derrida, Glissant returns to the tension between the geographical and conceptual definitions of East and West: "The Arawaks and the Caribs were nomadizing in the islands when the West coming from the East toppled over them" ("Pensée du tremblement," 86). The West that came from the East—namely, Europe—represents the violence of conquest, colonialism, and empire. The East, in a symmetrical response, comes to signify the nomadic prey of the West. In his poem *Les Indes,* Glissant insists on the ambivalence of the Indies, as illustrated by Christopher Columbus's and the conquerors' confused perception of the new continent as West Indies. The Caribbean is thus an imaginary East in a geographical West: "And the seaman even says that he believes, children, that there are two Indies . . . But the Indies are truth" (*Les Indes,* 77). The poet, in the voice of the storyteller addressing his children, associates the plural Indies with truth. Truth is therefore double. However, the two Indies, the multiple Easts, have different functionalities: "The suffering Indies follow on from the dreamed Indies" (101). The material conditions of slavery emerge from the exotic dream of the traveler.

that Glissant was a Vaudou practitioner, which would be ludicrous. But it is important to see that his friends inscribe him into a network of gods, which is perfectly in line with his philosophy and poetics of Relation. I call this a relational ecological sacred.

Glissant, when he autographed books for friends, colleagues, or students, would accompany his signature by the inscription "Under the Gaze of our Gods" and a drawn figure of a crying god with the face of an archipelago. The gaze and presence of plural gods is echoed in Glissant's 2006 dialogue with the philosopher Derrida, in a conference on trembling in which Glissant asserts not atheism but his awareness of the presence of plural gods that defies a monotheistic worldview: "Jacques resolutely worked within . . . the field of theology and even of teleology in which trembling intervenes as a category of the relationship to God. . . . But where I would like to push the discussion, is that I think that God is monolingual while gods are multilingual" ("Pensée du tremblement," 105).[33] Glissant's religion is not a theology in the sense of an organized discourse on God or gods or a doctrine that erects itself into science.

The closest philosophico-theological stance to Glissant's religion is the one admirably scrutinized by theologian and philosopher Catherine Keller in *Cloud of the Impossible: Negative Theology and Planetary Entanglement.* Keller investigates the hybrid philosophical and religious system of beliefs of negative theology, which sprouted from Neoplatonist, Christian, and Hebraic narratives (40). The foundational attitude of negative theology closely resembles Glissant's notion of positive opacity, the recognition that ethically respectful communities are based on the respect of the other's opacity and the avoidance of reducing the other to one's own transparency: "I am thus able to conceive of the opacity of the other for me, without reproach for my opacity for him [*sic*]. To feel in solidarity with him or to build with him . . . it is not necessary for me to grasp him" (*Poetics,* 193). What Betsy Wing translates as "to grasp" is *comprendre* in the original French. *Comprendre,* which can be translated as to understand, to comprehend, to comprise, or to grasp, therefore points to the gesture of taking within oneself—of ingesting, if you will—the other's difference within one's own system (digestive or rational). Glissant's opacity meets, on an ethical level, the theological thought that fourth-century theologian Cyril of Jerusalem and Greek philosopher Socrates alike qualified respectively in the following terms: "To confess our ignorance is the best knowledge" and "know what you do not know" (quoted in Keller, 40). As I was reading alternative forms of religion to better understand Glissant's notion of

à Valérie Loichot,
TOUT-MONDE
Sous le regard de nos Dieux!
Très affectueusement
édouard glissant

Édouard Glissant, *Under the Gaze of Our Gods.* (Glissant's autograph on author's personal copy of *Tout-Monde* 1993 © Valérie Loichot)

the sacred, I initially picked up Keller's *Cloud of the Impossible,* intrigued by elements of the title and subtitle of her book. "Cloud," "Impossible," Planetary," and "Entanglement" echoed Glissant's concerns with meteorological manifestations that escape scientific measurement, his concept of Tout-Monde or Whole-World, and his own notion of entanglement, which the Caribbean philosopher sees as the ultimate arrival of the thought operation based on Relation, "the entanglements of world-wide relation" (*Poetics,* 31).[34] Reading on, I became pleasantly surprised by the explicit presence of Glissant's thought in Keller's book, found in epigraphs and significant discussions having to do with relational thought and opacity. The surprise was welcome not only because it provided evidence for my reflection on Glissant's religious thought, but mostly because the Caribbean philosopher was conveyed to the field of Western theology, worlding it. Keller uses Glissant's definitions of Opacity and Relation to build her theory of "Nonknowing Relational Ethics" (228): "It is *mindfulness* of Relation that plies the ethical—as opposed to the corporate *mindlessness* of entanglement. In his luminous *Poetics of Relation,* Édouard Glissant, writing out of the legacy of North Atlantic slavery, supplies the missing clues to this doubling" (255). Keller was providing a theological response to the indignant critics of Glissant's demand to "the right to opacity" ("Now it's back to barbarism! How can you communicate with what you don't understand"; quoted in *Poetics,* 189) in her apophatic theology: "This is not the darkness of evil, but of the deep variegations of nonknowing that it may do ill to ignore or to manipulate" (7).

Glissant's religion is relational also in its etymological sense of *re-ligere,* to link again the physical and the spiritual, humans and humans, humans and plants, or ideas and ideas. In the same response to Derrida, and in order to illuminate his views on religion, Glissant turns to the following metaphor: "See the clouds of birds, the swarms of birds . . . you will never manage to count them precisely as they thrust in waves of crests and ravines, as they soar and fall in and out of sight, as they dive to take root . . . their unpredictability is that which relates them, and which swirls away from all science" (*Philosophie,* 83). Thus, Glissant's religion, linkage, or relation is unpredictable, dynamic, and also linked to an ecological environment that is incommensurable and incomprehensible. I use this last term not in the sense of the failure of thinking, but rather in an acknowledgment that the opacity of the world cannot always be reduced to rational, scientific, or theological doctrines.

"Vous ne me comprendrez jamais" ("You will never understand/ comprehend/comprise me"), Glissant would tell his students at the beginning of his seminars.[35] This lack of comprehension recalls Glissant's notion of opacity, which does not prevent relation with the other, but, instead, admits the obstacles to taking into oneself completely an object that is larger and more complex than the movements of "hands that grasp," or a mind that reduces the other to its measurement of comprehension.[36] As he advanced in age, Glissant turned more and more to nature and to an ecological consciousness to express his spirituality based on unpredictability, change, and the recognition that if we are all related, we also conserve an incommensurability that resists the comprehension of a reductive transparency. Glissant has called this a "respectful opacity" in *Poetics of Relation* (204).

Anicet's design of Glissant's tomb aesthetically and materially translates this spiritual and ethical conviction. Just a little over a year after the installation of the stone, the colors have already faded into a less solid black, into a less clear white, warped by earthy brown and greenish corrosion. The lines of divisions have already softened. The erosion of the artwork was part of the plan: "You should know that the work is not a decoration in black and white. It is living material; the cracks are the fissures of the soul; it is meant for people to partake in it, to clean it, to improve it. The public hasn't understood that yet."[37] The ceramic sign is participatory and invites fissures that are simultaneously unfathomable and relational. The breaks in the monument reveal the fragility of the stone, a vulnerability expressed in Glissant's *Pensée du tremblement.* The thought of trembling in the late Glissant is not a sign of failure but a resisting force to a "stiff systematic thought and excessive systems of thought" (*Cohée,* 128). *La pensée du tremblement* is a spiritual, ethical, and political gesture against fixed truth, rigid theology, or, worse, religious or political absolutisms.

La pensée du tremblement, which is unquestionably linked to the body of the poet rendered vulnerable and unstable by ageing and ailments, also proposes an ecology of being with the world: "To live the landscapes is to tremble the trembling of the world" (87). In *Cohée du Lamentin,* Glissant further connects human body and planet earth through the image of the quake: "The thought of trembling is the seismic thought of the world that shakes in us and around us" (87). Without citing him, Glissant rejoins Serres's seismic thinking, which is not catastrophic in the etymological sense of turning things upside down, but relational in the sense that it provides an ephemeral, albeit deep, moment of communication between the vulnerable planet and the lonely trembling human: "Who am I? A tremor of nothingness, living in a permanent earthquake. Yet, for a moment of profound happiness, the spasmodic Earth comes to unite herself with my shaky body. Who am I, now, for several seconds? Earth herself. Both communing, in love she and I, doubly in distress, throbbing together, joined in a single aura (Serres, *Natural Contract,* 124). The penultimate paragraph of Serres's *Natural Contract* shares a dense lexical field with Glissant's *Philosophie de la Relation.* His nothingness, tremor, seism, wavering, union, ephemerality, communion, evokes Glissant's insignificance, trembling, vulnerability of the human that specifically allows a deep relationality with planet Earth. While Glissant does not share Serres's tone of religious adoration, he nonetheless establishes a deep emotional, even ontological, bond between human and planet in a model whereby *poétrie* stands for Serres's communion in love. This ontological communion, for Glissant, amounts to a "suspension of judgment, of being perhaps, which Montaigne so brilliantly imagined, like an habitual visiting, not a possession of this earth, suggested by Amerindian thought, like the telluric function of Amerindian ancestral lines, never closed or excluding, sung by the peoples of the Africa of the Griots" (*Cohée,* 128–29). Glissant's vulnerable body—like Serres's, experiencing the earthquake—is also more apt to communicate with the world through its trembling, which is at once stifling tremor and vivacious vibration.

Serres could very well choose, as another example of his natural contract, the Cree relationship to nature as described by Jack Forbes, which has no need for the term *environment* since there is no environ where there is no center. The Cree, and more generally Indigenous epistemologies, also invalidates the need for the word "religion," since, like the word "environment," it implies cuts, borders, classifications, and an inside and outside. "Because of the "relatedness of *all* forms of existence," Forbes contends, "the ethics and moral values of Native people are part and parcel of their cosmology and total world view. Most native languages have no word for 'religion' and it may be true that a word for religion is never needed until a people no longer have it . . . Religion is, in reality, living" (Forbes, *Columbus,* 15). Serres uses the same antistructural argument: "So forget the word *environment* . . . It assumes that we humans are at the center of a system of nature" (Serres, *Natural Contract,* 33). While Serres draws examples from a European domain (e.g., the paintings of Goya or Millet) or from European-assimilated foundational texts (e.g., *The Bible* and *The Odyssey*), his choice of Jean-François Millet's "Angelus" as a privileged example of the closeness between humans, land, and religion allows his natural contract to resonate with Forbes's and with Glissant's own natural contracts where shared vulnerability and familiarity dethrone exploitation and possession. Millet's couple of peasants bowing to the field they have just labored, their humility and thanksgiving, the discrete faraway presence of a church in the background, blending in its gray with the horizon, illustrates a similar ecology. For Glissant, Serres, Forbes, and Millet, the weakening of life paradoxically entails a strengthening of the relationship between the poet, philosophers, humans, and their *entour*, the earth, linked through their respective approaching death, mortality, or to use a neologism, through their respective dyingness.

Writing on the Grave: "Nothing Is True, All Is Alive"

The epitaph on the grave reads like a riddle: "Rien n'est vrai, tout est vivant" (Nothing is true, all is alive).[38] The epitaph also serves as epigraph to Glissant's *Anthologie de la poésie du Tout-Monde* (13). The art of the riddle points in at least two directions: the philosophical mode of the fragment practiced by Heraclitus, a philosopher close to Glissant's heart because of his preference for the scrap, the aphorism, and thought in movement rather than fixed absolute truths. The riddle also evokes the *tim-tim*, or riddle, common to the Caribbean storyteller, inheritor of an African *Weltanschauung*.[39] The enigma is thus situated in both a Greek and an Afro-Caribbean philosophical tradition. But what does the riddle mean? First of all, it denies the existence of an absolute truth, and even of the very possibility of truth, in line with Glissant's religion in flux. Indeed, claiming that nothing is true opens up a paradox, since the utterance of the absolute proposal, "nothing is true," is also a denial of that very claim: if "nothing is true," then, the proposal itself is not true, a version of the classic "liar paradox" in philosophy. Then how do we interpret the second part of the inscription? What is the relation between the two terms? Is it one of explanation or simple juxtaposition? If all is alive, then all is in movement, in opposition to the rigidity of death or of an absolute truth. The maxim constitutes the logical consequence of the philosopher's relational aesthetics in a posthumous tense since it does not end with the author's own death, but instead continues in a relay with artists who continue his project, knowingly or unknowingly, and with the landscape that changes it. Since the riddle is an epitaph on a grave, Glissant invites us to reflect not only on his death, but on ours as well, to consider death as a transformational mode in movement and flux with nature rather than a stasis in being. This brings us back to Glissant's Caribbean and Rabelaisian thinking of the environment as a connected network of flows of death feeding life. As Alessandro Corio explains, "Reading Glissant from

the punctuation of the submarine earth.[46] This enormous womb-abyss, at the origin of new life and new cultures in a so-called "New World," is loaded with death. It is "pregnant with as many dead as living under the sentence of death" (6). The womb, also called "belly," is simultaneously site of gestation and digestion, a uterus-intestine that processes the enslaved bodies, sucks in their nutrients, and expels them as excrements. The site of mothering is inextricably linked to death: a womb-tomb.[47]

In *Philosophie de la Relation*, Glissant comes back to the tomb, which is no longer submarine but telluric: a collapse of earth. The passage from the underwater mass grave (*Poétique*) to the soil of where the mother is buried (*Philosophie*) indicates a shift from the haunting of millions of dead to the tribute to one, from the unknown to the known, the unnamed to the named, the terrifying womb-intestine of the slave ship to the poet's own mother. It is not, however, a simple passage from the collective to the individual, since the mother's tomb communicates with the Whole-World's community.

In Glissant's poem-essay, three subjects occupy the same structural position of being sunken into the earth: the poem, the poet's birth house, and the poet's mother, who, for the first time in Glissant's written work, is called by her full name: Adrienne Marie Euphémie Godard. This precise naming contrasts with the submarine womb-tomb of Glissant's earlier writing, which was unnamable, collective, enormous, and unthinkable: "And you can't make out one from two nor from two hundred million" (*Case du commandeur*, 64). The grave of *Philosophie de la Relation* becomes individual and private as the writer feels his own death drawing near. The poet's named real mother also seems to replace the faceless and abject womb-abyss of *Poétique de la Relation*. In *Philosophie de la Relation*, Glissant recounts his discovery of an "old, yellowish official document" stating that his mother's full given name was "Adrienne Marie Euphémie": "This constituted the very rare manifestation of a proximity to a mother, to my mother in particular, who was far remote from literary concerns, but who nonetheless had a buried intuition for the literary" (144–45). The full spelling out of the dead mother's name leads to the realization of a close proximity to "a mother," which Glissant defers calling (by *pudeur*, discretion, or respect) "more specifically, my own mother" (145). This newly found relation comes with the intuition of a subterranean ("buried") literary or poetic relation with the mother. The closeness increases, Glissant adds, when his mother "died and refused to be buried in the town of Lamentin, which sinks into the mangrove. Madame Adrienne wished to be buried in a wooden box in the naked soil, a ceremony both bare and unbearable . . . to refuse a grave is no ordinary thing in the land of Martinique [where] tombs are the Houses of the dead" (145). The mother's body is thus homeless, errant, exiled away from tomb or town. This thought, to the poet, is unbearable. But, at the same time, it is a materialization of his philosophy of errantry and uprooting.[48] The mother's unhomed body allows her to be everywhere: "Today, I can conceive that my mother, whose undeniable trace I barely sense between two of these monuments, completely fills the Lamentin cemetery." It is precisely this simultaneous disappearance under the earth and uncertainty of the site that links the mother to the poem: "But the poem . . . had slipped away under the first caving in of the earth. Let us remember: *that the poem was buried in a collapse of earth*" (15).

Philosophie de la Relation, as a genre, is infixable. It begins with the lyrical opaque bursts of Glissant's early poems, such as *Les Indes,* evoking the birth of the sacred simultaneous to the birth of the Earth. It is a philosophical treatise with conceptual elaborations on the thought of trembling. It also includes Glissant's autobiographical accounts of his last visits to Martinique. Like the poem or the departed mother's body, *Philosophie de la Relation* is nowhere and everywhere. The birth house, like the poem and the mother's body, is now engulfed in the soil: "The cabin was engulfed in a collapse of earth. As if all the births it had produced, and, by extension, my own, had reverted to a primordial abyss, quickly covered up by chaotically organized ordinary plants. Fragility of birth that carries you away . . . but, along with that same feeling, I always felt as if I was aging at the rhythm of the earth, an infinite speck of dust in the universe, myself dust (archipelago)" (117). This mature meditation on birth and death is marked by the aporetic and the oxymoric, best expressed through poetry. The birth, which "carries you away," is already death, and rebirth effected through the proliferation of ordinary plants. It links the infinitesimally small, the humbleness of the humus reduced to its minimal atom in the form of a speck of dust, to the infinitely large birthing and dying of the Earth. The breath of the poet married to that of the Earth is extremely close to Léopold Sédar Senghor's philosophy of a joint movement between the rhythm of the Earth and that of humanity.[49] It also brings to mind Aimé Césaire's *Notebook of a Return to the Native Land,* in which the poet allies utter humility ("Eia for those who never invented anything") to the dawn of the earth ("truly the eldest sons of the world"; 35).

It comes as no surprise, then, that, late in his writing, Glissant offers a long-postponed and long-awaited homage to his literary older brother, the

Martinican poet Aimé Césaire. The penultimate chapter of *Philosophie de la Relation* relates a journey to the birth house of "the poet." "The poet," presented as anonymous and therefore absolute by the use of the definite article, is only revealed to be Aimé Césaire later in the chapter. This deferred naming echoes the postponement of Glissant's naming of his own mother. In his last book, Glissant finally recognizes Césaire, his long-neglected poetic predecessor of a few years, as if death approaching would erase the tension between the two Martinican writers, competitors in life, by linking them to the archipelagic dust of poetry.

It also comes as no surprise that, while searching for his birth house, Glissant, instead of finding the dwelling, becomes lost in Faulkner's landscape: "If you get lost like this in a postage stamp (for example, Faulkner in his Yoknapatawpha), it means you really know it is yours" (142). The lived landscape of Martinique buried in the earth espouses Césaire's poetry and Faulkner's imaginary.[50] This is what makes the grave bearable to Glissant and to his visitors: the interment of his poetry within the Poetry of the world. The grave is Poetry.

An Ecological Sacred

One of the sacred forms at work in Caribbean thought, including that of Glissant, which I like to call a "relational ecological sacred," and which the philosopher himself terms "another sacred" (*Philosophie*, 148), frequently recurs in the works under examination in *Water Graves*.[51] Julien, Bailey, Walker, Taylor, Philip, and Danticat, among many others, champion the genre in their aesthetic creations that provide sacred objects and rituals through a connection among humans, aurochs, fish, coral, seaweed, swamp, sea, cotton, tar, railroad shards, salvaged window frames, preserved legal documents, trash, and mud. This relational sacred may or may not be linked to an institutionalized religion such as Vaudou, Christianity, or Kongo. In Danticat's *Claire of the Sea Light*, for instance, the relational sacred is deeply steeped in Vaudou rituals with the predominance of the sea deity, the *lwa* Lasiwèn. New Orleans artists Julien and Waters create works that are also steeped in Christian and Vaudou imagery and rites that include performative gestures of mourning, like Joseph Roach evokes in *Cities of the Dead*.[52] Whether attached to a religion culturally recognizable as such, all manifestations of the sacred involve a chain of solidarity, a connection with the planet and its elements, large as Gaia and small as a papaya tree: an ecological sacred.[53]

The relational ecological sacred can be universalized and undoubtedly inhabits regions of the world not predominantly struck with unritual.

French philosopher Michel Serres's *Contrat naturel,* to take but one example, looks strikingly similar to Glissantian thought. However universal the ecological sacred may be, I contend that zones of the unritual more sharply embrace it. It is more a difference of degree than of kind. Cultures touched by the dehumanizing experiences of the unritual of slavery, precarious migration, extreme poverty, and vulnerability to disaster experience a higher degree of forced proximity, which often turns into a solidarity with other living and even inert beings that have gained vitality.[54] In this regard, Monique Allewaert's theory of an "ecologically inflected mode of personhood" (*Ariel's Ecology,* 147) is particularly helpful. Instead of invoking dehumanization, Allewaert qualifies *parahuman* resistance of human subjects through assemblages with animals and plants as the formation and restructuration of dismembered human agency (85). This *parahuman* resistance is clear in Glissant's *Philosophie de la Relation,* in which plant life relays the mother's missing grave, as well as in Taylor's coral-human assemblages, in Danticat's *Claire of the Sea Light*—where frogs and humans relate in digestive and gestational modes—and in Zeitlin's *Beasts of the Southern Wild,* where little girl Hushpuppy befriends the terrible aurochs instead of becoming their "breakfast."

This *parahuman* relation extends to inert objects since, tragically, humans were legally reduced to a status of things, and since, in the context of underwater drowning, the remains of human bodies were locked up with balls, chains, and metal weights that continue to bind them, even in death and abysmal oblivion. It is one thing for drowned bodies to be enlivened with corals, as is the case with King Alonso's body in Shakespeare's *The Tempest,* or in Taylor's beautiful underwater sculptures. While tragic, Shakespeare's and Taylor's drowned bodies form a beautiful assemblage with vivid superorganisms:

> Full fathom five thy father lies
> Of his bones are coral made
> Those are pearls that were his eyes
> Nothing of him that doth fade
> But doth suffer a sea-change
> Into something rich and strange. (1.2.482–87)

It is harder to imagine this "something rich and strange," when underwater human remains can only be measured against metal, as evoked by Glissant's "balls and chains" tracing the underwater road of the slave trade evoke, or as documented by historians exposing the tragic measurement of humanity against ballast.

In 2015, the remnants of the Saõ José, a slave ship hauling between four hundred and five hundred enslaved humans from Mozambique to Brazil in 1794, was found off the coast of South Africa's Cape Town. Paul Gardullo, historian and curator at the Smithsonian National Museum of African American History and Culture (NMAAHC), explains that the number of humans on the ship can only be evaluated by the number of 1,500 iron blocks of ballasts initially boarded on the ship, necessary to offset the weight of human cargo. As indicated in a *New York Times* piece entitled "Grim History Traced in Sunken Slave Ship Found Off South Africa," "no skeletons or even partial [human] remains have been found in the wreck."[55] Thus, humanity—the absence of human remains—can only be *measured* (not seen or imagined) by the supplementary weight in metal that allowed the bodies, too light for cargo, to be transported to their plantation incarceration and social death. Gardullo, in a tone not dissimilar to Glissant's philosophical and poetic reflection on the balls and chains gone green, explains: "The more cargo that you have that is living, the more ballast you need, because live cargo moves and is not as heavy as, say, tubs of molasses . . . Ballast becomes a signature for slaving, and a direct corollary to human beings"[56] In its coldness, the language of theorems ("a corollary") sharply highlights the dehumanization of the enslaved. The particularly petrifying evidence—iron blocks of ballast signifying humanity—kills once more the transported human beings of the unritual of slavery by reducing them once more to thingness. The blunt discovery attaches emotion to scientific investigation, as maritime archeologist Jaco Boschoff, who dived multiple times into the site, admits: "'I'm a scientist, I'm not one for massive amounts of emotion'" but "'I knew immediately.'"[57]

As "Grim History" indicates, this scientific discovery was quickly followed by the need to ritualize: "Divers will place soil from Mozambique Island on the underwater site to memorialize the graves of the 212 drowned slaves." In addition, the museum will exhibit items pulled from the sea, with "recordings of voices describing the slave trade, "a place . . . for you to mourn and to remember." The project is in line with the ecological sacred. The ritual was not attached to any specific religion, for what specific religion could serve in a context in which the enslaved were severed away "from protecting gods and a tutelary community of Gods" (Glissant, *Poetics,* 5) and thrown into the immense unritual of sea bottoms? What remains is the need to mark a watery site as a specific grave that can be seen, uncovered, investigated, and given proper rituals. The teams of historians, scientists, and underwater archeologists of the joint initiative between the Smithsonian NMAAHC and the African Slave Wrecks Project, sponsored by the South African Heritage Resources Agency, do just that, as their recent recovering and excavation (Philip's "exaqua") of the Mozambique ship demonstrates.[58]

Indeed, once a shipwreck site is marked as a specific point at sea, once the slave ship is recovered as a seeable and tangible object, not an elusive passing, the process of collective mourning can begin.[59] Humans acquire a certain control over the immense pervasiveness of underwater deaths and limit the haunting. Significantly as well, the ritual is relational in that it links Mozambique, the place of origin of the kidnapped Africans, to their underwater death site through the sacred soil, which performs—albeit symbolically since soil dissolves in water—a proper ritual covering of bodies. If the first ritual is of the relational sacred kind, the second, performed at a museum, is based on a relaying of media. The experience of the museum's visitor is not just aesthetic, but an act of "mourning" and "remembering.

It is important not to confuse the sacred with religion, since forms of the sacred *can* happen outside of organized religious experience, as philosopher Jean-Pierre Dupuy contends in his *Mark of the Sacred* and as religion scholar Gary Laderman demonstrates in *Sacred Matters*.[60] Philosopher An Yountae, in his monograph on mysticism and religion in post- and decolonial thought, develops the notion of a "secular theology," "concerned less with making theological claims about dogmatic notions such as God or transcendence than with disclosing the overlooked political possibility lurking in mystical thought while probing the mystical depth implicated in political thought" (*Decolonial Abyss,* 5).[61] While Glissant is not a mystic in the sense of being illuminated by God or gods, it is clear that his works are mystical in that they host things obscure to human comprehension, as evidenced in his concept of Opacity. However, for Glissant's case, we should speak of a pragmatic mysticism in touch with the political implications that Yountae highlights. Perhaps more helpful than the term "mystic," which Glissant refrains from using, is his notion of religion. Indeed, Relation, in Glissant's etymological but also philosophical system, is linked to religion. Glissant inflects his central poetic notion of Relation with religion, which he describes as *re-ligare* (to link together again) or *re-legere* (to read again). Serres offers a poetic example of this sense of re-ligion in the profane image of Penelope weaving: "Day and night, Penelope never left her loom. In the same way, religion presses, spins, knots, assembles, gathers, binds, connects, lifts up, reads, or sings the elements of time. . . . The learned say that the word religion staple materiality. This act of self-creation is not a self-enclosure, a sterile tautology, since it begins to be recognized ("commença d'être reconnu") by *another* agency. *Reconnaître,* which can both mean recognition as identification, and *re-connaître,* as knowing again, knowing once more, knowing anew, points to a beginning that is not arrested in time, not even foundational, even abysmal, since it lets us imagine *another* moment of knowing, following the model of Borges's proverbial dreamer who dreams a man to realize that he himself is the figment of another man's dream in "Circular Ruins" (96–100). Like Borges's dizzying, unfathomable, relational, and reversible creation story, Glissant's is also inhabited not by certainty but by doubt: "Thus, should have been decreed, *perhaps,* in the prehistories of all world literatures, this same beginning. Its heading would point to a first and obscure composite of the intention of languages, well before the sharp lightning strikes of histories divide spaces and echoes of voices. It was before all humanity" (C'était avant toute humanité; 11). The appearance of Glissant's "other sacred" is thus not marked by an act of separation but inhabited by a lack of differentiation, by a "good" preracial, preethnic, prehistoric, prelinguistic confusion. This nonact was "avant toute humanité," which could be heard as "before all humanity," but also "before all, humanity"—both preceding humanity but also already intensely human: "It was all happening before races, languages, and stances differentiated and antagonized, and the poem had vanished in a sinkhole of the earth, in unknown darknesses, and with it all possibilities of languages, that we now had to recompose like broken roots" (13).

This sacred appears in a state of previolence: "The humanities [les humanités] had not yet fortified their differences with the stroke of bloody amputations" (12). It is more than a pre-Babel, more than a premonolingualism, but a prelingualism, where primeval onomatopoeia reigns both at the beginning and end of humanity: "The frenzy of the original *hahr-hahr,* that had prefigured the bells, before standing in for them once they fell silent" (14). Here again, Glissant meets theologian Keller in her discussion of the undifferentiation of Plato's khora, and its modern and postmodern revisions: "In one sense, there is nothing more hotly 'relational' than these Freudian, Lacanian, Kristevan, or Irigayan investigations . . . of the prelinguistic constituents of the subject. An indeterminate Khora, a formless matrix of affection and abjection, can be said to name an unconscious relationality (and so its own version of apophatic entanglement)" (*Cloud,* 220).

Let us repeat, *What is this other sacred and to what is it other?* An excursion into philosopher René Girard's thought on the sacred in

Judeo-Christianity is warranted, providing a sharp contrast with Glissant's and Keller's entangled origins. We would be hard pressed indeed to reconcile Glissant's sacred with Girard's theory of differentiating violence as foundational to human communities. For starters, Glissant's sacred begins with a "primordial poem" (*Philosophie,* 148) that intermingles grunts, unpredictable plants, and pervasive lavas, in an originating chaos that stands opposed to Girard's foundational differentiating murder.[66] On a systemic level, then, the sacred and the profane, instead of facing one another in separated realms, merge and mingle. Sylvie Glissant, claims that Glissant's writing unveils "a profane sacred, a sacred of the living" ("Une Vision prophétique du passé," n.p.). We could even claim that Glissant's noncategorical thought tolls the bell of the categories of sacred and profane altogether. However, while his thought points toward that horizon, it of course cannot be reached since Glissant still needs words, such as the very word "sacred," to speak and to write. If we push his logic through, this would amount also to the disappearance of language as a system of differences (Saussure), and perhaps even the end of thought. While Glissant's "avant toute humanité" may be utopic, thinking toward utopia, like walking toward the horizon to attempt to see its dissolution, makes us at least imagine the possibility of a world free of divisions and focus on lines that unify, rather than on lines that cut. As one of the narrators of *Anima,* by Lebanese-born author Wajdi Mouawad, explains, there are several types of lines: lines that separate and demarcate but also "lines that save us, conductive, electric, musical" (283).

For Girard, human communities simultaneously reveal and conceal the original murder just like a tomb reveals the presence of a corpse all the while cutting it off from sight: "All cultures and all religions are built on this foundation, which they then conceal, just as the tomb is built around the dead body that it conceals. Murder calls for the tomb and the tomb is but the prolongation and perpetuation of murder. The tomb-religion amounts to nothing more or less than the becoming invisible of foundations, of religion and culture, of their only reason of existence" (*Of Things Hidden,* 164). The poem, in Glissant, occupies the same place as murder in Girard's theory: it is concealed through entombment: "But the poem . . . had slipped away under the first caving in of the earth. Let us remember: *that the poem was buried in a collapse of earth*" (*Philosophie,* 15, emphasis in original). As opposed to Girard's murder, which communities conceal, Glissant's poem slips under the earth with an agency of its own, to then reemerge in a beautiful chaotic assemblage with plants. Glissant's mole poem, digging itself into subterranean passage, breathing

Roots, murmurs, flowers, trees, birds, and volcanoes enter in the composition of Glissant's original—which is not originating—violence. Glissant's *other sacred* is bound to take *another* path from Girard's, since it does not define a "domain of human control," but an ecological relationality, which humans do not transcend. As Glissant proceeds to define this predifferentiated sacred, the "before *all* humanity," or "before all, *humanity,*" represents a stage of personhood in which botanical, animal, and elemental forms knot up with the "poem."

The agents of Glissant's ecological sacred include: "Glycerias follement apparus" (Glyceria popping up in strange places; 12), "lisières déchiquetées" (torn-up forest skirts; 12), "arcs-en-ciel torturés [qui] n'étaient encore que des masses sans halo" (tormented rainbows as of yet masses without halos; 12); "les premiers brasiers de la terre" (the first blazes of earth; 12); "un oiseau innumérable" (an innumerable bird; 13); "le chuint cascadant des racines soulevées à vrac et toutes les boues qui résistent à la montée des mots" (the cascading hiss of torn-up root floors and all the muds resisting floods of words; 14); "[un] male papaye [qui] porte des fruits" (a fruit-bearing male papaya tree; 15). The list highlights at once the wholeness of the phenomena, which includes meteorological events, vegetal growths, volcanic beginnings, and the sap rising of words. The aesthetics of the juxtaposition also brings us back to the poem, which creates beauty and meaning through unpredictable encounters. In this ecological poem, human words are present, yet not elected as central, since they tangle up with autonomous agents such as "roots" and "muds."

Glissant's thinking of the origin is not all celebratory and retains an element of violence that dominated his early thought. *Philosophie de la Relation*'s story of nonoriginating origin clearly echoes another inaugural scene, to be found in his 1990 *Poétique de la Relation,* his classic "Barque ouverte." "The Open Boat" famously evokes the unthinkable nature of the experience of enslaved Africans in the Middle Passage, which the poet identifies, with its triple abyss composed of the hold of the ship, the bottom of the ocean, and the abysmal suffering of the enslaved, as the belly, *le ventre,* of the deported Africans. Already in "The Open Boat," the drowned humans attached to corroding balls and chains evolve in their assemblage with seaweed in the haunting image of the "boulets verdis" (greenish balls and chains). The essay provides a tomb, a monument, a prayer, a poem, and dignity to the millions who perished at sea in the absolute unritual of human trade.[72] Glissant's sacred also grows out of this historical state. The violence of the unritual forces *another* relationship to the dead that consists not in burying them, but of retrieving them.

The word "entombment"—and any existing word, for that matter—does not do justice to the act of retrieving the underwater dead. Philip coins the verb *to exaqua,* to remedy the failure of "unearthing" in the context of drowned bodies (see chapter 5).

Despite the similarities between the respective beginnings of *Poétique* and *Philosophie,* references to historical and political events seem to have disappeared from Glissant's late musings of *Philosophie de la Relation.* While I agree with Peter Hallward and Nick Nesbitt that the anticolonial ideology of an early Glissant is gone in his late work, I contend that the object of his politics has shifted. Glissant's late work takes not an apolitical turn, but rather a new political turn, an ecopoetic turn, a sacred-political turn, which becomes more and more concerned with what numerous biologists, chemists, geographers, environmentalists, economists, and cultural critics such as Michel Serres, Eugene Stoermer, Paul Crutzen, Bruno Latour, Dipesh Chakrabarty, Timothy Morton, among many others, have identified and theorized as the Anthropocene, an age in which the presence of human animals on earth has had enough of an impact to constitute a geological-scale epoch.[73] Humanity became a geological force. While Glissant does not explicitly cite any of the physicists, historians, and critics who have argued that the Earth has a future without humans and that the apocalyptic end we imagine or anticipate is not that of planet Earth but that of humans, his late thought tightly communicates with their theories. In Glissant's last public conference entitled "Rien n'est vrai, tout est vivant," philosopher François Noudelmann asks him: "Is there a politics of the living?," to which Glissant replies:

> If it's a matter of a politics of the living of planet Earth, I fully agree. But if it's a matter of a politics of the living of humans, I fiercely object, because the living of the Being develops, as I have said, on its own . . . and if we subject it to the scalpel in an attempt to create clones, we introduce in its chain of unpredictability—for the living is unpredictable—the predictability of death. As far as the living of the planet goes . . . I agree with the measures to be taken, with one restriction: are we sure to know the intimate laws, rules, and mechanisms of the functioning of the living of the planet? Absolutely not. Which raises a serious concern: obviously, we have to preserve forests . . . obviously, we have to act, but are we sure that the planet does not heal by itself, ever so slowly, even if, in the meantime, it crushes us? Are we sure that our fate—the fate of humans—is tied to that of the planet?[74]

Glissant's belief in the autonomy of the planet, his depiction of human violence cutting and dissecting the chain of the living, and the rather than forming a circle of community. Nevertheless, rectangles, or rather *hyper*-rectangles, multiplied, salient, and doubled, function as the dominant mode of representation and aesthetic mourning in the post-slavery and post-Katrina works of art I examine in this chapter. The rectangle, absent from the traditional hymn version of the song, appears in A. P. Carter's 1927 interpretation, "Can the Circle Be Unbroken?," in the shape of a window. Closely based on Carter's rendition, each stanza of the Nevilles' version refers to a window through which the mourning singer watches the funeral march: "I was standing / By my window / On a cold and cloudy day." The appearance of the rectangular window spotlights the position of a watcher removed from the procession rather than that of a casket carrier or a procession follower. It places the focus on the one who witnesses the funeral march, a seer who is nonetheless no stranger to the loss. The Neville Brothers' song indeed refers to the death of loved ones through heart-wrenching expression loaded with concrete adjectives referring to age and terms of endearment: "That's my little baby sister"; "That's my mother, my dear old mother." While based closely on Carter's song, which also laments the death of a mother, the Nevilles anchor the dirge in a cultural specificity inseparable from New Orleans:

> That's Chief Jolly
> That you carry
> I sure hate
> To see him go.

The term "Chief," in the New Orleans context, immediately calls to mind the head of a "Mardi Gras Indian" tribe. Mardi Gras Indian tribes are composed of mostly inner-city African American community members who parade in costumes reminiscent of Africa and meant to evoke Native American costumes in a gesture conjuring early solidarity between enslaved Africans and Native Americans.[2]

The song also allies its universality with a specificity grounded in place and culture, as well as reracializing the traditional Carter song into African American New Orleans consciousness. Digging deeper into the character of "Chief Jolly," we learn that the reference also attaches the song to the familial intimacy of the Neville Brothers, whose uncle George Landry was none other than "Big Chief Jolly." The song is thus deeply personal, a dirge to a family member and a city, while nonetheless retaining its universal function of mourning the loss of a loved one. Interestingly, an internet search indicates that the Neville Brothers' version has become emblematic of gang violence in the United States, thus gaining a specific function of mourning associated with urban violence.[3] The dedication of the 1989 album *Yellow Moon,* which is itself a collection of homages to the departed, anonymous and famous, personal and collective—as in the song "Sister Rosa," dedicated to Rosa Parks—points to this personal, familial, and historical tribute. The album is dedicated at once to the "entire Neville Nation" and to "sufferers around the world."[4]

In similar fashion, Bailey, Julien, and Waters simultaneously occupy the positions of bereft window watcher and casket carrier. Deeply entrenched in the effects of disaster (whether slavery or Katrina), and often direct survivors of disaster, these artists saw their works destroyed by the hurricane and its human-made aftermath. Like the art of their Africana predecessors and contemporaries such as Romare Bearden, Jacob Lawrence, and Victor Anicet, or of dissident world artists like Ai Weiwei who respond to human-made, natural, and political disasters, their work is both deeply personal and communal while also decidedly universal. Beginning this discussion with the Neville Brothers and with music is no accident, since this chapter is devoted to African American artists from the US South who *write in the wake* of Katrina and the Middle Passage and who, more crucially, *write Katrina's wake.* While the artists featured here are visual artists, music—in the form of rhythmic or polyrhythmic patterns, the inclusion of musical scores, the representation of musicians, or the incorporation of salvaged musical instruments—is omnipresent in their creations. Moten is right on point when he defines music, with its rhythms, moans, and whole-body involvement as a particularly sacred intervention: "Sound: suspended brightness, unrepresentable and inexplicable mystery of (music is the improvisation of organization) ritual is music" (*In the Break,* 45).

While contemplating and scrutinizing the sea of artistic production in the disasters of slavery and Katrina, what has struck me is the need to frame disaster with a marked insistence on, even artistic obsession with, rectangular shapes and containers. In order to become human, philosopher Paul Ricœur teaches us, one needs a narrative or other structures.[5] There is nothing surprising in the need to frame, contain, and control following a traumatic experience. Death also needs the framework of a narrative. As Danticat lucidly states in her *Art of Death,* "Death cannot write its own story. While we are still alive, we are the ones to get to write the story" (125). There is nothing shocking in the construction of revolutionary frames counteracting journalistic and police framing of blacks as looters and murderers (see chapter 3), nothing unexpected in the need to heal or to cure, to gather in an aesthetic spiritual container the medicine required to heal. The Kongo *nkisi,* its Plantation South equivalent of what the system of slavery had begun.[12] Bailey, Waters, and Julien feature disaster centrally in their works and use aesthetic objects for purposes of containing, remembering, healing, and overcoming the catastrophes of slavery and other meteorological and human-made disasters. While I provide more details on each artist in subsequent sections, the US visual artists Bailey, Julien, and Waters share a common belonging to the African diaspora, carrying the weight of the memory of the Middle Passage and plantation and postplantation violence and featuring them centrally in their works. New Orleans–based artists Julien and Waters experienced the flood firsthand, lost their belongings, and, more crucially, saw a partial or significant portion of their work tools and artistic production ruined in the hurricane and its aftermath.[13]

For these three artists, the materiality of the experience of disaster is married to a sense of the sacred. In the state of the unritual discussed in this book's introduction, the role of the artist is also that of spiritual guide and a performer of sacred acts who reritualizes the dead. This return of the sacred can take many paths, be it the performance of Christian, Kongo, or Vaudou rituals or the secular enactments of a relational or an ecological sacred.[14] In the unritual, the artist is the designated healer and spiritual guide. Aesthetic objects thus also take on an air of sacred objects. In the aftermath of disaster, in the context of human victims of the unritual, aesthetic works provide a grave or a postmortem ritual house of rest and peace. The multiple epitaphs to be found in these artists' photographs, paintings, or multimedia installations, the solid materiality of their frames, endow them with the properties of funeral monuments. At times, their qualities of grave, altar, or coffin are to be understood quite literally. For instance, in Waters's *Clarinets* series, New Orleans jazz instruments repose in cases that are presented as coffins adorned with the offering of cut flowers.[15] The multiplication of coffins, beyond a direct response to Katrina, has a historical resonance with the segregationist treatment of African Americans in the afterlife. A striking example of this practice can be found in Zora Neale Hurston's account in *Their Eyes Were Watching God* of the 1928 Okeechobee hurricane that devastated the Florida Everglades. After "the time for dying was over" and the "time to bury the dead" arrived (168), the gravediggers were charged with the impossible task of differentiating "black" and "white" bodies rendered inscrutable for having stayed in the water for too long. Only "white folks" were to receive a "cheap pine" coffin while instructions to process "colored folks" went as follows: "'Jus' sprinkle plenty quick-lime over 'em and cover 'em up'" (171). "'Don't be waistin' no boxes on colored,'" orders a lead guard (171). We thus understand Waters, Bailey, or Julien's insistence on building rectangles and coffins as a deeply set duty to give the dead a proper ritual.

These *rectangulists,* if I may define this disparate group as such without reducing their individual features to a static school, seem to work countercurrent to some artists of the African diaspora who have tended to privilege the circle or the spiral as a pattern.[16] Yet their preference for the rectangle coexists with its opposite force. Precisely as they frame their creations in rectangles or insert multiple rectangles in their works, the artists systematically break, subvert, dissolve, interrupt, or complicate the rectangles with a passion. On a basic visual level, rectangles crisscross with lines and circles, juxtaposed with other rectangles to form complex geometric shapes. Their frames partly dissolve or liquefy. Regular tessellations become interrupted by another shape or liquid substance. More than creating a visual curiosity, the interruption of the geometric grid and straight lines is heavy with sacred meaning, as the example of Bailey's use of the Kongo *Dikenga* (Kongo cosmogram) teaches.[17] Musical notes appear, pointing to a creative and unframable synesthesia, be it expressed in melodious harmonies or cacophonies. A bleeding blue or a splat of mud partially covering the rectangle opens it up to the watery threat or to an overflowing abject. Images of water complicate the meaning of rectangle in simultaneously contradictory ways: water that drowns, water that cleanses, water that bars access or allows passage. Shards of mirrors or sparkling surfaces open up the rectangle to dissemination and reflection. The mirrors also link the living and the dead, as curator of African art Susan Cooksey explains: "Mirrors and other shiny objects were meant to evoke the spirit of the deceased, so that she or he might provide guidance to the living" (*Kongo across the Waters,* 350).

Evolving organic and inorganic materials such as corroding metal, fading colors, rotting wood, or growing vegetation give the rectangle a transient nature. Assemblages made out of Georgia red soil, cotton, metal, human and animal hair, flowers, and indigo, allied with more conventional forms of aesthetic representations such as oil painting, watercolors, and photographs, impart a living characteristic, not unlike Anicet's tombstone or Taylor's underwater sculptures.

Some installations, such as Bailey's *Windward Coast,* are meant to be performative and to shift shape in each new exhibit space. Just like the fluctuating sea, Bailey's piano keys fill the gallery space they embrace, their shape never the same. On multiple levels, all the works of art under analysis here resist containment in one singular art frame, one single media frame, one single sense. Julien and Waters incorporate painting, quilting, flags, instruments, flowers, and other found objects in their photographs. Bailey adds musical or concrete soundtracks to his multimedia exhibits. In all of the works, the multiple media stand in a relation of solidarity or relation. This "relational aesthetics," as defined by art historian Nicolas Bourriaud, takes as its base "the realm of human interactions and its social context, rather than the assertion of an independent and private symbolic space" (quoted in Bishop, *Installation Art,* 116).

These works unanimously escape monolithic cultural frames and avoid blending varied cultural elements in their performance of creolization. Bailey collects Kongo, Carib, African American, and Jamaican signs in his creations. Assembled in the medicine cabinet, these elements are never blended but coexist in their screaming particularity. The Kongo Dikenga is recognizable as such, yet it forms another world in progress through the unpredictable product born from its juxtaposition with family portraits, and from the endless process left to the viewers' imagination. The artists' creolization, I argue, goes beyond the definition of creolization based on human difference, reaching a transspecies, transelement dimension whereby the animal, the human, the vegetal, and even the inorganic materiality of metal or stone are agents in solidarity. Creolization also acts in the juxtaposition, the co-living, of the dead, the living, and the realm of its liminal continuum.

For Glissant, creolization, in contrast with an impoverishing blending or melting pot, diffracts the objects in contact and paradoxically leads to beautiful and unpredictable results, such as jazz born out of the plantation system and slavery's horrors.[18] The artists build on the same paradox of an openness born out of enclosure, separation, and segregation, on the paradox of beauty born of extreme violence that Glissant identifies as a characteristic of the plantation in his *Poetics of Relation* or Philip as an amazing result of the inhuman system of slavery in her *Zong!* The plantation, for Glissant, is shaped by confinement: "It is an entirely pyramidal organization, confined in an enclosed space . . . whose technical mode of production is non-evolving since it is based on a structure of enslavement" (*Poétique,* 78). The astonishing fact, for Glissant, is that a supremely enclosed system provided the space and occasion for creolization, which he calls "open word": "Thus, the limit, which was the structural weakness [of the plantation system], becomes for us an advantage..In the end, captivity lost the battle. The place was closed, but the word that derived from it remains open" (89). Waters's clarinet cases, Julien's quilt, and Bailey's cabinets and the myriad possibilities they contain repeat, across the waters of the diasporic Americas, a "closed space" begetting an "open word."

While I could have introduced these contemporary artists in any order, the organizing principle of this chapter relies on the evolution of the rectangle in their works. While the rectangle is sovereign as a frame in Waters's creations, it becomes destabilized and vulnerable in Julien's *Katrina Quilt,* just like the leaning frame of a structurally compromised New Orleans house, disseminated and ultimately washed over in Bailey's *Voyage of No Return.* This progression is also that of ritualization and mourning, which begins with the need to frame the experience of death, to ritualize and provide a grave, to be able to embrace the living again in the fluidity and continuity of a performance or a wake.

Eric Waters: Clarinets in Peace

Like many contemporary artists born and bred in New Orleans, Eric Waters was at least doubly struck by the flood: first because he experienced it as a person, and second because his work, past and present, was deeply affected by it.[19] As for his past work, in 2005, floodwaters destroyed his home and the majority of his life's work, as if his last name held the premonition of his fate. As for the future, the flood was instrumental in changing the photographer's focus and mission, turning it into a gesture of preservation, remembrance, and sacred gesture. Before Katrina, Waters was especially known for capturing living scenes of Mardi Gras, second line dances, and other New Orleans performances.[20] He was a favorite portraitist among jazz artists, as well as a sought-after wedding photographer, which turned his attention, mostly, to the living. The vivid, saturated, and often primary colors he captured and the quality of luminous light of his *Mardi Gras Indians* series attest to boisterous life. Sliding by in rapid succession on his official website, these photos proclaim the unaffected purity of colors such as egg-yolk yellow, peacock blue, royal blue, hot pink, pastel pink, fire orange, earthy rust, deep purple, gold beige, grass green, and blood red, testifying, in their juxtaposition, to the primacy of life. The vibrant colors and fluff of the Mardi Gras Indian chiefs' plumage often fill the frame completely, refusing, in their excess of life, to be seized by the rectangular shape.[21]

Waters's post-Katrina series, *Clarinets—A New Orleans Metaphor,* stands in sharp contrast to the boisterous Mardi Gras Indian scenes.[22] While still based on music and performance, *Clarinets,* a collection of mixed-media still lifes composed of "30 modestly sized photographs in searing, saturated color," has as its central focus not sounding instruments under the hands and breath of living artists, but instruments at rest, instruments at peace.[23] Waters explains that

> the project began with a chance encounter with Dr. Michael White at the 2008 New Orleans Jazz and Heritage Festival. Upon seeing me, he said that I should photograph his clarinet collection, which was destroyed by the levees breach in New Orleans after Hurricane Katrina. This serendipitous moment gave birth to a collection of clarinet photographs originally called "A New Orleans Metaphor: Death and Dying in post levees breach New Orleans aka Katrina". A long title for a long journey taken by a collection of clarinets, some dating back to the 1890's. The words reverence, awe, irony, rejuvenation, hope, despair, anger, and beauty served as inspiration for the collection. The journey, once begun, became a consuming passion.[24]

Significantly, the idea was born out of a moment of solidarity, of relay, between the photographer, scholar, and musician Michael White.[25] Waters's *Clarinets* series has subsequently been preserved in a gorgeous, oversized hardcover book entitled *Solemn Sounds of Silence*. Waters's photographs are accompanied by seven poems by Atlanta-based writer Kevin Sipp that lyrically echo the photographs, offering reverence to the victims and survivors of both Katrina and social and racial oppression. The project of art after disaster must be a common and collective enterprise in which, as the clarinet project demonstrates, music, scholarship, photography, and poetry relay each other.

Waters characterizes his chance encounter with White as a moment of serendipity, a found opportunity in loss. One could easily read this as opportunism; to be sure, photography or art in the wake of disaster runs the risk of exploiting disaster with a lucrative goal devoid of moral, ethical, or even emotional value. It also runs the risk of reducing living and suffering human subjects to objects of consumption. Susan Sontag warns us against this risk: "Whatever the moral claims made on behalf of photography, its main effect is to convert the world into a department store or museum-without-walls in which every subject is depreciated to an object of consumption, promoted into an item for aesthetic appreciation" (*On Photography,* 110). The gesture of turning the world into an aesthetic object is particularly violent in the representation of suffering and devastation. Indeed, Waters's clarinet series, among other postdisaster works, has been described as flirting with "disaster porn," or the bottomless "appetite for the iconography of disaster," in an essay by art critic Cinque Hicks. Hicks categorizes Waters's *Clarinets* as part of that trend:

"The rhetorical gesture of the flowers and the sweetness of the blue and green hues distract from the artist's argument rather than augment it. By profoundly prettifying his subjects, Waters has made confections that slide down too easily. Disaster is made gorgeous and loss made romantic."[26]

I argue, however, that Waters's "prettifying" of disintegrating instruments, which are lost to their living use, is not in the service of art for art's sake or financial profit but instead functions to beautify a grave. The flowers are not merely decorative objects but offerings on a tomb. We would be hard pressed to read Waters, an artist who lost his home, his art, to the storm, and who now lives in Atlanta, far from his beloved city, as an exploiter, much less a pornographer, of the storm. Waters describes his *Clarinets* enterprise as a "consuming passion," evoking both the depth of his gesture of artistic giving, and the suffering he undergoes. The blue, brown, and red hues, more than pleasing to the eye, are deeply connected with a history of diaspora and grief: the blue of the blues, the red of blood, the brown of precious African woods, or, as poet Kevin Sipp seizes it, in the title of one of his poem paying homage to Waters' photographs, "Velvet the color of blood blues, Wood the color of bones" (*Solemn Sounds,* 2).

My reading of Waters's *Clarinets* as graves or funeral monuments to the dead by a mourning artist contests the interpretation of gratuitous prettifying. Many of the photographs in the series have as subject a frame that evokes a coffin or a grave: corroded and broken clarinet cases shaped like rectangles with softened angles.[27] One of the still lives (9) contains three clarinet bells placed vertically, turned into vases containing wilted roses, as if resting on a funeral monument. The bottom of the frame lies on the clarinet bell, which itself lies on a hard black stone rectangle the shape of a tombstone. The horizontal case turned grave contains metallic bits of instruments, shards of rotten wood, broken flower stems, and shreds of roughly textured black fabric partially dyed in black metallic blue. The rotten frame begins to deteriorate on the right-hand side, its content on the verge of pouring out, as if the frame were struggling to harness uncontainable pain. Rectangular framings are common in the series. At times, the frame disintegrates or is incomplete. Five clarinets stacked horizontally are framed by only three found pieces of wood, including one that looks like a clutch, desperately attempting to hold the instruments together, like a fragile collection of bones detached from their frame.

In another untitled photograph instruments of different sizes attempt to give a rectangular resting place to other clarinets and fail to do so; one leans dangerously while another is too short to complete the rectangle around a disposition of clarinet bridge keys and tone hold rings

a barely recognizable mess of melted clarinets, reaching the abstraction of unattached shapes and colors where rust melts into a verdigris blue, a verdigris blues.[31] All, in this ensemble, is movement of fluid, unpredictable curves and spirals that have said goodbye to their straight lines. They have relinquished their intended function and classification, since the clarinet keys could as well be human fingers or toes. The serpentine melted keyholes resemble eyes looking straight at the viewer. Joints, bells, mouthpieces, keys, and barrels form a still life of dismembered body parts. At the same time, the composition resembles the dense, fluid, animated lines of Cuban painter Wifredo Lam's masterpiece, *The Jungle,* in which animal, human, and vegetal limbs are in a state of becoming one another, of uninterrupted circulation. It also concretizes Glissant's emblematic figure of the rhizome, in which the growth is horizontal, vertical, and spiralic, where, when a root is cut, it grows again in a new direction.

Waters's rhizomatic work is an antirectangle. The composition evokes a fluid network of connections between the dead and the living. At the same time, however, the frequent presence of rectangles in Waters's creations also marks a necessary moment in the work of ritualization. I see the photograph reproduced on page 12 as a step beyond the necessary gesture of rectangulation. It reestablishes movement and flux only possible after the building of a grave or monument.

Two of Waters's photographed installations from the *Clarinets* series include an LP record with the inscription NoLa.[32] The "metaphor" in the series title, *Clarinets—A New Orleans Metaphor,* is used as a concrete word, a concrete object standing for another in an attempt to allow language to seize the ungraspable, to say the ineffable. In this case, the clarinet stands for the vastness of the destruction of a city whose name, NoLa (which could also be a beloved woman's), is inscribed on the grave-object like the name of the deceased or an epitaph. Waters's flowers—lilies of bright orange, yellow, and pink—can be spectacularly vibrant. The vividness is technically obtained by building color on film with the use of long exposure, which achieves a more saturated result than digital photography. Alternatively, other flowers suggest fragility in the delicate paleness of dried roses and desiccated lilies, whose grooves resemble veinlets of human skin or veils discreetly covering the corpse of the departed, be they vegetal, human, or, in this case, inanimate objects. Plump and desiccated flowers assembled in the same composition create a continuum between the living and the dead.

Why use clarinets as the privileged New Orleans metaphor? We could reasonably explain this by the serendipitous encounter between Waters

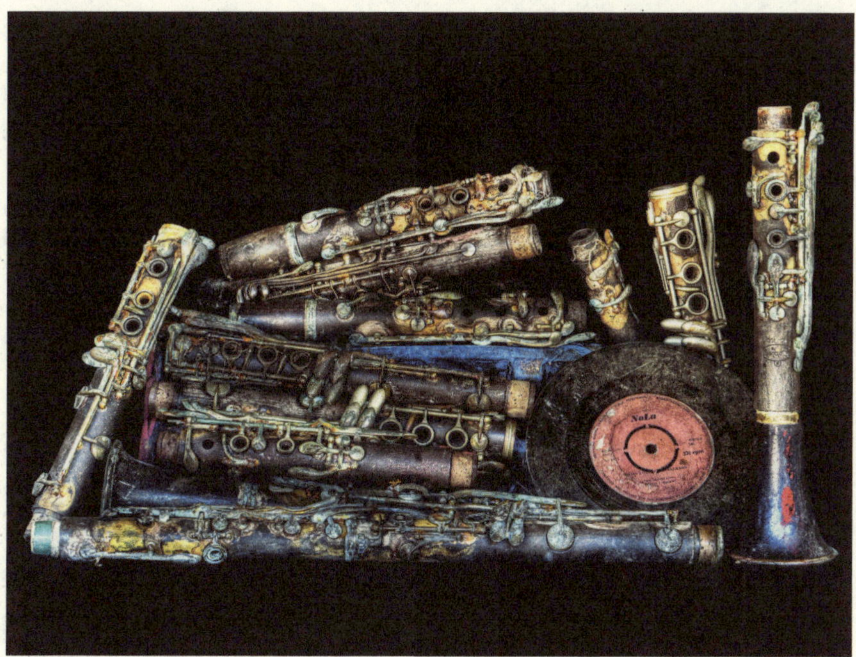

Eric Waters, *Untitled* from the series *Clarinets: A New Orleans Metaphor,* photograph, 2009. (© Eric Waters, courtesy of the artist)

and White. This alone, however, fails to explain the "consuming passion" that seized the artist. The clarinet is a form of musical expression that contributes to the multimedia and kinesthetic need of combining objects. It also contributes to the resacralization, the memorialization, in the wake of the unritual. Sound is central to the works, as is the sense of smell with the presence of flowers. The collection is also subtitled in some of its versions as "the solemn sound of silence," highlighting the irony of an instrument meant to produce sound, to articulate music, silenced by disaster. As art reviewer Catherine Fox writes, "A clarinet may not be significant in the grand scheme of losses endured, but somehow these pictures serve as a metaphor for Katrina tragedies large and small. The instruments speak precisely in their juxtaposition with other found objects that are given meaning and made to speak (through metaphor). But what story do the clarinets tell us? While central in early jazz between the 1910s and 1940s Big Band era, the clarinet has been neglected as a symbolic instrument of contemporary jazz, which tends to privilege the trumpet, the trombone, or the saxophone as its main representatives. Choosing a more discrete and complicated, less boisterous or powerful instrument than, for instance, the saxophone or the trumpet may also make a statement about neglected players in the contemporary jazz scene, paying tribute to a disused, neglected part of New Orleans history. The clarinets are also carriers of a deep transatlantic history. For instance, their wood—clarinets were often carved out of African hardwood, *mpingo* or African blackwood, and granadilla. The choice of this deeply historical, discreet, complicated instrument as opposed to the trumpet, which has become emblematic of New Orleans jazz through dominant images of Louis Armstrong, may also attempt to avoid repeating a stereotypical image of the city. The clarinet is not a loud emblem. It is a grounded metaphor.

In the same way, Waters's *Clarinets* compositions escape easy representations. They are neither "pretty" nor "gorgeous," two words critic Hicks used to qualify the series. Despite some pretty elements inserted into them, the works are not pretty in the sense of a pleasing, attractive, or decorative and diminutive beauty. Nor can these modestly sized photographs exhibiting corrosion, rust, rot, and fragility be considered "gorgeous" in a flaunting, excessive, sexual way. The works are beautiful, however, in their combined strength and vulnerability and in the contrasts they exhibit, like the dissonant beauty of the city of New Orleans. The vivid colors of the lilies against the subdued verdigris, celadon, turquoise, rusty-earth, and brass tones of the corroding metal are not decorative in function, but highlight the painful contrast of life and death in the aftermath of disaster. They also perform the simultaneously ironic and hopeful juxtaposition of the transient vividness of life, and of the patina of time and water on the devastated instruments. They belong to this deeply ironic form of art in the wake of disaster that Danticat evokes in *Create Dangerously,* with the striking example of the "chocolate angel" cut off in a background of a sky of blue, towering over human devastation: "In the entryway of a makeshift refugee camp, a large white tent with a striking image painted on it: a stunningly beautiful chocolate angel with her face turned up towards an indigo sky as she floats over a pile of muddied corpses" (169).

Epaul Julien: Open Quilt

Like Waters and like Danticat, (Eric Paul) Epaul Julien is summoned not only to create aesthetically but also to testify, to become a "journalist," a bearer of memory, and a convener of rituals in the wake of disaster and the unritual. His photographic and mixed-media work changed drastically after 2005.[33] Before Katrina, Julien was concerned mainly with "documenting New Orleans and Haiti" (quoted in Biguenet, *Before,* 68). While documenting these two sites of creolization and African heritage, Julien is too humble in reducing his work to mere documentation. His juxtaposition of images of characters captured in his present photography with aged family members demonstrates a complex relating of the rubbing between past and present, life and death. In *Before,* the in-focus portrait of a serene girl in a black cloak in the foreground of the photograph opens into the background figure of another laughing girl in a long white dress, her image blurred, fluid, and dynamic, her smile and dress flowing generously by the effect of blurring caused by a movement too fast to be captured by the photographic lens on a slow shutter speed (69). The placement of in-focus figures dissolved into the ghost-like presence of others through the apposition of photographs producing a double face (*Transcend,* 2004; *Angle Inferno,* 2001; *Unconscious Self,* 2005) pays tribute to the genre of spirit photography, which aims to capture the soul of the departed. Spirit photography, theorized by John Harvey, was practiced from the 1860s through the twenty-first.[34] As scholar Kimberly Juanita Brown indicates, its genre was a staple of "post-civil rights articulations of the ghostly return" and "hyperpresent." Brown argues to "visualize corporeal transcendence" of the "black female experience" (*The Repeating Body,* 140–41). The claim that photography can preserve the evanescent forms of spirits as a "permanent and scrutable artifact" furnishes a "conduit for communication between spiritual and material realms, and (in the case of photographs of ghosts) as an enduring consolation to the bereaved" (7). In this sense, spirit photography provides a path for remembrance in the state of the unritual. Julien, who often faced impending death, indicates that his photographs, through their evasive movement, "capture the spirit of things rather than things themselves."

The photograph entitled *Reflections,* produced a few years before Katrina, is set in a New Orleans cemetery identifiable by the above-the-water, grave-house monuments.[35] A main alley cutting through two rows of graves occupies the center of the photo. In the top half, a young girl holding an oversized umbrella shelters two young boys from the sunrays in a light rain. The girl gazes at one of the boys, who looks at the other boy, who, in turn, looks at the girl. Their triangular gazes establish a circle of communication and reflection. While the group is in focus, one of the smiling boys' hands flutters as if engaged in a hand game. The photograph is divided horizontally in its exact middle by the pool formed by stagnating rain water. The bottom half is the reflection of the children and the graves. The sepia tones give the photograph the patina of things past, in

Epaul Julien, *Reflections,* photograph, silver gelatine, 2003. (© Epaul Julien, courtesy of the artist)

contrast to the children's decidedly contemporary oversized shorts, pants, shirts, and basketball sneakers. *Reflections* is part of the series entitled *1803,* in homage to the birth of the Haitian nation, of which Julien's great-great-grandfather was a citizen. The series mixes portraits of residents of New Orleans and Haiti, such as a second-line dancer with umbrella and a Haitian mambo of Vaudou priestess, establishing a kinship between the two Creole sites. In the series, images of children playing in contemporary New Orleans and Haiti mix with photographs of the past, as well as with portraits such as *Mommy and Me,* a vintage-looking portrait of a toddler in his or her mother's arms. The double-exposure technique in *Mommy and Me* is reminiscent of vintage spirit photography and indicates that the past, the dead, still haunt us with their movements.

Geographic, temporal limits, and the frontier between life and death are softened and even erased by the monochromatic sepia tone uniting all the photos of the series, as well as by the softness of blurred lines. The artist adds sepia tones especially when portraying African American skin tones, which evoke warmth and life. Julien stays away from black and white photography, which, he claims, spreads upon the photographed subjects the tint of death with their blue and green overtones.

The still life with plump open papaya (*Papay,* 2002) and the portrait of a merchant selling sweet potato pies (*Sweet Potato Pie,* 2003) coexist with scenes of cemeteries and desolate landscape (*Barn,* 1998; *Home Solem,* 2003), establishing a fluidity between the pleasures of quotidian life and death. The work *Reflections* establishes a deep connection between present and past through the fluidity of the mirroring water, a relation that clearly becomes one between life and death in the space of the cemetery, a place of reflection, circulation, and communication. The line of water simultaneously marks the zone of division and passage between life and death, as in the Kongo Dikenga or in the Haitian cosmogony. Julien's object escapes the frame, since the top of the children's head is cut off both above and below, white, watery sky on top and white water reflecting white sky in the bottom giving no limit and no horizon, as if to focus on the relation meeting in the center of the photograph. This glimpse into Julien's pre-Katrina photography is meant to prepare the ground for interpreting his post-Katrina work. While his preoccupation with ancestors, with Vaudou, with Africa and creolization, with the relation between the dead and the living, with memorialization and sacralization of the past, and with his native New Orleans already inhabits his early creations, Katrina radically changed his work. Fleeing the storm, Julien had to leave behind most of his photographic equipment. Out of necessity, the artist reinvented himself and his works using techniques of bricolage, collage, and multimedia creations, working with personal artifacts and salvaged Katrina memorabilia while also incorporating more painting in his works.[36] The techniques, already practiced by pioneer visual artist Robert Rauschenberg in his *Combines* of the 1950s and 1960s, place Julien in greater aesthetic dialogue with Romare Bearden (for the collage), Bailey (for the construction of objects out of mixed media), and Walker (for the use of black, cut-out silhouettes). The interruption caused by disaster strengthens Julien's aesthetic connections with these artists' postslavery work. During his early exile, Julien created cut-out black silhouettes of musicians disintegrating as they play (*Before,* 72–73). One represents a young girl whose trumpet has escaped her vanishing arms, fists tightened in anger. The musical and spiritual heart of the city of New Orleans, also appears stranded in the mess of the installation, as if the cityscape and the city heart had also been irremediably changed by the flood. The salvaged window frame is painted over with pastels of pink, yellow, peach, and purple. Its integrity and its power of containment are compromised by vivid marks of red and blue bleeding on the frame, as if blood and water had invaded the work. In the bottom-right corner, the grid evolves into spiraling circles in a style reminiscent of Anicet's tombstone on Glissant's grave.

The sea or watery world has indeed invaded the picture. A proportionately large and protruding purple fish scale covers a section of the left-hand side of the piece. Stains of blue indicate the penetration of water in the architectural frame. Finger-painted stains of red evoke the trace of bleeding hands trying to break the walls or ceilings, as so many humans desperately did when were trapped in the attic by raising floodwaters. Pianos are overturned in a messy assemblage. A yellow toy pickup truck is stranded at the bottom of the piece, like so many cars and trucks remained strangely stranded on top of houses in the Lower Ninth Ward for several months, and even years, after Katrina.

The doorframe, as well as other objects or cut-out shapes, are covered by drawings of imperfect grids, circles, arrows, triangles, spirals, crosses, and other symbols drawn in blue by an awkward hand, perhaps in a rush. While the signs are left unexplained, the crosses closely resemble the X-code system used on houses by Federal Emergency Management Agency (FEMA) and the police in the aftermath of the flood to mark the presence of living or dead human and animal bodies, as well as to evaluate structural damage.[38] By using the FEMA X-code in his works, Julien essentially turns his artwork into buildings that, like the damaged dwellings of Katrina, bear the mark of a code that reduces human and animal casualties in a symbolic language devoid of ritualization or respect for the dead. The X, as we know, reduces the human to a nameless and faceless thing. In the landscape of New Orleans, however, and in Bailey's work, the indelible Xs are turned into art and endowed with sacred power, such as the example of an X on a green shack in Bayou St. John's Maurepas Street covered, but not completely erased, by the bright painting of a pink heart.[39] The dots around the heart are characteristics of the *vèvè,* or drawing, to let gods enter the world of the living in Vaudou tradition. The pink heart is one of the attributes of the Iwa Ezili, the Vaudou goddess of love, luxury, and beauty.

Like the transformation of the profane and violent X-codes into a form of beauty and mark of the sacred in the New Orleans cityscape,

Julien's blue inscriptions, while they resemble the X-codes, call to mind the *Dikenga*, a representation of Kongo cosmogony that uses rectangular geometrical forms interrupted by other lines to prevent the return of lost souls of the undead or of the dead not properly sacralized into the world of the living.[40] The two arrows present in the work could also evoke the Kongo practice of marking the circulation of the spirits of the dead, as historian of African art Carol Thompson explains: "Arrows point counterclockwise to chart the soul's voyage through life. A horizontal line marks the boundary between the living above and the ancestors below; it is also conceived as a mirror-like surface of water—the threshold between this world and beyond" ("Minkisi," 12). The presence of an African-derived cosmogony also marks Bailey's work, as I show below.

In what is arguably the most striking work of the 2006 mixed-media series *Katrina Quilt,* Julien engages even more directly with geometry menaced by disaster and the language of the X-codes. As its title indicates, the composition takes as its object a patchwork of the artist's own rectangular photographs of Xs on walls, of found handwritten inscriptions, painted over or digitally altered. The grid is composed of eight columns and seven rows. Bleeding colors and dissolving lines interrupt its square geometry.

The choice of the quilt as a form of memorialization and ritualization of the past is heavy with symbolism, since quilts are produced and presented as gifts on special occasions such as births, weddings, or funerals and are meant to bring the physical comforts of warmth and cuddling. But quilts can also act as political gestures on the part of the community to share an untold story, as with the domestic violence AIDS Memorial Quilt.[41] Mississippi-based artist Gwendolyn Ann Magee (1943–2011) quilted to celebrate the power of resistance and African American agency in response to segregation and racial violence. Her quilts represent the Gehennas that Europeans and their descendants inflicted upon Africans and African Americans. They feature the slave trade (*Expandable Cargo,* 2010), lynching (*Southern Heritage, Southern Shame,* 2014), chain gangs (*Five Year Hard Labor,* 2001), and Hurricane Katrina (*Requiem,* 2007).[42] Magee also manifests the beauty and creativity that persist despite attempts at dehumanization. The orange-red, which could evoke the flames of a devastating fire, also depicts the warmth of many suns. The green and black blues evoke the invasion of water while at the same time forming an aesthetically compelling tableau.

In her powerful online exhibit and analysis of Magee's fabric art, curator Dorothy Moye quotes Monica Hesse from the *Washington Post:*

own "X-signs," including this one, thus troubling the division between FEMA and Katrina survivors, official code language and creativity, order and madness.

Among some of the photographed residents' inscriptions included in Julien's quilt, a straightforward political inscription—"Is this America?"—criticizes the nation's response in a sharp irony, written on the star-spangled banner. In his four-part documentary, *When the Levees Broke: A Requiem in Four Parts,* Lee similarly refers to the neglected African American victims of Katrina and segregation as state of exceptionality within the nation: "This film document is in remembrance of all the Hurricane Katrina victims in New Orleans and in the Gulf states of Louisiana, Mississippi, Alabama, and Florida. Today, the people living along the Gulf Coast continue in their daily struggle to rebuild, revive, and renew in *these* United States of America" (opening credits, emphasis mine). Southern hospitality coexists with violent territoriality: "Welcome Bac'k Yall" [*sic*] stands next to "Looters will be shot." "Off to Gumbo," inscribed on another door, indicates the survival of New Orleans cultural specificity through the reference to culinary comfort and the ironic coexistence of rampant death with quotidian pleasures.[48]

The careful selection of the shots, as well as the framing, gives a sense that the work of art is not flooded by disaster, but instead frames it by manipulating information, provoking meaning out of the juxtapositions and complex structure. Julien's work is not a quilt, but the photograph of a quilt. It is not constructed out of three layers of fabric, but out of the arrangement of carefully chosen photographs. The rectangles are not united through the stitching, but through the collage technique of a photographer, which adds yet another level of framing and control. This control, this framing, however, is not perfectly geometric and retains, in its structure, marks of disaster. This imperfect symmetry nonetheless can also be seen as a gesture of control, a *medicine* for healing, and a door to the sacred.

The outside frame of *Katrina's Quilt* consists of a perfect rectangle attempting to frame other perfect rectangles. But, beginning with the fifth row down, the geometry is broken by the photo of an unstable shotgun house that cannot be contained by the frames and dangerously leans to show its imminent fall. The excessive use of frames and their ultimate demise in Julien's photographic object recalls the postdisaster work of Art Spiegelman's *In the Shadow of No Towers*. Similarly, Spiegelman's graphic novel account of the 9/11 attack and its aftermath is dominated by an abundance of frames that fail to hold their narrative together.[49] For cultural critic Martha Kuhlman, however, the crumbling frames of

Spiegelman's work do not indicate failure of narrative control, but rather a different form of control over the narrative that she calls "tressage," which could be translated as braiding or interweaving: "In Spiegelman's work, the centrifugal force of fragmented narratives is balanced by the centripetal energy of *tressage*" (*The Traumatic Temporality,* 856).[50] Tressage, the art of interweaving in a nonlinear way, is built, for Kuhlman, on "an elaborate substructure that contains hidden symmetries, visual analogies, and references that create a coherent whole" (861). Julien's *Katrina's Quilt* seems to be built on the same principle. While the shotgun house, the structural backbone of the work—and of New Orleans, for that matter—fails, like Spiegelman's falling towers, to hold its city in a centrifugal way, *tressage* holds the work, and the city, together by inviting the viewer to recreate multiple connections with the fragments that lead to multiple interpretations. For instance, the diagonal proximity of the inscription "Looters Will Be Shot" with "Welcome Bac'k Yall," depending on the reading direction, could be interpreted as hope or as cruel irony. The juxtaposition of the frames inserts a sense of the authorial control of the artist who recreated a narrative, providing for the viewer what Kuhlman calls "the delight of fitting these pieces together and figuring out graphic solutions to a catastrophic event that appears to defy representation" in the face of trauma (861). Spiegelman's and Julien's narrative control in the aftermath of disaster, be it 9/11, Katrina, or slavery, can only function through this interactive, collective, or "compositionist" model, to use philosopher and anthropologist Bruno Latour's word.[51]

In *Katrina's Quilt,* the choice of the single shotgun house as frame breaker makes a strong statement about the victims of Katrina. While revival Greek southern mansions constitute the dominant architectural style of iconic St. Charles Avenue, the most common New Orleans dwelling is the deep and narrow shotgun house, designed to save space in limited lots. Historians have argued that the shotgun house was inherited from West African architecture and brought to New Orleans to slowly overpower Creole cottages in New Orleans in the 1830s.[52] While the floor plan of the house can be explained by the material need of facilitating air circulation in subtropical environments, religious scholars also claim that the structure facilitates the circulation of spirits. While its name is often explained by the fact that one can shoot a bullet straight through the house, the meaning is also inflected by the term "shogun," which means "God's house" among the Yoruba people in West Africa.[53] Thus, the shotgun house is at once emblematic of a particular sociocultural economic reality and associated with sacred functions, growing deep.

As Julien explains in his interview in *Before,* and as our next featured artist, Bailey, amply demonstrates in his *Memory as Medicine* work, disaster art, especially of the nonexploitative kind performed by survivors or witnesses of the event, is also therapy: "Since I had left New Orleans without my photography equipment, as we traveled I began creating mixed-media collages with the few photographs I had or could reproduce. In the end, I lost ten years of work, and while the discovery of mixed media collage has been therapeutic, my work will never be the same" (*Inventing Reality,* 68).[54] As Julien's testimony indicates, the practice of art in the aftermath of disaster has paradoxically both devastating and healing effects. In addition to helping the artist/victim to cope, disaster art can also be therapeutic for the spectator/victim, as Dori Laub claims in the context of the Shoah: "Laub's explanation of how the Holocaust victims work through the process of coming to terms with their trauma is useful in this regard: To undo this entrapment in a fate that cannot be known, cannot be told, but can only be repeated, a therapeutic process—a process of constructing a narrative, or reconstructing a history and essentially of re-externalizing an event—has to be set in motion" (Kuhlman, *Traumatic Temporality,* 69). While trauma studies interpretation is helpful here, we have to keep in mind that Julien's work's potential for healing is first and foremost derived from the specificity of African-derived spirituality and sense of the sacred.

The therapy at work in Julien—what Bailey would call "medicine"—while shaped by disaster in that the story it tells has to be compositionist since it is built not on a house foundation but on shards, bits, and pieces, is also shaped by sacred beliefs. The art itself becomes medicine and sacred object at once, in the Kongo sense of *nkisi,* or medicine.[55] In this light, the interruption in flow can be seen as a putting at rest of the spirits of the dead still haunting the present because they haven't been properly rendered sacred. While the break in pattern in *Katrina's Quilt* might indicate disaster or the unritual, it can also be seen as a possible cure or protection against the haunting of the past. For Southwell Wahlman, "A break in a pattern [in quilts] symbolized a rebirth in the ancestral power of the creator or wearer. And a break in a pattern also helped keep evil spirits away. Evil is believed to travel in straight lines and a break in a pattern or line confuses the spirits and slows them down" ("Signs and Symbols"). The same is said precisely about shotgun houses, whose frames are not perfectly aligned, not so much to prevent a bullet from flying from front door to back kitchen, but to prevent the easy circulation of unwanted spirits through the house, presenting us with another case of omnipresent, yet imperfect, framing and geometry endowed with sacred function. Julien's tilted shotgun house, in its vulnerability, similarly paves the way to an open word that obeys neither the imperial logic of the grid, nor the destructive force of water and of social and racial oppression.

Radcliffe Bailey: Medicine for Disaster

Between June 26 and September 11, 2011,[56] the High Museum of Art in Atlanta organized a large-scale exhibition of works by Bailey entitled *Memory as Medicine*.[57] Thompson mounted the exhibition and edited the gorgeous companion volume in which she published a pivotal essay on the art of Bailey, focusing especially on the strong ties between his work and Kongo history, arts, and cosmogonies. While Atlanta-based Bailey, unlike Waters and Julien, is not a direct witness or survivor of Katrina, disaster is omnipresent and multilayered in his works. The Middle Passage, the recurrent holds of the slave ship and racism, Katrina, the Haitian earthquake of January 2010, and the Japanese Tsunami of March 2011, to cite a few, are all evoked. While anchored in African American and African memory, Bailey also offers an opening on creolizing and worldwide forms of disasters, providing a therapeutic and sacred function of art in their aftermath.

The title of the show, *Memory as Medicine,* is drawn from Bailey's 2011 creations in which he collects various objects associated with slavery and the atomization of the African body under the heel of the pseudoscience of racial superiority in physical medicine cabinets, exhibiting black bodies in a curiosity cabinet glass rectangles in a way reminiscent of his predecessor, African American artist Fred Wilson, who installed plastic skeletons in wood and glass vitrines that reproduced structures of "a natural history museum," as art historian Huey Copeland argues (*Bound to Appear,* 31). In his 1991 exhibit *Friendly Natives,* Wilson aimed to "demonstrate the pervasiveness of hierarchical modes of seeing, framing, and memorializing the other" (31). While reproducing modes of exhibiting black bodies in museums, Wilson placed his plastic skeletons in "cryptlike vitrines labeled with filial designations, such as 'Someone's sister.' Here, human remains are not merely specimens to be cataloged but depictions of subjects lost to history who were once enmeshed within the embrace of kinship structures" (quoted in Copeland, *Bound to Appear,* 31). Wilson, with his "cryptlike" cases and recumbent skeletons in glass coffins, provides a sacred shape to victims of the unritual.

Extending Wilson's gesture, Bailey incorporates twenty-nine severed heads of African American subjects with bald skulls, open mouths as if whispering, and semiclosed eyes as if receiving amazing news (*Cerebral Caverns,* 2011, wooden medicine cabinet and plaster heads, Thompson, *Radcliffe Bailey,* 110). While the first impression is that of the dehumanization and atomization of humans, the desecration of body parts turned into medical objects, the second is that of life persisting through an unstoppable dialogue in which the mouths, lips, ears, and eyes communicate messages to one another. The installation provides, like Wilson's, a place in which the black human subject lives in a network of communal relations despite the extreme fragmentation and atomization that attempt to arrest him.

The cabinet frame is a perfect square divided into four rows and four columns of identically perfect smaller squares. The circulating whispers, the unframable voices of the severed heads, the kinetic movement they create, however, constitute one of many cases of subversion of the prison grid. But, first, how can we understand "medicine" in the context of postdisaster artistic intervention? How does Bailey's "medicine" relate to the discourse on trauma, healing, memory, and sacralization? How does it fit in relation to European-based, African-based, and creolized forms of healing?

The etymological meaning of "medicine," from the Latin *medeor,* "to heal," "to cure," is related to the word *meditor,* "to meditate." This basic definition, then, evinces the tight relationship between the mind (soul) and the body, too often severed in Western contemporary medicine. While Bailey's concrete medicine cabinets recall Western medicine, Thompson convincingly demonstrates that Bailey's understanding of medicine escapes its framing. As she astutely demonstrates, the multiple cabinets, boxes, orifices, frames, and other containers in Bailey's art, as well as the title of "medicine," directly communicate with West African practices and understandings of "medicine," and most particularly with the Kongo *minkisi* (pl.) or *nkisi* (Thompson, "Minkisi," 101). In Kongo sacred practices, *minkisi* can be anthropomorphic or zoomorphic statuettes with a cavity, or other miscellaneous containers such as bags, baskets, boxes, bottles, urns, or pots that can contain "medicine." The "medicine" they carry includes a variety of objects such as nails, seashells, spices, fiber, metal, hair, feathers, and beads, which gain their healing (or harming) property through a metaphorical or metonymical relationship, through language, to the element at stake in the illness or predicament.[58] For instance, seashells, for their resemblance to a womb, are metaphorically associated with fertility. For their metonymic relationship to the sea, shells facilitate the link with underwater-dwelling ancestral spirits. *Minkisi* exist in the

Americas in the form of funeral urns or memory jars placed on funerary monuments in Georgia and the Carolinas; "bundles," which can be found in Maryland and as far as New England; or "pakè" or "gwo pakè" in Haiti.[59] The bag full of bones the character Pilate carries around her neck in Toni Morrison's *Song of Solomon* and the bundle in Glissant's *Case du commandeur* are forms of *minkisi.* As far as our reflection on the function of artist as healer is concerned, the Kongo *nkisi,* and its contemporary form in Bailey's works, connects aesthetic, healing, and sacred functions in one single object. The artist is thus a natural healer and practitioner of the sacred in the aftermath of disaster, which works against the current on contemporary Western divisions between the three functions.

We would be hard pressed not to see *minkisi* everywhere in the 2011 exhibit. Bailey's physical cabinets of contemporary medicine are convoked for their new artistic, healing, and sacred function. His mixed-media works often include photographs of original Kongo *nkisi* anthropomorphic statuettes.[60] Proliferating rectangles on his creations, including three dimensional ones, invite "medicine," or at least, the projection of content.[61] Boxes with wooden frames complete with glass and wood cabinetry, piano and violin frames, three-dimensional glass cases, salvaged doors and windows, canoes, wood and Plexiglas vitrines, glass containers, bottles, and candelabra all contain Bailey's medicine.[62] Thompson indicates that "their contents include a broad range of culturally charged objects, imagery, and raw material such as indigo powder, tobacco leaves, and Georgia red earth" ("Minkisi," 20). To add to Thompson's list, we spot silk flowers, dried flowers, and seashells, which are objects commonly found on graves whose aim is to communicate a message to the departed; we spot nails and sharp objects, which are reminiscent of the sign of divine intervention in Kongo *nkisi;* obsessively frequent miniatures of black slave ships and a "door of no return," recalling the communal experience of the Middle Passage; a baseball bat, which speaks to the artist's passion as a child; a cooking ladle, which brings to mind the centrality of cooking for female ancestors and relatives; and musical notations, piano keys, and other piano parts, which refer to the importance of music, jazz, and the blues.[63]

As in Waters's and Julien's works, music is omnipresent in Bailey's creations, either through material pieces of instruments serving as cases and frames or through its insertion in works by the representation of musicians, sound installations accompanying sculptural works,[64] or the inclusion of musical scores.[65] The three pieces in the 2011 series *Notes from Elmina* provide a potent example of the function of music as a vector for Relation and creolization in the Glissantian sense.[66] In the three works that can be seen as a triptych, sheet music of European classical scores serve as the canvas for three tableaux covered by colorful paint strokes that mask some of the scores while keeping them visible. If we read the triptych in the order suggested by the artist, we can reconstruct the narrative of the voyage from the coast of Africa, to the middle of the sea, to the new earth. *Notes from Elmina I* represents the fort of the town of Elmina off the coast of Ghana, used to collect captured Africans before they were sent on their westward sea journey. A red, black, and blue ship painted in minimalist strokes leaning toward the abstract awaits on an unchained sea and under angry skies painted with violent brush strokes of blue, green, orange and yellow. *Elmina II* and *Elmina III* share a similar construction. The classical music sheets continue to serve as canvas to similarly agitated strokes of gouache, watercolor, and ink drawing, but, added to the composition, a cut-out photograph of an anthropomorphic statuette stands in the center of each frame.[67] In *Elmina II,* the figure stands waist-deep in water. This figure has his feet planted on a ground of black, surrounded by rich and colorful flora. While we could read the three works as telling the narrative of the exile from Africa, the sea journey, and the arrival to a new land, the sceneries seem disconnected without this effort of the imagination and this added narrative from the viewer. What connects them though—their underwater currents, if you wish—is what Brathwaite has called a submarine history, built on underwater rhythms and currents, in his essay "Caribbean Man in Space and Time."[68] As cultural and art critic Manthia Diawara argues, in Bailey's *Notes on Elmina,* "We see the spaces that were separated before now connected by the poetics of musical painting; that which was lost is reconstituted and resurrected as one world under the groove of Bailey's notes on the ground, on the sea, and in the sky" ("Radcliffe Bailey," 135–41, 138). The broken continuity between the three landscapes or seascapes, as Glissant would have it, "the unknown," is recovered through music.

Yet why use these scores of European classical music and not the rhythms of African instruments and voices, as Brathwaite would have it? We can see this as another source of creolization born of a situation in which African, European, and other elements are thrown together quickly and violently in one space of co-living or co-dying. While Thompson's work of retracing Bailey's objects to their specific roots (be they Fon, Kongo, or Mende, etc.) acts as a revelation, we also should keep in mind that Bailey's art, while it builds on African roots, is also an art of creolization in which Africa is an undeniable trace, laying in a state of fragmentation. The 2010 collage

Radcliffe Bailey, *Notes From Elmina II,* gouache, collage, and ink on sheet music, 12 × 9 inches, High Museum of Art, Atlanta, 2010. (© Radcliffe Bailey, courtesy of the artist and Jack Shainman Gallery, New York)

entitled *Western Current* (acrylic and collage on paper, Thompson, *Memory as Medicine,* 63), represents in its center, pinned between angry sky and threatening sea, a disorderly heap of African statuettes overflowing a canoe. This tragic image of masks and statuettes that used to signify a network of Gods and beliefs, and are now piled up senselessly, as in the market of African artifacts, speaks to the disaster of the loss of continuity with ancestral spiritual roots, and to the desecration of gods now sold for decorative, aesthetic, or educational purposes in museums. As Wyatt MacGaffey sums it up, sacred objects such as "a nkisi in a museum is inert and in fact dead, in terms of its original function as a 'personified medicine'" (*Kongo across the Waters,* 176). The importance of Bailey's art is that these stranded elements unite again with new cultural forms to create new cultural assemblages. Without rehashing the poetic essay in which MacGaffey identifies motifs and gestures of creolization such as riffs, rhythms, and rhizomes in Bailey's art, I will quote the conclusive moment of his text: "Radcliffe Bailey's art, like Glissant's poetry and philosophy, takes us from the threshold of the Manichean logic of slavery and oppression into an imaginary realm of relationships between seemingly contradictory ideas and objects [that] come alive to assume new meanings" (138). This, for Diawara, is not a gesture of severing from Africa, but, rather, a gesture of "memory, origins, and the African diaspora's relation to the past." As poet and art critic Jake Adam York comments, Bailey's generous gesture is primarily a global one: "Taken together . . . the thirty-seven works in *Memory as Medicine* indicate another space, vast and organizing, beneath all others: the Black Atlantic. Whether evoked as an agent of the diaspora, as a ground for the slave trade, or as a temporal gulf that separates Bailey from his genetic past, each work recognizes the ocean's size and history, in image or in form."[69] Bailey goes even further in relegating to his work a world dimension: "'My art is not about the South, because the pictures are from the North. It's more about the world" (quoted in Thompson, *Radcliffe Bailey,*" 49).

To return to the musical scores, Bailey imagines them as the "soundtrack" of the scene of kidnapping, transplantation, and enslavement in the era of slavery and colonization: the melodious sounds of Mozart ironically accompanying barbaric acts. More importantly, perhaps, since Bailey is a visual artist, it is in the technique and aesthetics of the works that this clash of objects that "don't get along" can be best understood. The dissonance between the musical score and the narrative is augmented by the dissonance of colors within the works. Strikes of orange, magenta, fuchsia, bright grass green, burgundy; water blues ranging from pastel to royal to midnight blue; soft pastels; bright gouache; and saturated inks create a gaudy assemblage. As Bailey admits, "I put colors together that don't make sense to work together." Instead of randomness and lack of appreciation for equilibrium, this conscious gesture responds to a precise objective: "OK, this color doesn't get along with this color but let me find a way to make it work."[70] These "colors" that "don't get along" with one another, these strikes made of material paint, these inanimate objects gain a sense of personhood, a life energy. Whether echoing a Merleau-Pontian phenomenology of reciprocal intertwining of object and subject or an uninterrupted Kongo continuum of all things alive and *minkisi* endowed with life, agency, and power, Bailey's strokes of colors are agents of his process of memorialization of the dead and things past.[71] The materiality of art gains an ethical value of beings that do not make sense together, yet have to live together and make it work. This, too, is part of his ethical and sacred gesture of world creolization.

Whether paint strokes, music sheets, ocean shells, or Georgia red clay, the material objects that form the backbone of Bailey's art—while "culturally charged," as Thompson rightly indicates—are also associated with communal, familial, and individual hardship and trauma. Though creolizing and relating to the world, they are also grounded in place. Indigo, tobacco, and Georgia clay metonymically and metaphorically refer to the experience of slavery and postslavery cash-crop cultivation of the earth. Personal and familial memorabilia, including "more than 400 tintypes from a family album dating back to the late 1800s" given by the artist's grandmother, inhabit the works (Thompson, *Radcliffe Bailey,* 49). Fragments of railroad tracks, frequent in Bailey's works, refer not only to the collective experience of northbound travel to "freedom," but also to Bailey's personal and familial experience, in that his father worked on the railroad.

The 2005 mixed media *Self-Portrait* includes a mess of railroad spikes, sugarcane, paintbrushes, and sticks covered in thick black encaustic (Thompson, *Radcliffe Bailey,* 28). This mass of wrecked material inanimate objects is strangely called "self-portrait" in the absence of any anthropomorphic object, save perhaps the forked stick painted bright red in the center resembling the arteries leading to a heart. The "self-portrait" is highly collective. While the paint brushes evoke the artist's trade, the railroad spikes in their excessive presence refer to the artist's father's life of labor, the thick black encaustic that resembles tar recalls lynching and other forms of torture, and the sugarcane the collective experience of enslaved Africans in the Americas.

The greatest paradox expressed in Glissant's *Poetics of Relation* is that the prison system of the chattel plantation with its enclosed space and airtight pyramidal power structure gave rise to astonishing forms of openness, unpredictability, performativity, and creativity, which he also calls creolization and of which jazz is a manifestation (73). Similarly, Glissant's slave ship, which functions both as womb and grave, gave birth to an "open boat": "Our boats are open and we sail them for everyone" (9). Bailey's 2003 mixed-media collage *Batoe* materializes Glissant's boat, at once *bateau,* prison slave ship, and *barque,* or canoe, open to the air. The neologism Bailey inscribes in large, capitalized white letters, "BATOE," phonetically echoes *bateau,* boat or ship, while resembling "canoe" (Glissant's *barque*) in its spelling.

The collage consists of a photograph of three black men fishing from a canoe. Multicolored, invasive rectangles dominate the top (sky) and the bottom (depths of the sea). Adding to this rectangular oppression, the emblematic railroad tracks representing Bailey's father's life of labor bar the collage horizontally. Yet the boat is open, and the three men navigate it. In the center of the frame, layered, erratic paint strokes of clashing yellows, khakis, reds, and blues break open the oppressive symmetry. The rhizomatic and kinetic strokes give new roots and branches to the fishermen. In the center of the rhizome appears a serpentine figure, evoking the sacred figure of Damballah, considered as the primary creator of all life.

While pointing to the openness and connectivity these creations perform, I do not want to stop at a solely optimistic reading of Bailey's and Glissant's notions of the "open boat" or living rectangles. Despite the openness, the heavy black frames of the collages and the thick walls of the medicine cabinets still insist on the framing and oppression of the system. Some works, like 2008's *Voyage of No Return* (Thompson, *Radcliffe Bailey,* 53) a mixed-media piece inserted in a medicine cabinet, are, to use a phrase from the famous jazz standard, "decidedly blue." The late nineteenth-century tintype portrait of a beautiful young girl veiled by a translucent blue slave ship constitutes the center of the thick black frame. The young African American girl with cropped natural hair and gold earrings, dressed in black velvet and white lace, stares the viewer straight in the eye, as if to demand a response. She is determined and dignified. Her large, bright eyes are watery, aquatic. The artist has added a touch of paint in the corner of the left eye, to indicate a tear, perhaps. The blur of the contour of her chest makes her body look ghostly and at the same time fuses it onto the plinth of the miniature ship, which seems to act as

Radcliffe Bailey, *Voyage of No Return,* mixed media, 26 × 26 × 7 inches, 2008. (© Radcliffe Bailey, courtesy of the artist and Jack Shainman Gallery, New York)

her body's foundation, its grounding. She, like the boat, is turned into a statuette that rests on a plinth, arrested, exhibited as if in a cabinet of curiosity. A dozen rectangles, shades of green and blue reminiscent of the ocean, proliferate around the girl-boat. These rectangles have different textures: smooth, rough, covered in glitter. Some are glued right below the surface of the glass; some dwell in the depth of the three-dimensional piece. The proliferating doors are like the many reminders of possible pathways into the past. Yet these openings cannot be crossed again. The door of no return, as Trinidadian-Canadian poet Dionne Brand explains, "is not mere physicality. It is a spiritual location. It is also perhaps a psychic destination. Since leaving was never voluntary, return was, and still may be, an intention, however deeply buried. There is as it says no way in; no return" (*A Map to the Door of No Return,* 1).

In contrast with *Batoe,* which contains rhizomatic routes and roots of escape, the portrait of the young girl as a ship is irremediably fused with doors of no return and the transfixed memory of the Middle Passage. The superposition of images blending and blurring into one another and into the background suggests an unfinished story, a corpse neglected and left without a proper ritual, that continues to haunt the viewer. It asserts the presence of the spirits of the past in the present, despite the radical break that the transatlantic slave trade brought.

Diawara interprets the doors as openings to past and future: "In Bailey's works, the Door of No Return has become the Door of Many Returns, the door of Renaissance and of new relations, poetic, political, and social" (140). While it is true that Bailey's multiple doors and rectangles can serve as openings transfigured and inhabited by artistic energy, we cannot forget that this opening, in the context of postslavery as analyzed by Glissant, Brand, and others, cohabits with its extreme opposite. The open word struggles with so many closed doors for space in the artist's canvas. It is with this oxymoronic and painfully ironic relation between prison and flight, life and death, beauty and horror, that Bailey's work touches us and acts as a living grave, allying the stiffness of the material with the freedom of the spirit. This contraction in no way dismisses Diawara's reading of Bailey through Glissant's movement of creolization. On the contrary: Bailey's creolization, like Glissant's, is based on the conservation of the violence of the past in poetic and artistic expression. This is precisely what, for Glissant, distinguishes creolization from *métissage,* which often leads to oblivion through the blending of differences. If for Glissant *métissage* leads to oblivion, creolization is an expression of a dynamic, living memory.

When my students and I visited the *Memory as Medicine* exhibit in early September 2011, the work that astonished us most by its scale and the sheer disaster it conveyed was *Windward Coast.*[72] This shape-shifting installation was first exhibited in 2009 at the Solomon Projects gallery in Atlanta and at the Jack Shainman Gallery in New York. The work, which fills a large room, consists of a heaping mass of broken piano keys on top of which the plaster head of a black man covered in tar and glitter bobs just above the surface. This was, for me, a monument to the devastation of the Lower Ninth Ward, which I had seen in person, and of the Haiti earthquake, which I had witnessed on television and social media. For some of my students, it immediately recalled the tsunami that had ravaged Japan a few months before *Windward Coast*'s Atlanta installation. It is also likely that, when exhibited in New York, the work would have

Radcliffe Bailey, detail from *Windward Coast—West Coast Slave Trade,* piano keys, plaster bust, and glitter, variable dimensions, 2018. (© Radcliffe Bailey, courtesy of the artist and Jack Shainman Gallery, New York)

been often read as the piling up of the fallen Twin Towers. The caption for the work at the 2011 High Museum exhibit, however, qualifies it as a reference to the Middle Passage. In the companion catalog, Thompson argues that in Bailey's *Windward Coast* and *Storm at Sea,* "piano keys become sea. Both works evoke the Middle Passage, a defining experience that shaped the traumatic history of the black Atlantic world" (21). The lone anonymous human head stands, like the proverbial unknown soldier, for all graveless victims. The stratified and messy depth of the installations function as a fluid monument, a countermonument, or an aesthetic grave for disasters past and yet to come. It is true, however, that, along with this potentially universal gesture serving as an account of the dismay of humanity and nature, the work, once again, lies on a certain materiality and cultural specificity. In Bailey's works, as seen earlier, the particular and the universal are not in contradiction, but it is their very tension that constitutes the efficiency of his art. The head of the bust submerged to the chin is that of an African man or a man of African descent, which directly evokes victims of the Middle Passage, Katrina, or the Haitian earthquake.

The head, however, can also announce disasters to come for an inclusive humanity, such as the consequences of global warming on rising seawater levels in the age of the Anthropocene. The right to universality, after all, the right of being a man, is what Frantz Fanon and Aimé Césaire ultimately fought for.[73]

This is also what Bailey means when he claims that his art is for, of, and about the world. "Windward coast," the coast most roughed out by wind and strong sea currents, as opposed to the leeward coast, also clearly refers to the oceanic waters of the Middle Passage separating and linking West Africa and the Caribbean. The Windward Islands comprise Saint-Vincent, Grenada, St. Lucia, and Martinique, major arrival ports for the slave trade. Yet "windward," a maritime term, could refer simply and universally to the side of a coast most roughed up by sea or wind weather. Like Glissant, whose work's universal function can only "take" if grounded in the particularity and materiality of Martinique, Bailey's universal-leaning installation rests on its immediate relationship to local businesses. Bailey obtained the piano keys by developing a relation "with a business near his home where old pianos are disassembled and their parts recycled" (Thompson, *Radcliffe Bailey,* 22). A focus on the local can be seen in many of the featured artists' works. The grounding in the local does not lead to isolationist or "folklorist" attachment to the place, but instead allows reaching universality.

Windward Coast also issues an invitation not merely to contemplate but also to engage with the material. For art historian Claire Bishop, installation art is especially conducive to visitor engagement, the decentering or dispersion of the subject, and activated spectatorship (Bishop, *Installation Art,* 102, 128). She identifies these characteristics as particularly apt to involve the visitor politically or ethically, since meaning in installation art is "elaborated collectively rather than in the privatized space of individual consumption" (116). In terms of belonging to a political and ethical community, I argue that installations such as *Windward Coast* also place the spectator in a position of mourner invited to perform acts of religion, as in re-ligare, or "to link again," to respect the unnamed numerous dead.

Bailey's installation encourages the visitor to pick up a conch shell discretely placed in a corner of the room, lift it to her ear, and hear an uncertain sound resembling at once music and the sound of sea waves. The conch shell is closely associated with mourning rituals in the coastal cultures of the African diasporas. It is placed on graves from Florida to Martinique and is used as a horn to announce death in the Caribbean. For

Chamoiseau, it also links the present of the Americas to its Amerindian past: "The giant shell of the conch leaves no one indifferent. . . . When its contours balance out with time, it is truly majestic. The Amerindians consumed its flesh but also used the conch as a passage way between this and invisible worlds" (*Matière,* 76). Hence, picking up a shell in the Bailey exhibit carries the corporeal memory of interacting with the shell on a maritime grave and in a relational time. We later learn that "a sound artist recorded the reverberation of the disengaged piano keys as they dropped to the floor. The recording resembles free jazz and evokes rolling ocean waves crashing on a shore" (Thompson, *Radcliffe Bailey,* 22). It is precisely this kinetic and multisensory participation, the repeating crests and troughs of sound and music, this act of listening, guessing, and performing, that is key to Bailey's work, creating an open space that overflows the proliferating rectangles. As Thompson concludes her essay, "This emphasis on performance is key. Gradually moving from a primarily visual mode to a more multisensory and kinetic experience, Bailey's richly patterned polyrhythmic aesthetic conjures what might be regarded as a jazz aesthetic and structured spontaneity as a way of working" (*Radcliffe Bailey,* 97).

The installation moves us to take part in the ceremony, as in a wake or a *homecoming* in the funeral sense of the term, to pay respect as we gently put the conch shell to our ear. Bailey's work becomes a grave, not that of the fixed type, but as Joseph Roach has demonstrated in his *Cities of the Dead,* an act of performance.[74] As opposed to a fixed product, performance facilitates the "historical transmission and dissemination of cultural practices through collective representations" (25). Performance also, as in the New Orleans Second Line, provides a ritual for the dead.[75] Performance also frees up the bodies fixed by representations, social status, or history, as critic Stevin Blevins argues: "When unhoused [by performance] the artifactual body performs its archival past . . . the public history work performed by black writers and artists . . . not only reactivates historical traces housed by the archive but likewise unhouse the body as an artifact of history" (*Living Cargo,* 8). By putting rectangles, caskets, and other frames in motion, the artists precisely honored, aesthetically and ritualistically, the black victims of the unritual. However, as our next chapter shows, performance can also run the risk of rekindling the unritual at the very same time it pays homage to its victims.

Beyond their creative idiosyncrasies and sharp particularities, Bailey, Julien, and Waters resemble one another in the face of Katrina, disaster, and the unritual. At a formal level, the artists unanimously insert rectangles in their works while subverting them by multiplying them, dissolving them, opening them, up, mixing them with other objects in assemblages and performance. This gesture demonstrates the prevalence of rectangles in the acts of framing and fixing black and oppressed subjects, both in representation and lived experience. The framed subject is reduced to a stereotype, arrested or killed through the tacit laws of police racial profiling. Their aesthetics also rests on an ethics of art forms relaying one another, as in a relay race. In the face of the outrage of disaster, or the immensity of the unritual and its neglected dead, aesthetic productions as diverse as music, painting, photography, poetry, sound, collage, carpentry, or quilting relay one another in an attempt to approach the immense scale of disaster and to remediate the unspeakable disaster: what Blanchot defines as "the unknown name, alien to naming" (*Disaster,* 47), through the network of collaboration. Photographers, visual artists, curators, poets, and jazz musicians work as a team to solidify the fragility of their isolated art. Their aesthetics relay ethics and politics where they fail. In its drawing from installation art, memorials, sculpture, poetry, song, and fiction, this book hopes to do the same.

A pessimistic Kara Walker questions the efficiency of art and provides her own response: "What role can the visual arts play in reexamining one of America's greatest social failures? 'Not much'" (*After the Deluge,* 7). The visual arts, in their relationality, can do a little more. Collaboration between artists extends to the relation to the public viewer, who becomes a performer, thanks to the form of installation art so prevalent in these works, and thanks also to the parts of opacity and indecision that the public has to manipulate to create meaning. Objects—Waters's soldier clarinets, Julien's dynamic quilt, Bailey's changing sea of piano keys—gain agency. The artists are first- or second-degree witnesses, victims, or survivors of Katrina and slavery, and the works are political manifestos and remedies for healing. Above all, they stand for the absent sacred monuments and mourning gestures in the face of the unritual of slavery, Katrina, or disasters—past, contemporary, or to come. Artistic creations become dirges and requiems through their blanks and blacks; through the peace and music they contain or produce; through epitaphs, shrouds, tombs, or urns; through the offerings they make and the shrouds they throw. Naturally, they all deal significantly in water and its ambivalence: water is their threat and need, medium and barrier, saving grace and assassin, cleansing and toxic medium. Water is a threshold between worlds such as the Americas, Africa, and Europe, as well as between the worlds of the living and the departed. As seen in the introduction, water is expressed in Vaudou cosmology as *lot bo dlo* (the other side of water, the space of those who have migrated) and *anba dlo* (below water, the space of those who have died). Water facilitates passage and bars access. Hence the frequent presence in the works of ambivalent figures such as boat coffins or window graves.

3 Mami Wata the Formidable

Kara Walker's *After the Deluge* and Beyoncé's *Lemonade*

La Siren, La Balen,
Chapo'm tonbe nan la me.
Map fe kares pou La Siren.

—Traditional Vaudou song

ABOVE THE ocher waves of Maafa and the murky waters of Katrina rises the formidable and sacred Mami Wata. In visual artist Kara Walker's 2007 gouache "Middle Passages," the maimed body of an enslaved woman-child turns into a fierce siren figurehead. In the 2016 music video "Formation," singer-performer Beyoncé alluringly reclines on a police car in the city's flooded waters. This chapter revolves around the staging of Mami Wata in Walker's and Beyoncé's works both as a potential gesture of desecration, but also, and paradoxically, as a mark of the sacred in the face of the Unritual. Mami Wata not only provides insights into the artists' creations, but also helps question our understanding of two formidable women artists often criticized for capitalizing on catastrophes. As the great female ruler of the sea in Vaudou tradition, does Lasiwèn provide a power model for survivors, or does the presence of this erotic figure disturb the peace of the dead? Do Beyoncé and Walker perpetrate the unritual, or do they navigate such desecrated realms that their creative work is inevitably caught in muck? Finally, what does the perspective of the artist, in terms of class, ethnicity, gender, sexuality, city of origin, and personal relation to the disaster reveal about the legitimacy of her artistic interventions?

The mermaid, the siren, *la sirène,* under its Western guises from Homer to Hans Christian Andersen to Walt Disney, emerges as the creolized *lwa, orisha,* or divinity *Mami Wata, Lasiwèn, Lasiwèn-Labalèn, Manman Dlo, Lamenté, la Sirena, Yémaya* in her various Afro-diasporic avatars. For Kimberly Juanita Brown, she, in the form of Iemanjá, "serves as the necessary repository for all earthly slave traumas, having the requisite lack of material existence that spares her flesh and attack of the lash" (*Repeating Body,* 143). In the Mexican song "La Petenera," *la sirena* robs the mariners' souls and taunts Columbus himself, who resolves to sail no longer if God spares his life after the encounter: "Si Dios me salva la vida / No vuelvo a ser marinero."[1] With the powers to stop the conquest of the Americas, she is the *great and terrible,* the *formidable* female ruler over the sea.[2] The figure is widely venerated in West Africa in Igbo, Ewe, and Kongo religions and in the Americas in Santería, Orisha, and Vaudou. She connects the sacred realm of anba dlo (below the water) with the transatlantic crossing of lotbo dlo (across the water).[3] She unites the living and the dead as well as the sedentary and the diasporic. She weaves an underwater network between African, European, Asian, Amerindian, and American myths, becoming a figure of creolization par excellence.[4] With her fishtail and human torso, arms, and head she provides a fluid hybrid between the human and the nonhuman. In this sense, she foregrounds the concept of the ecological sacred displayed in chapter 4. In the Caribbean, she is portrayed as a whale (*la balèn,* which can be the siren's self, sister, or husband) or as the large aquatic mammal manatee. *Lamenté,* "manatee" in Creole, is one of her names in Guadeloupe and Martinique. Christopher Columbus mistook the sea mammals for mermaids, off the coast of Haiti on January 9, 1493: "'They came quite high out of the water' but 'were not so beautiful as painted, though to some extent they have the form of a human face'" (quoted in Drewal, "Mami Wata," 65).

Mami Wata is a deity of extreme beauty, health, and wealth, with attributes such as sweet perfumes, a lush mane, and plentiful coins and jewels.[5] She can lure humans, women and men alike, into their watery graves but can also offer them treasures of wealth and love. As in the Haitian Vaudou song of this chapter's epigraph—"my hat fell into the sea; I caress Lasiwèn"—when the "hat" (symbol of the soul), falls underwater, it encounters love and ternderness in its terrible death. Mami Wata is the lwa of ambivalence: sacred and kitsch, killer and lover, aesthete and provocateur.

Flirting with Muck: Kara Walker's Aesthetics

Visual and installation artist Kara Walker is best known for her cut-out black-on-white silhouettes representing violent scenes of torture and sexual abuse under slavery, often in a satirical manner toying with the grotesque. As some art historians and critics such as Gwendolyn Dubois Shaw, Kevin Young, and Sander Gilman have argued, her work also often flirts with the pornographic.[6] Significantly for the constellation of artists featured in *Water Graves,* Walker was Bailey's fellow student at the Atlanta College of Art (Walker was born in 1969 and Bailey in 1968) and shares his view on performance as a way to give proper ritual and heal the community in the aftermath of disasters such as Katrina.[7] Walker, like the artists featured in the previous chapter, mixes image and text. In line with Glissant's notion of a relational aesthetics, she incorporates the paintings and sculptures of others in her exhibits and books.[8]

In 2006, shortly after Hurricane Katrina and its ensuing human-made disaster, curator Gary Tinterow worked with Walker to mount the multiple artist exhibit entitled "Kara Walker at the Met: After the Deluge." Walker and Tinterow selected pieces from the permanent collection at the Metropolitan Museum that they exhibited with Walker's own cut-silhouette creations.[9] The exhibit included works of art as varied as an anonymous sixteenth-century painting of "Christ's Descent into Hell" (Walker, *After the Deluge,* 92–93) in the style of Hieronymus Bosch; a nineteenth-century Kongo *nkisi* anthropomorphic statuette; Winslow Homer's 1899 "The Gulf Stream"; William Turner's "Slaveship" ("Slavers Throwing Overboard the Dead and Dying"); and miscellaneous works representing hellish scenes of drowning, storms, and torture juxtaposed with Walker's own pre-Katrina production.

The structure of Walker's book is abysmal. It does not just tell the story of New Orleans or other waterborne disasters, but offers a compelling commentary on disasters past—the biblical flood; Maafa—and of disasters to come announced by apocalyptic scenes. It is also "an attempt to understand the subconscious narratives at work when we talk about such an event" (*After the Deluge,* 9). Walker states: "All the historical paintings and my images and typewritten texts precede the recent hurricanes, tsunamis, and to some extent, the global concern about rising sea levels." In the book born out of the exhibit, *Kara Walker: After the Deluge,* eleven folios are inserted in the text as if to represent the ineffable of disaster while providing a proper shroud for the dead. The black pages mark the book as a funeral monument and remind seers that their act is not just one of aesthetic contemplation but also one of mourning. Walker's idea of building an exhibit around the works of artists spanning centuries and continents speaks to the shared involvement of humanity, not just a group of exception, in the event. The fact that this exhibit responds to Katrina and disasters to come with a compilation, an installation collage made of works that preceded the event in time, makes a powerful statement about the prophetic property of art.[10]

In *After the Deluge,* the juxtaposition of miscellaneous works, as well as the black pages that connect them, resists framing. The multiauthorial composite book speaks to the impossibility of framing disaster in one single work of art or in the creations of one single artist. Indeed, the compilation speaks to the fact that one single artist cannot respond to the event. In many ways, the installation resembles Glissant's anthology *La Terre le feu l'eau et les vents,* in which the unpredictable juxtaposition of, for instance, a poem by François Villon against the hanged victims of the sixteenth-century European wars of religion with Billie Holiday's and Abel Meeropol's antilynching song "Strange fruit," speaks to the shared involvement of humanity in repeating events of discrimination, oppression, and torture. Disaster, for its immensity, has to be told through a relay of works and testimonies competing with one another. Disaster cannot be framed by one or any single image or painting and has to be expressed through collective expression and performance. Walker captures the issue in this dense reflection:

> I've seen music, dance, and Mardi Gras celebrations activate damaged, closed-off psychic spaces; they provided hope. But what role can the visual arts play in reexamining one of America's greatest social failures? 'Not much' is the pessimistic conclusion I came to, followed by a close examination of a line of thinking familiar to Blacks, as expressed by my grandmother: 'All you have to do in this world is stay black and die.' This phrase sums up multilayered experiences of suppression, resentment, and rage. I have asked the objects in this book to do one more thing. Instead of sitting very still, 'staying black,' and waiting to die, I have asked each one to take a step beyond its own borders to connect a series of thoughts together related to fluidity and the *failure of containment.* (9, emphasis mine)

For Walker, as well as for all the artists featured in this book, the fluidity of performance heals when frames kill.[11] Good frames, of the kind analyzed in chapter 2, provide, let's recall, coffins for the victims of the flood. They are akin to the framing of a carpenter rather than that of a shooter. We are now talking about bad frames, which include the framing by police and journalists that is featured in Walker's works. For Walker, "Paintings are neat containers of ideas about the commonplace nature of disaster."[12] The fixity of a still image and the framing of a painting or a photograph fix the subject in a dead position. Here, Walker repeats her grandmother's words of wisdom: "Stay black and die." The grandmother's warning evokes psychiatrist, poet, and revolutionary Frantz Fanon's description of the "white gaze" that fixes its object—in Fanon's case, the "nègre": "Locked in this suffocating reification . . . I stumble, and the Other fixes me with his gaze . . . the same way you fix a preparation with a dye . . . I explode. Here are the fragments put together by another me" (*Black Skin,* 89).[13]

In "Loot or find: Fact or Frame?" legal scholars Cheryl Harris and Devon Carbado evoke the phenomenon of fixing through a frame in their analysis of two photographs taken during the New Orleans 2005 flood. The two images seized—fixed—two groups of people in the same situation: wading through toxic waters, wearing t-shirts, carrying bags. Whereas the two subjects that appear to be white are described as "finders," the young African American man is framed as thief: "The captions that appeared with the two photos . . . were quite different. The caption for image A read: 'A young man walks through chest-deep flood water after looting a grocery store in New Orleans.' The caption for image B read: "Two residents wade through chest-deep waters after finding bread and soda from a local grocery store after hurricane Katrina came through the area" (87–88).[14] While the apparently white couple is portrayed as surviving, the black man is framed (in the photographic and police sense) and fixed (in the chemistry and Fanonian sense) as criminal. Harris and Carbado conclude: "We interpret events through frames—interpretational structures that, consciously or unconsciously, shape what we see and how we see it. In the words of one scholar, framing refers to 'understanding a story you already know and saying, 'oh yeah, that one.' As we process and make sense of an event, we take account of and simultaneously ignore facts that do not fit the frame, and sometimes, we supply ones that are missing. Thus, it is sometimes said that 'frames trump facts'" (91). In this model, as in Fanon's fixing gaze or Walker's grandmother's dictum "stay black and die," the dying happens figuratively through the projection of a static preconceived image on a living human being. But, crucially, the framing of the black subject as criminal—looter, thief, murderer, or rapist—can quite literally lead to the death of the human beings executed by electricity or lethal injection, or by the police, as they are suspected of a crime solely because of their "racial" belonging, as we have repeatedly seen in recent memory.[15] This loss of young black boys and men is on the scale of an epidemic, as Ward establishes in her memoir *Men We Reape*d, which she also called her "Southern Requiem." This racist madness, or, in Walker's terms, "racist psychosis" (9), deeply denies African American subjects their status as survivors, or, simply, citizens, by presenting them as aggressors. For Tamir Rice, Michael Brown, Christian Taylor, Brandon Jones, Wiliam Chapman, Darrius Stewart, and all those who remain unnamed, let us pause for a moment.

It takes a team of visual artists (Walker, Bailey, Julien, Waters), poets (Sipps, Brand), psychiatrists (Fanon), musicians (Terrence Blanchard), cinematographers (Lee), and lawyers to disrupt the power of the rectangle, since "fixing" and "framing" happen on the levels of the representations and experience of the living and the dead.[16] It takes a relay of voices to render the memory of the living and the dead in its fluidity and complexity. It takes a redirection of the gaze from the framed subject to the complex causes of disaster (technological, social, racial, economic, political) to begin to make sense of the unfathomable. The shifting of the gaze or redirecting of the spotlight cannot be accomplished with the addition of another frame. It has to be replaced by another way of seeing: "The story that has interested me in this book is the story of Muck" (Walker, *After the Deluge,* 7).

Muck resides in a material zone between the liquidity of flood waters and the solidity of the frame. "Muck," or "dung in a moist state," refers to the excremental, the viscous, the not quite solid yet not quite liquid, the messy, the stinky, the impenetrable, *and* the unframable.[17] Muck is among the unclassifiable substances that psychoanalyst Julia Kristeva describes as the ultimate threat to the subject: "Excrements and its equivalents (decay, infection, disease, corpse, etc.)," she claims, "stand for the danger to identity that comes from without: the ego threatened by the non ego, society threatened by its outside, life by death" (*Powers,* 71).

Another prevalent flowing substance in Walker's works is milk. Liquid, yet hefty in the substantial nutritional and emotional solidity that it creates, milk, misdirected, chaotically flowing, profaned, violated, stolen, pervades her works. In her outstanding reading of milk in Walker's works through the economics of slavery and capitalism, Patricia Yaeger contends: "While African Americans and Afro-Caribbeans were once defined as superfluous, as an expendable economic resource, I want to argue that this imagined superfluity has been met in twentieth-century Afro-southern and Afro-Caribbean art with superfluidity, with fictions that open the floodgates to 'the colonial difference'—foregrounding histories cast aside by canonical modernity" ("Circum-Atlantic Superabundance," 775). While we cannot deny this response from African American and African Caribbean artists with an excess of fluids and floods, Walker's muck, in contrast with milk, is not exactly, or not only, "superfluidity." The fluids of her work flirt with the thick black gouache that simultaneously flows and reaches a thickly textured materiality. This superfluidity does not go down easily and is interrupted by the frequent solidity and precision of traits of the silhouetted shapes and bodies, by the opacity of the unfathomable, and by the indigestible excremental violence of her works. In Walker's works, there might be superfluidity, but also the solidity of an opaque rock, impacting the viewer.

Muck, in Walker's work, is uncoupled from its pervasive associations with womanhood and woman's sexuality or cooking, as in William Faulkner's "woman's muck" (*Light in August,* 238) or to black and white southern womanhood (Yaeger, *Dirt and Desire, ix–x),* and attached instead to the very origin (cause, culprit) of these violent images, stereotypes, frames: "Racist pathology is the Muck, aforementioned. In this book's analogy, murky, toxic waters become the amniotic fluid of a potentially new and difficult birth, flushing out of a coherent and stubborn body long-held fears and suspicions" (Walker, *After the Deluge,* 9). Racist pathology and environmental disaster (toxic waters) blend in Walker's muck. The abject substance paradoxically—and horrifyingly—becomes the amniotic fluid of a new birth. We can ask what or who is being born from the abject, in the way Kristeva has theorized it, as a reaction of profound disgust to the presence of objects blurring the line between life and death, humanity and bestiality, or cleanliness and filth, such as the corpse, the skin on cooked milk, the wound, or Auschwitz. The abject, Kristeva observes, "draws me toward the place where meaning collapses" (*Powers,* 2).

We have to complement Kristeva's list with the massive situation of abjection created and reproduced by the capture, the rape (as in both abduction and sexual violation) of humans in the Middle Passage and during "chattel slavery." Walker's spillage of words and images, her aesthetic muck, reinvents language and beauty precisely where meaning collapses, at the risk of flirting with abomination. She does not do so by recreating structures, rectangles, a grammatical scaffolding, but rather by inhabiting the extreme border that, for Kristeva, at once defines the self and expels it: "There, I am at the border of my condition as a living being. My body extricates itself, as being alive, from that border . . . If dung signifies the other side of the border, the place where I am not and which permits me to be, the corpse, the most sickening of wastes, is a border that has encroached upon everything" (3). By dwelling in muck, Walker goes further than Kristeva in that it is no more a matter of "it is no longer I who expel, 'I' is expelled" (3–4, emphasis in original), but of "it is I/us who is/are the abject." This all-empowering gesture of the self amounts to its complete dissolution. Borders are gone. So are their menacing, and protecting, qualities: vulnerability at its height.

We can also wonder, then: How does muck manifest itself aesthetically in Walker's creation? It is in the black of the pages that dissolve the frame of the included works. See for instance, the untitled gouache and cut paper on paint board from Walker's 2001 "American Primitives," which stages the disturbing image of a threesome that at the same time evokes the position of circus acrobats engaged in fellatio leading perhaps to teethed castration (63). The piece's frame, to the left and right, opens up on the deep black gouache of ghostly limbs or branches. In the catalog, the gouache blackly bleeds into the black page of page 62, left blank in the black page, thus evoking the unframability of the horror of the scene and the failure of rectangles.

The diptych forming the 2004 gouache, cut paper, and collage on paint board "Middle Passages," reproduced on the facing pages 44 and 45, feature two severed pieces of a formerly united whole through flowing brushstrokes. The gouache, in its opacity and textured thickness, is the ideal medium to represent muck. The uncontained black, white, and tan gouache and collage depict, to the left, a tall ship capsizing; to the right, the stereotyped silhouette of a young African African woman or girl with a protruding belly and an air of terror on her face, sitting on a palm tree. The tree, looking like an offshoot of the boat, is severed from it. The other end of the tree, undistinguishable in its black ink from the young woman's body, looks like a disproportionate prosthesis standing in for a missing other leg, as if the woman was irremediably linked to the machine of the ship. The ship becomes part of herself and she herself is an indispensable part of the machine of slavery. The textured gouache of the tormented sea is rich in thick strokes in shades of brown and black. The sepia sky is streaked with thin filaments of blood. The orphaned woman's arms stretch out toward the orphaned ship, as if terrorized to see the boat drifting away and the wooden umbilical cord that attached her to the ship severed. Alternatively, the trunk of the palm tree can be read as a phallus or piercing instrument of torture. Umbilical cord or transpiercing phallus? Walker does not give us an answer, but instead provokes us to think about birth, rape, and torture as monstrously condensed in one visual object.

The fear of the individual woman-girl is also what Glissant calls the "fear of the unknown" (*Poetics,* 6) This state of mind, shared by the collective African diaspora, is the fear of a radically new world cut from the old, a cut reinforced by the distribution of the two sides of the diptych of a formerly united piece now severed by the impassible white gutters on the page. The white gutters offer yet another example of being framed by whiteness. Walker also playfully detours the function of framing—and of whiteness. Indeed, while "gutters" in the artistic sense refers to the margins and divisions of the page between inserted frames or objects, in a

Kara Walker, *Middle Passages (2),* gouache, cut paper, and collage on board, 15 × 15 inches, 2004. (Artwork © Kara Walker, courtesy of Sikkema Jenkins & Co., New York)

literal sense, a gutter channels muck and is thereby filled with muck. With her visual pun, the artist presents whiteness itself as both the conduit and site of muck, thereby exposing the abject nature of the white enterprise of enslavement of fellow humans.

Walker's subject's fear of the unknown is doubled by a fear of death by drowning. The severing from the ship implies that she will drown at sea, facing the likely risk of being torn apart by sharks.[18] She stands between the devil and the deep black sea in a nonchoice. She inhabits the impasse that Africana scholars C. L. R. James, Patterson, JanMohamed, and Glissant have each respectively called "hell," "social death," the "death-bound subject," or the lethal "womb-abyss."[19] Walker's troubled ocean

Kara Walker, *Middle Passages (5)*, gouache, cut paper, and collage on board, 17 × 17 inches, 2004. (Artwork © Kara Walker, courtesy of Sikkema Jenkins & Co., New York)

water is a death-bearing amniotic fluid of sorts. The potential death of the woman coincides with that of the ship, which could be read either as the death of a single ship or as the death of the system of selling and enslaving human beings that carries its own lethality. The leaning tree is growing from the belly of the sea—no land is apparent here—as if the underwater sea world confusingly gave birth to the fragile roots of an impossible, yet necessary, aquatic tree. We dwell in the ambivalence of the sea as a lethal abyss with a propensity to grow roots. Such an image recalls Glissant's lethal sea belly. Indeed, the sea-abyss is also the paradoxical site of birth and underwater roots, as commonly explained by poets and artists alike. For Glissant the underwater bottoms contain "signposts" of memory; for

Haitian artist Édouard Duval Carrié ocean depths are both a grave and a fertile soil for tree growth.[20]

Similar to the ambivalent character of the sea as a simultaneous site of life and death, the young woman's silhouette offers an optical illusion that allows us to read it in two ways. In her sideways topsy-turvy shape, where right and left are inverted, if left-facing the woman is the terrorized figure leaning toward the drifting ship for survival; conversely, if right-facing, she looks like a confident ship's figurehead, a horizontal diver, arms outstretched backward, poised head aligned, aerodynamically going forward with the wind. Walker reinforces her optical illusion with a verbal pun, since a "figurehead," in its political sense, qualifies a supremely powerful person. The woman's legless body, instead of being amputated, grows into the tail of a siren or Mami Wata, in continuity with the bow of the ship. This epitome of European ship figureheads shifts meaning when transposed into the Yoruba, Kongo, and Fon-derived religions of the African diaspora. In her classic 1953 introduction to Vaudou, *Divine Horsemen,* avant-garde filmmaker and writer Maya Deren highlights the powerful and ambivalent relationship Lasiwèn entertains with motherhood: "[La Sirène] is said to steal children and take them to the bottom of either the sea or of a stream, but is also known to bring them up" (Deren 208n78). Viewed through this lens, Walker's pregnant woman is then not only a victim of rape but also an agent of her own sexual reproduction with control over giving life or laying it down at the bottom of the sea. She becomes the powerful "Reine des Ambaglos" (Queen of the Underwater People), central to Haitian American artist Duval Carrié (as I will discuss in chapter 4).

But, again, Walker leaves us on a fence. The artist doesn't guide the direction of our gaze and makes us see simultaneously the helplessness and power of the feminine silhouette, or lwa. The two vulnerable objects—ship and woman—are spread apart on the extreme left and right of the frames, respectively, as if under quartering. Visually, the focal center of the piece is a gaping sea of thick muck. The stretching of the gaze away from the center also defies attempts at framing (the boat and woman threaten to puncture the frame) and forces us to see historical objects in the extreme periphery of our field of vision. Our gaze is quartered between two objects impossible to seize at once since they outstretch to the right and left of our vision span. This is not an easily readable linear story but one that hurts our gaze and challenges our imagination of a horrific—and unfathomable—individual and collective event. The tortured aesthetic construction challenges our position as a stable subject. As art theorist

Claire Bishop argues, instead of a "rational, centred, coherent humanist subject," art based on "decentring" the gaze creates a "person intricately dislocated and divided, at odds with him or herself" (*Installation Art,* 13).

Muck, manifest in the hampering meaning, also resides in the murky zone between the fragments inserted in the catalog, whether Walker's or other's creations, images or texts, paintings of photography, left for the seer to untangle. As critic Michael Bibler explains, "This disorientation—the feeling of being immersed in the images without recourse to a clear map through them—enacts the challenge to linearity that is embodied in the central image of Walker's project: 'muck'" ("The Flood," 3). This murkiness, which cannot be confused with obscurantism, establishes, like Glissant's opacity, a respectful relationship to the other, by not reducing an unsayable and nontransferable experience to a knowable fact. Walker's murkiness, like Glissant's opacity, erects an epistemology into an ethics by representing precisely that which cannot be translated, that which escapes a transparent representation. Reducing such inscrutable differences into transparency would amount to a mistranslation at best, or a violation of the other's experience at worst: "A generalizing universal is always ethnocentric" (*Poetics,* 117).

Muck is also in the filth included in Walker's work, which juxtaposes and blends scenes of a pastoral South with crude representations of a woman hanging by her feet ("They Say Water Represents the Subconscious in Dreams," *American Primitives,* 2001, 16–17), to perplex "Tambo" stereotypes dancing on the dismembered figure of a woman bleeding to death with her legs wide open exposing her vulva ("Untitled," 2002, 22–23) to a mother—*or is it a lover?*—screaming over the tortured body of her son/lover with a torn-open ribcage in the big wooden alley of a big house ("Big House," *American Primitives,* 30–31), among others.[21] This filth has been the object of criticism as tasteless exhibitionism, degradation, and pornography.[22]

Crucial questions and tentative answers arise from Walker's representations of barbaric acts leading to the dehumanization of the living and the desecration of the dead. Are images reexposing and redepicting representational acts of rape, torture, or maiming of the dead complicit in the repetition of violence, or do they raise consciousness so that such barbaric acts will never be repeated? What happens when these images fall into the wrong hands or are viewed with the wrong eye? Certainly, the positionality of the one who authorizes or circulates images of abject violence influences the appropriateness or decency of such reproductions. When Mamie Till-Mobley chose to leave her lynched, tortured child Emmett

Till's casket open and photographed, she certainly wanted the world to see the horror of lynching and not to perpetrate an act of desecration.[23] On the other end of the spectrum, postcards of photographed lynchings in which the agonized tortured or the maimed deceased were staged as spectacles for grinning white southerners. By its very nature, the postcard performed the ultimate act of defilement by allowing the spectacle of violence to casually travel without the veil of shame and decency.

Does *Without Sanctuary*—the companion volume to the 2002–3 *Without Sanctuary* exhibits, a collection of lynching postcards edited by James Allen—raise consciousness or perform a gesture of unritual?[24] Congressman John Lewis sees the collection as an important tool of memory: "Many people today, despite the evidence, will not believe—don't want to believe—that such atrocities happened in America not so very long ago. These photographs bear witness to . . . an American holocaust."[25] Ricardo Lacayo from *Time* magazine evokes *Without Sanctuary* as "a great and terrible book." Critic Susan Sontag features the exhibit and its companion book as the ultimate example of the ambivalence of representing past violence. Did *Without Sanctuary* satisfy "voyeuristic appetites" or an "obligation to 'examine'" (*Regarding,* 92)? Sontag answers this crucial interrogation by providing a series of further unanswered questions.

Paige Parvin in a 2002 issue of *Emory* magazine nails the unritual nature of the exhibit: "To stumble into the show unknowingly," she writes, "would be like tripping over a dead body in a public park."[26] I remember tripping into the exhibit twice in Atlanta. The first time, at Emory University, I felt a sense of nausea caused by unbearable images that neither my physiological nor rational system could process. The reaction was mostly about my helplessness to stomach what I was seeing despite years of experience teaching and researching slavery and postslavery literatures. The second time, at the Martin Luther King Jr. National Historical Site, the experience was much less about my own physiological and rational inability to process the utter unritual but, rather, about my own insertion in that history and present responsibility to it. The visitors that day were mostly African American Atlantans and travelers. The main discomfort came from the visibility of my whiteness, inserted in the spectacle, which put me in a position of guilt and shame. My whiteness merged with the close-up of the grinning hot-dog-eating white boy in the foreground of an image of a charred human body. I follow philosopher George Yancy's imperative in his book *Look, a White!* to make my own whiteness "visible" and "marked."[27] Leaving the exhibit, I asked myself how to bring that guilt and shame in an outward constructive mode in line with a heightened consciousness of my own whiteness: an act that Yancy qualifies as "heavy laden with great responsibility" (*Look,* 6). At the least, the exhibit encouraged me to keep teaching what are called "difficult texts" in the hope that some of my students will bring a critical, humanities-based mode of interpretation in their respective careers and actions as lawyers, teachers, public health officers, traders, creators, and medical doctors.

Over a decade later, I am writing on the "great and terrible book." However, I will never teach or show these postcards to my students. They go beyond my capacity to rationalize and think critically. While I bought, and teach, Walker's artistic representations—which are representations, not photographs, of real tortured, maimed, and lynched humans—I did not buy *Without Sanctuary,* which could be seen, if found, for instance, by my children, as an act of unritual, perhaps for their lasting ability to degrade the victims of such acts, alive or dead.

The exhibit, however, with its spectators' heightened feelings of rage, guilt, or empathy, provided a performance that provided a context, a community (albeit a community made out of pain and violent history), a wake. Beyond its visual dimension, the exhibit "Without Sanctuary" had a soundtrack: "Strange Fruit" written by Abel Meeropol and sung by Billie Holiday. The singer's sober piano accompaniment and the deep raucous sadness of her voice, the pained vibration of her vocal cords, the irony of the lyrics, the grimaced syllables, and the final visceral cry interrupted by definite silence, brought the spectator goose bumps, sadness, tears, nausea, appropriate for an act of mourning. This is the sort of body performance that Moten qualifies as ground-breaking: "Here lies universality: in this break, this cut, this rupture. Song cutting speech. Scream cutting song. Frenzy cutting scream with silence, movement, gesture" (*In the Break,* 39). Through its performance of imbricated interruptions, "Strange Fruit" carries the exception of the suffering black body into universality. It acts as a powerful dirge to counteract the unritual of the tortures, their postcard images, and their contemporary display in Atlanta. Unfortunately, the book version does not come with the sober veil of decency offered by the exhibit's soundtrack.

I feel a similar, while not identical, trouble, when viewing an image from Spike Lee's post-Katrina documentary *When the Levees Broke.* Lee's "film document" exhibits the indelible image of a frail elderly African American woman in a wheelchair who is dying as the film progresses, and whose son desperately tries to get help for her. Ethel Freeman's eventually lifeless body, left alone in a corner of the New Orleans Superdome, is discarded, to quote Fanon, as "an object among other objects" (*Black Skin,* 89).[28] The obscenity lies not in the woman's death, but the fact that the death's exposure by the disaster of Katrina externalizes private moments such as dying and death to the outside world: intimacy is turned inside out, skin is turned inside out. The human catastrophe of Katrina reveals what critic Hortense Spillers describes as a "body whose flesh carries the female and the male to the frontiers of survival and [that] bears in person the marks of a cultural text whose inside has been turned inside out" (*Black Skin,* 207).

Lee's obvious intent is to expose the evidence of the political neglect of the town, the environment, and its racist politics. As "Requiem," the title of the documentary's first part, indicates, the film has a ritual funerary aim. The song from the opening credits, "When the Saints Go Marching In," which to a casual viewer could appear as an upbeat, hence tasteless, accompaniment to the images of mass-scale disaster indeed serves as a dirge and as a commentary on the apocalyptic nature of the event. The unofficial anthem of New Orleans, "When the Saints Come Marching In" is indeed a traditional funeral march whose apocalyptic lyrics are based on the imagery from the Book of Revelation.[29] New Orleans jazz trumpet player Terrence Blanchard's "A Tale of God's Will (A Requiem for Katrina)," used as soundtrack, provides the musical dirge for Lee's visual requiem. However, despite the best intentions and arguably sacred soundtrack, I am left perplexed by this visual second indecent exposure, so to speak, and wonder how the departed woman can be covered with a shroud of decency. When I happened to discuss this scene with artist Eric Waters as we were comparing memories of New Orleans, he was, unlike me, not shocked. For Waters, the Katrina clarinet-case shroud maker, the outrage resided only in the neglect of racism, not in Lee's representation, which he saw as necessary for the world to see what happened. Poet Patricia Smith's "Ethel's Sestina," which stages the same, now named, elderly woman in her wheelchair, offers the readers Mrs. Ethal Freeman's imagined last words: "Nobody sees me running toward the sun / Lawd, if they think I done gone and fall asleep / They don't hear Come" (*Blood Dazzler,* 46). The poem precisely avoids repeating the spectacle since the viewers "don't see," yet hear, Ethel's story.

Walker's art walks the tightrope between opening the viewers' eyes or kicking them in the gut. A similar controversy marked her 2014 exhibit, "A Subtlety," where she was accused of degrading black women's bodies by repeating racist stereotypes.[30] However, in contrast with Lee, who filmed human subjects, Walker works with stereotypical images, not human subjects, instead. To me, the danger of Walker's art lies more in the reception and the public's reaction rather than her representation. "A Subtlety," turned into a digital show that escaped her control with images of obscene selfies taken with the giant mammy-sphinx's vulva. Visitors who entered the exhibit were provided with no information about the show or the history of slavery and exploitation it evoked.[31] Only in the last few weeks of the exhibit were visitors given a pamphlet educating them about slavery and racist stereotypes. What made the show unsettling is that its public component heightened spectatorship due to the nature of installation art, as art historian Claire Bishop has theorized, and also because Walker imagined, and even trapped, the visitors as a fundamental part of her exhibit's interactive and observational aims.[32]

Walker's art engages the gut as much as the mind. This is where its power—and vulnerability—lies: as Walker explains, "I have a visceral reaction which I don't really want to go away, and the problem with making this kind of work is that you're always producing, re-enacting that reaction. It starts to feed on itself" (*After the Deluge,* 33). The question of the circulation of violence from the event to its representation, to the artist's gut reaction, and to the spectator's gut reaction is then raised. What genealogy of violence does Walker's art feed on and reproduce? How can we, as scholars and educators, stop the violent visceral cycle and reinstate a rational analysis that would lead to action? Gilman puts his finger on it when he wonders, in "Confessions of an Academic Pornographer," his piece on Walker, "How do you put images in quotation marks in a critical text?" (28). It is our role as academics to provide the quotation marks, which, in the state of the unritual, act as a shroud of understanding and respect. If I do teach Walker, it is never in a comfortable way. Her images, in my view, have to remain hidden from the eyes of children and people next to me when I am reading on the bus.

In a seminar on Caribbean Literature and Cannibalism a few years ago, my students and I examined Walker's silhouettes in postures of abject violence. Before discussing the piece critically, I asked the participants to write on a pink index card the first three feelings that they experienced, in an attempt to test Walker's contaminating "visceral reaction." I collected the cards and wrote the responses on the whiteboard without names attached, to preserve students' privacy and to give a sense of our group's collective gut reaction. The answers were even more troubling than I had expected, including strong physiological—gut—reactions. The list included "jarring sensation," "piercing sensation," "breathlessness," "loss of appetite," "repulsion," "revulsion," and "nausea." These are the physical experiences of subjects confronted with terror and the abject, as Kristeva evokes: "I experience a gagging sensation and, still farther down, spasms in the stomach, the belly; and all the organs shrivel up the body, provoke tears, and bile, increase heartbeat, cause forehead and hands to perspire (*Powers,* 3). The thirteen seminar members expressed emotions and feelings of anxiety, discomfort, dread, erotic confusion, titillation, interest, shock, vulnerability, embarrassment, exposure, confusion, disbelief, guilt, shame, alienation, haunting, anger, fury, rage, desperation, and fear of being caught looking.

Once the first impressions were collected, we discussed them critically, observing how vulnerable our position was in front of Walker's art. We acknowledged that our multiple reactions were shaped in part by our positionalities in relation to the history of slavery and the forced enslaved, whether we self-described as African American, white, Asian, or other.[33] We observed the passage from shame to rage and indignation that could free up a path from an inward stance of seclusion to an outward feeling of action. As art critic John Berger explains in "Photographs of Agony," it is not enough to be filled with despair. "Despair," he claims, takes some of the other's suffering to no purpose. Indignation demands action" (34).

We pondered how, as teachers, future lawyers, doctors, or political activists, we could take that indignation to educate, inform, and legislate. We then observed that our feelings of shame and rage had been similar to those expressed by Fanon toward racism in *Black Skin, White Masks,* a text we had read in an earlier seminar. We proceeded with analyzing aesthetically the functions of the black silhouettes that were stereotypes rather than persons. A student brilliantly offered that the use of the color black, the absence of color, which our brain visualizes for us in some way, facilitated our identification with and projection into the figures and our implication in the history of oppression and racism. We ended the discussion with a word from Kevin Young, who claimed that "Walker is less an artist of history, whether racial or artistic history, than a historian of fantasy" ("Triangular Trade," 37). The class discussion provided us with Gilman's missing "quotation marks." It allowed us to distinguish our emotional response from critical analysis, and thus to become better critics and activists.

We also began to provide a "critical shroud" of decency for the photographed drowned of slavery, Katrina, and victims of pandemic epistemic racist representations. The veil of decency I referred to earlier, so often missing from the raw artistic representations by Walker, Lee, Allen, or, as I examine later in this chapter, by Beyoncé, is for the spectators to build the adequate interpretive frame. The veil is not in the representation but in an act of working through in the psychoanalytic sense, which involves the processes of repeating, elaborating, and amplifying interpretations. Using the term "*working through,*" then, involves the idea of a therapy toward a desired cure.[34] We should then ask: When the artistic experience of the unritual is transposed into the language of psychodynamic cure, what and who are the trauma, the pathology, the analyst, and the analysand? It seems that the trauma is, generally, the act of unritual, the apocalypse of slavery, the unveiling of human decency; the pathology, racialized violence; the analysands, the entire community of artists and spectators; the analysts, that very same community of artists and spectators, tormented and tormentors; the analyst's labor, the deciphering, interpreting, and criticism of the unritual. In this way, such art is not an art based on catharsis, on evacuation of a feeling, of, according to the Aristotelian definition "a purification of the soul of the spectator by the spectacle of the chastising of the tormentor."[35] There is neither pleasure, nor purgation, nor spectacle, nor the ultimate extraction of evil, but, rather, a highly interactive, communal, performative, and enduring relationship between the artist and the spectator. The absence of veil calls for the spectator/critic/citizen/human to provide that veil through interaction (aesthetic, psychoanalytic, critical) with the work. The working through provides the veil, an affective shroud, through the pedagogical process. The issue is not the moral purification or "purge" of the Aristotelian model, but a pedagogical political action, and the sacred gestures that such representations call for.[36]

This essay in scholarship strives to expose our shared vulnerability through the undecidability of Walker's works. With the same motivation, literary scholar Karla Holloway subtitled her book of criticism *Passed On: African American Mourning Stories* "A Memorial." While it flirts with the abject, it is necessary to show how Walker's art contains acts of resacralization in the face of the unritual. *After the Deluge,* I would like to argue, functions like a sacred place—more specifically, like a flooded graveyard that the viewer could visit, pausing in front of each image as if contemplating a tomb, under the guidance of the vulnerable and powerful Mami Wata of Walker's "Middle Passages" collage.

Bill Haber's photograph of an African-American woman reproduced in *After the Deluge* (8) stands in sharp contrast with the sea figurehead. The overweight woman, wading through oil-coated, chest-high toxic waters, carries in one hand her soaked, bagged belongings; in the other, a twelve-pack of bottled water. The thirsty woman in the midst of a flood is no ancient mariner but a citizen of Lee's refrain in *When the Levees Broke,* "These United States of America." She is also a subject of world poverty in a race-and-class-inflected catastrophe that impedes her walk to nowhere. Taken from a back angle that fails to reveal her face, the image erases her selfhood under the weight of a generic poverty. Just like the grave of an unnamed soldier signifies the unknown soldier, universally, she is the universal poor. Haber's waters extend beyond all four sides of the shot and offer no visible shore or shelter in sight. The toxic water's beauty, in its spectrum (spectral) rainbow of violet, turquoise, emerald, sapphire, and indigo, sharpens the depth of the abominable. However, Walker's added strike of genius—and respect—is to place the image of the human citizen after a Kongo *nkisi* "male power figure" (2) and in the company of other sacred images and figures such as Joshua Shaw's "The Deluge Towards Its Close" (80–81), Pieter Nolpe's "The Bursting of St. Anthony's Dike" (82–83), and "Christ's Descent into Hell" by a follower of Hieronymus Bosch (92–93). In her "great and terrible" artwork, more than provoking astonishing contrasts between proper acts of mourning and the obscenity of the unritual, Walker establishes a continuity between the quotidian and the sacred whereby anonymous vulnerable humans coexist with saints, power figures, or martyrs.[37] The great *and* terrible paradox for the artist is the imperative of birthing beauty in the most degrading state of desecration of the dead and dehumanization of the living. Aesthetician of the African diaspora Moten encapsulates it in the words "terribly beautiful" ("Blackness," 143).

Flirting with Death: Beyoncé's Siren's Song

Beyoncé Giselle Knowles is to popular music what Kara Walker is to contemporary black art, albeit on a different scale of wealth and visibility. Both women make money from their art in contrast with other struggling artists. Moreover, both artists have been accused of desecrating memories of the dead and exploiting human suffering, specifically that of black lives, in order to make a profit. Beyoncé's music video "Formation," released just one day before her 2016 Super Bowl appearance, which shocked mainstream (read "*white*") viewers as an invasion of black politics, with its political lyrics and squad of ladies dressed in Black Panthers attire and sporting Angela Davis-style Afros.[38] All the while, the twin video of the live performance, starring a luxury-garbed Beyoncé reclining on a drowning police cruiser in the toxic waters of New Orleans, has been seen as a perpetration of the exploitation of trauma and black suffering in post-Katrina devastation. In this book's lingo, Beyoncé's critics would call it an act of unritual.

Curator and New Orleans native Shantrelle Lewis, who has participated in post-Katrina revitalization artistic endeavors, compellingly condemns the singer's exploitation of suffering:[39] "In 'Formation,' which invokes both Katrina and the Black Lives Matter movement, Beyoncé attempts to politicize black tragedy and black death by using them as props for popular consumption. . . . While some people are gagging at the idea of Beyoncé atop a New Orleans Police Department squad car . . . I'm reliving trauma. . . . I am remembering images of bloated bodies of grandmothers and grandfathers, cousins, uncles, great aunts, and nieces that drifted through the floodwaters like discarded pieces of scrap wood."[40] Beyoncé lasciviously reclining on a police car in her luxury dress and fit Mami-Wata-body violently clashes with images of unhealthy bodies, such as that of the water-carrier featured in Walker's *After the Deluge*. The performer's victorious pose can be taken as an insult to the victims of the unritual, which Lewis describes as discarded inanimate objects. Explaining similar accusations, Copeland reports that Walker's harshest critics similarly claim that she "trivialize[s] human suffering and recklessly reproduce images of black abjections, which are effectively naturalized when divorced from their historical context" (*Bound to Appear,* 198). Playing devil's advocate, Moten explains the impasse black artists face in their historical duty to expose the suffering of African Americans, which, if their art gains visibility, inevitably leads to a success based on the spectacle of suffering and, conceivably, to perceived narcissism: "How does one give expression to these outrages without exacerbating the resistance to suffering that is the consequence of the benumbing spectacle or contend with the narcissistic identification that obliterates the other or the prurience that too often is the response to such displays?" (*In the Break,* 3). In addition, if we adhere to my theory that Beyoncé is cast in "Formation" as Mami Wata, her triumph may not only be selfish narcissism but also a gesture to reconnect the victims of Katrina to the sacred. Mami Wata's corresponding lwa Ezili provides a similar spectacle of lust in a ravaged Haiti: "The place of torture becomes the scene for a charade of love," Dayan comments on the ceremony in honor of the powerful woman lwa (*Haiti,* 65).

By way of contrast with Beyoncé's "Formation," Jesmyn Ward's account of the devastation of Hurricane Katrina in the fictional community of Bois Sauvage, based on the author's own hometown of DeLisle on the Mississippi Gulf Coast, avoids the pitfalls of cultural appropriation.

Ward wrote *Salvage the Bones* in the direct aftermath of hurricane Katrina, which she experienced and survived: "I lived through it. It was terrifying and I needed to write about it" (263–70, 263). The novel takes place in the Pit, a mud-filled hole that serves as home, prone to flooding and sliding, recalling Walker's abject muck. It explores the lives of four teenage siblings prematurely thrown into adulthood by abject poverty, environmental racism, sexual violence, hunger, and trauma, all culminating with the utter destruction of hurricane Katrina. There is no Gucci glamour in the Pit. There are only a few sporadic moments of sacredness and tenderness, manifest in the references to Greek myths offering only brief solace ("for a moment, I was Psyche or Eurydice, or Daphne. I was beloved"; 16); in the fleeting holiness of animals and plants ("the puppy appears like the heart of a bloom. It is as still as a flower's stigma"; 18); "[China, the pit bull] is a weary goddess"; 40); or in the care between humans and dogs or brothers and sisters ("call me sister"; 258). In *Salvage the Bones,* "water meant death" (216). It will take Ward over ten years after Katrina, with the publication of *Sing, Unburied, Sing* in 2013, to see water not only as a lethal weapon but also as the realm of protective Yemaya, "the goddess of the ocean and salt water, with her shushing and her words" (159).

While Beyoncé does not share Ward's position of direct survivor, she is not a total stranger to the catastrophe, because of her direct parentage and connection and commitment to the black lives lost to Katrina and racial violence. While the lush image of the superstar riding a police car in her Gucci dress clashes with the poverty-struck victims of Katrina, Beyoncé provides plentiful context in her video in contrast with Walker's silhouettes presented in their isolation on blank walls or pages. As Copeland explains, it is the lack of historical context that banalizes images of suffering (*Bound to Appear,* 198). The video's montage avoids this trap by featuring emblematic images of violence done to black subjects throughout the centuries balanced with African American successes and heroic moments. Real footage and fictional images include, for instance, a crew of African American women and girls in antebellum cotton gowns and Storyville-style *plaçage* attire, referring to the commodification of black women now ruling over the plantation house; a young *Mardi Gras Indian* dancing in a lush purple costume; parades of second-liners; locals peeling crawfish at high speed; a portrait of Rev. Martin Luther King Jr. on the cover of "The Truth" with the caption "More than a dreamer"; a black horseman resembling a Buffalo Soldier; a jubilant congregation; and graffiti screaming "Stop Shooting Us." The montage of images in quick succession accelerating centuries of black exploitation and black power ends with a hooded teenage boy dancing in front of a police squad with arms outstretched while the uniformed men raise their arms in surrender in front of the new prophet. The presence of actor Quwenzale Wallis, tennis star Serena Williams, and the "Mothers of the Movement" blurs the lines between fiction and historical events.

The squad of dancing ladies "*slaying*" a cocky femininity allies the sensuous to the political. Rock and roll magazines *Les Inrockuptibles* and *Rolling Stone* applauded the video for its political stance. *Rolling Stone* claimed that "in the era of #BlackLivesMatter, 'Formation' felt downright necessary. [Beyoncé's] Super Bowl performance, with nods to Michael Jackson and the Black Panthers, was pretty awe-inspiring too."[41] The French *Les Inrockuptibles* qualified it as "a video both aesthetic and militant, featuring images of a Katrina-ravaged Louisiana, an ode to Black Panther women, and a more confident than ever Queen Bey, as the Popess of an ultra-sophisticated black power."[42] This victorious female black power conjures the divinity Mami Wata in Beyoncé's performance.

Like the New Orleans artists featured in the previous chapter, Beyoncé and her squad pile up disaster upon disaster creating a narrative made of fragments and shards, not to undermine historical and political narrative but, rather, to practice a "tressage" or "weaving" in graphic solutions in which the viewers have an active role to play in assembling the parts. The raw juxtaposition of the killing of young black men and of Katrina victims left uncommented does not diminish but invites the viewer to weave together the united pieces of a puzzle of environmental and racial violence. To use critic Martha Kuhlman's words, Beyoncé invites her viewers to "[fit] these pieces together and figure[e] out graphic solutions to a catastrophic event that appears to defy representation" ("The Traumatic Temporality of Art," 861). Undeniably, the spectacle of "Formation" can revive trauma by replacing the pain, discrimination, and poverty of New Orleans victims with the triumphant rule of Beyoncé sitting on the police cruiser like Mami Wata on her watery rock. At the same time, it can also facilitate active viewing and listening as a way to put the pieces of a hurt community back together again. Like Walker, Beyoncé leaves her viewers on a fence.

The triumphant figure of Beyoncé is also a call to rule. As she sings "you just might be a black Bill Gates in the making / I just might be a black Bill Gates in the making," she is standing on the police car with her arms outstretched in the same triumphant pose as the hooded young boy. Paradoxically, militant black power merges with the capitalistic strength of entrepreneur and world's wealthiest person Bill Gates. While Beyoncé's wealth is far from equaling the business magnate's, she shares with him his philanthropic outlook. Wealth is also an attribute of Mami Wata, whom art critic and curator Henry John Drewal calls a "'capitalist' par excellence" for her abilities to "bring good fortune in the form of money" ("Mami Wata," 60).[43]

Critics have widely commented on citationality in Beyoncé's "Formation." References ranges from African American science fiction writer Octavia Butler to French advertising film director Jean-Paul Goude.[44] The video was directed by world citizen Melina Matsoukas, who is of Greek, Jewish, Jamaican, and Cuban descent. The opening sequence amazes with its masterful montage, juxtaposing in quick succession shots from documentary footage and filmed material of Beyoncé and her crew.[45] The video opens with Beyoncé squatting on the sinking police car with her poised red and white smock and combat boots to a soundtrack of percussive electronic pulse. The montage cuts to a black man's gold teeth, whose brilliance provides a visual link to the shot of a New Orleans street at night, with a black man riding a bicycle and police lights flashing in the background. A cut follows to the desolate underbelly of Interstate 10 at the mouth of Canal Street, a site of pervasive homelessness at the heart of the city. Next comes a tracking shot of ravaged shotgun houses that evokes a cinematic "drive-by shooting." The very quick sequencing renders impossible any framing, whether by a camera, or by gun. Returns Beyoncé in black funeral attire, eggplant-purple lipstick, and oversized silver necklaces, reminiscent both of chocking instruments of torture and African neck adornments. She stands on the front porch of a Greek Revival plantation house flanked by two sternly dressed black men acting as bodyguards, claiming a space that has long been reserved for white plantocracy and excluding African Americans, who had to use the back door.[46] We then return to real footage of people dancing in a small, smoky, dark apartment with a high back-lit window; flooded boat houses; and a pastor preaching at a funeral, with a close-up on Beyoncé's face and bust singing the first words of the song confronting "haters" and paparazzi. The artistry of the meaning-making montage is undeniable.

The catch, however, is that Matsoukas *borrowed* significant sections of the clip from "The B.E.A.T.," an independent documentary directed by Chris Black and produced by Abteen Bagheri.[47] She used not only single shots but the montage itself, which constitutes the signature and aesthetic property of its creator. For instance, the gold tooth leading to the ambulance light was Black's. While this is not the place for an intellectual property trial, we can nonetheless conclude that this case walks a fine line between theft and citationality, solidarity and greed, individualism and community building.[48] An article from *Les Inrockuptibles* concludes that "the political and aesthetic power of the song is a bit stained" by the controversy. The journalist adds, to the director's credit, that "Matsoukas worked extremely hard in synchronizing montage and music" ("Qui est Melina Matsoukas?").[49] Indeed, the lyrics—cowritten by Beyoncé and rappers Michael L. Williams II, Khalif Brown, and Asheton Hogan—collated upon the montage, create original nexuses of meaning. Take, for instance, the juxtaposition of Beyoncé's "Texas *bamma*" shout and the shot of the basketball player wearing an "[Ala]*Bama*" jersey, creating a compelling image of a Black South in which Texas and Alabama are both claimed as sites of blackness and in which popular sports and luxury fashion, masculinity and femininity coexist.

While not perfectly honest, "Formation" provides a platform for working through trauma, as critic Regina Bradley puts it: "Katrina is . . . a springboard for re-rendering southern trauma and its association with blackness. Trauma is the spring board of southern blackness."[50] As in my earlier discussion of Walker, I mean "working through" in the psychoanalytic sense of a cure, which involves the processes of repeating, elaborating, and situating the traumatic moment in a context and a narrative. In addition, Beyoncé provides a model of "working hard," necessary to reconstruction in the aftermath of catastrophe, be it Katrina or the murder of black subjects with impunity.[51] No one can deny that Beyoncé has worked hard on this album, *Lemonade,* and her endeavors to reach the worldwide visibility and power she gained and to make visible the too often invisible: "I dream it, I work hard." Her lyrics turns on its head the insidious stereotype of idle black women, which gives the illusion of rendering them responsible for their economic plight, as Patricia Hill Collins has famously exposed in *Black Feminist Thought.*[52]

This citationality flirting with intellectual theft is also arguably part of a creolizing engine made explicit in the following lyrics: "My daddy Alabama, my ma Louisiana, you mix that negro with that Creole make a Texas bamma." The ingredients of the recipe for a black feminist creolization include provocative, Mami Wata-style elements. "Negro," as many critics have argued, refers to Beyoncé's assertion of blackness with her reference to "Jackson Five nostrils," not without humor and irony. "Creole" could be understood in the sense of a mixed-race person, or, in its more localized sense, as a New Orleans Creole or a light-skinned African European person with French origins. The strong references to the "country" ("can't take the country out me") and the set of New Orleans for the video corroborates this local definition of Creole. This recipe for a neocreolization of already-creolized sites and objects could refer both to Beyoncé's strong sense of self and as a mode for a community. Read autobiographically, the performer's recipe for mixing mirrors Beyoncé's family line. While the artist's father, Mathew Knowles, was born and raised in Alabama, her mother has Louisiana African, Native American, and Acadian roots. Born in Galveston, Texas, Célestine Ann Beyincé-Lawson's ancestors are from Iberia Parish, Louisiana. Through the mother line, Beyoncé is a descendant of Acadian leader Joseph Broussard, also known as Beausoleil (1702–1765). The Acadian hero—literally, BeautifulSun—transmitted his name to the Cajun band BeauSoleil, led by Michael Doucet, who also provide their own musical recipe for creolization: "BeauSoleil avec Michael Doucet take the rich Cajun traditions of Louisiana and artfully blend elements of zydeco, New Orleans jazz, Tex-Mex, country, blues and more into a satisfying musical recipe."[53] Beyoncé's lyrics thus transpose the star's roots: "My daddy Alabama, My Ma Louisiana, you mix that negro with that Creole make a Texas Bamma." The word "bamma" comes as a term that doesn't refer to racial or ethnic identity, but rather, to a rural, "country" self who lacks a sense of style.[54] Of course, Beyoncé revises the definition by projecting onto it the epitome of global luxury fashion. Beyoncé sets the record straight that Texas is also a black and Creole state. This grounding in the Lone Star State is reinforced in another song from *Lemonade,* "Daddy Lessons," in which the singer names the state thrice—"Texas . . . Texas . . . Texas"—thereby stating her birth right. Her choice of the country music style, albeit creolized since it opens with New Orleans brass instruments paired with western harmonica, also settles her blackness into a musical genre mistakenly considered as only white. Her performance, with her invitation to the Dixie Chicks to join her at the fiftieth installment of the Country Music Awards in 2016, continued that assertion.

While gratifying, the autobiographical explanation is not altogether satisfactory. Too many bloggers or critics fall into the trap of interpreting Beyoncé's works as transcriptions of her life, a trend observed in simplifying readings of black or minority artists.[55] A simple illustration of this is that Beyoncé's father is still alive and well, whereas the daddy persona of *Lemonade* has died. I see, in Beyoncé's recipe for creolization, an ode to the complex and tortured history of the southern United States, which takes us beyond a white-and-black binary model. In her naming of three major southern states, Texas, Alabama, and Louisiana, we can hear an echo of Nina Simone's 1964 "Mississippi Goddam," which became a civil rights anthem, in which the jazz singer accuses the states with rampant racial violence, the killing of black schoolchildren, and lynching in an upbeat showtune: "Alabama's gotten me so upset / Tennessee made me lose my rest / And everybody knows about Mississippi Goddam." In contrast with Simone's anthem, however, which confronts the southern states in a moment of rage motivated by justice, Beyoncé's "Formation," performed in the midst of our contemporary civil rights struggle, puts the emphasis on claiming and inhabiting the southern states in a gesture of ownership. The lines "My daddy Alabama" and "My ma Louisiana" are reminiscent of Martinican poet Aimé Césaire's claim to the southern United States in his *Notebook to the Return to a Native Land* as sites that belong to him since they were built upon black suffering and trauma: "What is mine . . . Virginia. Tennessee. Georgia. Alabama" (15–16). Beyoncé's possessive "my" and Césaire's "mine" are to be understood as a singular plural encompassing a collective. "What is mine" for Césaire is what belongs to my race and my community of the oppressed; for Beyoncé, "my daddy" and "my ma," while autobiographical, are also to be understood in the allegorical sense of "countries," constituting homes for communities. "You can't take the country out me" could indeed refer to her "country girl" (bamma) style, carrying hot sauce in her bag, but also to the insertion of the creolized persona featured in the song (black, creole, Texan, etc.) in the centerstage of the "country" as nation. To be sure, Beyoncé performed "Formation" during the intermission of the Super Bowl, the most watched television broadcast in the United States and on an unofficial national holiday during February, Black History Month. The claim is reversible. Beyoncé also claims, "*They never take the country out me.*" She declares that in the heart of the all-American televised spectacle inextricably lives its black identity. Beyoncé's gesture is thus a highly visible media response to the exclusion of African Americans from the US nation. In her political siren's song, Beyoncé's tells the nation, *You can't take the US out me.* In her ritualistic Mami Wata call, Beyoncé installs the memory of the dead on the altar of the most visible spectacle for the living: the US Super Bowl.

"Formation," the twelfth and last song of Beyoncé's album *Lemonade,* begins with a relentless synthesizer beat that grips the entire song. The pulse is composed of three throbs, the first two regularly mimicking a steady heartbeat. The third, dimmer syncopated beat regularly follows the heartbeat, interrupting it like an echo, or a gunshot. Hence, from the start, the song introduces the regular pattern of basic life, the heartbeat, and its constant echo of the ultrasound machine of a body on life support, or the interruption of the beat—perhaps by a gunshot, or a fearful arrhythmia. Even before Beyoncé's deceptively soft raspy whisper enters the song with harsh words of confrontation, the minimalist beat has begun telling us a story of life and death. It has introduced the theme of threatened black lives that will explicitly appear throughout the song in the lyrical and visual accompaniment. The song is written in F minor, which Austrian composer Franz Schubert described as the key of "extreme grief," "funereal lament," and "longing for the grave."[56] As much as the beat, the key transports us into a realm of life inhabited by the threat of death. Far from Schubert's aesthetics, the choice of New Orleans bounce music for the song nonetheless similarly indicates the conflation of celebrating the dead and the living. As Pulitzer Prize–winning journalist Wesley Morris puts it, "[Beyoncé] knows how to use bounce music to have it work both ways: funereally and as fun."[57]

The video version also revives the dead into the world of the living. It opens not with the beat but with the voice of Messy Mya, purple-haired New Orleans rapper and comedian, murdered at twenty-two years of age. Messy Mya first asks, "What happened at the New Orleans?," hence introducing in the song victims of gun violence and calling for truth about Hurricane Katrina and then announcing his return: "B . . . I'm back, on popular demand."[58] Mya's "voice from the grave," Bradley puts it brilliantly, "'haunts' the track and like a brief séance, delivers a message to the living."[59] As Dayan eloquently writes in what serves as an epigraph to the introduction to this book, "The dead do not die. They haunt the living. Both free and unfree, the undead still speak in the present landscape of terror and ruin" (*The Law,* 195).

Arguably, the explicitly erotic lyrics and images of "Formation" could at best distract from the memory of the dead, at worst desecrate it. However, eroticism may also very well help to celebrate the memory of the dead, if we look at the force of *Eros* interacting with *Thanatos* as irremediably linked in a universal sense, or, in a more specific context, in the sacred realm of African-derived religions of the Americas such as Vaudou and Santería, as constantly coexisting forces.[60] Critic Bradley puts her finger on it when she remarks on Beyoncé's cultural literacy in African derived religions, spirituality, and imagery: "Is it possible that Beyoncé, in her red and white dress, was summoning Mami Wata, the water deity who could be both a healer or lure travelers to their watery grave? . . . One possible intention here is a visual reminder of the many unknown souls that drowned and possibly took their place by Mami Wata's side during

Katrina."[61] Indeed, Beyoncé reclining on a police car recalls Vaudou imagery of Lasiwèn, Mami Wata, or Yemaya reclining on her stone, luring men with her beauty, in a space between solid and liquid that is threatening to all but to her own amphibian self.[62] She establishes contact between the dead and the living, and among water, sky, and earth, as the figure of Lasiwèn so often does. In Danticat's novel *Claire of the Sea Light,* the narrator's departed mother adopts the shape of the water deity, as she connects the image of the girl's dead mother with the reminiscing of her father: "She was his Lasirèn, his long-haired, long-bodied brown goddess of the sea. With an angélic face like a bronzed Lady of Charity, Lasirèn was, it was believed, the last thing most fishermen saw before they died at sea, her arms the first thing they slipped into, even before their bodies hit the water" (*Claire,* 34).

Beyoncé also visually calls to mind visual representations of the water goddess in Haitian Vaudou that depict the deity adorned with a colorful necklace, combing her luxurious golden hair, with a fishtail of red and white scales.[63] In her red-and-white fish-scale Gucci dress, the performer gazes at the viewer in an inviting pose, with parted lips and offered body. Symbol of luxury, eroticism, and destruction, Lasiwèn, as analyzed earlier in the section on Walker's *Middle Passages,* stands in the ambivalent place between threat and salvation, since she has the power to deliver both: she can drag people underwater and bring them back alive to the surface. In Vaudou theology, Lasiwèn, the powerful and beautiful water deity, is a figure of ambivalence. She can be both male and female. She is often paired with labalène (the whale), alternatively double or husband, as in the Creole song of the epigraph. Lasiwèn is an avatar of the lwa Ezili, also a figure of sexual fluidity.[64] As Dayan explains, "Bearing the trappings of exquisite formalism and femininity, she subverts the role she affects. In her many aspects, Ezili reveals a sexual ambiguity . . . Ezili also chooses women as well as men in 'mystic marriage.' The customary gendered relations between men and women do not matter" (*Haiti,* 63). Beyoncé's pansexuality is made evident in "Formation" in the fashioning of her own body of lavish curves and badass muscles; in the pairing of a flimsy dress with combat boots; in the expression "my cocky fresh." Hilton Als points out that "Formation" is "remarkably gay."[65] Queer theorist of the Black Atlantic Natasha Omise'eke Tinsley agrees when she qualifies the Beyoncé of *Lemonade* as queen of queer love.[66] Lasiwèn's, as well as Beyoncé's association to water realm, facilitates multivalent passages of love and desire. As critic Eric Solomon demonstrates in "Southern Currents," the fluidity and liminality of water is a particularly apt conduit to multidirectional love and desire.[67] Sexually fluid and aggressive, she can also be a figure of tenderness, as expressed in the Vaudou song. The headpiece of "Chapo'm tonbe nan la me" (My hat fell into the sea) metaphorically refers to a soul or consciousness rapted away. Alternatively brazen gorgon and gentle manatee, Lasiwèn seizes those who amorously stroke her: "Ma'p fe kares pou La Siren" (I caress the siren).

Beyoncé piles up the liminal in the figures of the amphibian, the hybrid, the queer, the creolized, and the living dead. Her embodiment of Mami Wata transposes the sacred space of Vaudou cosmogony in the post-Katrina watery zone of unritual.[68] Water, as often observed in this book, simultaneously separates and relates. This ambivalence, the coexistence of the dead and the living, of the dangers and absolute necessity of water, is particular to zones of environmental, racial, and class vulnerability such as southern Louisiana, where the dead coexist with the living not only metaphorically but also experientially. With each flood, the dead, within or without caskets, literally resurface.[69]

In the penultimate shot of "Formation," the singer sinks along with the police cruiser. She is descending underwater but certainly not dying. The last shot of the video reveals a triumphant Beyoncé waving goodbye from an antebellum home in her antebellum dress. Wesley Morris of the *New York Times* astutely comments: "The image of Beyoncé in that dress atop the cruiser has some Toni Morrison poetry to it. You don't know whether the shots constitute a baptism or a drowning."[70] The reference to Morrison, especially in light of *Beloved,* highlights the presence of death in quotidian life. Not unlike Danticat ending her *Farming of Bones* with main character Amabelle entering the river in a gesture that her readers can interpret both as suicide or baptism, Beyoncé gives "Formation" an ambivalent ending.

This permeability extends beyond the single "Formation." Indeed, in *Lemonade* as a whole, the visual narrative establishes a fluid continuity between the singles as Beyoncé transverses liquid spaces while seamlessly entering a new song. Many of the scenes are set near water or underwater. Take, for instance, "Denial," in which Beyoncé swims and breathes, a perfect amphibian, in the astonishingly well-preserved, submerged bedroom of a Big House. The song's video opens with a shot of Beyoncé wearing a black cloak, jumping off a high rooftop onto the street in what appears to be suicide. The concrete of the buildings and roads dissolves into a black watery pool, allowing the potentially lethal gesture to turn into a gracious dive. The artist, now underwater, opens the silver zipper of her garment. Her black mantle has turned into the emblematic hoodie of Trayvon Martin and so many other threatened lives of black men and women.

As the black pool morphs into the bright light of a submerged antebellum room, Beyoncé swims, Ophelia-style, Lasiwèn's cousin, with poetically drifting, foamy hair. Water philosopher Gaston Bachelard indicates that in Shakespeare, Rimbaud, Mallarmé, and Poe, Ophelia, a siren-like figure, is defined by her magnificent floating hair: "For centuries, she will appear to dreamers and to poets floating on her brook with her flower and her tresses spread out on the water" (*Water and Dreams,* 83). The liquid mane provides a link with the floating hair of branches and weeds, and with the river like "living tresses." Beyoncé's receptive body, her mossy hair, greenish skin, and glassy eyes unquestionably evoke Ophelia. Yet, in contrast, the artist easily breathes underwater. She is no suicidal woman, but an amphibian being. She creolizes and enlivens the European myth with its Afro-diasporic cousin Mami Wata. She is no drowned muse for the poet but a powerful artist. While incorporating European myths in her style, Beyoncé expresses "a Southern black femininity so black that its African roots show" as Tinsley maintains.[71]

Beyoncé's sacred is unapologetically African diasporic and female ruled. Beyond her incorporation of Orisha and Vaudou deities, she leaves her blood mark on the West's sacred book. "Denial" features Beyoncé reciting verses by Somali British writer Warsan Shire. The poem begins under the sign of the sacred: "I . . . fasted for sixty days, wore white, abstained from mirrors, abstained from sex . . . confessed my sins, and was baptized in a river. I got on my knees and said, 'Amen.'" The lyrics soon verse into what could appear as blasphemous as in Walker's abject: "I bathed with bleach and plugged my menses with pages from the Holy Book." Indeed the monotheist religions of the Book (Judaism, Christianity, and Islam) define women's menses as pollution.[72] The detour of the Book as menstrual dressing may appear, in this context, utter blasphemy. However, in Beyoncé's cosmogony, the gesture is presented in the same breath as a list of rituals including confession and fasting. Menses, the externalization of liquid feminine transmission, a salute to sexuality and motherhood, by its association with the pages of the Holy Book, may very well attain a sacred status, instead of desecrating the Bible. Significantly, red is Ezili's signature: the color of the perpetual wound of her stabbed heart. Before a ritual offering or sacrifice, Ezili, Deren specifies, demands "absolute cleanliness, one of her "special traits" (*Divine Horsemen,* 139). The bleach bath preceding the blood flow of Beyoncé-Shire's verse adopts the Vaudou sequence. Woman's blood on the Bible indelibly inscribes Afro-diasporic religiosity and femininity on its biblical doublet. The figure of Ezili, Lasi-wèn, Mami Wata, embodied by her powerful avatar, Beyoncé opens the door to the sacred for the victims of the unritual. Like Walker's art, however, the rule of Beyoncé Mami Wata alias Ezili in *Formation* is not to be idealized. It resides in the filth that comes with luxury in excess. It throws an affront and a dream in hurricane-battered zones of vulnerability and poverty. Dayan remarks the same effect of Ezili in Haiti: "In the poverty of rural Haiti . . . what does serving the implacable, demanding, and luxurious Ezili mean? . . . For Haiti's poor . . . she compels an exuberance of devotion that plays itself out in a surfeit of matter. Those who do not have are possessed by the spirit of those who did" (*Haiti,* 64–65). Both necessary and insulting, Beyoncé's *Lemonade,* as well as Walker's *After the Deluge,* grow their sacred on inherited muck.

4 Drowned

Ecological Sacred in Jason deCaires Taylor and Édouard Duval Carrié

The sea doesn't matter, what matters is this: we all belong to the sea between us. (El mar no importa, lo que importa es esto: todos pertenecemos al mar que nos separa.)

—Richard Blanco, *Matters of the Sea* (*Cosas del mar*)

THIS CHAPTER takes as its object the artistic gesture of drowning. Sculptors, painters, narrative writers, and performance artists of the global Caribbean immerse their creations, themselves, or their spectators in bodies of water to provide aesthetic graves or memorials for the victims of the unritual.[1] In their ecocritical gestures, artists highlight parallels between the discounting of the life of the destitute and that of the planet. They urge us to see ourselves in the potential position of the vulnerability of the drowned, given the environmental crisis we are facing. Whether oceans, streams, artificial lakes, museum atriums, or indigo tableaux, figurative or literal bodies of water paradoxically connect and anchor via the flux and fluidity of water. *Todos pertenecemos al mar que nos separa.* Technically speaking, inanimate objects do not drown but sink. I argue, however, that the submerged objects under investigation are animate enough—by the spirit that artists and spectators insufflate into them, by the living relation that they form with their ecosystem—to drown.

Heftily anchored in the underwater sculptures of contemporary British-Guyanese sculptor and environmental activist Jason deCaires Taylor and in the *anba dlo* creations of Miami-based Haitian painter Édouard Duval Carrié, this chapter also follows an archipelago of other underwater contemporary artists linked by a "submarine unity," to invoke Brathwaite's famous concept.[2] Thus, Taylor's and Duval Carrié's respective creations form a lively, evolving, *relational sacred* ensemble with the other artists' works. These underwater aesthetic creations often relay the sacred, to the point at which the artist can become mistaken for a religious practitioner.[3]

This gathering features, from Martinique, painter Patricia Donatien and sculptor Laurent Valère; and from Haiti and its diaspora, novelist Danticat, singer and Vaudou practitioner Erol Josué, and painter Frantz Zéphirin. While produced in our extreme contemporary moment, the models discussed here extend deep and wide. I occasionally refer to twentieth-century thinkers and artists of the drowned such as Derek Walcott and Romare Bearden. Kongo cosmogony, biblical accounts of the flood, the Egyptian Book of the Dead, the memory of the Maafa or Middle Passage inhabit the creations. Prophetically, and tragically, the practice of submerging aesthetic objects in order to memorialize the dead enfold toward a future of multitudes of humans drowning to escape war, famine, or oppression. Geographically, the model of aesthetic consecration I feature extends to other regions of the world where seas and oceans have increasingly become mass graves for migrants and refugees.

The act of drowning I evoke espouses a spectrum ranging from literal to imaginative, and from material to theoretical. Indeed, when sculptors Taylor and Valère submerge their creations, they do so literally in the shallows of the Caribbean Sea and the Atlantic Ocean. Performance artist Civil literally walks into the Atlantic in Ghana. Other gestures rely upon ekphrasis, or the representation of an artwork of a different form within their creation. For instance, Danticat features a drowned wooden sculpture in her novel *The Dew Breaker,* and Bailey submerges musical scores in his painting *Notes from Elmina* (Thompson, *Radcliffe Bailey,* 86). Yet again, other artists represent the underbelly of water in their paintings more straightforwardly, such as Donatien in her "Soul amer," Bailey in his "En route," or Duval Carrié in his "Grand départ." Like artists Bailey and Julien, the creators of beauty featured in this chapter are highly polyvalent, drawing techniques from a variety of media, scientific disciplines, or past careers, as Taylor admits:

> Strangely enough, my time as a paparazzo photographer gave me the skills I needed to create a visual diary of my work. Art college gave me the technical skills I needed to make molds and armatures, understand materials, and look at space differently. Naturally, my years as a diving instructor helped me work out the physics of water, and gave me an understanding of how coral and marine life function. My theater and set design work taught me about load bearings, cranes, transportation logistics, and, perhaps more important, it gave me the ability to think on a large scale—essential if you're going to realize anything in the vast context of the sea. (*Underwater Museum,* 8)

Just like artists immerse themselves in a sea of techniques, skills, and epistemologies in order to approach the vastness of the sea, underwater death, and the endangerment of species, they also submerge their audience. Taylor and Valère encourage visitors to snorkel or dive equipped with mask or oxygen tank, reminding us of Walcott inviting his reader to play an active role in the poetic creation by taking a plunge. In "The Sea Is History," a poem sounding the intermingled past of the Middle Passage and biblical exiles "locked up" in the sea, the poetic voice playfully tempts the reader: "Strop on these goggles, I'll guide you there myself" (*Collected Poems*, 365). Writer and performance artist Fabienne Kanor locks up her captive audience into a stuffy black room inducing claustrophobia and the sensation of smothering in her performance piece "Le là d'où je viens" (The there where I'm from), combining memories of the Middle Passage, contemporary experience of sea migrations, and the artist's own exile. Duval Carrié enchants his spectators into an aquarium-like space that holds both haunting and restorative power in his "Indigo Room" installed in the atrium of Fort Lauderdale's Museum of Art. Literary critic Steve Mentz pronounces that the "ecological future is for swimmers, not sailors" (*Shipwreck*, 181). Artists and critics claim in unison that dealing with the sea must be a participatory and communal enterprise. *Todos pertenecemos al mar que nos separa.*

"Drowned" is based on this paradox: that the extremely isolating submersion of objects and persons can produce precise, common, and recognizable sites of mourning. Watery realms of unritual graves are nowhere and everywhere at once, absolutely lost and omnipresent.[4] Water is, by definition, the site were no grave can be had, but, at the same time, it is also a site that can be sacred everywhere—for instance, Varanasi, where ashes and bones thrown into the Ganges River both ensure their holiness and their connection with vegetal, temporal, and spatial expenses.[5]

Not all sites of drowning, alas, share the sacredness of the Ganges. Take, for example, Danticat's novels and short stories, which multiply abject sites of drowning, from her short story "Children of the Sea," in which a young mother throws her dead infant and herself overboard in the Atlantic ("they went together like two bottles beneath a waterfall"; *Krik? Krak,* 26); to Amabelle's parents submerged in the Massacre River in *Farming of Bones* ("my parents had no coffins"; 93); to the three-year-old boy taken by the waves in "The Book of Miracles" (*Dew Breaker,* 71). All episodes poignantly identify water graves as sites of absolute loss and condemnation to eternal haunting since survivors can neither retrieve the bodies of their loved ones nor give them a place of rest. In "The Book of

Miracles," one of the interconnected stories featured in Danticat's novel *The Dew Breaker,* Anne, a Brooklyn Haitian woman, is horrified every time she encounters a cemetery. She imagines her baby brother, who had "disappeared under the waves" on the Haitian beach of Grand Goyave at age three: "Whenever [Anne] passed a cemetery . . . she imagined . . . his tiny wet body bent over the tombstones, his ash-colored eyes surveying the letters, trying to find his name" (71). Such is a state of unritual when there was no grave in the first place, but only an unmarked watery site and a child left to wander to find his own name, his own grave, in utter loneliness.

Perhaps an even more sharply cruel nongrave is the limbo space of the in-between, the neither-land-nor-sea, the beach, embodying in space the purgatorial limbo of eternal pain. In her familial and political saga about the island of St. Thomas, *Land of Love and Drowning,* Tiphanie Yanique tells of an unwanted stillborn child's entry into the world. His parents are the only ones to know that "the child had almost existed" (219). The father Kweku "took Owen Arthur's baby body and flung it over the balcony. He did not look to observe if it had hit land or sea" (219). In the limbo of the unknown, the unwanted infant is forever fixed in unritual, a state of eternal unknown, which Glissant describes as even more severe than exile and the "incredible Gehennas" of the Middle Passage (*Poetics,* 5).

The fictional child of Yanique's novel calls to mind another similar, yet highly visible and nonfictional, image: that of the dead body of three-year-old Alan Kurdî, fixed in a photograph as if sleeping peacefully. Eternally, like Danticat's fictional drowned boy, the young Syrian Kurd boy will remain in our memories, abandoned on a cold Aegean beach, in the limbo where the wet sand meets the wave, with his blue and red first-day-of-school outfit and new shoes (Roland Barthes's *punctum*), his face hidden in the sand and away from us, eternally haunting, eternally condemned to limbo, framed by the photograph in this state of unritual.[6] Turkish journalist Nilüfer Demir said she *froze* when she saw the tragic little boy's beached body: "There was nothing to do except take his photograph," she said. "This is the only way I can express the scream of his silent body."[7] Once again, the relay between sound and sight, between image and scream, comes to the rescue in the shock of unritual.

Demir's photograph helped raise consciousness and energized international response to the worldwide refugee catastrophe. It also named one of the thousand unnamed victims drowned in the Atlantic and Mediterranean and, in this, helped in the act of remembrance. However, it gave the countless victims only one single name, one single face for the thousands of drowned victims.[8] In addition, some have described the image and its viral spread as "dead-child porn."[9] Indeed, doesn't photography repeat once more the killing of the child by exposing him, vulnerable, graveless, aestheticized? Unritual puts us in an ethical limbo between the necessity of documenting and raising consciousness and the risks of beautifying terror.

In the wake of Demir's photograph, perhaps with the aim to respectfully memorialize Alan Kurdî's desecrated body, a multitude of memorial and aesthetic gestures flourished worldwide. Anonymous hands placed shrines of flowers and candles on the beach. Indian sand artist Sudarsan Pattnaik installed a larger-than-life blue, red, and flesh- or sand-colored sculpture of the boy, no longer tiny but immense, with the underlying caption: "Humanity washed ashore / SHAME SHAME SHAME."[10] Finnish artist Pekka Jylhä sculpted the boy in the same posture and colors as in Demir's photograph and placed the figure in a glass coffin encasement, as if to provide a sacred resting place in, troublingly, not a proper cemetery but a museum space. The *Daily Mail* questioned whether Jylhä's piece, "Until the Sea Shall Him Free," was "touching or creepy."[11] Famed Chinese artist Ai Wei Wei posed on a beach in the dead child's posture for a black-and-white photograph described by Niru Ratnam in *the Spectator* as "Crude, Thoughtless, and Egotistic."[12] Creating around the unritual is risky business and often walks the fine line, as we have seen with the examples of Beyoncé and Walker, between empowering the disempowered and performing desecration yet again.

This detour into another region of the world—the immense water graveyards stretching between Africa, the Middle East, and Fortress Europe—demonstrates that our Caribbean artists aesthetically and politically resonate with the world. By inhabiting, populating, and reimagining the undersea with their aesthetic creations, artists reestablish alliances and connections where slave traders, polluters, or politicians had inflicted immense harm to humans and their habitat. I return to this world-echo in this book's epilogue.

Anba Dlo

Martinican sculptor Laurent Valère is best-known for his CAP 110 monument discussed in chapter 1. While less immediately visible in scholarship and on the surface of our earth, his drowned *Manman Dlo* (*Mami Wata*) is nonetheless monumental. Submerged very near the shore, in the Bay St Pierre in Martinique in 2004, *Manman Dlo* is the first of several installations by the artist.[13] *Manman Dlo*'s new underwater companion, inaugurated in 2016, is the divinity Yemaya, a curvaceous, reclining mermaid partially silted in sand. Valère's *Manman Dlo* materializes the great ambivalence of the underwater realm, or, in Haitian or Martinican Creoles, the *anba dlo*. The twenty-ton sculpture represents a gigantic head facing upward toward its human snorkeler visitors. What first strikes the viewer is its wide-open mouth. Is the figure thirsty for rarefied air? Is she perishing or gulping sacred water? She is at once silent in her underwater refuge (every submerged scream being mute) and extremely sonorous. She reminds us of Philip's reflection: "I have often since wondered whether the sounds of those murdered Africans continue to resound and echo underwater. In the bone beds of the sea" (*Zong!* 203). For the visiting scuba diver hyperaware of her own breath, the statue's visible act of breathing becomes highly noticeable.[14]

Were we to lip-read *Manman Dlo,* we could make out a long "ooooh" indicating the contemplation of awe, or an "Ommmm," the nebulous cosmic healing sound and sacred syllable of Buddhism and Hinduism. The short forehead flattened into an orb, the rectangular bone structure, the pupilless eyes half-open, the thick lips, the gigantic twenty-ton body chiseled from a great rock resembles the colossal Olmec heads. Thus, Valère's creation roots his contemporariness into the sacred and political Meso-American past. We remain in awe and stupefaction in front of the relational sacred she represents.

In 2006, two years after the underwater installation of Valère's *Mamandlo,* Taylor founded the world's first underwater sculpture park. According to the artist's website, "Situated off the coast of Grenada . . . it is now listed as one of the Top 25 Wonders of the World by National Geographic. His latest creation is MUSA (*Museo Subacuático de Arte*), a monumental museum with a collection of over 500 of his sculptural works, submerged off the coast of Cancun, Mexico."[15] With the joint purpose of producing beauty and of providing pH-adapted supports for coral regrowth, Taylor submerges hundreds of sculptures in the coastal waters of Mexico, Antigua, the Bahamas, the Canary Islands, and the Indonesian Gili Islands, among other locations. His subaquatic work—devoted to themes as varied as slavery, migration, mythology, gardening, and mass production—welcome growth of new underwater life forms that become at once unrecognizable and hauntingly, dynamically beautiful.

The piece "Vicissitudes," from the exhibit *TamCC* at T. A. Marryshow Community College, is an underwater installation of twenty-six human figures, alternating between woman and man, all facing outward toward

Laurent Valère, *Manman Dlo,* underwater sculpture, St. Pierre Bay, Martinique, approximately twenty tons, installation date, 2004. (© Laurent Valère, courtesy of the artist)

the sea. When I first saw it circulating on social media, the image immediately provided for me a visualization and concretization of Glissant's drowned Africans in his "Open Boat":

> Whenever a fleet of ships gave chase to slave ships, it was easiest just to lighten the boat by throwing cargo overboard, weighing it down with balls and chains. . . . These underwater signposts . . . still bring to bring to mind, coming to light like seaweed [ces évidences d'algue], these lowest depths, these deeps, with their punctuation of scarcely corroded balls and chains. In actual fact the abyss is a tautology, the entire ocean, the entire sea, gently collapsing in the end into pleasures of sand, make one vast beginning, but a beginning whose time is marked by these balls and chains gone green. (6)

Taylor's installation concretizes a sea melancholia composed of human faces and skulls in different stages of corrosion. Despite the close proximity of the heads, which evokes the human bodies that lynchers, torturers, and traders often joined together for convenience or spectacle, their humanity endures. It materializes that which, for Glissant, can neither be experienced nor even imagined.[16] Taylor returns to the drowned their visibility and establishes their humanity, despite the corrosion, or rather, precisely thanks to this corrosion and new assemblages between the human and the nonhuman. *Vicissitudes,* moreover, embodies the lesson of Glissant's "Open Boat"—namely, that it is precisely that which cannot be communicated, the experience of the abyss of slavery, of sea depths, of attempted massive dehumanization, that constitutes relation and poetry: "We know ourselves as part and as crowd, in an unknown that does not terrify. We cry our cry of poetry. Our boats are open and we sail them for everyone" (9). Like in Glissant's call, Taylor's human figures holding hands form an outward-facing circle, an invitation to take part in a *ronde,* a ring game, in an open community.

Taylor's intent, however, was not to invoke the Middle Passage. Instead, his primary motivation for vicissitudes was ecological: as described on his website, "His site-specific, permanent works are designed to act as artificial reefs, attracting corals, increasing marine biomass and aggregating fish species, while crucially diverting tourists away from fragile natural reefs and thus providing space for natural rejuvenation."[17] Despite the artist's initial intention, the seascape corroborates the common interpretation in social media and criticism that "Vicissitudes" is also about the Middle Passage. The water sites of Taylor's museums on the touristic Caribbean coasts of Grenada, Aruba, and Mexico unequivocally envelop the grave murmur, the smothered scream of sunken humans.[18] As Tanya

Jason deCaires Taylor, *Vicissitudes,* underwater sculpture, Molinere Bay, Grenada, installation date 2006. (© Jason deCaires Taylor; all rights reserved, DACS/ARS 2019)

Shields specifies: "These pieces are lodged in Grenadian waters that are the cemetery to so many people—Carib leapers, European pirates, African slaves—and they reflect the turbulence of memory and bearing witness" (*Bodies and Bones,* 49).

The very site of the installation was so strongly associated with the Middle Passage that it prevailed over the artist's intention. The memorial agency of the landscape is arguably stronger than the artist's, since the landscape is already itself monument, in a context in which written historical records, textbooks, or human-made monuments *about* or *to* the memory of the enslaved or disappeared Amerindians are seriously lacking: "(Our landscape is its own monument," proclaims Glissant in his *Caribbean Discourse:* "its meaning can only be traced in the underside. It is all history)" (11, parenthesis in original). The landscape is thus always already memorialization in no need of human construction. It is also a countermonument, to use James E. Young's term (more below), since it dwells not in the concrete, the durable, and the erected, but with traces, evolving shapes, and present manifestations of an absence that manifest themselves from below. This below can be seen as the opposite of the above of an erected monument: it pays tribute both to those at the bottom of a hierarchical pyramid of power (the enslaved, the oppressed, the crushed landscape) and to those coming from the sea floors and abysses.

Glissant's "Open Boat" reads the sea as a palimpsest in which the water's surface, like paper, hides a much denser and haunting subtext in its depths. While regattas, maritime sport ships, surfing, snorkeling, and nautical sports cover the surface of the Caribbean and the Atlantic and the touristic imagination of the Caribbean, they suggest, "coming to light like seaweed, these lowest depths, these deeps, with their punctuation of slightly corroded balls and chains" (*Poetics,* 6). While holding abominable, anonymous, and innumerable deaths, the space below water simultaneously acts, in the Caribbean and African diasporic imaginary, as a sacred site. Following a linguistic slip from English to Creole, we witness a radical change in the imagination of the underwater. Indeed, in Haitian or Martinican Creoles, *anba dlo,* literally below the water, defines the place where life came from and to which life returns. In Haiti, the *anba dlo* is also called *Guinen,* or Guinea, a metonym for ancestral Africa.[19] As Hume encapsulates: "The sea has been the unifying metaphor to explore the passage of African religious grammars across the Americas. This is most noted in the Haitian concept of the afterworld . . . where spirits cross the kalunga or marshy watery abyss leading back to Africa" (Hume, "Death and the Performance," 132). The *anba dlo* is also the space where life returns and where the living, the departed, and the unborn interact, as Jenson so aptly summarizes in her conversation with a Vaudou song:

> Witness the words of one of the best-loved Vodou songs: "Anonse o zanj nan dlo / Bak odsu miwa" (Announce to the angels [spirits] down in the water / the boats above the mirror). Offerings to these lwa, sent out on little boats or barks from rafts or boats in a zone about three miles from the shore, are only considered to have been successful in locating passage to the underwater world if the boats sink. . . . The Middle Passage in this sense is built into the metaphysics of traditional Haitian spiritual life. ("Writing of Disaster in Haiti," 106)

In other words, religion practitioners and artists alike, often working on a continuum, transfigure what could be an immense space of unritual into a sacred site.[20]

Caribbean poets and artists of the sea deal in the depth of the sea rather than with its oft-touristic surface. The poets, novelists, sculptors, and painters of the *anba dlo* in the Caribbean are innumerable, so great is the force of water in the everyday imagination of the islanders. Their underwater cemeteries host waves of drowned humans from the slave trade to the more recent deaths of Haitian exiles. The latter have gone to *lòt bò dlo,* "the other side of the water," which refers both to destinations such as the United States or Canada, and to death, the other shore of life.[21] We could begin a list with Walcott's "Sea Is History," and other innumerable poems; Brathwaite's *Caribbean Man in Space and Time* who sees the unit (fragment) and unity (relation) as submarine; Danticat's "Children of the Sea," which evokes the drowned bodies of Haitian migrants; Yanique's *Land of Love and Drowning;* Emile Ollivier's *Passages;* and Marie-Célie Agnant's *Le Livre d'Emma,* to cite but a few.

The list is equally inexhaustible for visual artists. Romare Bearden marks ancient Greek texts with the memory of drowned Africans in his hybrid neo-Homeric slave epic in the series "Odysseus Collages." Quilter Gwendolyn Magee represents the drowning of brown bodies shackled to one another for a surest death by drowning in an abysmal sea in her 2010 "Expandable Cargo."[22] Bailey has numerous creations representing the undersea as his 2005 mixed-media piece in Plexiglas "En Route," with the photograph of a black man in a canoe giving a ride to the collaged image of a Kongo nkisi figure. In "En Route," right below the surface, a disparate collection of African masks (*Are they museum artifacts? drowned ancestors? tutelary community?*) stare directly at the viewer. Bailey's *Notes from Elmina II,* a 2011 mixed-media gouache, collage, and ink on paper, exhibits a Kongo power figure solidly planted and imperturbable in the aqua, turquoise, mustard, pink, red, midnight-blue, and black strokes of nervous sea waves. The piece is a literal palimpsest, since the artist placed the different layers of paint strokes and photographs on a classical musical score, opposing a synesthetic strategy to the unritual. Internationally renowned Miami-based painter and mixed-media artist Edouard Duval Carrié represents the *anba dlo* with an extreme complexity, an erudite sacred imagery, and mind-blowing aesthetics. Deborah Jenson argues that "the space *anba dlo,* so prominent in the work of the Haitian painter Edouard Duval Carrié, symbolically bridges the cultures of the New World and Africa through the waters that divide them" ("The Writing of Disaster," 106). Duval Carrié's works featuring the underwater, a selection of which I analyze here, are too numerous to list.[23] Some of his titles explicitly refer to the creatures of this realm, whom he names the *Ambaglos,* a mythical people of the sea that bear a name like a nation.[24] Duval Carrié's 2003 mural, "La triste et malheureuse histoire des Ambaglos" (The sad and unfortunate history of the Ambaglos) features eight male and female humans floating adrift in the underwater.[25] The fluid scene is installed on a grid of twelve panels that could decorate a luxurious living space. It is also reminiscent of ancient funeral art, such as Etruscan murals: rock-cut paintings used to decorate sepulchers. Like the Etruscan visual memorials, such as "Man in Flight," found in a tomb of Tarquinia, and produced around 530 BC, Duval Carrié's mural represents human figures in movement intricately connecting with the natural world. "Man in Flight" appears to float in an ethereal space and connecting with offshoots of vines and plants as well as a couple of birds. In Duval Carrié's piece, vine-like flowers and plants form a rhizome among themselves and with the human figures that appear to grow out of them. White flowers in full bloom stare at us with curious dilated orange eyes. The women and men float with eyes closed, arms outreached, limbs surrendered to water. While the title—"La triste et malheureuse histoire"—undeniably points to the Middle Passage, the painting's serenity clashes with the horrors of the slave trader's forced drowning of human beings. The expression on the faces is peaceful. The sea liquid is not blue or violet but painted in ochre and bright oranges, evoking soil and sand rather than sea-depths. If some of the figures are complete, others only feature a head and bust. However, these partial bodies do not look like severed bodies from the mouth of sharks. There is no blood to be seen and the borders between the bottom of busts and the amniotic-like liquid are round and smooth; the heads and busts come out first, as if in the middle of the birthing process. The creation then offers a serene sense of the wholeness, beauty, and sacredness of the body that defies its title. The underwater spirits appear in a state of rebirth, rather than in a tragic fate, thereby in harmony with the sacred sense of the *anba dlo,* a place of departure, connection, and rebirth instead of finite death. The composition is "a floor panel that is meant to be used either as a floor or even as the bottom of a pool, since everything in the African cosmogony happens in the water."[26] The artist's gesture reaches beyond representing the *anba dlo* and gives it the intent of literally submerging it. Duval Carrié identifies New Orleans Congo Square as an ideal site for the shallow pool, which would there fill with rainwater.[27] Once again, water art connects the cousin diasporic zones of Haiti, Florida, and southern Louisiana, which had been separated by sea and by the unritual. *Todos pertenecemos al mar que nos separa.*

Duval Carrié's painting "La Reine des Ambaglos" sits in an artist's frame with four brass pegs. The water goddess featured in the work, too, connects the geographically discrete underwater zones yet connected sacred sites of the Greater Caribbean. The work features in its bottom and center a giant indigo figure of a woman with wavy hair flowing in a yellow underwater, pointing with her index finger and looking with an accusing eye in the same direction, her stern face represented in profile.

Edouard Duval Carrié, *Reine des Ambaglos,* mixed media on canvas in artist frame, 137 cm, 1999. (© Edouard Duval Carrié, courtesy of the artist)

The blue figure is adorned with white *vèvès,* Vaudou markings used to facilitate passage and communication between the living and the lwas or gods.[28] Like her underwater nation, the Ambaglos of "La Triste et Malheureuse Histoire," the queen appears to grow with underwater roots, offshoots, and flowers. The underwater plants continue to grow above water, as if to show the continuity between the space of the living and that of the departed and the unborn. The queen's floating hair strands form an intricate web with the flowers and stems. The water is a grainy, textured ochre yellow, thus allying the aquatic and terrestrial as communicating space and rendering the *anba dlo* a fertile land. While below water, the figure is not drowned in it but stands before it, as if untouched by the sea occupying the second plane, in her foreground position. Her head is also slightly taller than the body of water. She is untouched by water because she is water, both because of her immense size and because she is blue: her indigo skin and hair adorned by *vèvès*-like waves. Above the water float the silhouette of humans and boats, in the center an open boat—a large canoe with humans standing, pointing, and lifting their hands in the air in gestures of protest, accusation, or warning. Two tank ships, signaling contemporary militarization, perhaps US Coast Guards, surround the canoe. The canoe is reminiscent both of the slave ship and of the rickety boats of Haitians migrants fleeing dictatorship. Duval Carrié, in dialogue with her interviewer who interprets the boat as "less a slave ship than the boats Haitians took over to the United States," replies that "it is a continuation of the same story . . . After Independence, [Haitians are] still as destitute as they were when they arrived. They're still on the move. It's a resonance from the past and an accusation of the present'" (Sharpe, "Plunder and Play," 566).

Several layers of oppressive history coincide on the surface water, while the queen divinity Ezili Danto prevails, standing undisturbed, gigantic. Human skulls painted in the same color and style as the *vèvès* appear above and below the water surface. A mast adorned with a flag figures upside down, a sunken Christian cross. Above the surface, its mirror image (reminiscent of the song and ceremony evoked by Jenson) reveals the cross of Legba, the powerful *lwa* of the crossroads and passages. The square is pinned down with four brass pegs representing human heads and seashells, looking complicit in their shared mission of guarding the entrance of the painting-temple like four vestal priestesses or guardian *lwas*. The painting points fingers to the guilty and demands justice, occupying the sea, vanquishing politics and history with the power of the sacred. Moreover, as art critic Edward J. Sullivan asserts: "Duval is . . . a creator of environments—universes where his fantasy commands the players in his complex dramas to act out rituals and ceremonies" (*Continental,* 12).

The Miami-based artist's three-dimensional installation, "The Indigo Room or Is Memory Soluble," at the Fort Lauderdale Museum of Art best concretizes his *anba dlo* universe. Installed in 2004 to commemorate the bicentennial of the Haitian Revolution, the piece, a collaboration between Duval Carrié and high school students from the Dillard Center for the Arts, engulfs the visitor in a womb of memory. The ordinary space of the installation, the atrium room of the museum, which also hosts restrooms, water fountains, and elevators, juxtaposes the sacred space

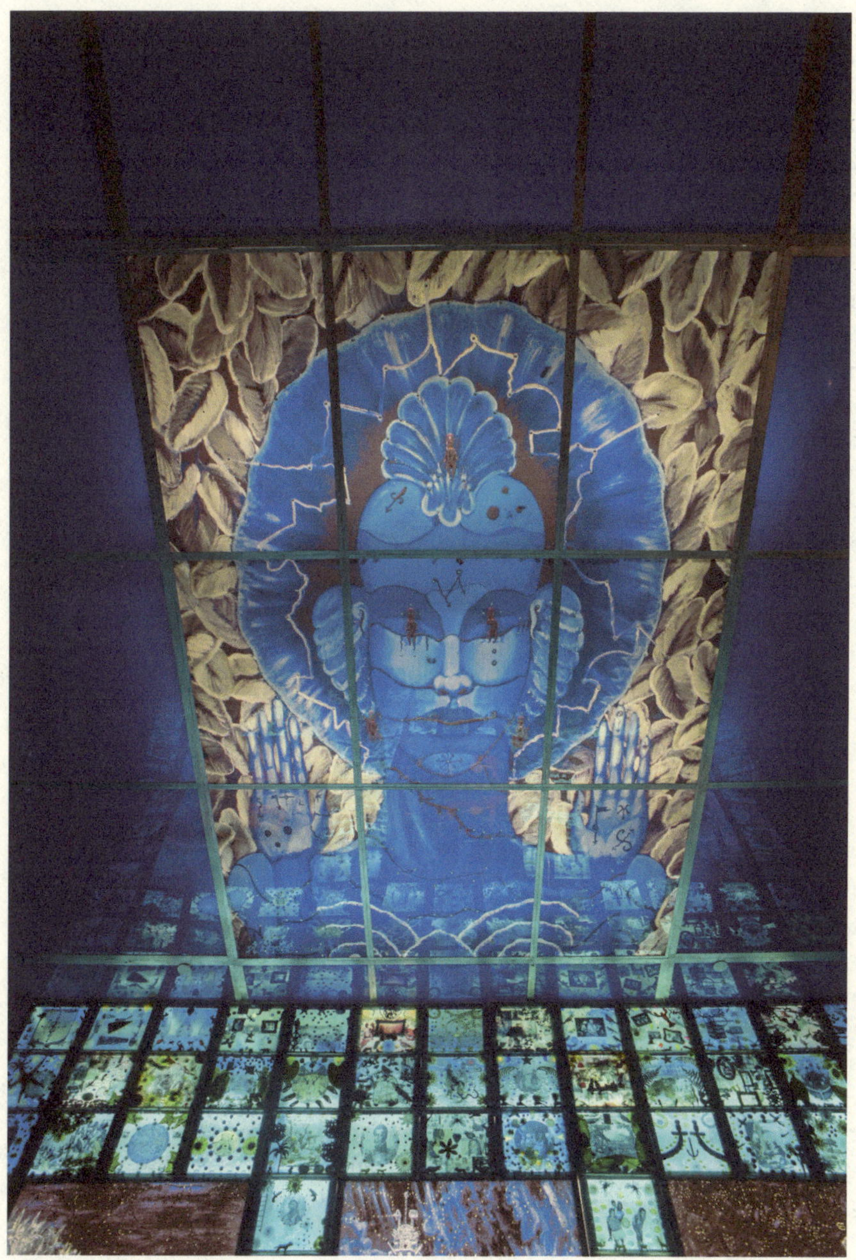

Edouard Duval Carrié, *Indigo Room,* installation at the Museum of Art Fort Lauderdale, 2004. The entire mural measures 4.94 × 3.63 meters. (© Edouard Duval Carrié, courtesy of the artist; photograph by the author, 2017, © Valérie Loichot)

with everyday acts. It also guarantees that most museum visitors will at least pass through it, and perhaps even interact with it by contemplating it or taking selfies with its reflective surface. The choice of the modest location also ensures that the installation will be of long duration. The visitor who steps into the room finds herself gasping for air in a dark yet luminous space dominated by greens and blues. She feels sucked in by the depth of each of the panels, which juxtapose layers of objects and paintings in each of the memory boxes, glowing from the bottom with artificial light and reflecting (indeed *drowning*) the visitor's image in its multiple mirrors. To view the ceiling painted upside down, I found myself having to bend backward as in the touristic or funereal limbo dance. My image reflected on the ceiling by a dull indigo silvering appeared blurred, featureless, submerged, ghostly. As in the Vaudou song quoted earlier, "Bak odsu miwa," the world was turned upside down and the realm of the visitor was drowned into the world of the Ambaglos. In turn, the sacred underwater realm reflected upon the life of the living visitor, the critic, the tourist, the memory-seeker, the mourner.

As a natural mirror, water is particularly apt in adding a sacred dimension to Duval Carrié's work. Indeed, the mirror, or its avatar as watery surface, is a recurring object in Vaudou and Kongo religions, where it is conceived as the dwelling of the spirits of ancestors. Kyrah Malika Daniels evokes its centrality and downward pull: "Making the connection between the spirit world and water, humans came to associate spirits with a downward divine realm, as bodies of water are typically ground-oriented, such as oceans, lakes rivers, ponds, and even waterfalls, which fall downwards" ("Mirror Mausoleums," 967). Duval Carrié's pull for the visitor to look up at the surface of the water and realm of the spirits introduces a significant shift in which the living viewer is placed in the position of the departed, creating a troubling interchangeability between the realms of the dead and the living.

On the ceiling panel thrones a giant head of Ezili Danto, whose formidable power as mother of children and matrix of memory transpires in the figures of the brown babies sitting in her eyes like pupils and resting on her chin, hair, and seashell crown.[29] Duval Carrié explains that the powerful *lwa* is the ultimate mother, the one who hears and sees.[30] Thus, the painting takes on an agency that turns the viewer into an object of scrutiny and interlocutor. Philip, featured in the next chapter, acknowledges the same *anba dlo* agency by inviting in her spiritual underwater coauthor Setaey Adamu Boateng, "the voice of the ancestors revealing the submerged stories of all who were on board the Zong."[31]

The triptych adorning the wall facing the water fountains represents Gods in exile, a common trope in Duval Carrié's œuvre. From left to right, "Le Départ" features the lwas on leaving a tropical land resembling Haiti on a barque; "La Traversée," shows them at sea fleeing a military boat; In "L'Arrivée," they disembark on a grassy beach with a cityscape resembling Miami. The three panels are framed by over a hundred squares, each realized by a Dillard student in collaboration with Duval Carrié. Not unlike the visitor to a grave featured at the beginning of chapter 1, the viewer has to kneel or squat in order to examine the panels, some of which are placed at floor level. Some, high on the wall, escape the eye's scrutiny. Each square tells its own narrative, but also creates innumerable meanings in juxtaposition with others, through the principle of "tressage" at work in Julien's "Katrina Quilt." To take but one example, the squares to the right of "La Traversée" juxtapose a portrait of General Toussaint Louverture with one Dillard student's family photographs. Seashells, ferns, dragonflies, pebbles, and miniature horses adorn the squares, opening up a network of connections between the individual and the collective; the personal and the historical; children at play and war; the animal and the aquatic; and the human, the animal, and the vegetal. The communication between the individual and the collective motivates the creation in the first place since Duval Carrié shared its authorship with dozens of cocreators, a perfect illustration of the art of the relational sacred.

Duval Carrié's main themes and tropes—the relationality between human and plant, between sacred and profane; the use of water as mirror and palimpsest; the paradoxically simultaneous haunting and agency of the (un)drowned—are also at work in Cap-Haïtien-born, Haiti-based Frantz Zéphirin's creations.[32] A self-taught artist, Zéphirin is also a Vaudou practitioner. If his art is internationally acclaimed by art collectors and often exhibited in Europe, Latin America, and the United States, his work is less discussed in US academic circles than Miami-based Duval Carrié.[33] I linger here on one of Zéphirin's untitled paintings labeled with the cabalistic number 0687550.[34] Zéphirin's composition is divided equally between an above and below, an *odsu dlo* and an *anba dlo*. Where the line of horizon would divide sky and sea stands a thick limbo where ten human heads stagnate, gazing intensely. The ten heads have complexions ranging from chocolate to dark brown, mahogany to dark gray, and with a multitude of eye colors: sapphire, coral, amber, jade, turquoise, and moonstone. They are quasi-identical in their mask-like features, yet singularly distinct, as if to mark at the same time the collective nature of their group and their individual existence. This singularity of a larger collective is a trait often found in narratives or representations of the Middle Passage where the enormous numbers of the anonymous drowned need a singular face in order to speak to our consciousness. Their clenched teeth, dilated nostrils, and outstretched eyes are frozen in an expression of fear witnessing horror. Their liminal position increases the proximity and specular relation between the above and below. Should we turn the painting upside down, the above could easily become a below because of its aquatic colors and its floating limbs and hands. Here again, we witness the mirror of the Vaudou song quoted above: "'Anonse o zanj nan dlo / Bak odsu miwa'" (Announce to the angels [spirits] down in the water / the boats above the mirror; Jenson, "Writing," 106). A frequent Vaudou trope, the sky reflecting in the water mirror, or vice versa, is a prevalent trope in literature as well. For instance, the naming of unborn child Claire Limyè Lanmè (Claire of the Sea Light) in the eponymous novel happens in the liminal space of a "patch of the sea" reflecting the moonlit sky and "being lit from below" (*Claire of the Sea Light,* 33) upon the surface of the sea where the unborn child's parents are doing "some night fishing" (32). The narrator reminisces about the now-departed mother of the unborn child not only as a living earthly woman but as the sacred water deity Lasirèn (34). The water is thus not a dividing line but a site of passage, flux, communication, and confusion between the realms of the unborn, the living, and the dead.[35]

Zéphirin's *anba dlo* is occupied by a giant mouth, armed with paddles (like a boat) and teeth (like a cannibal). The open mouth reveals in its cavity a single eye watching and four cyclopes all intently gazing at the viewers. On the top half of the painting and above the sea, a giant vegetable-eye, green and striated like a leaf, mirrors the giant vegetal mouth at the bottom of the painting and under the sea. Disembodied heads and floating outreached hands and forearms surround the eye.

Using the same mirror structure as Glissant who qualifies the sea abyss as the "reverse image of all that had been left behind" (*Poetics,* 7), Zéphirin nonetheless departs from the Martinican poet's imagination of the slave ship, since Glissant sees it as a belly "pregnant with as many dead as living under sentence of death" (6). Instead, here the swallowing ship uses the mouth, another part of the digestive tract, as opposed to the Glissantian belly, which is at the same time intestine and uterus. While part of the same process of devouring and ingestion of humans by the slave trade, the use of the mouth, in contrast with the belly, could indicate

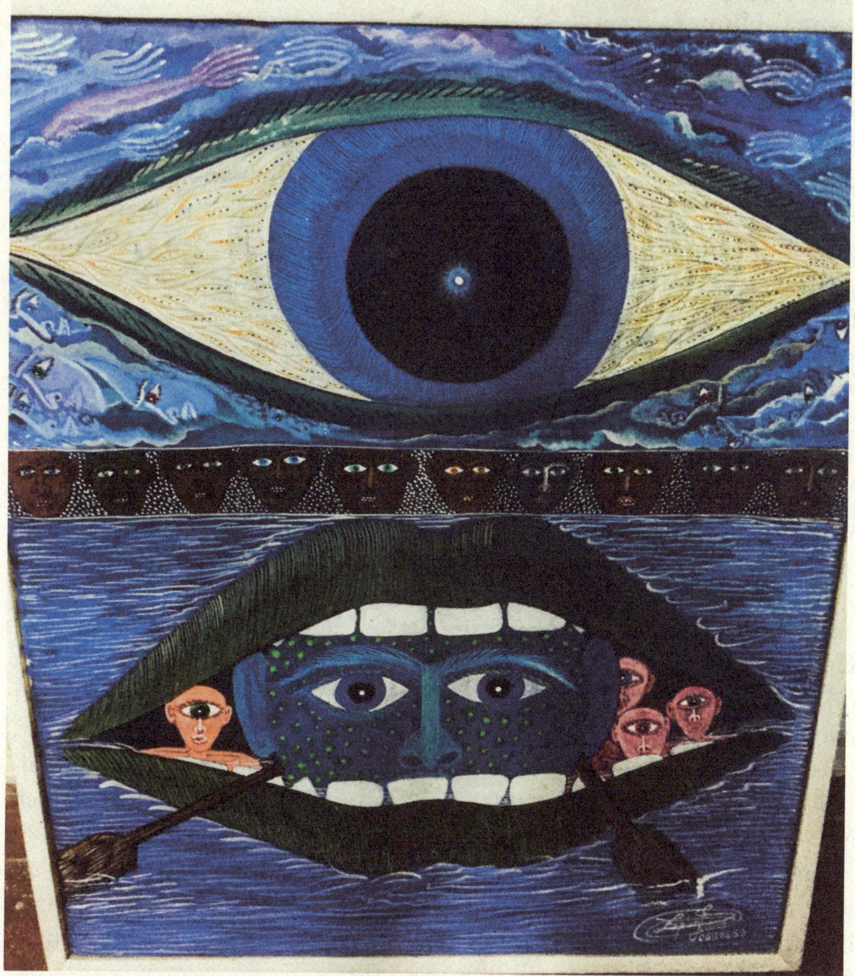

Frantz Zéphirin, untitled, numbered 068750, oil on canvas. (© Frantz Zéphirin, courtesy of the artist)

the possibility of speech since the widely mouth could also be emitting a sound, an "Aaahhhh" scream as well as devouring, reminiscent of Valère's *Manman Dlo*. But for both Glissant and Zephirin, the drowning gives way to an open word, a communication between the dead and the living. In this system, the human, the animal, the vegetal, the seashell, and the skull form new alliances of solidarity.

Animal-Human-Vegetal-Sacred

Zéphirin describes himself as a "historist animalist" (Russell, *Masterpieces of Haitian Art* , 173), highlighting the crucial participation of nonhuman species in the formation of Caribbean histories. Quite often, if not universally, poets and artists of the sea dwell in animal, vegetal, or even mineral objects, forming assemblages with humans in their quest to fathom the depths of the unconscious, memory, or history. French poet Lautréamont, one of the leading poets of the sea, expresses it clearly in *Les Chants de Maldoror:* "Old ocean, men—despite the excellence of their methods, although aided by scientific means of investigation—have not yet managed to measure your vertiginous depths; despite them using the longest and heaviest sounding poles. Fish are allowed there but men are not. I've often wondered which was the easier to fathom: the depths of the ocean or the depths of the human heart!" (24–25). The sea depths, which Lautréamont associates with the abysmal human heart, is then best known by nonhuman animals. Written in the 1860s, these words still ring true, since the abysses of the sea are still the least explored and fathomable parts of the earth and its immediate outer space. For Lautréamont as well as for our Caribbean Sea artists and poets, it is not only a question of superiority of nonhuman animals—or plants, for that matter—over their human kin, but a question of shared history, relay, solidarity, and, as I argue, of sacred alliances. In "Sea Is History," Walcott's "History" "really begin[s]" (54) not with biblical moments such as Genesis, Exodus, or Song of Solomon, or phases of Caribbean history such as Emancipation (all cited in the poem as false starts), but rather with the arrival of "synods of flies," a "secretarial heron," "fireflies with bright ideas," "bats like jetting ambassadors," and "mantis, like khaki police" (*Collected Poems*, 367).

Literary critic Monique Allewaert, in *Ariel's Ecology,* coins the term "para-humanity" to define an "ecologically inflected mode of personhood" at work in the Caribbean (147). The proximity between plants, nonhuman animals, and human animals is, for Allewaert, not a source of dehumanization, but rather a restructuration of human agency putting "animals, parahumans, and humans, in horizontal relation (that is to say para or beside each other) without conflating them" (86). Allewaert's definition illuminates the "historist animalist" artists and poets under analysis in this chapter for whom humans are constantly "para," near, with other forms of beings animate or inanimate (tree, coral, fish, rock, etc.) in their quest to remember the past. In addition to Allewaert's reconstruction of the notion of historical, social, and philosophical personhood, I emphasize a reconstruction of the sacred through these interspecies alliances.

Sea poets are also tree poets. A frequent sacred practice in the Antilles consists of "twinning" a newborn with a tree by planting the placenta or the umbilical cord in the roots of a tree.[36] As explored in chapter 1, Glissant is entwined with his vegetal double, the acoma tree. Duval Carrié similarly paints himself as a tree with roots growing underwater and above the ground. Notably, his "Self Portrait as an Uprooted Tree" (*Continental Shifts,* 149) symbolically sketches the artist, devoid of any human shape or features, as a tree grounded—rather, uprooted—in an indigo sea floor and sky. Its branches and roots extend into flowers, seashells, Ezili hearts, and Vaudou *vèvè* drawings, illustrating a clear ecological sacred. Paradoxically, the death-bearing underwater site is a fertile terrain. It becomes a sacred place, a Vaudou altar, in the height of profanation.[37]

The shift between unritual and a renewed sacred operates when we slip from the English term *underwater* to the sacred-laden Kreyòl term *anba dlo*. The Vaudou song "Depi M Soti Lan Ginen" (Since I left Guinea) provides a compelling example of the present intersecting with the past, the human interacting with plants and minerals, and the abominable transfiguring into the sacred.[38] In Haitian *houngan* (priest), dancer, and singer Erol Josué's performance of "Depi M Soti Lan Ginen," the earth shakes in a way that makes us tremble.[39] The song's lyrics introduce the image of slave traders probing ("sondé") the diasporic subject. The probe, like a maritime instrument used to test the bottom of the sea, or like a surgeon's tool examining the depth of a wound or cavity, fails to fathom the bottoms of the ocean or human body alike, fails to empty it of its content, like an ulcer-searching probe usually would. Instead, the "probed" flourishes in an explosion of life and power:

Depi m soti lan Ginen
Moun yo ape sonde mwen
Se mwen menm, Rasin o
. . . .
Mwen soti anba dlo
. . . .
Se vre, Jou yo konnen sa m sèvi
Latè va tranble
Jou yo konnen non vanyan mwen
Kanno va tire
Se mwen menm, Gwo Wòch o.

> (Since I came out of Guinea / Those people have been probing me / It is I, the root / . . . / I came out of below water / . . . / It's true, on the day those people find out whom I serve / The earth will shake / It's true, when they hear my valiant name / The cannon will fire / It is I, Great Rock.)[40]

Like in Duval Carrié, Zéphirin, Taylor's respective imaginations, *anba dlo* enables alliances between humans and other realms such as the vegetal (roots) and the mineral (rock), which become agents.[41] *Anba dlo* facilitates the persistence of humanity by illuminating the survival of sacred alliances with divinities ("Jou yo Konnen sa m sèvi") and the enduring proper name, which inscribes the human in a symbolic communal system ("Jou yo Konnen non vanyan mwen"), leading to a warrior-like political resistance ("vanyan" and "Kanno va tire").

Taylor's art similarly enables alliances between the human drowned, underwater roots and growths, and the sacred. His underwater sculptures installed around the globe recreate structures friendly to the regeneration of species threatened by human alteration of the environment by providing long-lasting supports for coral regrowth, fish, sponges, algae, crustaceans, and microscopic organisms. His official website includes an encyclopedic "Environment" rubric, in which are listed the inhabitants of the shallows (lobsters, hermit crabs, mantis shrimp, starfish, urchins, coral, sponges, surgeonfish, damselfish, etc.), their common and scientific names, their generic and family classifications, their anatomy, their digestive, reproduction, and dwelling habits, their biotopes, and the alliances they form with the anthropomorphic and nonanthropomorphic sculptures. Photographs of these symbiotic relations creating a new habitat for the living from statues evoking underwater deaths permeate his website.[42] To take but one example, the drowned collective of people of the MUSA collection at Isla Mujeres, who were once submerged in the smooth concrete of their skin and clothing, are now covered in new life forms that establish new meanings. The head of the drowned woman (see fig. 19), which, with her empty eye sockets, might have once appeared cadaveric is now bursting with the life of multicolor sea moss and a white sea egg, which now adorns her chest like a decoration, or an ambivalently erotic prickly caress. The presence of death in Taylor's installations is neither forgotten nor presented as an ending, but, rather, as a continuation in a symbiosis benefiting both the statue and the urchin, one of the many shallow-water threatened species, which can there find a habitat.[43] In his 1992 *Natural Contract,* Michel Serres announces that, with the course of history such as it is and the increasing separation and violence of humans

Jason deCaires Taylor, *Silent Evolution,* underwater sculpture, MUSA, Cancun Underwater Museum, Mexico, installation date 2009. (© Jason deCaires Taylor; all rights reserved, DACS/ARS 2019)

onto their natural habitat, the solution is one of death or life through symbiosis: "This is history's bifurcation: either death or symbiosis" (34). Taylor's art appears to be the concrete manifestation of Serres's "Natural contract," which the philosopher presents as a necessary addition to a "social contract" that has ignored and destroyed its nonhuman participants for too long. Humans must relinquish their parasite status to embrace symbiosis: "A symbiont recognizes the host's rights, whereas a parasite—which is what we are now—condemns to death the one he pillages and inhabits, not realizing that in the long run, he's condemning himself to death too. . . . Conversely, rights of symbiosis are defined by reciprocity" (38).

Marine Biologist Helen Scales comes to the same conclusion. In her essay devoted to Taylor's ecological mission, she highlights the crucial ecological role of coral reefs while pointing out the minimal space they take on our planet: "Coral reefs cover less than one percent of oceans but are thought to be home to a quarter or even a third of all marine species" ("From Polyps to Ramparts," 20). Bursting with life, coral reefs are highly vulnerable since, as Scales explains, "The seas have become thirty percent more acidic since the industrial revolution since they absorb a lot of carbon dioxide. . . . Scientists estimate that by 2050 . . . only fifteen percent of the world's reefs will be able to keep growing." While small on the measure of human destruction of the environment, Scales argues that such "collaborations between scientists and artists can help engender a more emotive response to nature's troubles, to spark interest, and inspire action" (29). The slow but steady disappearance of corals and other marine species is of the type that ecocritic Rob Nixon calls "slow violence," which "occurs gradually out of sight . . . dispersed across time and space . . . a violence that is neither spectacular nor instantaneous, but rather incremental and accretive" (*Slow Violence,* 2). Hence, Taylor's response is unhurried in its evolution, not immediately visible in its underwater site, patient in its accretive assemblages and hopeful for a long regrowth. Slow violence requires a slow aesthetics.

While much attention has been paid to the link between the aesthetic and the ecological in Taylor's work, less has been written on its sacred dimension, which interacts with the latter two. One could easily see in the symbiotic ensemble of the sea-urchin–woman a figure of the sacred, reminiscent of the many religions stranded together in the Caribbean. The urchin spines could resemble the nails of the crucifixion of Christ, or those planted in Kongo nkisi for divine intervention.[44] While it may not have been Taylor's intent, the very election of the *anba dlo* as a site of aesthetic production renders his art sacred by default. Caribbean geography, whether aquatic or terrestrial, is inhabited by religious or sacred figures reminiscent of Kongo, Christian, Vaudou, or more idiosyncratic religions, such as the *Quimbois*.[45] The *diablesse,* featured in Taylor's mythology, is a common figure of *Quimbois* across the Antilles: "And then I found La Diablesse . . . In her deep and dark watery ravine she looks sinister. In French, her name means She Devil and she comes from an old Caribbean folktale. The fish swam in and out of the rib bones of her skeletal body. Her face is hidden under a wide-brimmed hat. When she was made she had eye sockets but now they are filled with sea plants. Her skirts are weeds flowing in the water like petticoats."[46] The Diablesse's attributes are highly reminiscent of the *lwas* of death in Vaudou such as Gédé or Manman Brigitte: skeletal-faced, with empty eye sockets, a wide-brimmed hat to hide her face, and a luxurious, coquettish attire. Located in Moliniere Bay off the West coast of Grenada, Taylor's Diablesse, with her skeletal mask, flowing white hair, petticoat, wicker body shill, and oversized hat made out of rectangular metallic blades[47] recall contemporary Haitian art such as that produced by the Atis Rezistans of the Grand Rue in Port-au-Prince.[48] The fish passing through the empty eye socket presents a compelling example of the interaction of life and death based on passages and returns rather than on a finite frontier.

From *Anba Dlo* to *Anthropocene*

As amply demonstrated, the haunting memory of the slave ship and the sacred of anba dlo inhabit Taylor's underwater art—or, rather, Taylor's creation inhabits their site, in symbiosis. The present of the Caribbean Sea is inhabited by yet another threat, widespread and anchored in the deep temporality of the Anthropocene, that of climate change. Other artists featured in this chapter like Donatien, Duval Carrié, and Danticat relate to the same cause. Water fluidity and expanses connect the historically linked ravages of the Middle Passage and forced migrations with the endangerment of vegetal, animal, and coral species in the Anthropocene.[49]

Along with ecological theorist Timothy Morton, Taylor could contend that his art is "not only a historical claim but also a geological one. Or better: we are no longer able to think history as exclusively human, for the very reason that we are in the Anthropocene" (*Hyperobjects,* 5). Beyond their aesthetic value, Taylor's sculptures have a specific ecological purpose. The artist handpicks material such as pH-neutral concrete to allow corals to grow—I quote the artist—"just like children."[50] By building a coral reef accessible to tourists, snorkelers, and divers, the underwater sculptures also serve as diversions, to preserve "natural" sites of endangered coral reef. Taylor wishes for his installations to "benefit the natural world and not needlessly occupy space on an already cluttered planet." To that end he "installed over five hundred water sculptures and created more than one thousand square meters of habitat space for various types of marine life" (8–9).

In 2011, near Isla Mujeres in Cancun, the sculptor immersed a life-sized replica of a Volkswagen Beetle designed to attract crustaceans. In the installation fittingly called "Anthropocene," a backward-facing crouched human in a fetal position becomes one with the womb-like smiley car that seems to have more of a face than its human companion. A year postimmersion, the corroded carcass's visible holes attract growing seaweed, a school of fish, and an occasional human diver. But what connects the drowned human and the sunken Beetle in Taylor's incongruous and shocking juxtaposition? The corrosion and constant evolution of the sculptures (both anthropomorphic and not) indicate that they will eventually resemble each other in their new coral shape. In his museum collection, Taylor seems to imply that the genocide of slave trade and the ecocide of massive industrialization are part of the same epoch-changing continuum. The Beetle also evokes another strike against humanity practiced on a global scale. The VW Beetle, then still called VW Type 1, began as Adolf Hitler's dream of a car for every German. The apparently inconspicuous vehicle, which later became the innocuous symbol of the hippie generation, might then link, in this sea continuum, the genocides of Maafa and Shoah with the Ecocide, broadening even further Taylor's project, and materializing a form of "multidirectional memory," to use Rothberg's concept.[51] The installation's situation in the Caribbean Sea gives an additional twist to Taylor's ecological concern. Indeed the overuse of cars and the disposal of their carcasses pose a significant ecological problem in the Caribbean. For instance, in Martinique, which has one of the highest number of cars per capita (1.4, 2011), car cemeteries not only pollute ecologically and visually but are also vectors of propagation of dengue fever, Zika, and other mosquito-borne disease. The choice of a sunken Beetle for Taylor, the car reclaimed by environmentally concerned activists, might also be an act of hopeful direction toward environmentalism, or else sorrowful irony.

Martinican visual artist Donatien compellingly ties the Middle Passage, contemporary ecological ruin, and sacred signs in her artistic production as well as in her scholarly projects on literature and spiritual

Jason deCaires Taylor, *Anthropocene,* underwater sculpture, MUSA, Cancun Underwater Museum, Mexico, installation date 2011. (© Jason deCaires Taylor; all rights reserved, DACS/ARS 2019)

practices. *Soul Amère,* her 2013 exhibit at the CMAC (Centre Martiniquais d'Action Culturelle) in Fort-de-France, visually connects these consecutive yet continuous—and even simultaneous—events and states. The sixty works in the exhibit "invite [spectators] to stroll in an imaginary place where all sorts of mythical creatures recreate a fragmented history, bearing the marks of an acerb contemporariness oscillating between globalization and crisis."[52]

The multilingual title of the exhibit immediately announces this complex layering of past hauntings and future threats. Literally, *Soul Amère* translates as "bitter soul," referring both to a spiritual presence, to a form of music—*la musique soul,* in French, refers to "the music of Black Americans characterized by purity of inspiration and sincerity of expression" (*Le nouveau petit Robert*)—thereby establishing contact with *lotbo dlo,* between different sites of the African diaspora across the water. Orally, the title could be heard as *sous la mer* (below the sea, *anba dlo*), *sous la mère* (below the mother), or even *saoûle la mer / la mère* (drunken sea / mother), indicating a thick enmeshment of water, motherhood, music, bitterness, drunkenness, and sacredness. The painting "Paradise Island" immediately elicits sacred art.[53] Its composition in three horizontal levels resembles Christian representations of hell, purgatory, and paradise, such as in Dante's *Divine Comedy* or in Hieronymus Bosch's "Garden of Earthly Delights." It also reminds us of the mirror image in Duval Carrié and Zéphirin where the odsu dlo reflects in the anba dlo. The three-layered structure could also be read as the three levels of the psyche, consisting of the subconscious, the unconscious, and consciousness or, yet, as the historical sedimentation of history in the Caribbean Sea. Instead of a choice between sacred or profane, Christian and Vaudou, historical and psychoanalytic, Donatien's "Soul Amère" takes all into account and presents them in a continuum.

If we read the painting from top to bottom, the first level represents a pale blue sky, a bright orange sun, ocher *mornes* or hills, three palm trees, and two written signs pointing to "Hotel" and to "Paradise Island." While the palm trees could be quickly dismissed as touristic icons, especially in light of the inscription "hotel," they also signal a native resistance since palm trees, solid and always upright, have a propensity to find water in circumstances of drought or hardship. Palm trees also have a ritual function, especially with respect to Ayizan, the lwa of market and commerce in Vaudou.[54] The sun is all but mild and comforting. Rather than the sought-after touristic commodity, its color, vivid and merciless, with rays of metallic spikes, is Aimé Césaire's great and terrible "sacré soleil vénérien," "sacred Venerian sun" (related to Venus) or "damned venereal sun" (related to STD; *Cahier,* 7).

The interstitial panel of Donatien's "Paradise Island" is also the largest. It is the recognizable *anba dlo* in which three human fish hybrids, mermaids, or *manman dlo,* hang head down. Their feet or tail are attached to the ground above, suspended between land and water, and linked by umbilical cord to the three palm trees, as in the African-derived practices of "twinning" between human and tree. The figures have a sacred African mask for a face, hands held in prayer or perhaps in shackles, their bodies resembling the case of a Pharaoh's sarcophagus. Their bodies are held in limbo to signify the constant haunting of past drowned bodies in the transatlantic slave trade that forces them into an eternal purgatory. Nonetheless, these figures also bear marks of multiple sacred rites. Their bodies rest in peace in an indigo sea, covered with spiral signs, which also may mark the presence of a certain sacred, nonlinear conception of time.

The bottom level figures the polluted bottom of a shallow sea. Where coral reef, sea shells, sponges, and other forms of aquatic life should be dwell piles of colorful discards: two cars (again, Beetles), a pair of open scissors/a mouth threatening to cut or swallow, discarded shards of wood and metal, arrows, a metal shipping container bearing the inscription "Consumption & Co.," a canoe overflowing with piles of dirt and garbage, in a senseless mess. If the top of the painting pictures an oppressive tourism, its bottom figures a space of hyperconsumption smothering the island. As for the middle, it represents its "soul": large, yet threatened from above and below, from past and future, from a landscape shaped by colonization and tourism and a bottom polluted by excessive capitalistic consumption.

The color blue is no surprise in the context of a sea painting. However, the indigo hue of the sea and its midnight-purple highlights bear significance. Indigo evokes the cash crops produced by slaves and indentured workers in Martinique (where indigo was produced between the eighteenth and nineteenth century) and in the rest of the plantation zone in the Antilles and continental America and also connects the underwater back to its Yoruba past, and even further back to India ("indigo," from the Latin *indicum,* means "from India").[55] Indigo blue thus serves both as grounding in the Martinican experience, and as a channel toward other geographic zones or times of the African diaspora. It conjures the bluesy jazz standard composed by Duke Ellington, "Mood Indigo," which defines that special blue as the bottom of the feeling of the blues: "You ain't never been blue / Till you've had that mood indigo / That feeling goes stealing right down to my shoes." Blue indigo, with its link to the depth of melancholy and sadness of the blues, gains yet another level of sadness and vulnerability with its connection to the Martinican notion of *blès.* In her *Exorcisme de la blès,* Donatien uses this concept derived from the lived experience of the suffering Creole body. An elderly Martinican woman confesses to Donatien: "'la blès an, cé bagaï an tan lontan'" (The blès is a thing of long ago; 3). "The aesthetics of the blès," Donatien adds, "is neither apology for illness or decadence, nor for pleasure in pain [volupté de la souffrance]. It acts in a structuring and energizing reactivity to suffering" (17).[56]

The *blès,* bodily manifestation of a past trauma, phonetically and semantically evokes the blues, a similar transfiguration of suffering into creative energy. It brings to mind the French word *blessure,* or "wound," and hence its derived concept of vulnerability. Vulnerability indeed comes from the late Latin *vulnerabilis,* a "wounding," from *vulnus,* and therefore inscribes the Martinican body in a community of shared pain and experience.[57] Remarkably, the French word *blessure* shares an ancient etymological parent with the English word "*blessing.*" Both descend from the Anglo-Saxon word *bledsian,* itself derived from *blód* or "blood."

Bledsian evolved into "blessing" "originally perhaps to consecrate by sprinkling blood."[58] Hence, the wound propitiously attracts the sacred, a manifest reality for our underwater artists.

Taylor and Donatien thus connect the anba dlo with the Anthropocene in order to link past, present, and future; communities anchored and global; and humans and their vegetal, animal, and inanimate neighbors.[59] Danticat's 2004 novel *The Dew Breaker* offers a compelling counterexample, in which a drowned sculpture severs all connections to past, sacred, memory, and environment.[60] The interconnected stories of Danticat's composite novel revolve around a torturer under the Duvalier regime, now living in Brooklyn and masquerading as a prison survivor. The multifaceted character takes chameleon names according to who calls him. He is, for his daughter, "my father"; for his wife, Anne, "her husband"; for the disembodied narrative, a dislocated entity alternatively called "the Voice" and "the fat man"; for one of his victims "a large man with a face like a soccer ball and a widow's peak" (105); for a witness who saw him murder his family as a child, "the barber;" for his New York customers, "a phantom"; and, for the man who recognizes him as his parents' slayer "choukèt laroze" (the dew breaker) [Danticat, *Dew Breaker,* 116)] A pastor, before dying under the torturer's hands, leaves "a wound on the fat man's face . . . a brand that he would carry for the rest of his life" (227). The unnamed man with many monikers is disconnected from himself since "the fat man" and "the voice" are discrete entities. He lives into a lie that is the opposite shell of his identity of slayer under the mask of a victim. In his US life, the only signs that mark him to the reader as the torturer are his girth, his widow's peak, and, most strikingly, a "blunt, ropelike scar that runs from my father's right cheek down to the corner of his mouth, the only visible reminder of the year he spent in prison in Haiti" (5). The scar erases his face, making it a mask, at once dissimulating his former identity and screaming it out loud.

Her daughter loves him obsessively despite all and makes him the unique model for her sculptures: "I'm not really an artist. Not the way I'd like to be. I'm more of an obsessive wood-carver with a single subject thus far—my father" (4). The opening story of *The Dew Breaker,* "The Book of the Dead," referring to the ancient Egyptian funerary text that the father reads compulsively, begins with the disappearance of the narrator's father: "My father is gone" (3). The reader soon learns that he has kidnaped the statue made to his own liking, which her daughter intended to sell to a wealthy Haitian Floridian. The sculpture is described in great detail, becoming salient and vivid in the narrative through an exhaustive ekphrasis detailing its material, size, and posture: "A three-foot mahogany figure of my father naked, kneeling on a half-foot square base, his back arched like the curve of a crescent moon, his downcast eyes fixed on his very long fingers and the large palm of his hands. . . . It was the way I imagined him in prison" (6). The posture is one of humility, in its literal sense of proximity to the soil, or *humus,* and in the sense of a modest state of mind. The disproportionately large father in real life is made little in its three-foot realization, in his diminished, kneeling, curved-upon-himself, downard-looking posture. The body becomes one with the elemental, feminine, melancholic figure of the moon and with the tropical native hardwood exploited during slavery and colonization, in the form of "twinning" evoked earlier. Like a sculptor of words, Danticat lingers on the texture, shape, and properties of the carved wood under the hands of her sculptor-character: "I'd used a piece of Mahogany that was naturally flawed, with a few superficial cracks on what was now his back . . . they seemed like the wood's own scars" (7). In a reverse image to Toni Morrison's *Beloved* character Sethe who has a tree on her back growing from the wounds of the whip (*Beloved,* 17), Danticat's mahogany inherits the scars of the father's back. This arboreal growth, like the symbiotic relation at work in Taylor's underwater sculptures, establishes a zone of contact and growth between the human and the tree, between the flesh and the vegetal, albeit in a relationship of wounding and pain, not of healthy rejuvenation. The father insists on calling the sculpture "my statue." "Statue," as in the Latin *statuo* ("to place," "to set"), refers to a static and durable sculpture representing a human or animal figure. A statue almost always provides the three-dimensional image of a person worth celebrating or memorializing. "'I don't deserve a statue," the father proclaims (19). As a result, he steals his daughter's creation and discards it in a lake. Indeed how can one possibly memorialize a torturer?

Not all types of underwater sites function as *anba dlo.* Thus far, I have focused on sea waters as sacred, connective, and fertile fluids marked by death and unritual. However, as Bachelard demonstrates throughout *L'eau et les rêves,* sea, rivers, ponds, viscous muddy waters each carry a specific relationship to memory and imagination. Danticat's novels feature a multitude of bodies of water each with a proper, and oft-shifting, imaginary. Take, for instance, the river in *The Farming of Bones* that carries Amabelle's parents away and that offer her a site of baptismal renewal at the end of the novel; consider the sea in *Claire of the Sea Light,* which serves as, alternatively, a cosmic mirror between living daughter and departed mother, and a brutal rogue wave taking fishermen away. In *Children of the Sea,* the sea provides neither *anba dlo,* nor *lotbo dlo* as it fails to bring young mother and infant to the shores of Florida or to the sacred space below. In *The Dew Breaker,* Danticat introduces yet another body of water: the stagnant pool of an artificial lake. In his reflection on Edgar Allan Poe's waters, Bachelard indicates that stagnating waters imply a particularly stale relationship to a lingering death: "Silent water, somber water, stagnant water, unfathomable water, so many material lessons for a meditation on death. But it is not the lesson taught by Heraclitean death, by a death which bears us afar with the current and like a current. It is the lesson of still death, a death in depth that stays with us, near us, in us" (*Water and Dreams,* 68–69). Bachelard's mute shallow waters are the opposite of an *anba dlo,* which would shepherd the departed into another realm. In addition, Danticat's stale lake is artificial and severed from its immediate environment. It is "a man-made lake, one of those marvels of the tropical city, with curved stone benches surrounding a stagnant body of water" surrounded by "the highway, and the cars racing by. . . . It is muddy and dark, and there are some very large pink fishes . . . looking as though they want to leap out and trade places with us" (15). The dark, muddy, stagnant water seems to be an appropriate place to discard the effigy of the father-torturer.

Danticat's lake, like Donatien's shallow sea, features an Anthropocene water that has become a dump for dead memory. Like the piles of trash at the bottom of Donatien's sea, the daughter's sculpture has become meaningless, ruined, and sterile: "The cracks have probably taken in so much water that the wood has split into several chunks and plunged to the bottom" (15–16). In contrast with Taylor's creations, which are meant to create new alliances, the carving's wood is meant to rot in oblivion. Danticat's giant pink fish, perhaps invasive Asian carps threatening the survival of other fish life in US waterways, do not want to relate but rather to "trade places" with the humans who contemplate the murky surface of the lake. If Danticat's novel is chiefly about the violence of torture under dictatorship, the haunting presence of the artificial lake also directly points to the devastating effects of manicuring, controlling, and segmenting nature in the Anthropocene.[61]

Something should be said about the eponymous water of the novel's title: the dew. The aqueous droplets of vapor deposited on grass and plants at dawn form what Bachelard calls complex waters throughout his *Water and Dreams,* residing between the aqueous and the ethereal. Their dissemination in multitudes of dewdrops provides a fresh, renewed, ephemeral, nonmonumental relation to memory, the past, and the dead, which I explore in the following section.

Coral or the Power of Frailty

Philosopher Georg Wilhelm Friedrich Hegel features, along with architecture, unyielding sculpture—"temple of the mind"—as the ideal form of beauty since it is not marred by frailty: "The spirit which sculpture represents is that which is solid in itself, not broken up in the play of trivialities and passions" (*On Art,* 121). But certain types of events and gestures, small and big, individual or collective, local or planetary do not "deserve a statue" (*Dew Breaker,* 19). The fragmented, disjointed, and wounded Caribbean history is best represented by a broken object: "Break a vase, and the love that reassembles the fragments is stronger than that love which took its symmetry for granted when it was whole. . . . It is such a love that reassembles our African and Asiatic fragments, the cracked heirlooms whose restoration shows its white scars" (Walcott, *Twilight,* 69).

Hegel's ideal of architectural or sculptural monuments has been challenged in the aftermath of shameful historical events, such as Nazi genocide, which can neither be monumentalized nor cannot *not* be remembered. Literary and Judaic scholar James E. Young has theorized what he calls "counter-monuments" and explored their manifestations in postwar Germany: "To [the postwar artists'] mind, the didactic logic of monuments, their demagogical rigidity, recalled too closely traits they associated with fascism itself: against the traditionally didactic function of monuments, against their tendency to displace the past they would have us contemplate—and finally, against the authoritarian propensity in all art that reduces viewers to passive spectators" (Young, "The Counter-Monument," 274). The challenges to "rigidity," "didactic function," "authoritarianism," and "spectator passivity" are also particularly helpful in understanding the postslavery Anthropocene art of the Caribbean, which similarly represents a shameful, hurtful, and incomplete memory of a partially disappeared people. Like post-Shoah countermonuments, memory art produced in the aftermath of the Middle Passage needs "brazen, painfully self-conscious memorial spaces conceived to challenge the very premises of their being" (271).

Such an installation, the Harburg monument, shares striking similarities with Taylor's underwater art: "As more and more names cover this 12-meter tall column, [the monument] will gradually be lowered into the ground. One day, it will have disappeared completely and the site of the

Harburg monument against fascism will be empty" (276). The German countermonument and Taylor's sculptures are both bound to evolve and to eventually disappear. They are works of creative vulnerability, of life enduring precisely thanks to its transient and relinquishing nature. They reach power through frailty. They demand intervention and cooperation, whether through human or coral signatures. However, we also need to question their dissimilarities. In contrast with the Harburg monument meant to turn into absence, Taylor's art, in its very disappearance, will gain renewed presence and life in its assemblage with coral reef. Not all catastrophes are equal in their relationship to the past. While the Shoah and Maafa share the massive extermination of two groups of people—Jews and Africans—in the millions, their relationship to tangible archives and other material records of the past are sharply different. As Glissant puts it plainly, descendants of Africans in the Americas were "naked migrants" with no familiar tools, religious icons, family photographs, letters, legal documents, historical records or any tangible archive (*Discours antillais,* 66). Thus, the countermonuments of slavery, instead of aiming for an eventual absence, forge a relational presence that acts tangibly in lieu of the missing material records of the past.

Taylor's art, like other countermonuments, defies the three principles of Hegel's aesthetics: "1. We suppose the work of art to be no natural product, but brought to pass by means of human activity; 2. To be essentially made for man 3. To contend an end" (*On Art,* 51). In a perfect inverted symmetry, Taylor's creation (1.) becomes art when it passes through the agency of ecological nonhuman activity; (2.) is primarily made for the regrowth of the coral reef; (3.) continues in constant evolution without an end since it disappears to merge with its biotope. Taylor's relinquished authority is precisely what facilitates his creations' strength in their disappearing persistence into coral life, obeying the principles of a Glissantian relational and ecological aesthetics. Leupin identifies the divergence between Hegelian and Glissantian aesthetics: "But Hegelian history of arts is finalist, beginning with the fusional poem and ending with a final evolution. . . . Once this goal is reached, art is exhausted and philosophy has to relay it] (*Edouard Glissant,* 196).

Taylor's website provides multiple examples of this beauty reaching full bloom precisely when it changes through ecological alliances. The statues in Taylor's underwater museum in Cancún, Mexico, are meant to be overtaken by coral within only a few years: "In a stifling warehouse filled with bodies—ceramic replicas and false starts—[Taylor] fusses over their lips and noses. Gets the hair just right. Adjusts their clothing. Then he sinks them in the sea."[62] Taylor's project also brings to mind Glissant's underwater grave, hosting greenish sunken balls and chains corroded by the sea (*Poetics,* 6). These human remnants become monuments when they fuse with the landscape. Taylor's sunken community concretizes Glissant's theoretical claim that "our landscape is its own monument" discussed earlier. Not only do landscapes constitute monuments, but, more crucially, monuments revert into landscape in an unbroken continuum of living memorialization. Take, for instance, Taylor's statue made out of the cement cast of Joachim, a fisherman from Acapulco, the central piece of "Man on Fire": "His pitted and textured skin were [*sic*] ideal to promote coral growth" (*The Underwater Museum,* 110–11).[63] Joachim's scarred skin, which could be seen as the result of wounds or illness, marking a departure from classical standards of beauty, becomes, in Taylor's art a conduit for aesthetic and life creation. "Man on Fire," submerged eight feet under at the MUSA, Cancún, now forms a fertile assemblage with coral, his human traits almost unrecognizable by the work of the coral, alternatively morbid (if considered as an anthropomorphic work) or strikingly beautiful (if envisaged as coral growth).

The assemblages of coral and concrete generate vivid tableaux of pale yellow, tangerine orange, moss green, bleeding red, light pink, and dainty white.[64] This astonishing beauty is not fixed in a Platonic world of ideas but energizes movement and passage. Noudelmann contrasts Glissant's aesthetics with Plato's or with that of other philosophers of "truth": "In contrast with this 'beautiful' indexed on the 'true' (platonic 'beauty') or with this formal beauty (the aesthetics of shapes), Glissant seeks beauty within life and its transformations" (38). Taylor's too is an aesthetic of transformation.

Taylor's (and nature's) relational ensembles can also become unremarkably gray, formless, and, ultimately, indiscernible as works of art. Thus, Taylor relinquishes not only his statues but also his very aesthetic gesture, which can become secondary, or even instrumental, to his ecological goal. As James Buxton concludes, Taylor's "underwater society" will be eventually "totally assimilated by marine life, transformed to another state—a challenging metaphor for the future of our own species."[65] This is a lesson for humanity: that after asserting our monumental strength, we have to relinquish the primacy of our species. *The recognition by humans* of our own damage onto Gaia must come with the realization of our fragility and vulnerability, bred in part by the planetary impact of our own industrial and colonizing hubris. It is through trembling, through the ephemeral, through vulnerability, that we can survive in relation. Coral life is particularly apt to perform a durable ephemerality through its relational properties. Its worldwide presence in shallow tropical waters provides an apt example of submarine relations between vulnerable zones in the Atlantic, Pacific, and Indian oceans. Coral reefs are screaming evidence for the urgency of preserving life on the planet as we know it. Indeed, "about 60% of the world's reefs are at risk due to human-related activities."[66] It would be ludicrous to see initiatives such as Taylor's as a practical solution to reconstruct quickly disappearing reefs on the planet. However, we can hope that his art may increase the visibility of their endangerment.

Coral is also visible for its regrowth in its unpredictable and relational sites and shapes. Coral resists human categorical thinking. While we now know coral is an invertebrate from the *Kingdom Animalia,* it is often perceived as vegetal because of its stillness and resemblance to flowers, branches, or vegetal shoots. In his *Scala Naturae,* Aristotle classified corals as "zoophyta" ("plant-animals").[67] Until the eighteenth century, it was believed that coral was of the *Kingdom Plantae.* Early biologist Buffon situates the polyp as "the last of animals and the first of plants" (*Oeuvres,* 138). Contemporary biogeographer Charles Sheppard underlines that corals are classified as "anthozoans, a word derived from the Greek words 'flower' and animal,' which describes the appearance of each polyp" (*Coral Reefs,* 25). This hybrid and liminal position makes the coral both biological and geological, argues Sheppard (1–20). The extremely diverse ecosystems of coral reefs ally plant and animal life with mineral materials "in symbiosis both at an enormous scale and at the level of the single cell algae that grows on the coral tissue itself" (28–29).[68] In symbiosis with these scientific paradoxes, coral collects aesthetic and affective ones. If used as a precious adornment in jewelry, it also conjures death underwater, since some forms of corals secrete exoskeletons with calcium carbonate, just like bones. Coral allies beauty to the macabre.

Coral is to water what a rhizome is to earth. While Glissant elects the rhizome as a privileged example of the dynamic movements of relation and creolization, coral can also constitute an apt example for the properties of change, evolution, symbiosis, boundary blurring, compositeness, of relation.[69] Indeed, as Scales sums up: "Each colony of reef-building coral is itself built from thousands of polyps that look like miniature pulsating flowers. . . . Inside each polyp are millions of cells, clustered like tiny marbles. These zooxanthellae, nicknamed 'zoox,' give corals their bright colors and make life possible in parts of the ocean where nutrients are in short supplies" (*Underwater Museum,* 19). Taylor himself defines his art as relation: *"It's environmental evolution, art intervention as growth, or a balancing of relationships."*[70]

Far away from the Caribbean Sea, but in an Indian Ocean similarly shaped by creolization and coral life, Mauritian poet Khal Torabully uses coral as material paradigm and metaphor for his concept of *coolitude,* cousin to Caribbean creolization.[71] What he terms "coral imaginary" resembles Glissant's "Relation" and Taylor's vulnerability. The expanding, horizontal, multirelational coral provides a symbiotic metaphor for the "coolie" Indian and/in the creolized world of Mauritius, instead of a model of cultural purity and hierarchies. By endorsing Césaire, who famously claimed "My negritude is not a rock" (*Cahier,* 46), Torabully implicitly challenges Hegel's conviction of the superiority of the solid and fixed: "Coolitude is neither cobblestone nor rock, but coral. An image nigh, tactile, both strong and fragile, which I offer as a way to imagine the world, as a way to allow diverse imaginaries and cultures to find peripheral byways, crystallizations, accelerations, and not only errantries."[72]

A little over ten years after its submarine installation in 2006, Taylor's *Vicissitudes,* with which I opened the chapter, provides such creative connections. The constant evolution of coral and other marine life enhances even more the relationality that was already at work in his original twenty-six human figures holding hands in a circle. The agency of coral, fish, and crustacean has now unequivocally related the memory of the Middle Passage, with the present and futurity of the Anthropocene. Once bare, the anthropomorphic statues are now covered in coral, providing a hospitable habitat for fish, barnacles, urchins, and sponges. Their previously nude-colored skin is now astonishingly pink and orange. Their waning human form extends in unpredictable growths, stimulating memory and imagination and demanding interaction.

Taylor's sculptures, in sharp contrast with the drowned Africans of Glissant's abysmal depths, are placed in shallow waters in accessible shorelines. Most sculptures are submerged only four to eight meters deep and can be seen, touched, by the casual snorkeler and scuba diver. What does this shallowness reveal? In a chapter of Cohen's *Prismatic Ecology* entitled "Violet-Black," Stacy Alaimo argues that the animals of the sea abyss, since they are out of human sight, are also the most neglected beings, those most deprived of rights: "So little is currently known about sea animals and ecosystems, so rarely do they figure into ethical and political consideration." The deep seas, she adds, "epitomize how most ocean waters exist beyond state borders, legal protections, and cultural imaginaries" (233).

A direct sensorial experience of the sculptures would be necessary to fully grasp the sounds and silence, water temperature and currents, biotope, and challenges such a visit poses to the human body—all crucial dimensions of Taylor's complete aesthetic accomplishment.[73] Taylor's artistic production diverge sharply from Hegel's belief that only sight and hearing are relevant to the aesthetic experience. These purportedly "inferior" and pleasurable senses distract from the static "symmetrical," "purified" "Temple of the God" or "Temple of the Idea" (Hegel, *On Art,* 120–21): "For smell, taste, and feeling have to do with matter as such . . . these senses cannot have to do with objects of art, which are destined to maintain themselves in their actual independent existence, and admit to no sensuous relation" (67). Water's currents, temperature, and optic filter enriches even further the multiple sensory interaction of the diver experiencing Taylor's installations. One of the principles of Mentz's manifesto, "Seven Shipwrecked Ecological Truths," corroborates Taylor's watery aesthetics: "Oceanic reality is distortion. Water distorts the senses, changing and diminishing visual perception while muting hearing. The overpowering taste and smell of salt fill our mouths and noses as we pass into the sea. Its fluid touch envelops our skin. Inside this massive body, nothing appears the same" (*Shipwrecked,* 180–81). The perceptibility gained through Taylor's art is not about giving control to the human eye over objects, since the sculptures are in constant, silent, unpredictable, and beautiful evolution in water. The installations urge human seers to relinquish control over the stability of their perception. They make human visitors aware of a multiple and reciprocal agency that decenters the anthropocentric gaze. To use Alaimo's words, it is a call to "envision posthumanist perspectives that renounce mastery, transcendence, and stable, terrestrial frames of reference that center the human subject within visible horizons" (*Exposed*, 245).

Taylor's installations are meant to exist in a worldwide—seawide—network of relations, as opposed to Hegel's "objects of art, which are destined to maintain themselves in their actual independent existence" (Hegel, *On Art,* 67). I mean Relation, in the Glissantian sense, as a process (not a product), as a progress (not an end point), as a network (not a temple). This Relation is a totality (involving all elements at work in Relation), which is not totalitarian (with the election of a central truth), and which demands participation (not unmoved contemplation).

The participatory role of the viewer, while it could be seen as a general rule in countermonumental, non-Hegelian forms of art, is particularly heightened in drowned art, and in the aftermath of human-caused catastrophes such as the Maafa, the Shoah, or global climate change. As Young astutely remarks, "The citizens of Harburg and visitors to the town to add their names here to ours. In doing so, we commit ourselves to remain vigilant" ("The Counter-Monument," 275). In the same vein, as I have shown in my discussion of the "Indigo Room," and as Sullivan formulates, Duval Carrié's art is unconditionally participatory: "We, the viewers, become participants in the sacred rituals suggested by the combination of painting, sculpture, textile, and other objects" (Sullivan, *Continental Shifts,* 12). Participatory and relational art are tied with ethical and sacred imperatives. Spectators are asked to step out of their comfortable positions as viewers and become cocreators. Art historian Claire Bishop evokes the property of installation art to foster an "activated spectatorship," which implicates the viewer politically and ethically (*Installation Art,* 102). Duval Carrié's installation, in addition, activates the viewer's sacred reverence for the dead.

One could dispute that the difficult accessibility of Taylor's installations defeats the purpose of such a consciousness-raising visibility. Underwater sculptures, indeed, are only accessible to a happy few. Vists to Antigua or Mexico require wealth and mobility, as well as swimming and diving skills. I would retort, however, that Taylor's website is widely accessible in the liquidity of its slideshow, in its interactive, criss-crossed, and nonlinear construction, in its constant growth (the evolution of sculptures is meticulously documented and updated). Philosopher Serres would agree that world-wide-web-based sites provide access to a relational, liquid, and immense world: "A major contractual actor of human community, at the dawn of the second millennium, weighs at least a quarter million souls. Not in heft and flesh, but in crisscrossed networks of relations and in the number of world-objects at its disposal. It acts like the sea" (*The Natural Contract,* 16).

This web presence, in which the multiple, the transient, the connected, the aquatic, embodies the impetus of life, challenges teleological truth and monumentality. It brings to mind Glissant's epitaph featured in chapter 1: "Nothing is true, all is alive." The Heraclitean aphorism too invites us to let go of our human certainties. In his late writing, Glissant explains that "the living is a continuity, which, even when it ends, enters the rest called death to prepare another continuity" (*Francofonia,* 212). Glissant, Taylor, Duval Carrié, and our other sea artists teach us that the sacred resides in the relation, the relaying, the relating of life and death, huge and tiny, human and nonhuman, rot and beauty, chaos and growth. The artists, and their spectators-interactors, give the dead an imperfect yet appropriate—living—grave, whether in the shallows of the sea, the blue indigo of a museum atrium, or the liquidity of a website. *Todos pertenecemos al mar que nos separa.*

One of the lessons of this chapter is that sculpture paradoxically needs to be fluid in order to provide effective forms of remembrance and reverence. The next installment of this book, "Poetry as Grave," apparently contradicts this finding. More than with incongruity, though, we are faced with chiasm. Just as rocks must become liquid, impalpable words must become concrete. It is precisely this encounter of the fluid and the solid, of the permanent and the vulnerable, and of the tomb and the wake that provides the most valuable aesthetic tribute to the unritual.

5 Stone Pillow and Bone Water

Natasha Trethewey's *Native Guard* and M. NourbeSe Philip's *Zong!*

Underwater . . . a place of consequence.

—M. NourbeSe Philip, *Zong!*

You drifted your life like a river drifts its currents. . . . At least there's one thing you knew for sure: books are boats and words their crew.

—Emile Ollivier, *Mille Eaux*

Natasha Trethewey's *Native Guard* and M. NourbeSe Philip's *Zong!* could not look more different in form. Trethewey builds structure out of broken shards in her regular sonnets, in the perfect symmetry of a palindrome. Conversely, Philip works ardently as a rock breaker, shattering legal documents into elemental monosyllables and sounds, reducing them to malleable material in order to recompose an at once extremely fragmented and sculptural poem. While their respective gestures seem opposite, both poets are sculptors who shape the raw materiality of words into highly significant forms. As poet and critic Evie Shockley explains, Philip places constraint on these poems "by limiting her corpus, her linguistic body, her material to the case" ("Going Overboard," 811). With different aesthetics, Trethewey, too, works under enormous formal constraint. Both poets, are, as Philip describes her own craft, "sculptors of words: I use the text of the legal report almost as a painter uses paint or as a sculptor stone" (Philip, *Zong!*, 198). This shared passion for the hard materiality of words has a lot to do with providing graves, stones, or monuments to the neglected, forgotten, or desecrated dead.

The hardness of words also acts as a pale substitute for the hardness of lost bones. Hence Trethewey's and Philip's obsession with skeletal structures and itemized bones. Trethewey sees history as a "scaffolding of bones" while Philip avows, quoting Derrida's *Specters of Marx*, "'haunted by 'generations of skulls and spirits,' I want the bones" (Philip, *Zong!*,

201). As we know, finding the remains of the dead is a necessary step toward healing personal and collective traumas. In her introduction to a series of interviews with Hartman and Philip, critic Patricia J. Saunders ponders: "Can we understand [slavery] by returning, yet again, to the archive, in the absence of bones, of tombstones, to try to identify and localize the remains of the enslaved?" ("Fugitive Dreams," 2). Derrida in *Specters of Marx* similarly insists on the need to find the departed's solid remains in order to begin the process of mourning. In "Notanda," Philip quotes forensic anthropologist Clea Koff who worked in the aftermaths of the Rwandan and Bosnian wars: "Families need proof, Koff says—they come looking for recognizable clothing and say, 'I want the bones'" (201). The bones provide the material intersection of three imperatives: psychological, sacred, and legal. Finding the bones of a loved one facilitates the mourning process and the expelling of ghosts; exhuming the bones allow families or nations to mourn; retrieving the bones provides forensic evidence for individual or large-scale legal trials.[1]

This need for evidence and the involvement of the reader as a forensic artist, an interpreter of evidence, is at work in both *Native Guard* and *Zong!* In "Evidence," Trethewey brings to light the bruises and swellings on her mother's body that the court neglected to see. In "Zong! #24," Philip exhumes the body on the ship as evidence for the murders that the trial failed to address:

evidence is
sustenance is
support is
the law is
the ship is
. . . .
the trial is
the rains is
the seas is. (42)

Water is the realm of these material proofs. However, while we could say that Trethewey's rivers carry memories, solid bones, that lead us back to the past, Philip's ocean has drowning capacities that sink us in an immense tautology, an abyss. *Native Guard* is primarily telluric, and it hosts perhaps the driest graves of this book. Nonetheless, its bloodstained rivers and Mississippi Gulf Shore sands and islands, with their unmarked graves and even *ungraves* of African American soldiers, sharply connect to our water unritual. In a recent poem entitled "Liturgy" from her 2018 collection *Monument,* Trethewey explicitly connects her own mother's grave to the unmarked ones of victims of hurricanes and floods. Invoking the presence of an unnamed survivor, the poet writes of "her daughter's grave, my mother's grave—underwater—on the Coast" (119).

Before the 2006 publication of her third collection of poems, a double elegy to her murdered mother and to Louisiana's black Union soldiers entitled *Native Guard,* Tretheway switched publishers—from Graywolf to Houghton Mifflin—to secure a hardcover. The hardbound book-object would provide a solid grave for the victims that a softcover would not. It would confer a small immortality to the dead, longer than that of the more transient paperback. In a similar vein, poet M. NourbeSe Philip claims that the concrete solidity of her 2008 poem *Zong!* (e.g., alphabetical units as rocks, calligrams as tombs, hardcover as headstone, poem space as graveyard, water as bone) memorializes those departed without national or personal monuments. Philip explains: "I use the text of the legal report almost as a painter uses paint or the sculptor uses stone" (198). Trethewey and Philip—from Mississippi and Tobago, respectively—spotlight the absence of individual graves and collective monuments that would celebrate the memory of the victims of the American Civil War, domestic violence, and the Middle Passage. Such poems associate the hard with the soft, the stone with the flesh, the bone with the water, the metaphorical with the material, the static with the performative in order to provide both at once a lasting grave and a living wake.

Stone Pillow: Natasha Trethewey's *Native Guard*

In *Native Guard,* such assemblages of extremes take shape under the sign of a rock-hard pillow, which appears in two crucial moments of the collection. In "Graveyard Blues," the poet, visiting her mother's tomb, meditates: "I wander now amongst the names of the dead: / My mother's name, *stone pillow* for my head" (*Native Guard,* 8, emphasis mine). The central piece of the collection, "Native Guard," a long elegy in diary form dedicated to the memory of African American Union soldiers, calls for the ethical and historical imperative to remember: "

> These are things which must be accounted for:
> slaughter under the white flag of surrender—
> black massacre at *Fort Pillow;* our new name,
> the Corps d'Afrique—words that take the *native*
> from our claim. (29, emphasis mine in first italics only)

The two passages are related by the presence of two solid pillows, one of stone, the other the solid structure of a fort. In addition, they both refer to names: the name of the mother standing for her absence, and the misnaming of the Native Guards (more on this later). They are also related by the more discreet yet significant punctuation mark—a colon—used in both stanzas. In "Native Guard," the colon introduces a to-do list of things to remember and to account for, as in accounting, justice, or reparation. In "Graveyard Blues," the colon associates the collective ("the names of the dead") with an individual example ("my mother's name"). Both places that house the pillow reside in in a memorial site of death: the graveyard and battleground.

"Graveyard Blues" features the poet drifting around the graveyard and resting on her mother's grave: "I wander now amongst the names of the dead: / My mother's name, stone pillow for my head" (*Native Guard*, 8). The stone pillow presents an oxymoronic space between softness and hardness, comfort and discomfort. Interpreted quite literally, the image of the poem brings to life the daughter placing her head atop her mother's name inscribed on the gravestone. We imagine a performance, a tender gesture from mother to daughter for which the tombstone becomes a bed. The mother's name is the symbolic—and dead—expression of a body that no longer is. Once connected to a warm body, it is now inscribed in cold stone; where there once was a bosom, a mother's breast for the daughter's head to repose, there is now only rock. In her 2017 commencement address at Emory University, Tretheway explains that the mother's name is laden with grief and anger; ultimately unsayable, the mother's last name is also that of her murderer, Trethewey's stepfather, who battered and killed her. In her address, the poet explains that the last verse of "Graveyard Blues"—"my mother's name, stone pillow for my head"—feels like a "kind of cold comfort." She then unexpectedly confesses:

> But the fact was, my mother had no stone, and in that moment, having written a beautiful [pause] lie, I had to confront an uncomfortable truth about myself, that I had erased her from the monumental landscape, that because of me, she lay in the ground unmarked, not properly memorialized, like all those black soldiers whose stories I was trying to tell. Because I could not think of a way to inscribe her name. Because the name she had when she died was still the name of her ex-husband, her murderer, a troubled Viet-Nam Veteran with a history of mental illness, a man who had been my step-father for ten difficult years. I had never put her name on a stone, above her grave, where someone passing by it might read and be compelled to speak her name aloud. You see,

> it had never occurred to me that I could inscribe her maiden name, the person she had been when she entered this life. It was a failure of the imagination.[2]

Trethewey's choice of a public confession at the forum of the very public event of a university's commencement ceremony speaks to the simultaneously very private and very public nature of her poetic mission. It also raises the need for the individual responsibility to speak (for the poet) and for collective action (for the class of graduating seniors about to be sent into the world). Yet the cold cruel stone, as well as the courageous confession—historical and intimate—in what should have been a stern academic setting also provides a place of comfort, we can imagine, through the mother's first name, and the tears, sighs, held breaths, and reddening faces of people in the audience. More generally, stone pillows carry a similar ambivalence. They can evoke utmost solitude, precariousness, orphanhood, and desolation, as in photographs of African and Middle Eastern refugee children resting their exhausted necks and heads on rocks or paving stones on European streets.[3] They can also be objects of comfort, beauty, and aesthetic sophistication such as the stone-, porcelain-, or jade-decorated pillows of ancient Chinese dynasties. Trethewey's stone pillow is all that: painful and necessary, like her poems and her intimate public interventions.

The pillow, which caught this reader's attention, is one among many thumbtack words that attach the narrative of the murdered mother to that of the massacred black Union soldiers, as well as the narrative of domestic violence to the racist violence of the state. While I return to "Graveyard Blues" and "Native Guard" further on in the chapter to expand on their qualities as sacred sites, I will note for now that *Native Guard* is itself organized as a makeshift graveyard, through its structure and paratext (its cover art, front matter, dedications, and epigraphs). This textual apparatus that lives outside the poems, outside the individual graves, named and unnamed, provides the gates, signposts, and labyrinthine structure of an actual cemetery. Its elements make the reader pause, wander, err, go astray, delay, read inscriptions, epitaphs, explanations, contemplate portraits on unknown tombstones, dream, muse, hum, and pause in at once aesthetic and mournful postures before finding a beloved's grave or facing a shattering engraving.

At first sight, the book-graveyard seems to be clearly organized and segregated like cemetery sections would be. The poems in section 1 (*Native Guard,* 5–15) are devoted to memories of the poet's mother. Section 2 (19–31) chiefly focuses on the Louisiana Native Guards and, more specifically, on the need to provide memorials to the bayoneted Union soldiers whose blood reddened the Mississippi at Fort Pillow, Tennessee, and to those who survived. Section 3 (35–46), however, troubles the neat frontier between familial and national history, between individual mother and collective Native Guard, and, as we implicitly learn as we read the poem, the oppression of black women, women in general, under the yoke of domestic violence, and the betrayal of African American soldiers by the very state they served. Section 3 marries the two narratives by intermingling poems devoted to the mother, to the personal trauma to the poet and family of "miscegenation" and sly attacks from the Ku Klux Klan, and to the Native Guards. Common words link these two narratives like nails. In addition to "pillow," the words "monuments," "headstones," "ghosts," "boats," "native," "bed," "nation," and "history" also provide channels of communication between the individual and the collective, which become one only through the same experienced violence of racist-based segregation, and through the beautiful art that the recipients of that violence create, whether it is the poet's poem or the soldier's journal on an overcrowded manuscript.

As in a raw cry of pain, an expression of surprise, or an ode to the sharp cruelty of individual and collective experience, *Histoire* and *histoires,* history and histories, in the eponymous poem of the collection the poet/journal writer sighs and sings: "O how history intersect" (*Native Guard,* 26). The exclamatory "O" emblematic of lyrical poetry and descendent of the omega of Greek lyrical poetry places the text of the soldier's journal in the realm of the lyrical, thus blurring the line between politics and aesthetics, the soldierly and the sentimental. The alliterations built on the juxtaposition of the moaning, howling sounds "O" and "aw" ("O how") and on "h," indicating sighs or lament, further intensify the emotional charge of the verse. The transitive verb "to intersect" is used in an intransitive way, lacking an object, therefore absolute and self-sufficient. It is not that the individual intersects with the collective, or miscegenation with battery and military violence, or race with gender, or past with present. "O how history intersects" is all of these at once without needing to be attached to, or limited by, any of these examples.[4] The sharp pain expressed with the "O" and alliterations of pain reside in the plainness, the bigness of intersection in itself, intersection per se, which lingers in an unresolved pain. The subjects of history are stuck at a giant, messy, inescapable, yet productive crossroads.

As the reader enters the graveyard poem, she finds orientation signposts in the four strategically placed epigraphs, which all seem to memorialize a certain block of this memory, and intersect. As the "relational" artists examined in past chapters, Trethewey calls upon other art forms in order to approach the unspeakable unritual. While two epigraphs are excerpts of poems (by poets Charles Wright and Walt Whitman, respectively), two others are song lyrics (one by Nina Simone, the other a plaintive gospel spiritual and bluegrass dirge). The poems ask the reader for a reflective pause of mournful contemplation before entering the sacred space of the book-graveyard. The general epigraph to the book, on the page immediately following the opening dedication "For my mother, in memory," features the words of white poet Charles Wright, born in 1935 in rural Tennessee (a loud echo to the Fort Pillow Massacre, also in Tennessee). Wright immediately followed Trethewey's two terms as poet laureate of the United States (2012–14 and 2014–15), also a noteworthy coincidence and legacy, where the rural white poet from Tennessee follows the rural black poet from Mississippi. In "Pastoral," the poet claims this inheritance from her father: "*My father's white,* I tell them, *and rural*" (*Native Guard,* 35, emphasis in original). Between Wright and Trethewey, there is thus a shared zone of rural South intersecting with race. Interestingly, the intersection of rural and southern reaches the highest ladder of poetic honor in the United States (they are also both Pulitzer Prize winners in poetry). Significantly, as well, the younger black rural poet precedes the older white rural man in this lineage of the most distinguished poets of the United States, thereby reversing centuries old trends (but "O, how it intersects").

In the epigraph drawn from the poem, Trethewey elects one of the greatest poets concerned with death and morning in America. Wright referred to three of his trilogies as "The Appalachian Book of the Dead." The verses are taken from the poem "Meditation on Form and Measure" from the collection *Black Zodiac* (26). Part of the epigraph reads: "Memory is a cemetery / I've visited once or twice, white" (n.p.). The choice of the lines as the poem's epigraph reminds the reader that the excursion into memory provided by Trethewey's book is akin to a visit to the sacred site of a cemetery. The enjambment, severing the adjective "white" from what it modifies, isolates the color white, which could be the dominant shade of marble on tombstones, but which, in Trethewey's gesture of inclusion, also suggests the segregation of cemeteries into white and black sections.[5]

Trethewey's other literary epigraph comes from Walt Whitman's classic 1855–92 *Leaves of Grass,* an excerpt that makes profuse use of the lyrical O of the ode, exclamation marks, and abundant sensual adjectives: "O magnet South! O glistening perfumed South! My South! . . . Good and Evil!" (*Native Guard,* 33). Despite his exuberant praise, Whitman points to the intersection of the two extremes of "Good and Evil" complicating, or defining, his love for the South. This announces Faulkner's character Quentin Compson, whose confused love for the South closes the 1936 novel *Absalom, Absalom!:* "I don't hate the South, I don't hate it" (*Absalom,* 306). Compson, like Whitman, overuses exclamation marks and phony emphasis to mask a complex love and hatred relationship for a region simultaneously very beautiful in its landscape, stimulating sensory experience, and by the ugliness of enslavement of humans and lynching. This is also reminiscent of the excruciating irony present in the juxtaposition of sensual "scent of magnolia / sweet and fresh" with the "scent of burning flesh" of Abel Meeropol and Billie Holiday's 1939 "Strange Fruit." For Trethewey, all of this encapsulates the painful intersection of love and hatred for the South, and especially Mississippi, which turned the poet as child into a "what," not a "whom": "She is married to a white man— / and there are more names for what grows inside her" (*Native Guard,* "My Mother Dreams Another Country," 37) and to words that turn her into thing, animal, or monster: "*—peckerwood* and *n—— / lover, half-breed* and *zebra*—words that take shape / outside us" (*Native Guard,* 40, emphasis in original; in the original, the slur is uncensored). Before her entrance into the world, and during her entrance into the world, the young Natasha Trethewey is, like Frantz Fanon's proverbial black man, turned into an object among other objects, "overdetermined from the outside" (*Black Skin,* 95) What's different from Fanon, though, is that Natasha and her mother are both reified, for their racial classification, but also because they escape such a classification as the well-placed enjambment makes plain: "n—— / lover."[6] The enjambment at once separates the racial slur and the state of lover. Love is thus severed from race, just as the antimiscegenation laws—which were still in use in 1966, the poet's birth year—forbade Natasha's parents' "interracial" love, prevented their relationship as just "love," and criminalized the child of that love. The break between the two verses also emphasizes the gap, the moment of gasping that a racist would experience in contemplating this in the pitiful eyes of this "odd" couple. It also overdetermines Natasha and her family by the crime of love flowing across racial barriers. If "n——" represents the abject; the criminal abject is the "n—— lover."

Trethewey directly identifies with Faulkner's character Quentin at the end of her "Pastoral": "*You don't hate the South?* they ask. *You don't hate it?*" (*Native Guard,* 35, emphasis in original). She also recognizes herself in allegedly mixed-race Joe Christmas from Faulkner's *Light in August.* Christmas, too, is trapped in the tortured situation of the legal impossibility of being mixed-race, which leads the Mississippi town mob to lynch him. They bear the same name, Christmas, or a version of it: "Natasha is a Russian name—/ though I'm not; it means Christmas child, even in Mississippi" (*Native Guard,* "Pastoral," 36). Faulkner's character was abandoned on the church's steps on his birthday, December 25, and named after the Christian holiday. Natasha, Russian version of Natalia (literally, "child born on Christmas"), therefore has a lot in common with Faulkner's character: two "miscegenated" children who bear the name of a sacred Christian holiday linked to the birth of Christ, to the ultimate Nativity, *nativeness, native.*

However, this is where Natasha's and Joe Christmas's similarities end. The child poet inherited her name neither through the Bible nor through Faulkner but through Leo Tolstoy's *War and Peace,* which her father was reading at the time of her birth (*Native Guard,* 36). She was born not at Christmas but "near Easter, 1966, in Mississippi" (36). "I know more than Joe Christmas did," she writes. The poet *knows* more than Joe Christmas; the poet is a native of Mississippi, yet also of a place much larger than Mississippi, as she extends in the worldwide dimensions of poetry and literature, through the Russian epic novel. The signposts Trethewey offers with both the epigraphs and the literary allusions found within the body of the poems indicate that she is inextricably anchored in the quotidian and historical experience of racial violence in Mississippi, and, at the same time, at ease in the "more" that the world of literature (including her own *Native Guard*) provides. She is also in a position of *knowing,* of performing agency, placing her in the distant position of a witness, a thinker, a guard of knowledge, not in the bulldozed subjectivity of Faulkner's character X-d out in the graphic form of his name: X-mas.[7]

This foray through Faulkner and "miscegenation," far from being a digression, refracts our discussion on life and death, criminalization, and memorialization, and the relationship between the law, the unritual, and the sacred. Indeed, the mixed-race character, whether in Faulkner or Trethewey, is who or what dwells outside of the law and, as a consequence, outside of the sacred. Like the unrecognized Native Guards who need to be integrated into the official historical discourse and lay on the battlefield, "their bodies swelled . . . unburied" (Trethewey, *Native Guard,* 46), the mixed-child, or *métis,* begs to enter the limits of the law instead of being thrown in the margins of a community, the margins of illegality, just like corpses of unbaptized enslaved Africans were thrown in the swamp a stone's throw away from the canefield instead of the cemetery. It is no surprise, then, that Trethewey's book of poems is organized into three sections, devoted roughly and respectively to the mother, the Louisiana Native Guards, and the *métis* child. Language expels the latter from the category of humanity—"and there are more names for *what* grows inside her" (*Native Guard,* "My Mother Dreams Another Country," 37, my emphasis)—and makes of it some *thing* legally dead:

> I return
> to Mississippi, state that made a crime
>
> of me—mulatto, half-breed—native
> in my native land, this place they'll bury me.
> (*Native Guard,* "South," 46)

Times have changed, if ever so slightly: Natasha knows more than Joe Christmas, for the antimiscegenation laws were overturned one year after Trethewey's birth on June 12, 1967, with *Loving v. Virginia,* and in the last words of *Native Guard* Trethewey demands reparation for the criminalization of her birth by Mississippi state law, in the form of the sacred recognition of her death by the same state: "this place they'll bury me" (*Native Guard,* 46).

The two other cemetery markers serving as epigraphs come from the world of song. When I teach *Native Guard,* I devote a session to the epigraphs and ask students to do research about the songs so that they can *know more* and to bring an interpretation of their choice to class. As serious readers, when a song is given the space of its own page, we are not only to read the words but to hum the tune and sing the lyrics, if we *know* them, or to use the technological tools that now put many an interpretation of these songs at our fingertips. In any case, the inclusion of song lyrics in a literary text asks us to pause, perhaps to listen, to sing, to reminisce, to imagine, and to feel. In a book such as *Native Guard,* conceived as a memorial to the dead, song excerpts introduce a sonorous dimension that introduce a ritualistic dimension, as Moten so poetically puts it: "Sound: suspended brightness, unrepresentable and inexplicable mystery of (music is the improvisation of organization) ritual is music" (Moten, *In the Break,* 45). Thus, the book is at once stone and movement, death and life, tomb and wake. The song enlivens the fixed hardcover of the book, the rocks of the words, and the scaffolding of the verses. This is a phenomenon often observed in *Water Graves;* for instance, *Without Sanctuary,* the exhibition on lynching paired unbearable photographs with the soundtrack of Billie Holiday's "Strange Fruit" (chapter 3); and the mixed-media artists featured in chapter 2 (Bailey, Magee, Waters,

Julien) incorporate musical instruments, scores, vibrations, lyrics, or literal piano keys in their creations.

The first epigraph from song world is a punchy line from Nina Simone's 1964 "Mississippi Goddam": "Everybody knows about Mississippi" (*Native Guard,* 17). Simone's title may elicit giggles for its rawness, but, more importantly, it brings a profound understanding of the multivalent violence inflicted upon African Americans in the southern states. We notice that Trethewey only quotes part of the title—"Everybody knows about Mississippi"—slashing out the interjection "goddam!" We wonder whether the ommission is due to politeness or if it changes the meaning. Indeed, "everybody knows about Mississippi" gives a broader understanding and emphasizes the crucial importance of "knowing." We then notice the fast-paced, upbeat show tune, in sharp contrast with the crimes denounced in the lyrics, and comment that Trethewey's poem presents the same cruel irony of the beauty of Mississippi and its ugly history. "Mississippi Goddam" lists hound dogs set on humans, the school segregation and murder of black schoolchildren, housecleaning for poor pay, and stereotypes of laziness as examples of this oppressive history.

Yet, even before we can analyze, think, compare, Simone's interpretation touches our affect. Indeed, the singer's raucous cries, the anger on her face, the urgent hitting of piano keys intensely contrast with the lyrics "Go slow!," ventriloquizing politicians who halt desegregation. The performance takes us through anger, pain, shame, disgust, and outrage. It makes us pause, the way one would in front of the spectacle of the brutal murder of African American troops, or of Trethewey's mother. It make us notice the reverberation of our feelings in relation to our contemporary outrage of the unsanctioned murder or battering of black men and women by the police. We may then sing, mourn, and yell together, while joining our voice to past, present, and future protests.

The students' examples of "Wayfaring Stranger" attracted more polyvalent responses. The dirge is defined as "traditional" in Trethewey's epigraph (*Native Guard,* 3). Therefore, it is not specifically linked to a specific movement, time, community, or performer. The versions students brought to class were interpreted by black and white performers including Johnny Cash, Emmylou Harris, the Hope Gospel Singers, and Jack White. We first stopped to analyze the lyrics: "I'm going there to meet my mother / . . . / I'm only going over Jordan / I'm only going over home." We noted that the river Jordan is a symbol of baptism that crosses lands literally and symbolically in the Judeo-Christian tradition. We also discussed "going home" as a trope of the afterlife in the African diaspora, as reaching the other side of life and meeting again lost land and deceased beloved ones. The lyrics are particularly moving because we know that the book is the poet's return to past images of her departed mother. In this light, the "I" of "I'm going there to meet my mother" can be interpreted as the poet "going home" in a book, *Native Guard,* which has become her vessel to travel there. Listening to the equally plaintive interpretations that the students brought makes us pause, feel, and perhaps cry. For instance, Jack White's rendition, with its sobbing fiddles, heavy banjo strum imitating the footsteps of coffin-bearers, raucous voice breaking, and nasal moans ending in a whisper, makes us listen and perhaps even join in the singing.[8] The musical breaks Trethewey includes in her epigraphs invite the readers to share in the performance as if they were at a wake.

Getting into the heart of *Native Guard* takes time, preparation, and contemplation. The book invites us to dwell in its paratext: its epigraphs, titles, and book cover. While I have already referred to the solidity of the hardcover as stone pillow, as tombstone, it is now time to linger on the inscription on the grave. In the center of the journal manuscript is a rectangle with the picture of a grey textured tombstone; in the tombstone's middle read the words, "Native Guard," and right below, "Poems."[9] If we read this inscription as one reads the marking on a grave, *Native Guard,* the collection of poems is the dead. It could refer to an individual guard, but it also functions as a singular collective just like the proverbial "unknown soldier," whose function is to memorialize, through the adjective "unknown" every individual single soldier of a multitude of unknown soldiers. The inscription "poems" acts like the inscriptions at times found below the name of a deceased such as "beloved wife and mother," "blacksmith," or "baker." Since "Native Guard" is gender neutral, then, one could imagine that the native guard could be the mother, as well as the poet. "Guard" clearly refers to the troops, but also to the poet herself, who "guards"—protects, defends, keeps in safety, accompanies for protection, watches by way of caution or defense (all definitions from *Merriam-Webster's*), and also guards the entrance to a sacred space, through her poems.

As for "native," the collection housed under that word opens up onto a wide range of definitions. Beyond its historical reference to the Louisiana Native Guards, it also refers to the state of being born in a land, as the poet is a Mississippi native ("in my native land," *Native Guard,* 46). "Native" shares with the word "nation" the Latin root of "birth": "Nation: L. nation, from natus, born." To be native is thus a claim to a belonging to the nation, a claim for full citizenship, a crucial claim for a poet whose birth was considered crime, and, more generally, a crucial demand for African

Americans who were considered second-class citizens. "Native" becomes equated with the right to belong to a country (land *and* nation) for Natasha and for the black troops as well. In the poem "Native Guard," the fictional journal-writer deplores their renaming: "our new name, / the Corps d'Afrique—words that take the *native* / from our claim" (*Native Guard,* 29, italics in original). In the renaming from Native Guard to Corps d'Afrique, which happened in 1863, the soldiers' identity are violated on several levels. If we take "native" as someone belonging to a soil, and, by extension, to a nation, then the Union fighters are expelled from the country they serve and associated with a continent of origin, a faraway and long-ago Africa. By the use of the French term Corps d'Afrique, they are once more displaced from the nation they serve and amalgamated with an undistinguished corps (body) of black soldiers serving a colonizing nation, such as the *Tirailleurs Sénégalais,* corps of colonial infantry of the French army formed in 1857.

As I discuss the word "native" as a desirable name for the African American troops, I cannot but think that this gesture, while appropriate and even necessary, also appropriates the name of prior and contemporary natives of the country—the Natchitochez, the Opelousas, the Avoyel, the Choctaw, the Chickasaw, the Biloxi, the Koasati—who have left so many marks and names on the landscape and history of Mississippi, but who appear only as a pervasive absence, a haunting ghost, in the book *Native Guard.* The bygone *native American* lies in the repositories of beds and names of rivers: "The Yazoo fills the Mississippi's empty bed" (*Native Guard,* 19). The names of the rivers of the state of Mississippi, which used to be full of meaning, are now empty shells, unreadable epitaphs, whose meanings have been erased by colonial history and now sound to us like poetry for the forgotten: Yazoo, Pascagoula, Tombigbee, Tallahatchie, Chickasawhay, Buttahatchee, Amite, Yockanoukanie, Okatoma, Homochitto, Hatchie, Tangipahoa. The Mississippi—"big river," "great river," "father of waters," "father of all rivers"—has retained its meaning and successfully links the "old native" to the "new native," the Native American chant to the African American blues, as in "Ol' Man River," the song eternalized in the 1936 second version of *Showboat* by baritone and civil rights activist Paul Robeson. But the Mississippi river makes us drift away from *Native Guard.* Or does he? "Ol' Man River, that Ol' Man River, he must know something but don't say nothing. He just keeps rolling. He keeps on rolling along."[10]

The words of the title *Native Guard* thus take us on a linguistic, poetic, and historical journey that reveals the complex web of relations at work in the book. Native-nativity-Natalia-Natasha-Native-Guard-nation are linked, etymologically and semantically, in an inextricable network that connects human to country (as soil and nation), right of birth to citizenship right, politics to sacred, as well as their possible violent severing from one another.

If the hardcover is the tombstone, if the title is the name of the dead, then, the excerpt from the journal printed on the cover is the writing on the grave. The parchment-colored cover jacket of *Native Guard* is filled, front and back, with a "diary page reproduced in *Thank God My Regiments' an African One: The Civil War Diary of Colonel Nathan W. Daniels.*[11] Daniels (1832–1867) was the "Union white commanding officer of the African American 2nd Louisiana Native Guard Volunteers, he and his men were removed from mainland military activity and confined in obscure duty on Ship Island, ten miles off the coast of Mississippi" (Weaver, *Thank God,* xv). Once again, historical past and individual present converge, since Trethewey was born in Gulfport, Mississippi, a few miles away from Ship Island.[12]

Colonel Daniels was also an ardent abolitionist, as his diary reveals: "Thank God it hath been my fortune to be a participator in the grand idea of proclaiming freedom to this much abused & tortured race. Thank God my regiment an African one, that I have been permitted to assemble them under the banner of freedom to do and die for their country and liberty—The 2nd Louisiana Regiment of Native Guards will yet have a name in history" (Weaver, 68). The diary entry, dated April 11, 1863, is barely legible, as it is a literal palimpsest of two superimposed texts. The first layer of writing is horizontal, the one written on it horizontal transversal (what Weaver calls "cross-writing") and marked more insistently, with heavy quill marks and ink blots, as if to make it more visible. The obscured writing is indicative of the lack of paper Officer Daniels had at his disposal in his forced retreat on Ship Island. However, symbolically, when Trethewey choses this particular page as her book cover, she uses it to indicate a sedimentation of history, the copresence of two obscured histories, and the need to make the illegible legible, the occulted revealed in the poems that follow. Indeed, Trethewey could have chosen neater pages from Daniel's journal. If we consult the manuscript available on the Library of Congress website, some pages are clearly legible, with only one layer of text and plenty of room for the writing to breathe.[13]

Also significantly, as Weaver's transcription indicates, April 11 is the day of the first Second Louisiana Native Guard Infantry Regiment battle against the Confederates: "My men fought nobly . . . all behaved well, and particularly Major Dumas who had men shot down all around him"

(Weaver, 83).[14] Indeed, African American soldiers were often relegated to noncombatant positions in an attempt to lessen their bravery or equality as soldiers.[15] Trethewey also choses this particular diary entry to put forth the bravery, military prowess, and, ultimately, integral service of the black regiment to the nation.

Trethewey returns to the diary in the central and eponymous "Native Guard," the longest poem of the collection (*Native Guard,* 25–30). The elegy is built around date entries, imitating the structure of the journal and conveying a poetic historical document complete with dates. The poem picks up central formal and content elements of Daniels's diary. Formally, it includes entries with some dates overlapping with Daniel's, with others extended before and after the time limits of the historical document. The landscape and meteorological and ecological conditions are the same, on this barrier sea island at the mercy of storms and the elements, which also obsessed Daniels in his daily writing:

> Here, now, I walk
> ankle-deep in sand, fly-bitten, nearly
> smothered by heat, and yet I can look out
> upon the gulf and see the surf breaking
> tossing the ships (*Native Guard,* 26)

Major Dumas, Daniel's immediate subordinate, appears here in a hierarchically superior position to Trethewey's diary writer: "Dumas was a fair master to us all" (29)—"fair" referring both to his reasonable character but also to his light complexion. Weaver teaches us that "Colonel Daniels confiscated the diary from the house of Hamilton McNeil Vance, a Confederate citizen and cotton merchant in New Orleans. Vance and his wife had been writing alternatively in the book, describing their fears as the Yankees approached" (Weaver, *Thank God,* 20). In Trethewey, too, the journal is a confiscated good, like sugar or molasses could be, a staple, a node of survival:

> We take those things we need
> from the Confederates' abandoned homes:
> salt, sugar, even this journal, near full
> with someone else's words, overlapped now,
> crosshatched beneath mine. On every page,
> his story intersecting with my own. (*Native Guard,* 25–26)

While Trethewey, in a hermit-crab move, occupies Daniels's shell—a bit like Daniels inscribed his writing in the empty space left in the

Confederates' diary—she infuses it nonetheless with her own politico-historical priorities, and, of course, poetry. Their palimpsest histories merge in a text that is inseparably poetry and history. We learn that her journal writer is neither a white abolitionist, like Daniels, nor a man of color born free, like Dumas, but, rather, a Native Guard, likely a private, "born a slave, at harvest time, / in the parish of Ascension" (*Native Guard,* 25). The specific mention of the Louisiana Parish located on and around the Mississippi River between Baton Rouge and New Orleans gives the diary-writer a clear grounding in the space of rural Louisiana, largely dominated by sugar plantations. "Ascension" evokes the upward trajectory from slave to guard, but also alludes to the sacred Christian holiday, thereby presenting the former slave as a man, both in the historical and sacred realms.

Ironically, the journal writer who keeps track of names and "things which must be accounted for" (*Native Guard,* 29) has no name: perhaps to allow the readers to project any other unnamed soldiers neglected by history into his position. Of his functions on the desolate Ship Island, we know much. Historical character Dumas taught him to read and write. He is the chronicler of events happening on the island, recording events in his journal, and writing notes to family members on behalf of his illiterate colleagues. He is also a botanist and naturalist: "I studied natural things—all manner / of plants, birds I draw now in my book: wren, / willet, egret loon" (*Native Guard,* 28). In addition to his tending for the living, he tends for the dead: "Now I tend Ship Island graves, mounds like dunes / that shift and disappear" (29). His writing, drawing, tending thus memorializes and sacralizes where the two gestures had been failed by official historical narratives or state structures. His writing solidifies the ephemeral, such as the sand graves, emblematic of the tombs of African Americans disappearing under the biased wind of history and historicity.

"These are things which must be accounted for," writes the guard of memory. (*Native Guard,* 29). Beyond watching the small, yet macrocosmic, Ship Island, Trethewey's writer keeps track of more extensive historical records, such as the death of African American soldiers in battle or massacred in places like Pascagoula, Mississippi (28) or Fort Pillow. The poem "Native Guard" is the site where we encounter our second "pillow," which echoes the poet's mother's name on the grave: "stone pillow for my head." The individual and the historical intersect. The journal writer evokes the Massacre of Fort Pillow, Tennessee, on April 12, 1864, in which four hundred surrendering Union soldiers, most of them black, were slaughtered. As historian Richard Fuchs relates: "The affair at Fort

Pillow was simply an orgy of death, a mass lynching to satisfy the basest of conduct—intentional murder—for the vilest of reasons—racism and personal enmity" (*Unerring Fire,* 14). In his *Personal Memoirs,* Ulysses S. Grant describes the gruesome massacre in which the blood of soldiers bayonetted and put to the sword turned the Mississippi river into a water grave: "The [Mississippi] river was dyed . . . with the blood of the slaughtered for two hundred yards" (483). Trethewey's fictional memory-keeper continues the official historian's accounts in an entry from 1865. Significantly, Daniel's original journal had ended in September 1863. Thus, incomplete history provided by archival records continues in the poetic work in a practice of relation and relay that we have so often encountered in *Water Graves.*

Much has been said about African American poetry using history as a privileged object. As Shockley observes, "There has been a noteworthy trend in American poetry toward the historical poem" ("Going Overboard," 791). She adds that the case is particularly sharp for "African American poets writing from similar positions of exclusion and marginalization" who made "poetry tell on the willful blindness and smothering silence of an 'authorized history' that has located the story of our past, by and large, in the places and occupations filled by society's most powerful people." Trethewey herself evokes the unequal representation of history: "Some names shall deck the page of history / as it is written on stone. Some will not" (*Native Guard,* 28). Similarly, Trouillot's *Silencing the Past* reveals the blanks of history whereby a revolution, the Haitian Revolution, was unspeakable in historical discourse. Glissant argues, in the same vein, that in postslavery contexts fiction writers and poets need to pick up the torch where historical records fail to archive the past.[16]

While I wholly embrace the evidence of historical lacunae in the representation of histories of the oppressed and with the role of the poet (or the artist) to relay and complement the partial and incomplete historian's work, I rather prefer the expression "poem of history" to "historical poem."[17] The latter reduces the living movement of the poem—its rhythms, alliterations, enjambments, repetitions, metaphors—to a skeleton, a "scaffolding of bones," (*Native Guard,* 30) to use Trethewey's phrase. It would also put poetry in a service relation to history. "Poem of history," on the other hand, identifies history as a main concern of the poem, but dwells within the realm, the laws, and the aesthetics of the poem. Trethewey does not need to provide a historical account of the Louisiana Native Guards (Weaver already did this) but, rather, insufflate life within it. Let me explain by taking a detour through the poem "Pilgrimage" (*Native Guard,* 19–20).

The poem "Pilgrimage / *Vicksburg, Mississippi*" presents itself with its title and place epigraph under the double sign of the sacred and history. "Pilgrimage" evokes the journey of a traveler or a stranger to a shrine, a holy, or devotional place. Vicksburg immediately calls up the 1863 siege of the city, one of the last strongholds of the Confederacy, which eventually surrendered to Union forces. Perhaps lesser-known in our historical consciousness, Peter Cosby, a black man, was elected as sheriff in Vicksburg in 1874. White supremacist and members of the "Red Shirts" held the sheriff in custody and ran him out of town. In the following weeks, white mobs massacred African Americans in and around Vicksburg. Historian Emily Crosby estimates that three hundred blacks were killed.[18]

Trethewey is not writing a *historical poem,* so she does not document with facts and figures this dual side of history. However, her *poem of history* sharply records the pain and tension of this duality. "Pilgrimage" is based on the poet's journey to Vicksburg, perhaps on a weekend tour, such as those advertised on the "Vicksburg Pilgrimage" tourist website.[19] Before focusing on the town, she muses on the meandering of the Mississippi River, which extends as much in space as it allows for time travel: "Here, the river changed its course . . . as one turns, forgetting, from the past" (*Native Guard,* 19). The poem is heavy with funerary words ("skeletons," "ghosts," "graves") associated with spaces and structures from the past: The Mississippi is "a graveyard / for skeletons of sunken riverboats." Official statues embody a frozen death: "Here, the dead stand up in stone, white / marble, on Confederate Avenue." The enjambment highlighting the word "white" reveals the connection between the cold materiality of marble and the "white" side of history. Frozen in this official and one-sided version of the past, "the whole city is a grave." While the dominant (white, Hegelian) version of the history of Vicksburg will bring to mind the dead Confederates, the knowledge of the marginalized history of Sherriff Cosby's capture and of the ensuing bloodshed brings to the surface the unsanctioned murder of black men. While the poet lies in bed in one of the many Vicksburg mansions transformed into a guest house, "the ghost of history," she writes, "lies down besides me, / rolls over, pins me beneath a heavy arm" (*Native Guard,* 20). The ghost of history is personified in what we can imagine as a strong man, a predator, fixing the "I" of the poet in place, forbidding her to move or to fight, perhaps in the violent embrace of a sexual aggressor. In contrast with this frozen, cold, male, white, violent history, the "I" resists: "I stand" (19). The subject continues to perform an alternative history by imagining it through the mind of an unnamed and marginalized character: "They must have seemed like catacombs, in 1863, to the woman sitting in her parlor . . . I can see her listening to shells explode, writing herself / into history." The shift between past and present tense indicates this passage from a dead past to a living one.

The power of memory in Trethewey's poems of history lies in her selection of events evacuated from official historiography, in her practice of multiple archives (the body, the library, the landscape), in her recreation of long-gone characters' living voices, in her challenging of individual and collective history by showing "how they intersect," in her transformation of landscape from dead scaffoldings to flowing rivers, in her practice of a Bakhtinian plurivocality or a sedimentation of landscape according to Glissant. Glissant's assessment that "our landscapes are our own monuments" has been one of *Water Graves*'s leitmotifs. In the absence of official statues, plaques, monuments, tombstones, trees, rivers, islands, and rocks act as markers and sites of the past.

The last poem of *Native Guard,* "South" (45–46), insists both on the absence of human-built monuments and on the relaying function of elements of nature and landscape. The military formation, the Native Guards, whom the poet imagined in the skinny palm-trees, appears skeletal: "I returned to a stand of pines, / bone-thin phalanx" (45). The black soldiers who perished in combat at Fort Hudson are left in a state of unritual, as the terms *un*buried and *un*marked, sharing the same privative prefix, indicate:

> Port Hudson where their bodies swelled
> and blackened beneath the sun—unburied
>
> until earth's green sheet pulled over them,
> unmarked by any headstones. (46)

Nature, covering the desecrated bodies is the only decent griever, the only guard of ritual, covering the bodies with a green blanket of decency. Trethewey repeats a common war elegy trope, as does Arthur Rimbaud in his war sonnet "Le Dormeur du val," written in the aftermath of the Franco-Prussian war: "Nature, berce-le chaudement: il a froid" (Nature, cuddle him tight: he is cold; Rimbaud, *Poèmes, 67).* Trethewey, like Rimbaud, pairs things natural with what would be their—missing—human or human-made equivalent via an abundance of juxtapositions, similes, or metaphors: "pines" with "phalanx"; "tangle [of vegetation]" with "dialectic"; "magnolias" with "afterthoughts"; "flowers" with "white flags"; "palmettos" with "symbols of victory"; or "land" with the "vanquished"

(*Native Guard,* 45). Things of nature bury, remember, cogitate where official acts and discourses lack.

The poem "South" acts as elegy, mound, grave, for at least four entities. The most obvious ones are the dead combatants: "I returned to a country battlefield / where colored troops fought and died" (46). The poet's contemplation of the cotton field awakens the memory of the enslaved: "I returned / to a field of cotton . . . as slave legend goes—each boll / holding the ghosts of generations" (45). The multitude of unsung humans who worked the land find an endless repository in the ever-growing and multiplied plants of cotton. The poem is also an ode to the devastated land victim of urbanization and tourism: "Mangrove, live oak, gulfweed / razed and replaced by thin palms." We know how much the mangrove—this site of ecological renewal, of the rot of death and renewal of life, of complex biotopes and ecological alliances, this liminal space between earth and sea, protecting the coastal land from the vulnerability to hurricanes and floods—is precious to the survival of coastal human and nonhuman communities. The beaches near Trethewey's birthplace are fabricated out of the mangrove, human-made. Unlike Trethewey, who is literally native to the land and expelled from it, Mississippi Gulf Coast beaches are *unnative* yet naturalized through discourses and practices of tourism. Their surface of white sand, sparkling waters, and palm trees strip the past of its visibility and depth. Forgotten are Biloxi Native Americans who gave their name to the place, as well as civil rights leaders who fought to desegregate the Jim-Crow Mississippi beaches from the early 1950s to the late 1960s.[20]

In the final words of the poem (and of the book), the poet asserts her own right to a proper treatment and burial in the land that saw her birth:

> I return
> to Mississippi, state that made a crime
>
> of me—mulatto, half-breed—native
> in my native land, this place they'll bury me. (*Native Guard,* 46)

While I have already discussed this arresting passage earlier, it's worth noting here that the "I" of the poem, the land, and the history of racial oppression are inextricably and painfully joined; that the individual and the collective intersect through the word "native"; and that Mississippi is an indissoluble mess and haven mixing the political ("state"), the earth ("native land"), the community (they). People and place fuse in the awkward grammar of the poem's last words: "This place they'll bury me."

There's nothing linear, hierarchical, or teleological in Trethewey's representation of history. What the poet calls an "understory" (*Native Guard,* 45) appears as a geological sedimentation, whose superimposed layers would each have something to reveal about the particular in which the alluvia were washed away. And, indeed, "South" is visually organized as a series of alluvia. The poem consists of seventeen couplets in which the last verse is offset to the right and thus at once both relegated to the margin and emphasized, in what we could call a poetics of sedimentation.

If nature offers the initial shroud, mound, tomb, graveyard, wake, and war memorial, the poet, too, provides the sites, rites, and structures of decent remembering for the victims of the unritual. She is *industrious* and *does,* to paraphrase her description of the ants' work in "Monument." Trethewey reclaims history, reshapes its contours and fluxes in the disciplined control of form evident in all her poems. Her graveyards are not square and enclosed, her sonnets do not end on a terminal mortality, her epitaphs open up to multitudes of individual and collective departed, such as the Native Guard, who, as I have discussed, can be a multitude as well as a single loved one.

Many have commented on Trethewey's formalism. Meta Duewa Jones characterizes Trethewey as a "consummate formalist," who infuses her poetry with "the beauty of [a] sculpted language, her scrupulous attention to visual and historical details and her finesse with poetic forms" ("Reframing Exposure," 407). I want to argue here that Trethewey's fine work on form provides not only aesthetic satisfaction, but also inflects her vision of death, temporality, and memory, and facilitates the practice of open, performative, and interactive sacred gestures for her readers. For instance, what is perhaps the most historical poems of the collection, since it relies directly on archival material, "Native Guard" is also remarkable for its innovation in form, its manipulation of time breaking away from the linear, teleological temporality of a Hegelian history, and its invitation to the reader. The first and last verse of the long poem include the same words: "Truth be told, I do not want to forget" (*Native Guard,* 25) and ends with "a scaffolding of bone / we tread upon, forgetting. Truth be told" (30). Formally, the inaugural and final verses introduce a circularity that implies a lack of closure, and a continuity between present, past, and future, fighting against the finality of death and implying a continuity between life and death, as we have seen in many examples in *Water Graves.*[21] "Truth be told" could be used in casual conversation to confess a thought by means of honesty: "Truth be told, I do not like Brussels sprouts." However, the phrase's prominent position at the very beginning and the very end of the poem makes it sound instead like an ethical and religious imperative. Crucial truths need to be brought to the surface, as in the legal space of a trial, or in the sacred space of the "testimony service" or truth-telling in African American churches.

The circle of repetition is complicated by the chiasm it shelters: "Truth be told . . . forget"; "Forgetting. Truth be told." In Greek epic poetry and oral literature, chiasms are used as a mnemonic structure to ease memorization. The structure therefore demands interaction with the reader, begging him to remember. The mnemonic function of the chiasm is particularly relevant in Trethewey's structure, since it refers precisely to forgetting. The symmetrical form also highlights the contrast between the willful desire not to forget ("I do not want to forget") and the unavoidable forgetting encountered when we stumble upon objects that have ceased to contain meaning ("a scaffolding of bone"). While all of Trethewey's poems are all carefully crafted in sonnets, pantoums, or narrative poems in tercets or quatrains that convey thoughts through their structure, I focus here on three particular poems, whose striking architecture highlight Trethewey's relation to and performance of death, memory, temporality, and the sacred.

"Myth" (*Native Guard,* 14) represents perhaps the most desperate attempt at stopping time and stopping the mother's death. The poem, composed of eight regular tercets separated in the middle with an asterisk, is a perfect palindrome. Each verse of the first section is repeated in an inverse symmetrical structure in the second part of the poem (ABCDEFGHI / IHGFEDCBA). It is an amplified and multiplied chiasm of sorts, which, like the chiasm of "Native Guard," attempts to capture the passage of time in its edifice. The poem recounts the repeated tenuous moment between sleeping and waking, when the poet feels her mother to be alive, before she once again vanishes once the daughter is fully awake. The nine-syllable simple statement—"I was asleep while you were dying" (*Native Guard,* 14)—opens and closes the poem. It creates a parallel between an "I" and a "you" caught in different, yet not quiet differentiated, states of sleeping and dying. The gerundive temporality inscribes them not in the fatality of an event, as a past preterite would—"I was asleep when you died"—but in a shared undefined duration. The state of dying puzzles the mind by its odd liminal time not yet revolved but irreversible.

The writer places her poem under the sign of "Myth" and thereby asks the reader-turned-detective to look for evidence of that myth in the poem. As we try to disentangle the puzzle, we note an intruder in an otherwise plain and quotidian English language: "The Erebus I keep you in, still trying / not to let go" (*Native Guard,* 14). While Erebus is primarily the divinity of darkness in Greek mythology, it also refers to a particular place, the Erebus, where the departed arrive immediately after their passing. It precedes Tartarus, place of permanent darkness and oblivion. Erebus is then particularly apt to define this liminal place between the sleeping and the dying, between the dead and the living, that have not quite parted from one another. The palindrome attempts to seize that liminality with its enclosed structure and fails. Indeed, the frequent repetitions in the poem indicate not the repetition of everyday life but the traumatic repetition of the event of death, which cannot be processed. Death errs in the stale time of the symmetrical prison, the wishful Erebus, of the poem: "You'll be dead again tomorrow" (14).

We could stop with this explanation of the title by the explicitly named "Erebus." However, the obvious clue hides less visible evidence. Erebus hides another Greek myth, which speaks to the agony of not being able to retrieve the dead from the living: "So I try taking / you back into morning, sleep-heavy, turning / my eyes open, I find you do not follow" (14). If Erebus is the site of the myth, its heroes are Orpheus and Eurydice. Orpheus, the most venerated ancient Greek poet and musician, who could charm all living beings with his lyre, failed to bring back Eurydice from Erebus, when he turned around to look back. Eurydice died from a snakebite after trying to escape the grip of a satyr who had attacked her. The story sounds familiar: the poet grieving the death of a woman whom a man-beast assaulted. Like in the myth, the lyre and its perfectly symmetrical structure fail to bring back the dead into morning. The myth of Orpheus and Eurydice is transposed to a daughter-mother relation whereby the mother's loving daughter has to walk in Orpheus's shoes.

Perhaps because the space of myth provides a collective resonance to the poet's individual story—or because it embellishes the sordid murder of a woman in a case of domestic violence upon an African American woman that would be relegated to the confines of the back pages of a local newspaper and to the confines of the law, myth is a frequent haven in Trethewey's *Native Guard.*[22] In a poem written ten years later, "Imperatives for Carrying On in the Aftermath," Trethewey redresses the neglect of law with the power of myth: "Or / the juror who said, *It's a domestic issue—/ they should work it out themselves*" (*Monument,* 2). "Genus Narcissus" (*Native Guard,* 7) relies on the Greek myth of Narcissus alluding to another kind of chiasmic confinement since the young man met his fate while contemplating his beautiful reflection, and fatally drowning in his water grave. It is a bit surprising that Narcissus, representing excessive self-love, would be found in a poem dedicated to the memory of the mother. However, "Genus Narcissus" poignantly links narcissism and survivor's guilt to the memory of the departed mother. While the versification itself does not form a symmetrical enclosure like the palindrome that is "Myth," the sense of confinement is relayed by word repetitions, and by an abysmal practice of poetic and semantic referentiality through the word "daffodil," or, according to its scientific classification, "genus narcissus." From a literal standpoint, "Genus Narcissus" evokes the time when, as a little girl, the poet would pick yellow daffodils on the road back to school: "Gathering up as many as I could hold / then presenting them, in a jar, to my mother" (*Native Guard,* 7). The trope, as Trethewey explicitly avows, is old and tried. She uses for an epigraph the verses of seventeenth-century lyric poet Robert Herrick: "Faire daffadills, we weep to see / you haste away so soone" (*Native Guard,* 7). The young child's lonely road from school picking daffodils implicitly, yet clearly, evokes William Wordsworth's "I Wandered Lonely as a Cloud": "When all at once I saw a crowd / A host of golden daffodils."[23] The romantic poet too is taken by the beauty of the daffodils, in a Narcissus like obsession: "I gazed—and gazed—but little thought." The adult poet Trethewey glowers upon the child's naïve narcissism: "Childish vanity. I must have seen in them / some measure of myself—the tender stems / each blossom a head lifted up" (*Native Guard,* 7). What "Genus Narcissus" reveals about the adult poet's state of mind is quite the opposite: extreme self-deprecation linked to the guilt of not having saved the mother, while too taken with herself, and not seeing or hearing that the ephemeral flower, carried a dual prophecy: "*Be taken with yourself* / they said to me; *Die early,* to my mother" (14, emphasis in original). In contrast with the structure of the chiasm which attempts to confine fleeting moments into a closed structure, like Narcissus's mirror, into their ABBA structure, the simple ABAB parallelism of the last two verses of "Genus Narcissus," indicates that mother and daughter have parted on parallel, yet irreconcilable, roads.

Arguably, "Graveyard Blues" (*Native Guard,* 8) represents Trethewey's most striking formal coup. The poem recalls, in a repetitive, dragging, and nauseating rhythm, the interment of the poet's mother witnessed by her daughter. While its title defines it as a blues, the poem is also a sonnet composed of fourteen verses organized in four tercets and one final couplet, which brings a new turn to the poem, proclaims a definite resolution: "I wander among the name of the dead: / My mother's name, stone pillow for my head." This is of course, the central claim of the poem, which I already commented on at length. While adopting the classical European poetic form, Trethewey reclaims it by combining with not only the name, but also patterns of the blues. As poetry critic Jahan Ramazani explains in a chapter of *Poetry of Mourning* devoted to Langston Hughes, "The blues itself has 'always already' been a miscegenated form, commingling Western rhyme and meter with African rhythm emphasis and repetition" (140). The poet's feat is that she "miscegenates" it one more time, by coupling the structure of the blues with that of the sonnet. Ramazani's term particularly resonates with Trethewey's poetry since miscegenation is, as we have seen, as the center of the poem. This neomiscegenation of form, so to speak, directly addresses the tortured yet indispensable dual heritage of the poet, herself the daughter of the white Canadian poet Eric Trethewey and the blues-laden African American social worker Gwendolyn Ann Turnbough.

And, indeed, "Graveyard Blues" is unquestionably sonnet and blues at once. The last line of the first three tercets adopts the twelve-bar blues verse, which, as Ramazani argues, "can accommodate almost any subject from suicidal depression to erotic bliss, fitting nearly everything into its three rhyming lines, the second repeating the third" (139). Trethewey faithfully adopts the AAA/BBB/CCC blues rhyme pattern with the first two rhyming words of each tercet repeating: "down/down/sound," "hand, hand, . . . man," "away, away, she lay," "holes, holes, rolls" (*Native Guard,* 8). The internal repetitions emphasize even more the repeated lament of the blues with its structure of systematic repetition with a change: "It rained the whole time . . . Rained from church to grave," "When the preacher called out . . . When he called for a witness" (8). In the first and fourth stanzas, alliterations featuring long and heavy nasal diphthongs with dominating "o" and "a" sounds imitate the plaintive moans and sobs of the blues ("down," down," "sound;" "home," "holes," "home-going," "road," "holes," "slow," "down," "rolls").

Such a miscegenated aesthetics embraces an equally mixed sacred and legal practice. Words such as "graveyard," "church," and "grave" could be common both to the European elegy and the American blues. The following verses, however, indisputably evoke an African American funerary ritual: "When the preacher called out I held up my hand; / When he called for a witness I raised my hand" (8). The raised hand indicates that the daughter is ready to tell the truth, according to the liturgy of "testifying." Simultaneously, the hand held up calls to mind the scene of the legal trial, when one swears on the Bible to tell the truth and nothing but the truth. Recall that Trethewey engaged in a legal battle against "Dekalb County," Georgia, for not protecting her mother against her then-predator, who would eventually become her murderer.[24] Responding to the unritual is then not only a matter of providing sacred rituals, but also of legal justice and reparations. This dual imperative is at the core of Philip's *Zong!*

Bone Water: M. NourbeSe Philip's *Zong!*

While it is possible, albeit extremely difficult, to recover bones from a mass grave in Bosnia, Philip explains, retrieving the bones that the ocean drowned is impossible. Language itself fails in describing what such a retrieval would look like. Philip dismisses "exhuming" as an appropriate word. Indeed, exhuming comes from "ex-humus," out of the soil. From this linguistic void, she coins the term "exaqua": "What is the word for bringing back bodies from water? From a 'liquid grave'? . . . I find words like resurrect and subaquatic but not 'exaqua.' Does this mean that unlike being interred, once you're underwater there is no retrieval—that you can never be 'exhumed' from water? The gravestone or tombstone marks the spot of internment, whether of ashes or the body. What marks the spot of subaquatic death?" (*Zong!*, 201). If we conceive of the poem as retrieving bones and reconstructing evidence, it will need to adapt its forensic tools to the particular conditions of an oceanic search: the incommensurable fathoms and width of the seas, the constant mobility of waves and currents, the movable sediments, and the disintegrating properties of salt water. Thus, the poem itself will be adaptable, mobile, floating, yet resting on the random flotsam and jetsam left behind by shipwrecks and the murders of humans thrown overboard. The poem, as I describe below, brings back meaning into the chaos that it *exaquas,* by associating a hard poetics of bones with a liquid aesthetics of water. I analyze this mixed poetic gesture in the remainder of this chapter, focusing first on the general structure of the book *Zong!,* comprising all its elements (the poems, the glossary, the notanda, the transcript of *Gregson v. Gilbert,* etc.), then moving to a reading of what I will henceforth call the *poem per se* ("Os," "Sal," "Ferrum," etc.).[25]

Philip's poetics of liquidity and morsels is far from unique in Caribbean and post–Middle Passage literatures, where poets have to work from shards and fragments of the past. Haitian Canadian writer Emile Ollivier, another sea poet, lyrically comments on the vastness and mobility of water and the apparently feeble function of broken seashells: "Vast and complicated palimpsest of memory! Past like the sea, you excavate the sands of life to leave behind you broken shells in which we can still hear the sea. Is it naïve to think that the world, its scent and music can be rebuilt from broken shells?" (*Mille Eaux,* 134). *Zong!* performs, on a larger scale, Ollivier's shell reconstruction, and mends Walcott's broken vase, whose fragments hold more signification than the intact object: "Break a vase, and the love that reassembles the fragments is stronger than that love which took its symmetry for granted when it was whole. . . . It is such a love that reassembles our African and Asiatic fragments, the cracked heirlooms whose restoration shows its white scars" (Walcott, *Twilight,* 69). The strength of Walcott's object comes from the fact that it contains more pain than its original.[26] The cracks allow readers and viewers to project their own pain, and thus to compose a community precisely, through its fissures. Similarly, Shockley associates the blanks of *Zong!* as "aching white space" ("Going," 810). Critic Jenny Sharpe suggests that "silences in official archives" on which *Zong!* is based "are not only holes to be filled with meaning—missing-pieces of a counter-history—but also spaces of an affective memory with the past" ("The Archive," 470). The artistic creation not only registers pain, shame, wonder, or rage, but also demands it from its viewers or readers.

In Philip's case, the intact object, unlike Walcott's vase, is not rebuilt from love but from law. It is the court transcript that ultimately condemned the slave traders who threw overboard approximately 140 African captives in order to collect insurance money, turning humans into jetsam.[27] While moved by law, the trial does not do justice, since it incriminates the traders not for their inhuman crime of killing human beings but for having fooled the insurers. The verdict sanctions not the crime against humanity but the financial fraud and swindling: "It has been decided, whether wisely or unwisely is not now the question, that a portion of our fellow-creatures may become the subject of property. This, therefore, was a throwing overboard of goods" (*Gregson v. Gilbert,* quoted in *Zong!,* 211). In contrast with Walcott's vase, it is not a question, for Philip, of reassembling fragments, but rather, to create some love, justice, reparation, or ritual in a situation of absolute unritual in which the law itself offers no recognition of the African victim's humanity. The drowned humans are locked up in a status of movable goods that forbids, legally and sacredly, any mourning within the context of the law. The law itself, Philip argues, "in its potent ability to decree that what is not, as in human ceasing to be and becoming an object, a thing, or chattel, the law approaches the realm of magic and religion. The conversion of human into chattel becomes an act of transubstantiation the equal of the metamorphosis of the Eucharistic bread and wine into the body and blood of Christ" (196). While the Eucharist converts quotidian staples such as bread into sacred substances, the transubstantiation operated by law has the opposite effect: it turns sacred human lives into commodities. If the law governing the enslavement of humans gains a magic and sacred aura, to believe Philip, it is a malevolent one. As herself both a lawyer and a poet, Philip must rectify the law, reverse the sense of transubstantiation by giving humanity and sacred back to the victims of the legalized unritual, through her poetic creation. Poetry—poiesis as act of making—relays a faulty, even criminal, law.

Not surprisingly, then, Philip's book *Zong!* is composed of disparate, yet complementary items: the spine and cover; the cover art; the front matter; some dedications; several epigraphs; the acknowledgments; six sections of the poem per se ("Os," "Dicta"—which are missing from the table of contents—"Sal," "Ventus," "Ratio," "Ferrum," and "Ebora"); a glossary; a manifest, a notanda, and the 1783 *Gregson v. Gilbert* court transcript. They are all presented on the same plane, hierarchically unmarked, the poems complementing a legal document, which complements a linguistic glossary, which complements an essay in critical theory ("Notanda"), and vice versa.

Even before the poem begins, the authority of *Zong!* is complicated and multiplied. The spine lists the authors as "Boateng and Philip" (more on this soon). The first sentence of the acknowledgments begins to explain the dual author's mystery: "A work like *Zong!,* although apparently authored by one person, only comes into fruition with the assistant of support of many others" (*Zong!,* xii). *Zong!,* like many of the creations featured in *Water Graves,* is therefore a communal endeavor in the face of the enormity of disaster and unritual: "*Zong!* is the Song of the untold story; it cannot be told yet must be told, but only through its un-telling" (last sentence of "Notanda," 207). The untelling begins with relinquishing the author's sole authority. As Sharpe explains: "The book spine presents Philip and Boateng as co-authors, and Boateng is described on the book as 'the voice of the ancestors revealing the submerged stories of all who were on board the Zong.' The fictitious Ghanaian ur-ancestor can be searched (and found!) on the Internet as the book's 'author'" ("The Archive," 471). The author's gesture of letting go of her own authority makes sense in the understanding that the writing of the disaster, as Maurice Blanchot reveals in *The Writing of the Disaster,* is not the gesture of writers writing disaster, but of disaster writing itself from innumerable sites. A single author cannot face this multifocal event. However, a poet can attempt to write the disaster by multiplying sites of authorships, which automatically entails her to sacrifice her sole authority. Philip explains: "In allowing myself to surrender to the text—silences and all—and allowing the fragmented words to speak to the stories locked in the text, I, too, have found myself 'absolved' of 'authorial intention'" (*Zong!,* 204). It is not only that contemporary poet Philip coauthored the book with Boateng. More complexly, sites of authority are multiplied throughout the text, its black letters and white silences.

On all pages of the poems constituting "Os" (from "Zong! #1" to "Zong! #26," 3–45), names of drowned Africans are listed below the bottom margin. Like Donatien, Valère, Duval Carrié, Taylor, and other *sea artists,* Philip connects the underwater realm to the above-water. Graphically, a dividing (or joining) line marks the horizon between an above and a below, between the present of the poet and readers and the past of the departed (3–56). The line connects "*those who have died but continue to work on behalf of the living*" ("Notanda," 196, italics in original). Shockley convincingly argues that "those named under the lines are the '*underwriters* of the text' . . . an interpretation that both attends to their visual placement and recalls the gesture Philip makes on the title page, where she indicates that Zong! is the account 'as told to the author by Setaey Adamu Boateng'" ("Going Overboard," 814).

In the second book, "Dicta," names are abruptly replaced with blank spaces. The blanks, or silences, could also arguably act as coauthors of the text, since the victims of the Middle Passage constitute an enormous collective of humans locked in anonymity. Literary critic Myriam Moïse similarly interprets these silences as places that the reader can fill and therefore contribute to the text's authorship: "Silence can also be exploited by the reader who becomes a co-producer of the text" ("Grasping the Ungraspable," 31). In his essay on biopolitics in Philip and Glissant, Alessandro Corio similarly argues: "We [readers] act like detectives trying to recompose the fragments of this poetic puzzle" ("Anagrams," 337).[28] Offering tips on methods for reading her *Zong!,* Philip explains that the poem "suggests something about the relational—every word or word cluster is seeking a space directly above within which to fit itself and in so doing falls into relation with others either above, below, or laterally. This is the governing principle and adds a strongly visual quality to the work" (*Zong!,* 203). While she does not quote Glissant, Philip's use of "relational" reminds us of the process of understanding and being that the Martinican philosopher opposes to static thought.

The named coauthor, Boateng, is also part of this relational mode. "Setaey Adamu Boateng" appears on the internet only in connection to Philip's *Zong!* It is thus likely that Philip constructed it, since there are no other searchable occurrences of the name. The name Philip built constructs her (us) in return and stimulates our poetic imagination through the sounds and words it contains: "sea," "sea chantey," "Adam," "boat," "boating," "c'était" (it was), "attends," "wait," and many more words in the multilingualism of *Zong!*. The intriguing name leads our imagination into the lyrics (chantey) of an origin (Adam) and past (*c'était*), lost at sea. Setaey Adamu Boateng, Philip specifies, is the voice of drowned ancestors, the voice from the rich and sacred *anba dlo* that connects the dead, the living, and the yet-to-be-born or the yet-to-read. The presence of Boateng also counterbalances the dominant voice of the poem per se, which is that of the white slave trader, as Philip explains in an interview with Saunder: "Once I submitted myself to the text, once I made that decision, I could not say, 'No, that voice [the slave trader's] can't be in there': it disturbed me profoundly, it still does, but so it goes. There were things that came out of the text, phrases like 'nig, nig, nog,' . . . that made me feel nauseous as they would surface."[29]

As I remarked earlier, the structure of the book is composite and multivocal. Before entering the poem per se, the reader peruses a series of dedications: "For Lord Yeates, Ti Miss Maam, & the many, many others. Also for Kudakwashe" (*Zong!,* v). This homage to a composite collective made of the Irish "sea poet" Yeats; a possibly intimate acquaintance, "Ti Miss Maam" (which could evoke all the unnamed "mammies"); an unnamed collective, "the many, many others"; and "Kudakwashe," a Bantu name meaning "will of God." The reader then discovers an epigraph by Dylan Thomas about sinking in the sea and ensuing rising hope, and another from Shakespeare's *Hamlet,* evoking a "time out of joint," announcing the skewed temporality of *Zong!* After the acknowledgments comes the poem per se itself, divided into six fragments titled with five Latin words and one final, Yoruba word: "Os," "Sal," "Ventus," "Ratio," "Ferrum," and "Ebora," meaning, respectively, "Bone," "Salt," "Wind," "Reason," "Iron," and "Underwater Spirits." The Latin words indicate the poems' grounding in the masculine and Western dominating language of the law. The Yoruba word opens up the poem onto a West African sacred horizon.

Immediately after the poem per se comes a glossary, which lists words from the poem in various European, Middle Eastern, and African languages present in the slave trade and in legal discourse such as Arabic, French, Latin, Portuguese, Shona, and Yoruba. The lexicographic order of the document appears as a surprise after the chaos of the poem per se, as if a navigation map were usable in the midst of these troubled seas and memories. The "Manifest," which immediately follows, is puzzling at best. It is organized in discrete columns listing "African Groups and Languages," Animals," "Body Parts," "Crew," "Food and Drink," "Nature," and "Women Who Wait." The categories indicate a failure of itemization and the impossibility of containing uncontainable dynamic beings such as "Women Who Wait." The attempt at Aristotelian categorization precisely there to point to the failure of categorization reminds us of Argentinian writer Jorge Luis Borges's whimsical categories in *The Book of Imaginary Beings,* a whimsical zoological treatise that juxtaposes real and imaginary beings, static encyclopedic definitions of arrested beings, and entries defined not by their being but, rather, by their actions or conditions. For instance, "The Gnomes," "The Dragon," "The A Bao A Qu," "Animals That Live in the Mirror," "An Animal Dreamed by Kafka," "The Pelican," and "The Bird That Makes the Rain" populate Borges's fanciful zoo. Philip's manifest goes beyond a theoretical criticism of Aristotelian categories. Looking like ledgers used to list humans on board ships or on plantations, Philip points to the absurdity—if not the crime—of itemizing humans into accounting lists ("Women Who Wait": "Ans, Clara, Claire, Eva, Eve") and juxtaposing them with lists of consumable goods ("Food & Drink"; "ale, bear, bread, carp, cider"). I have already analyzed in depth the "Notanda," (plural form of the Latin word *notandum,* meaning "things to be noted," to be remembered, akin to memorandum), in which Philip unveils her methodology and motivations for writing *Zong!* Its position between the material created by Philip and Boateng and the two-page transcript of the *Gregson v. Gilbert* court case serves as a buffer zone. This juxtaposition of varied texts (poem, theory, court case) responds not only to a principle of *bricolage* in the absence of sufficient historical records, but also to the imperative of allying different discourses in order to approach the truth of the experience. In her 1989 "Discourse on the Logic of Language" (*She Tries Her Tongue,* 29–33), Philip had already used this method of creative juxtaposition of legal, medical, colonial discourses, and poetry, crowding the poem's pages vertically and horizontally in order to tackle a pain-struck mother-child relationship in enslavement. "Discourse" already contained in seeds the method and story of the long poem *Zong!*

The relation between the aforementioned sections is not only successive but also intrinsic. Indeed, the poem per se is built entirely of words, syllables, or letters found in the two-page court transcript, at times meaningful words or phrases, at times nonsensical. Like Glissant's poetry as pottery, Philip sculpts the words, the matter, the dough of the court case into sounds, words, and phrases, forming new assemblages. She explains:

"The text, the reported case—is a matrix—a mother document. . . . I devise a dictionary with a list of each of the 'mother' words followed by the words contained in that particular word—for instance, apprehension yields hen, sion, pare, and pear, to list a few possibilities. . . . I think of these poems as the flesh—the earlier 26 poems are the bones" (200). She brings the monolingual English words of the case into a Babel multilingualism of Arabic, Dutch, Fon, French, Greek, Hebrew, Italian, Latin, Portuguese, Spanish, Shona, Twi, West African Patois, and Yoruba. Beyond this linguistic diversity, letters form elementary prelinguistic sounds: "grunts, plosives . . . is this perhaps, how language might have sounded at the beginning of time?" (*Zong!,* 205). Philip asks. This prelinguistic realm is very close to Glissant's sacred original poem made out of grunts, snarls, and roars introduced at the beginning of *Philosophie de la Relation:* "The frenzy of the original *hahr-hahr*" (14) announcing the birth of a prelingual and primeval sacred (11). To take one example, the first page of the poem per se resembles the white beach of a page where shards of words, letters, lost languages, have scattered like pieces of a shipwreck ("goo," "g," "ne," "ah," "a," "wa," "d," "ter," etc.). Philip calls it a "language of grunt and groan, of moan and stutter—this language of pure sound fragmented and broken by history. This language of the limp and the wound" (*Zong!,* 205). Paradoxically, this breaking up of language to its prehuman sounds marks the emergence of a poem written under the mark of the sacred by Philip and her coauthor, Setaey Adamu Boateng, the hallowed voice of the drowned ancestors.

I have asked students and various family members to read this first page out loud. As a witness of their utterance, a new text, that which is formed on their face, emerges. It is a text of puzzlement, hesitation, playfulness, impatience, surprise, awe, frustration, revealed through their grimacing, stumbling, stuttering, or slipping through the words. It is first and foremost an affective reading, more than a rational one. Perhaps the most moving and meaningful reading was my eight-year old son who accepted the initial sequence of repetitions and gaps—"w w w," "w," "a w," "w a t," "er"—with the least surprise. On his face, eyes, and lips surfaced a submarine language, the first babbling sounds of an infant entering the realm of language. The series of "w's" moved, quite smoothly, from the elemental sounds to the word "water," which is, of course, the realm of the poem. Water is also the first desired object of the enslaved, who, as *Zong!* tells us, were dying of thirst: water. Water represents both the threat of an enormous death and the basic condition of survival. This interpretation read from my child's lips is only one of many

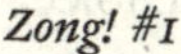

Zong! #1

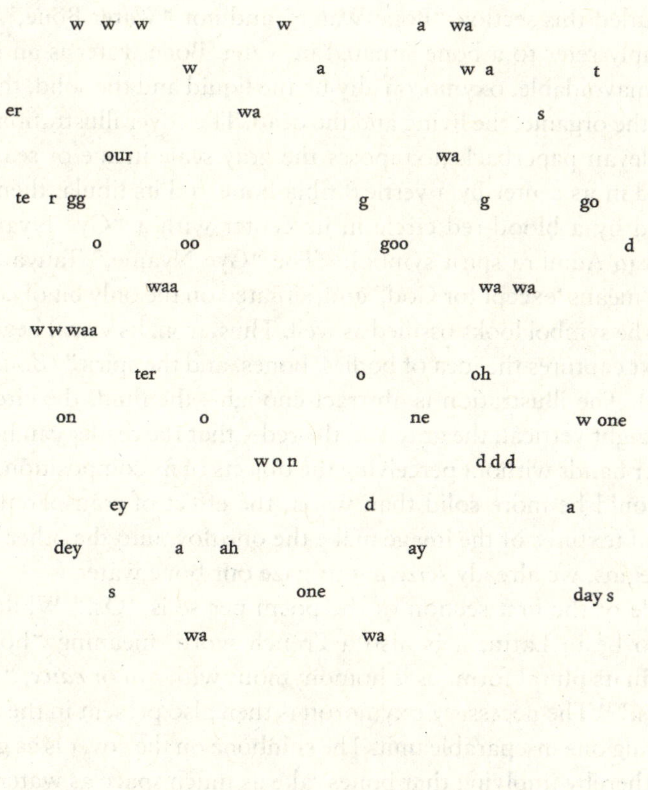

w w w w a wa
w a w a t
er wa s
our wa
te r gg g g go
o oo goo d
waa wa wa
w w waa
ter o oh
on o ne w one
won d d d
ey d a
dey a ah ay
s one day s
wa wa

Masuz Zuwena Ogunsheye Ziyad Ogwambi Keturah

3

M. NourbeSe Philip, *Zong!,* p. 3. (© M. NourbeSe Philip, courtesy of the author and of Wesleyan University Press)

valid ones since he, like all practitioners of the Latin alphabet, read from left to right and top to bottom. However, nothing indicates that *Zong!* should be read in that order. The reader is dumped there with no map, like the captives of Glissant's "Open Boat," who enter a river-sea with only one middle and no sides: "The banks of the river have vanished on both sides of the boat. What kind of river, then, has no middle?" (*Poetics,* 7). A reading from bottom to top would present the disintegration of language from words to monosyllables, to sounds, grunts, and sighs. According to the sense of the reading, which is open to the readers' choice, we can either move from birth to survival, or from articulate language to the disintegration of being.

I have titled this section "Bone Water" and not "Water Bone," which would simply refer to a bone situated in water. Bone water is an impossible, yet unavoidable, oxymoron allying the liquid and the solid, the inorganic and the organic, the living and the dead. The cover illustration of the 2008 Wesleyan paperback juxtaposes the gray-scale image of sea waves interrupted in its center by a vertical tibia bone and its fibula, themselves interrupted by a blood-red circle in its center with a "Gye Nyame," a West African Adinkra spirit symbol.[30] The "Gye Nyame," Tanya Shields explains, "means 'except for God,' and, situated on the only bit of color on the cover, the symbol looks ossified as well. Thus, from its visual beginning, Philip's text captures the idea of bodies, bones, and the spirit" (*Bodies and Bones,* 33). The illustration is abstract enough—the fluid, the circle, the almost straight vertical; the gray and the red—that the reader can hold the book in her hands without perceiving the objects of its composition. While a bone should be more solid than water, the effect of transparency and marriage of textures of the image make the one flow into the other. Before the text begins, we already seize in our gaze our bone water.

The title of the first section of the poem per se is "Os." While "Os" appears to be in Latin, it is also a French word, meaning "bone" or "bones." In its plural form, *os* is homonymous with *eau* or *eaux,* "water" or "waters."[31] The necessary oxymoron is then also present in the section title, forming one inseparable unit. The shinbone on the cover is as gigantic as water, thereby implying that bones take as much space as water in our imagination of the drowned. The quest for bones is ubiquitous in water deaths or in mass graves. Bones are iconic in Tanya Shields's *Bodies and Bones,* in which she explains, "the bones of the enslaved Africans at the bottom of the Atlantic constantly cause me to consider the lack of value placed on and in black lives. Bones are everywhere" (4). Shields also reminds us that skeletons form a "fundamental human connection" (4).

The cover image of *Zong!,* as well as the disjointed words and syllables composing the poem per se, present this bygone skeletal structure as shards of fragmented bodies. These fragments lying around can be seen as the passive state resulting from the literal cutting up and objectification of humans under the action of slave traders. However, it is first and foremost a subjective act of revenge. "One approach," Philip explains, "was literally to cut up the text and just pick words randomly . . . most similar to the activity of the random picking of African slaves—selected randomly then thrown together, hoping that something would come of it—that they would produce something" (193). What is being murdered and cut up is the legal report of the Zong case, which fails to do justice to the murdered humans: "I murder the text, literally cut it into pieces, castrating verbs, suffocating adjectives, murdering nouns, throwing articles, prepositions, conjunctions overboard, jettisoning adverbs: I separate subject from verb, verb from object—create semantic mayhem, until my hands bloodied, from so much killing and cutting, reach into the stinking, eviscerated innards, and like some seer, sangoma, or prophet who, having sacrificed an animal for signs and portents of new life, or simply life, reads the untold story that tells itself by not telling" (193–94).

What appears first and foremost is the expression of subjectivity with the repetition of the "I" of the poet ("I mutilate," "I murder," "I separate"). The poet turns murderer and torturer in this act of revenge displaced upon a text. How can such a repetition of violence avoid the endless cycle of violence in the tortured-torturer relationship? Philip's act avoids this cycle by operating two types of transubstantiation. First of all, the revenge is displaced onto words, not real bodies, which, in itself, is not an act punishable by law. The author's hands are figuratively, and not literally, bloodied. She takes her revenge from the literal to the metaphorical, from the domain of the law to that of poetry. While the poetic acts rests on violence, it does not maim living beings. It also differs from catharsis since the author (and arguably her readers) are not experiencing a spectacle of violence, but committing violence through their poetic action, their *poiesis.* Another transubstantiation is that of the poet into a prophet. The poet turns *sangoma,* a healer and a seer in Zulu communities. Revenge leads not to endless violence but turns its gaze toward a future and attains a sacred phase of healing and a survival of life.

From a sacred perspective, the oxymoron of bone and water fuses two disparate, yet complementary, funerary practices: the tomb and the wake, the fixed and the performative. The legal transcript is, for Philip, "the tombstone, the one public marker of the murder of those Africans on board the *Zong,* locating it in a specific time and place. It is a public monument, a textual monument marking their murder and their existence, their small histories that ended so tragically" (194). The case, with its structured, articulated, and whole frame is thus the skeleton, the geometric coffin, or the hard grave. But such a fixed, dialectical, and rigid monument is not enough, since the tragic story of these many lost bodies and bones cannot be seized. "Re-reading [Derrida's] *Specters of Marx,*" Philip indicates, "confirmed me in my earlier feeling that *Zong!* is a wake.

It is a work that employs memory in the service of mourning" (202). The poem per se is to the *Gregson v. Gilbert* case transcription what the wake performance is to the rigid tomb.

As critic Almas Khan argues, *Zong!* is close to the performative, oral, feminine, genre of the lamentation: "I would thus dub *Zong!* an experiential text in that it is felt more readily than it is described linguistically, like many lamentations" ("Poetic Justice," 19). Building on Jahan Ramazani's theories of the elegy, Khan explains that, formally, *Zong!*, with its "irregularities of meter and rhyme (if present at all), jarring juxtapositions, searing ironies, elisions, fragments, multiple languages and voices" (20) is an anti-elegy. Moreover, he adds that "'the elegy is historically a form written by men and about men' [quoting Patricia Saunders, *Lamentations and Modernity,* 51) . . . Contrastingly, 'the lamentation [is] composed by women and expressive of their experience' (quoting David Kennedy, *Elegy,* 13). Indeed, Philip explains that *Zong!* is akin to musical performance: "Many is the time in the writing of this essay when my fingers would hit an S rather than a Z in typing *Zong:* with the exception of one letter the two words are identical; if said quickly enough they sound the same" (207). Philip concludes her "Notanda" with her association of *Zong!* with a song that is decidedly feminine and African: "Why the exclamation mark after *Zong!*? *Zong!* is chant! Shout! And ululation! . . . *Zong!* is Song! And Song is what has kept the soul of the African intact when they 'want(ed) water . . . sustenance . . . preservation'" (207). The high-pitched, loud, oscillating, wavering, trilling ululation is the sacred utterance of women in Africa, the Middle East, and Asia who accompany a wedding or a funeral procession.

Philip's poem is a song "full of sound and fury," to quote Faulkner via Shakespeare. Indeed, we hear *Zong!* as much as we read it. We hear its sound and fury as much as its silences as in its loud thrills. Sharpe emphasizes the engagement of hearing in our experience of the poem: "Listening to the poem elicits the uncanny sounds of those who were lost at sea. The experience of hearing "Zong! #1" when compared to seeing it on the page, is to hear the silences in the legal case filled with ghostly sounds from the past. . . . When vocalized, a breaking up of the words . . . creates a linguistic stutter that becomes a plea, a gurgle, a chatter and moan" (Sharpe, Jenny, "The Archive," 475). Surprisingly, in her own performance of *Zong!*, Philip, while making silences and stutters evident on the page by marking breaks between words, also smooths out some of edges. Most notably, her voice moves from the text above the dividing line and the names under the line back to the text above without marking a break. For instance, her performance of "Zong! #14" goes as follows: "Master and mariners Adunni

Akanni Akanbi Alade Alayande the this the that the frenzy," nonmarking the dividing line between above water and anba dlo. It is as if her oral performance provides an additional dimension to her written word, reestablishing a fluidity between the separation of above and below, between the living and the dead. Her quiet, grave, and steady tempo is that of a commemorative ceremony in which the names of the dead would be read, heard, and inscribed in the memory of utterer and listeners.

Philip invites us to *see* the poem as much as *read* and *hear* it. She claims that her work is akin to that of painters and sculptors. This emphasis on seeing places her in a long tradition of visual poetry, which blurs the line between writing and drawing, writing and painting, writing and sculpting. I will not attempt to summarize the long history of typographic, visual, or "concrete poetry," but will nevertheless highlight formal and thematic resemblances between Philip and other visual poets. Critics have pointed to the resemblance between *Zong!* and the 1897 poem "Un coup de dés jamais n'abolira le hasard" (A Throw of the Dice Will Never Abolish Chance) by French poet Stéphane Mallarmé. Indeed, the two poems share a striking resemblance. Visual poetry is steeped in the ancient tradition of calligraphy, from the Greek "beautiful letters," which uses typographical marks to paint using the space on the page to imitate an object. Ante-surrealist Polish-French poet Guillaume Apollinaire named his 1918 collection of visual poems after his own neologism of "calligrammes." Perhaps the most emblematic is Apollinaire's WWI poem expressing the French resistance to German troops in his "Tour Eiffel." While both Apollinaire and Philip's poems oppose a visual aesthetic construction to a political and human tragedy, there is no such erection of a monumental Eiffel Tower in *Zong!,* no unifying symbol of a community, but, rather, a poetics of fragments and wreckage, an antimonument.

My question, then, is, How do we read wreckage? How can we make sense out of a story that cannot be told, yet cannot not be told? How do we maintain memorial and ethical imperatives in the shipwreck of language? Is *Zong!* a linguistic failure? I think not. As Philip claims, "The resulting abbreviated, disjunctive, almost non-sensical style of the poem demands a corresponding effort on the part of the reader 'to make sense' of an event that eludes understanding, perhaps permanently" (*Zong!,* 198). The reader, a "more than two hundred year old . . . echo" of the disoriented terrified Africans on board of the Zong (198), needs a boating map (*boating* is one letter away from *Boateng,* coauthor of *Zong!*). My sea map, or reading method, of the unreadable poem per se goes as such. I don't pretend that it's the only possible one but one that helps me make some sense of the apparent chaos or shipwreck, one that replies to the "corresponding effort on the part of the 'reader' to 'make sense' of an event that eludes understanding, perhaps permanently" (198). My method follows some linearity inasmuch as I navigate the poem following the section headings that appear as stable rocks in the poem currents ("Os," "Ventus," etc.). From there, it becomes combinatory. One of the challenges of the visual poem is that we are asked to see structures as much as to read words. In each section, I will therefore zoom out, to identify patterns of meaning or dismemberments on the page, skeletal structure or broken bones, and zoom in to see or read details—bodies, limbs, organs, molecular units. Some of the books lead to much more interpretation than others since the reading of such an open book would be infinite, and since some of the books speak more to the topic of water and rituals. Hence, I call on at "Os," Ventus," "Ferrum," and "Ebora," leaving "Dicta," "Sal," "Ratio," to other navigators. I bring with me, like all readers, my own expertise and disabilities. While I speak French, I do not speak Fon. This simple fact will make me see—and not see—patterns that are transparent to some and opaque to others.

The first twenty-six poems of the book, collectively titled "Os," are, for Philip, the "bones" of the poem, while the others are its "flesh" (200). Taking a step back to see the poems, we begin to make sense out of the apparent randomness of somewhat horizontal fragments. "Zong! #1" (3–4) fills up the entirety of the page with blocks of words and syllables not aligned in any cohesive way. The pages looks like an archipelago, with visible islands highlighting the white of the page that becomes its oceanic site. In Zong! #s 2, 3, and 4 (5–7), words and verses stand up in more vertical objects. These pages evoke the resistance of the living and the necessity of an ethical and legal imperative. Zong! # 4, for instance, places vertically, yet, in an offset way, the following words:

this is
not was
or
should be
this be
not
should be
this
should
not
be. (*Zong!*, 7)

The text as a standing figure is reminiscent of a similar technique used by Martinican poet Aimé Césaire in his *Notebook of a Return to the Native Land.* Similarly, his mostly horizontal text stands up as he evokes the revolt of slaves on the ship (""Standing / and / free," 48). Like the humans holding hand in the circle of Taylor's "Vicissitudes" (see chapter 4), words and letters provide a ring around a sea of silence in the main part of "Zong! #5" (9–13). "Zong! #9," "Zong! #10," "Zong! #11" (17–20), "Zong! #18" (31–32), and "Zong! #24" (41–42) are organized in parallel columns like those of a ship or plantation ledger listing the enslaved humans among other economic possessions. In these poems, numerous words and phrases emerge from economic and legal discourses, such as the word "means" (31–32) or "evidence" (41). The last poem of "Os," "Zong! #26" (45), is a dense paragraph like a compact rock. The thirteen-line block alternates various words and phrases systematically with "was" without punctuation marks: "was the seas was the costs was the could was the would was the policy was the loss . . ." (*Zong!,* 45). The regular recurrence of "was" is left for the reader to interpret. It can either relegate the Zong event in a gone past, or as the legal reference to an evidence, leading us either to oblivion, or to justice. "While the word placement, at first sight, appears chaotic, this analysis of what we *see* in "Os" demonstrates that there is an order, or rather, a series of imperatives at work in the poem. The meaningful visual objects of an archipelago, a standing figure, a ring, columns, a rock, show that the poet, too, is writing disaster, as disaster writes.

Let us now zoom in on a particular section of "Os." Every other verse of "Zong! #24" (41) is the verb "is." The last section of page 42 lists nouns all accompanied with "is." From this passage loaded with legal lexicon ("evidence," "law," "trial," "the case," "murder," "ground," "justice") resurges an ontology marked by the systematic recurrence of "is," giving back to humans and their lands their very being from which law attempted to strip them

jamaica is
tobago is
islands is
the case is
murder is
justice is
the ground is
africa is.

Despite this long and systematic list, the poem ends with a sharp contrast marking the end, the death, the mourning of enslaved Africans. The regular column ends after a blank space, with two word-verses offset respectively to the right and left of the column: "negroes / was." However, this low point, placed at the bottom of the page as if at the bottom of the sea and memory, is not the last word on the assertion of being. It recurs again strongly, and in Latin, the language of law, in a section of the poem "Ratio":

soul *sum* *sum sum sum* i am
sum i am i am *sum* sum. (*Zong!*, 117)

The title "Ratio," as in ration or reason, reminds us of Descartes's assertion of being, "Cogito, ergo sum." However, reason, too closely associated with rational thinking and economic thinking that provided ground for enslaving other humans, leaves way to the soul, which is: "Soul sum." Soul, the immaterial essence, the animating principle of life, the spiritual principle, is what escapes rational economic thinking and the annihilation of being. While the italicized "*sum*" defines it as foreign—more precisely, as Latin—the absence of capitalization in "sum" marks it as an English word, synonymous with amount or calculation, trapping yet again the being of the enslaved in their economic reduction to thinghood. While this ontological scream can potentially be seen, read, and heard, it is lost in a sea of words (*Zong!*, 117) and could easily go unnoticed, like a message in a bottle.

"Ventus" (77–98) begins with an epigraph from Thomas More: "The poem is a detective and the detective a poet" (78). I took this advice seriously and began looking for evidence in the shards of words apparently scattered by the wind (*ventus* in Latin). Looking for units of meanings, pencil in hand, I approached "Ventus" like the word search puzzle it strongly resembles. I found, for instance, the following units of meaning: "song le / *sang el* / *le sang*" (79); "tes *moi* / *je* am he / am she" (84); "l eau / *omi* / water / *omi omi* under" (84). No doubt did I see units that became specifically visible to a French speaker, and no doubt Yoruba or Portuguese speakers will see countless other multilingual combinations according to the language they speak or the life they live. My own interactive, self-influenced evidence made me draw the following conclusions: song (*Zong!*) appears where there is violence and where there is a lack (song is connected to *sang*, or blood) and to *sans* (homophonic of *sang*, "without"). I understood that there is a shared multilingual struggle with equivocal pronouns where subjects, objects, feminine, masculine are forcibly detached from their humans, as in the slave trade erasing subjectivity and sexual marker.[32] The lines "tes *moi* / *je* am he / am she" (84) represent what I call an ontological knot: a place where subjectivity happens in compound of linguistic units yet to be attached to a subject. I also understood that multilingualism allows for a fluid, continuous circulation of meaning since the word "water" flows in at least three languages and makes music

omi
omi
l eau
l eau
water clair
the
sound
of the oud
rouse s me. (82)

L'eau means water in French; *omi,* as the glossary indicates, means water in Yoruba (184). In addition, *Omi*—and this is not specified in the glossary, but brought back through my meager knowledge of Arabic—means "my mother," "mamma."

Philip reveals that one of the most painful moments of her research (her quest) was her reading a copy of the slaves' record of those aboard the Zong ship. In a document listing mostly "negroe man" and "negroe woman," one exception caught her attention: "'Negroe girl (meagre).' There are many 'meagre' girls, no 'meagre boys. This description leaves me shaken—I want to weep" (194). The slight adjective allows the imagination to bring back to memory a human being, a vulnerable little girl at that, in a sea of dehumanized, depersonalized humans-turned-items. I had a similar feeling of sharp pain and persistent nausea, when I read in French the word "p tit mort":

her
mort
her
p tit mort. (84)

"Le petit mort" could translate as "the little dead child," probably a boy since a "little dead girl" would be "la petite morte." In French, the subject is more able to disappear since grammar does not require use of the subject. The adjective does the trick. "p tit" (instead of the grammatical form petit) refers to an intimate, familiar language, that of a mother, the "her" of the segment, for instance, for her child. The phrase recurs throughout the poem like a haunting. In the last book, "Ebora," the "p'ti mort" reappears frequently: "le p'tit mort / sense of mortality" (176); "le mort / le p'tit mort" (177); "le p'tit mort" (written over the word "mère"—mother—perhaps although not fully legible; 178). "Le p'tit mort" constitutes my own personal haunting: one that will remain unseen to many other readers, like so many drowned humans remain unseen, yet undeniably there.

"Ferrum" is built as a dense archipelagic zone in which the words become increasingly complex and illegible with the multiplication of fonts and letter rocks of impenetrable meaning: "rt tend the m" (144); "nce of g" (145); "urs ru / n to groù / te o" (148). "Ferrum" ends, however, with a concrete poem in the form of a literal isosceles triangle (with two equal legs). The triangle, with its base above, resembles a boat floating above water, in equilibrium. The words composing the triangle are proper names written in an elegant antiquated cursive. The African names—"Bektemba . . . Nuru Okunade Dolap Moya . . . Ade"—resume the list that had drowned into invisibility at the end of the book "Os." The names resurface in the text, but are still locked up in the triangular hold of the slave ship or in the confines of the triangular trade. They dwell in the ambivalent place of rebirth and death that the slave ship is, as C. L. R. James and Glissant have showed.[33]

While *ferrum,* the iron, can refer to an instrument of torture, it is also the signature material of Ogun, blacksmith god of war and iron in the Dahomey, Yoruba, Fon, and, ultimately, Vodun religions. The triangle, associated with the title of the book "Ferrum," thus marks a phase of solidity and construction, of transformation of metals, of earth and fire. One of the *vèvès,* or symbols, of the *lwa* Ogun Feraille or Ogu Feray has as its base the same isosceles triangle, which can also represent an axe blade. "Ferrum" leaves its readers in the ambivalence between the tortured and the godly, the maimed subject and the maker of iron, the erasure of the past and the poiesis—the making—at the heart of poetry. Philip herself becomes the blacksmith Ogun.

Significantly, I cannot find on my keyboard the typographical marks under the letters "e" and "o" in "Ebora," the last book of *Zong!,* which indicates the otherness of the word, the presence of a language that cannot easily be seized by our Western technology. "Ebora," the only book title in a language other than Latin in *Zong!,* guides us into a realm that has reached back to sacred waters and to West Africa. *Ebora,* the "Glossary" indicates, means "underwater spirits" in Yoruba (184). The letters and words contained in the last book are literally washed out like faint aquarelle paint. The letters, while still legible for the most part,

Ogu Feray, Vèvè, drawn by Zoë Wakefield.

have entered a process of erasure, reinforced by the presence of the verb "erase" in the section: "erase this"; "erase me" (181).

In his remarkable *Shipwreck Modernity,* Steve Mentz comments on the interaction of "wet" and "dry" narratives in literary accounts of shipwrecks: "The poetics of shipwreck thus uses its two distinctive modes, the wet and the dry, to represent the subjective experience of historical change. Wet narratives emphasize disorder, disorientation, and rupture; they narrate experiences in which the casual ways of doing things get broken or fragmented. . . . But narrative cannot bear absolute immersion for long, and nearly all shipwreck stories also contain a dry countermovement that attempts to make sense and meaning out of disaster" (11). For Mentz, a dry (organized, cohesive, nonchaotic) narrative must prevail in order to counteract the force of the shipwreck writing itself and its introduction of chaos into our words and worlds. This is the phase of the disaster writing itself in Blanchot. However, while herown shipwreck narrative undeniably includes an interaction between the wet and the dry, Philip comes to an altogether opposite conclusion. Her last book ends with the prevalence of wet letters and exhausts itself (without exactly ending) in the middle of a sea of letters with no end and no beginning, with no head or tail. Is it then the acknowledgment of the impossibility of mastering the collective trauma of the slave trade? Rather, in her logic of relinquishing authority, the acknowledgment of humans' vulnerability and of being in fragments with worlds as multiple as the languages and shards of language present in *Zong!,* staying wet, staying watery is our best chance at survival and life in nonhierarchical categories. *Zong!* is an example of Relation according to Glissant, based on the same principles of nonhierarchical categories, opening in uncountable directions, continuous despite cuttings, unexpected connections, vulnerability, and coliving in fragments. *Zong!* is a performance of a Glissantian relational sacred, which defies an Aristotelian-based categorical logic that arbitrarily trapped a section of a spectrum of humanity in an airtight cell, relegating it to thinghood.

Like the markings on Glissant's grave—or on any aging grave, for that matter—the letters in "Ebora" are typed over others, turning the poem into a palimpsest, an illegible yet undeniable presence-absence, in which inscriptions of different times complete and obscure one another. A sharp sense of urgency surfaces with the multiplication of the word "os" (bones) and its anagrammatic offspring "sos": "sos sos sos," "os / *os,*" "save us *os,*" "bone souls," "water parts" (177). The oxymoron introduced at the beginning of this section, "bone water," is repeated here in the dissolving of bone in the immaterial soul and the solidifying of water in "water parts." Words clashing sometimes give way to happenstance multilingual neologisms such as "*os*mortality" and "*os*aces" (182). "Os mortality" collides mortality and bones (water). "Osaces," derives from the word *os* (bones) and evokes the word *rosace* (a rose motif), with its aesthetic sense of a symmetrical flowery motif on stained glass, and its medical sense of the pathology of skin rashes ("rosacea"), leaving us yet again in this ambivalence place between art and pain.

The last page of the poem per se is the most illegible, because of its increasing visual cacophony of words. If we consider the text as painting, it becomes a blurred abstraction, a blotch of a brushstroke, like in J. M. W. Turner's *Slave Ship: Slavers Throwing Overboard Dead and Dying—Typphon Coming On* that Ian Baucom has so convincingly interpreted.[34] Some words I can distinguish, in Philip's painterly letters, is "take every thing" [written over] / *cum grana* [illegible] / with a grain of salt" (182). This is what I see as the last significant lesson of the poem—and I insist on the subjectivity of my choice, since there cannot be one final reading of "a language of the limp and wound" that can (or cannot) be read from left to right, right to left, transversally, stutteringly, compulsively, emotionally, tearfully, nauseously, and angrily. "Take everything with a grain of salt" refers to the instability of a story, its link to subjectivity, doubt, gaps in knowledge, and the necessity of positive skepticism, or what Glissant would call "opacity" (*Poetics,* 189–93).

The phrase also refers to salt, which can make our food taste better. Metaphorically, can salt make the unimaginable horror of the violence of slave traders onto the enslaved go down more easily? In the context of

Zong!, and more generally water deaths, the grain of salt means thirst, like in Coleridge's proverbial "Rime of the Ancient Mariner": "Water, water, every where / Nor any drop to drink." The use of the Latin phrase "cum grano," under Philip's pen, indicates the manifestation of legal language. It may also refer to the registered origin of the phrase "taking with a grain of salt" by Pliny the Elder—"cum grano salis"—which provides an antidote or prophylactic against poison.[35] In this case, *Zong!* itself may be the recipe enhanced with a grain of salt that may lessen the poison of the slave trade and its mass murders. Salt is also a shared substance between seawater and human blood. "Human blood is salty," Sharpe points out, "and sodium . . . has a residence time of 260 million years" (*In the Wake,* 41). Thus, for Sharpe, the chemical is a constant reminder of the presence of black people, in the "residence time of the wake," in the nowness of the sea, of the world. In Ward's novel *Sing, Unburied, Sing,* salt is at once a corrosive destructive substance and a nourishing sacred ingredient, when mixed with water and femininity: "The tears and the ocean and the blood could burn a whole through the nose. The saltwater woman, the woman Leonie crawls toward over the rocks as she says, 'Mama, Mama'" (*Sing,* 244–45). It is also the substance of Mami Wata, "Yemayá, the goddess of the ocean and salt water . . . her arms all the life-giving waters of the world" (*Sing,* 159). Salt, let's not forget, is the purifying ingredient that one puts on her finger and places on her tongue before a ceremony. This association to sacredness is reinforced in *Zong!* with the placement of the word "vedic"—Hinduism rituals—immediately below the expression "grain of salt." *Zong!,* beyond its function as tomb *and* performance, conveys us to a collective ceremonial of mourning and purification, by putting a grain of salt on our tongue, that awakens us to consciousness.[36] We, writers, activists, and humans faced with ongoing massive earth-wide, sea-wide catastrophes, will need more than one grain of salt to kindle our eyes, consciousness, and action.

Epilogue

porque soy agua
porque estoy contaminada
y contamino a las amistades
dulces y blancas

(because i am water,
Because i am contaminated
And i contaminate white and sweet
Friends).

—Raquel Salas Rivera, "el obrero se limita a producir el valor de su fuerza de trabajo"

Because you,
You are precious cargo, Marwan . . .
How I pray the sea knows this.

—Khaled Hosseini, *Sea Prayer*

THE AESTHETIC creations featured in *Water Graves* dwell in the deep time and extended space of world catastrophes. Pairing images from Katrina and Maafa with reflections on earlier shipwrecks and the Great Flood not only emphasizes the spiraled repetition of the past, but also announces floods to come. The navigation between Kongo cosmogony, the Judeo-Christian Bible, Vaudou religion, creolized Caribbean and American religious rites, and idiosyncratic and secular forms of honoring the dead point not to the necessity of a given religion, but to the universally shared need for the sacred. Chamoiseau has called the latter type "un sacré profane, un sacré du vivant" (A profane sacred, a sacred of the living; "Caribbean Discourses," roundtable, n.p.).

This book's poetic and artistic corpus prophesized the ferocious 2017 hurricane squad of Harvey, Irma, José, María, Nate, and the aptly named Ophelia, which has caused devastating damage to Texas, St. Martin, the Virgin Islands, Cuba, Dominica, and faraway Ireland and continue to shape networks for a transoceanic consciousness.[1] Puerto Rico's María is an amplified reminder of New Orleans's Katrina, with five thousand victims and ongoing structural issues that remain unfixed.[2] Recent hurricanes continue to reveal the vulnerability of the land, and, above all, the governmental neglect toward citizens relegated to a second or third class, or to a state of noncitizenship, because of their race, ethnicity, language, culture, or geographical position in "isolated" islands.[3]

The cloak of water unritual has planetary dimensions. The drowned of the Gulf of Mexico, the Caribbean Sea, and the Atlantic Ocean form an underwater nation with the "boat people" of the Pacific, with East Indian indentured workers forced into an exiling taboo for crossing the *Kala Pani* or "black waters" of the Indian Ocean, and with many other seafarers.[4] Rohingya Muslims from Bangladesh and Myanmar are similarly struggling in the Indonesian seas. Sharply in our consciousness, the lethal abyss of the Caribbean resonates with the Mediterranean. Massimo Sestini, similar to Glissant in his "Open Boat," captured the despair of sea crossers in his aerial photograph of an open boat, ready to burst with the vulnerability of humans.[5] The frame of the Bergamese ship, which can barely contain its human cargo so dangerously sitting on the rails, lets us imagine, if we can, myriad other dead bodies abyssed in the sea. Barthes's *punctum* is the single lifesaver: a lamentable tire, which may save one of the hundreds of passengers. The hands and eyes plead the sky, the helicopter, and, therefore, us. The arrow-like shape of the boat ironically contrasts with the stagnation of human bodies piled up on the ship, and with the vertical fall toward the bottom of the sea of the drowned, past and future. The luminous navy blue of the sea contrasting with the frank white wake of the ship and the magenta, royal blue, orange, yellow, blue, pink, or green of the migrants' t-shirts offers, counterpoint-wise, the urgency of the humanitarian crisis. The light and dark skins of the women, men, and children indicate the opposite of a successful intercultural mixing. Here, a multinational identity, a whole humanity, is implied (the viewers) and in danger (the passengers).

As Chamoiseau vividly claims, "The Africans' continent at the bottom of the Atlantic . . . meets with a stunned exactness its double in the Mediterranean" (*Frères migrants,* 24–25). The UN reported that in June 2018 alone one out of seven humans who attempted to cross the Mediterranean lost their lives at sea, a significant increase since 2017, when the percentage, already tragic, was one out of thirty-eight.[6] The lives lost to the waters of the Gulf of Mexico, the Western Atlantic, and the Caribbean Sea tragically resonate with those of African and Middle Eastern asylum- or security-seekers drowning by the thousands in the underwater cemetery of the Mediterranean and Eastern Atlantic to reach Fortress Europe. Grim circuits are established between the Caribbean Sea and the Mediterranean. In *Poetics of Relation,* Glissant famously, if schematically, contrasts the Mediterranean Sea and the Caribbean Sea as, respectively, centrifugal and centripetal, concentric and diffracting (33). The movement that defines them both in our Now is decidedly downward. The abyss of the drowned of the Middle Passage of Glissant's "Open Boat" diverges little from the Mediterranean underwater grave. Neither concentric, nor openly, ethically eccentric, the Mediterranean is now characterized by a swallowing vortex. Its pull is "down, down, down," to paraphrase George Washington Cable, who, in "Belles Demoiselles Plantation," described as such the movement of another water grave, the "merciless, unfathomable . . . Mississippi" (Cable, *Old Creole Tales,* 142).

Caribbean scholars, poets, and artists thus find themselves drawn to the Mediterranean and Eastern Atlantic, and reciprocally. In *Sartorius,* Glissant evokes the outpouring of corpses that "today . . . reach us through mud and waters, who are always amongst the mass of the destitute and the abandoned" (57). Chamoiseau's *Frères migrants* extends to the Mediterranean what our artists of the unritual extend to the greater Caribbean. The "Déclaration des poètes," an appendix to *Frères migrants* composed of sixteen articles, calls for the ethico-political need to acknowledge the lives and deaths of tragic sea wayfarers as worthy and sacred: "The poets declare that the entire Mediterranean is henceforth the Place of homage to those who perished there" ("Article Thirteen," 135).

Italian social theorist Alessandro dal Lago mixes rare historical evidence, the imagination of the abyss, and poetry (Glissant's triple alliance) to reconstruct the narrative of the 2005 fatal journey of young Senegalese migrants, whose rickety canoe drifted off at sea instead of reaching the intended Canary Islands. Maritime currents made the pitiful boat drift away to the coast of Barbados, where the eleven remaining bodies were "virtually mummified from the sun and salt spray" ("Watery Graves," 1). The sea currents, tragically repeating the journey of the triangular trade from the shores of Africa to the Caribbean, reaffirms the historical depth of the unritual, and the grim connection between transatlantic slavery and contemporary treatment and fate of human beings, human rejects whom nobody wants. As novelist Khaled Hosseini writes in his 2018 illustrated album *Sea Prayer:* "Afghans and Somalis and Iraqis and / Eritreans and Syrians . . . All of us in search of home / I have heard it said we are the uninvited" (n.p.).

Like Chamoiseau, Dal Lago addresses the readers' sense of responsibility: "We locked them up in the fort on Gorée, corroded by salt spray. . . .

We suffocated them in the holds of ships and enchained them on plantations in the Antilles. Think how the mummified fifty-two drifting toward Barbados were guided in the wakes of black slave ships. Portuguese and Spanish, French and English all exploited the same current, that great conveyor belt of warm water where the vortexes of the Pacific and the Gulf Stream merge ("Watery Graves," 11). Dal Lago's drowned and desiccated humans are, in his own obsessive refrain, "no longer alive" and "not yet dead" (8). They form routes of "underwater signposts" (Glissant, *Poetics,* 6) drawn by currents—whether of sea, wind, or capitalism—and fashioning in return currents of solidarity. Glissant's "boulets verdis" or greenish balls and chains, like Philips's fractured bone-words or "os" (*Zong!,* 1), belong to the same family as Dal Lago's "remains of bodies now turned to marine flora and fauna" ("Watery Graves," 8). Where sculptor Taylor recognized infinite renewal of life in the new alliances of sculptures, coral, fish, and plant life, dal Lago sees desperate beauty: "The calcium phosphate that once flexed muscles now coagulates into coral, and delicate fingers turn to mother of pearl. What once were strong arms like our own now flower into sea anemone." Are Taylor's and Dal Lago's conclusions decidedly opposite? First, we should consider that while Taylor recreates the guise of humanity in his concrete sculptures, Dal Lago's "Watery Graves" is built on a news item about the literal death of human beings. As Chamoiseau moralizes in *Frères migrants,* these bodies are "people, not rocks, not plastic weaves, persons, persons in the thousands, [who] stack amass assemble in a viscous lace where the weaves of life and death no longer stand apart, and who huddle in shivering rags" (22–23). We should also note that while Taylor's admitted priority is ecology, at least in his early works, Dal Lago's is humanity. However, as the book has asked, can we prioritize the survival of one over the other? As all our artists and writers scream out, the two are joined in a common struggle for survival under the currents of land and human exploitation.

A remarkable feat of Dal Lago's "Watery Graves" is the demonstration of Europe's entanglement with these world disasters. Throughout the piece, justice—both human and sacred—puts Europe and the "West" on trial: "Because if," Dal Lago's last words declare, "you don't curse all those who with a mere stroke of a pen have killed their brothers by the thousands, turning their gaze away from the cargo and profiting from the shipwreck . . . you are impeding justice. And therefore, you be damned" (12). It is not just the drowned, the destitute, the victims of war and famine who risk dying, but a common humanity (of brothers *and of sisters as well,* we insist). The healing process and political solution must begin with the recognition of European, North American, or white, responsibility. As Aimé Césaire encapsulated in his fundamental *Notebook of a Return to the Native Land,* Europe, Old Europe, feeding on "the fine liqueur of a Gulf Stream," stiffens under the weight of its crime: "Listen to the white world . . . its stiff joints crack under the hard stars / hear its blue steel rigidity pierce the mystic flesh" (*Notebook,* 97). Brand, Moten, Philip, Rankine, Trethewey, and so many others have shown that the fate of black being is "in the wake," to use Sharpe's words. In addition to the wake of a (slave) ship, that of "the disturbance caused by a body swimming," or that of a ceremony to the dead, wake crucially "means being awake and, also, consciousness" (*In the Wake,* 21). It is high time for white scholars like myself to be in heightened consciousness, to show our responsibility and imbrication in this underwater spectrum, this underwater specter. "A child who dies in the Mediterranean Sea recaps the disgrace tolerated for millennia by human consciousness and thereby accuses us. And those who let him die" (Chamoiseau, *Frères migrants,* 127). Not recognizing the imbrication of all guilty and victims in this underwater landscape would let ethics die, and with it, humanity. Let's hear Chamoiseau: "Such a collapse generates a loss of ethics, and when ethics fail, beauty falls" (*Frères migrants,* 20).

After his Caribbean sites (Cancún, the Bahamas, Antigua), Taylor submerged his sculptures in and around Fortress Europe. Installations can now be found in London's river Thames, and, more significantly for *Water Graves,* in Lanzarote, a volcanic formation of the Canaries situated 140 kilometers from the Moroccan shores and 1,000 kilometers from Spain.[7] Like in MUSA (Museo Subacuático de Arte), his 2016 installations in the "Museo Atlántico" of Lanzarote is still primarily ecological. The museum's website reads: "This museum project is creating a huge artificial reef made up of a series of pH neutral cement sculptures which, over time, will help the marine biomass flourish and facilitate the reproduction of species on the island."[8] While the artist's *Vicissitudes* eerily recalled the drowned Africans by their very presence in an underwater site marked by that history, Taylor did not then express an awareness of the human dimension of his sculptures in relation. In his 2016 work, the artist justifies the choice of Lanzarote not only because of its status as a UNESCO biosphere reserve but also because it is the site of the contemporary human tragedy of African migrants and refugees who have drowned in these waters. His work has become increasingly conscious of human politics, as in the *Crossing the Rubicón* installation in the Canary Islands, a monument to the oft-tragic and futile attempts

Jason deCaires Taylor, *The Raft of Lampedusa,* underwater installation, Lanzarote, Spain, installation date 2016. (© Jason deCaires Taylor; all rights reserved, DACS/ARS 2019)

to create barricades and barriers in the sea, which "emphasizes that the notions of ownership and territories are irrelevant to the natural world" ("The Underwater Museum"). In one of twelve installations, *The Raft of Lampedusa,* the commentary pasted upon Taylor's own photograph of the sculpture reads: "Reflecting on the human crisis based on Géricault's painting. It represents how sailors were abandoned in the shipwreck off the coast of Senegal. The sculpture aims to show the parallelism between that controversial situation and the current refugee crisis, where many people are being abandoned by society, due to a lack of humanity. Making us think of hope and loss at the same time, paying tribute to those who have lost their lives in their journey. The shape of the boat is inspired by dinghies that arrive at the island of Lanzarote.[9]

The installation conflates times, spaces, and arts. Wordplay connects Taylor's *Raft of Lampedusa* to the political gesture of French Romantic painter Théodore Géricault's 1819 *Raft of Medusa,* which raised consciousness about the incompetence of the ship's captain and the newly restored French monarchy deemed responsible for the wreck of the frigate Méduse off the coast of Mauritania. This, and the conflation between the Eastern Atlantic of the Canary Islands and the Mediterranean, connects water deaths across time and seas. Lampedusa, the Italian island situated between Sicily and Malta, has become a tragic flagship for the unraveling refugee crisis, with the thousands of Africans and Middle Easterners who attempt to reach this outpost of Europe, and, specifically, for the October 3, 2013, wreck of a fishing boat in which 366 clandestine migrants perished. Significantly, Géricault's painting of the desperate, dead, and dying includes four or five visibly African passengers. Similarly, Taylor's nine sculpted passengers are discernibly African. Indeed, the sculptures "were cast from actual migrants who arrived on refugee drafts."[10] The narrative that Géricault, Dal Lago, and Taylor provide makes visible the perennial state nonbeing imposed upon black humanity that Sharpe has theorized (*In the Wake,* 17–22).[11] But it also highlights the common responsibility of all of humanity in these deaths. Taylor's sunken "Raft of Medusa" offers, in his words, a "stark reminder of the collective responsibility of our global community."[12]

The pervasive theme of Taylor's Canary Islands sculptures is the ecological sacred scrutinized in chapter 4. The artist explicitly advocates for the sacredness of the ocean in order to mobilize humans to protect the planet, especially its water depths that escape most humans' sight: "We don't protect our oceans enough, and one way of thinking about this is that we don't regard our oceans as sacred. And we should."[13] "Immortal" features the sculpture of a man, casted from a Lanzarote fisherman, reclining on a pyre made out of concrete sticks. It connects living human bodies and departed ones; water, fire, and earth; and funerary practices from ancient Greece, Hindu South Asia, and the Irish Bronze Age, among other locations on the planet. *Hybrid Garden* represents part-human and part-cactus figures who are bound to evolve in their assemblage with ocean life. The half–mountain goat, half–human child gazing into a mirror in "The Portal" reminds us that human animals, nonhuman animals, plants, and corals are imbricated in a relation of survival and responsibility in underwater fluxes. The mirror in the water, which Taylor claims is "intended to portray water within water, an interface or looking glass into another world, the blue world," perhaps coincidentally, perhaps knowingly, repeats the cosmic underwater mirror, the *miwa anba dlo,* which, in Vaudou, functions as a site of passage between the worlds of the living, the dead, the unborn, the quotidian and the divine.[14]

Taylor's massive installation *Crossing the Rubicón* features a single door surrounded by a metallic gate where plants grow, toward which smart-phone bearing humans crowd. The rectangular gate resembles the door of no return, which Dionne Brand identified as a pivotal "spiritual location" for kidnapped Africans and their descendants. For the enslaved humans packed in the barracoons of Gorée and Elmina, the door of no return was the last sight of telluric Africa, the last dividing frame opening up onto the horrific unknown that the ocean and slavers promised, "a place where a certain set of transactions occurred, perhaps the most important of them being the transference of selves" (Brand, *A Map,* 18). For contemporary exiles and refugees fleeing war, violence, insecurity, or famine, "dead or living under sentence of death" (Glissant, *Poetics,* 6) drowned in Taylor's installation and in the literal depths of the Mediterranean, what does the door signify? An entryway into freedom? Into Fortress Europe? Into the afterlife? Into a sure water death? Into the heedless future of technology-zombified humans? The artist sees in it a symbol of hope. The one single door, extended by a wall that can be traversed from above and from all sides, "is intended to be a monument to absurdity, a dysfunctional barrier in the middle of a vast fluid . . . [which] emphasizes that the notions of ownership and territories are irrelevant to the natural world."[15] Chamoiseau expresses a similar sentiment toward the inevitable failure of segregating walls: "Here . . . the coast-guards, the wall-guards, the border-guards, are exhausted from their failure to contain! . . . Fluxes have the vitality of a Biblical beginning" (*Frères migrants,* 15).

Taylor's and Chamoiseau's ethical utopias cohabit with the inconceivable numbers of victims, not merely of the ocean, but also of the walls that attempt to segregate it, as they do humanity. Taylor's works, Chamoiseau's words, and the creations explored in *Water Graves*—as well as this very book—aim to open up the walls of the Lanzarote, lazaretto, lazzareto, lazaret of the planet and to halt the building of new walls, ideological or physical, which Chamoiseau and Glissant call "stiff preservations of stone, iron, barbed wires, electric fence, or enclosed ideologies" ("When the Walls Fall," 262).[16] Water, formidable water, may rectify this stiffness, this *rigor mortis,* when it is fully endowed with its sacredness, beauty, and relation.

Notes

Introduction

1. In Swahili, *Maafa* means "great disaster": "The Maafa is a continual, constant, complete, and total system of human negation and nullification" (Jones and West, *Making It,* 178).

2. "In an age of global warming, there is no background, and thus, there is no foreground. It is the end of the world, since worlds depend on backgrounds and foregrounds. *World* is a fragile aesthetic effect around whose corners we are beginning to see" (Morton, *Hyperobjects,* 99).

3. All translations from French, Creole, Spanish, and Italian are mine unless I cite an English edition in the works cited.

4. Elizabeth M. DeLoughrey highlights the direct link between measuring water and measuring time: "The Atlantic Ocean, specifically the routes of the maritime slave trade, was the constitutive space for our modern and global measurement of time. Longitude to this day is based upon the movement of eighteenth century British ships traversing oceanic space" (*Roots and Routes,* 57).

5. Cecilia Chen, Janine MacLeod, and Astrida Neimanis edited *Thinking with Water,* a remarkable collection on water across the disciplines, from which MacLoud's essay is drawn.

6. On the properties of liquidity influencing black aesthetics, see the "mackeys" research group website: Georgia State University, http://liquidblackness.com/, accessed May 27, 2019.

7. "And souls take their spirit from the waters." Heraclitus's *Fragments,* in Diels-Kranz, *Die Fragmente der Vorsokratiker,* 5th ed. 1934, 12.

8. Humanities-based Oceanic studies is a deeply set and ever-growing field. See for instance, Paul Gilroy's classic *Black Atlantic,* Jacques Corbin's *La Mer: Terreur et fascination,* Ernesto Bassi's *Aqueous Territory,* and DeLoughrey's *Routes and Roots,* inspired by Brathwaite's notion of "tidalectics," or "the movement of the water backwards and forwards as a kind of cyclic motion, rather than linear" (in Mackey, "An Interview," 42–59). Mentz's *At the Bottom of Shakespeare's*

Ocean offers a wonderful bibliography of oceanic and sea studies in the chapter "Reading the New Thalassology" (101–12).

9. I elaborate on the concepts of *anba dlo* and *lotbo dlo* in chapter 4. For now, I will simply say that they are prevalent in creolized, African-influenced religions of the Caribbean. *Anba dlo* refers to the world below water, often inhabited by the spirits of the unborn and the deceased. *Lotbo dlo* refers to the other side of water, either as the other shore the departed have reached in the afterlife or left behind in their Middle Passage exile, or, in contemporary imagination, migrants from Haiti who live in the United States or Canada. The terms thus refer both to spirituality and history.

10. About the connected histories of Katrina, institutional racism, and slavery, see—among the wealth of scholarship, fiction, and testimonies—Vincanne Adams's *Markets of Sorrow, Labors of Faith;* Chris Rose's *1 Dead in Attick;* Natasha Trethewey's *Beyond Katrina;* and Jesmyn Ward's *Salvage the Bones.* Anissa Janine Wardi's *Water and African American Memory* revises definitions of ecocriticism in light of the interconnections of race, economics, history, religion, spirituality, and the environment in African American southern literature. See particularly the conclusion to Wardi's book "Mud, Blood, and the Blues: Hurricane Katrina and the Floodwaters of the African Diaspora" (117–41). "The Wrath of the Atlantic," Wardi compellingly claims, "drowned the city of New Orleans in a historical parallel to those who, for more than two hundred years, drowned in the currents of the Atlantic" (139).

11. For a thorough discussion of the "Dikenga Kongo," see religion scholar Dianne Stewart's "Kumina" (611–13).

12. "Echo from Cuba, Haiti, and all points of the Caribbean, Central America, to / Carve lives into New Orleans, Caribbean North, into neighborhoods like Gentilly, / Sugar Hill, Tremé, Pallet Land, and so many others" ("Sankofa NOLA," *Second Line Home,* 5).

13. On connections between this northern and southern Caribbean, see for example Ned Sublette's *The World That Made New Orleans,* Nathalie Dessens's *From Saint-Domingue to New Orleans,* John Wharton Lowe's *Calypso Magnolia,* and Eric Solomon's dissertation, *Southernmost Currents.* Solomon, for instance, shifts the focus from a terrestrial to a "terraquaeous" comprehension of new southern literature, including the southern United States, the Caribbean, and, as its pivot, the Florida straits. For a discussion of the shifting definition of where the Caribbean begins and ends, see Tatiana Flores and Michelle A. Stephens' Introduction to their *Relational Undercurrents* (15–27).

14. For an expansive and in-depth reading of the sacred in the Anglophone, Francophone, and Hispanophone Caribbeans, see, for instance, Keith Cartwright's *Sacral Grooves, Limbo Gateways* and Anny Dominique Curtius's *Symbioses d'une mémoire.*

15. See Dubois's *Haiti,* especially 4–10: "The Plantations consumed the landscape: observers at the time already noted that alarmingly large areas of the forests

had been chopped down for construction and various precious woods to Europe. And they consumed the lives of the colony's slaves at a murderous rate" (4).

16. Read scientists Simon Lewis and Mark Maslin's *The Human Planet,* in which the authors contend that colonialism in the Americas changed the earth's very makeup that began the Anthropocene. See also Mentz's discussion of Lewis and Maslin's theory in "Enter Anthropocene, Circa 1610": "Lewis and Maslin state that 1610 marks 'an unambiguously permanent change to the earth system' generated by the ecological mixing of the Americas, Europe, Africa, and Asia" (Lewis and Maslin in Mentz, 48).

17. In his essay on the "Art of Death" in contemporary Haiti, anthropologist Patrick A. Polk indicates that "gleaming choreographi[es] of sequin, bead, and banner" signal "an "encounter of the mundane and the sublime" by bringing "the glare of the other side up close and personal" (120). See the section "Encountering the Glittering Face of Gede" (120–31).

18. I adhere to Laderman's notion that religion can be expressed outside of institutionalized structures such as those of Judaism, Christianity, Islam, or Hinduism, or Vaudou: "Religious thoughts . . . are not all necessarily about God. . . . They are instead grounded in perceptions and experiences of the sacred . . . nonetheless a word signifying religious cultures or communities tied together emotionally and cognitively, but also spiritually and materially by vital rituals" (*Sacred Matters,* xiv). In the postslavery world examined in *Water Graves,* spontaneous, improvised, and bricolaged sacred expressions are often a necessity. This is equivalent to what Vincent Lloyd defines as the "new sacred politics," which emerges "from the grassroots" and "taps into post-denominational religiosity" of groups such as Black Lives Matter and the tribal leaders of the Standing Rock Sioux Reservation protesting the Dakota Access Oil Pipeline ("MLK Day").

19. "Rituals of remembrance," according to Hume and religion scholar Dianne Stewart "'reconstitute kinship across time and space'" (Stewart, quoted by Hume, "Death and the Performance," 111).

20. Tombs "exist to honour the dead, but also to hide them in so far as they are dead, to conceal the corpses and ensure that death as such is no longer visible" (163).

21. In a similar mode, Walter Mosley, branching away from his crime fiction and novel writing, coins the term *untopia* in his recent treatise on political philosophy: "I would like to present a word that I feel needs to be added to the lexicon of modern political language; that word is *untopia*" (11).

22. See Patterson, *Slavery and Social Death,* especially 35–75.

23. "Already 'dead' and buried, the zombie is brought back to a life of semi-consciousness to serve as a slave on a plantation" (Hurbon, *Les Mystères,* 61).

24. Maya Deren identifies two types of zombies in Haitian Vaudou: "A Soulless Body. The soul may have been removed by magic from a living person, or the body of someone recently deceased may have been brought up out of the grave

after the soul has been separated from it by regular rites of death. The purpose of this is to make use of the body as slave" (*Divine Horsemen,* 338).

25. See Césaire, *Cahier,* 25–26.

26. For an interactive digital mixed-media graphic novel also attempting to fabulate the archive of the Vietnamese drowned, see the extraordinary and devastating creation entitled "The Boat," based on the story by Nam Le and adapted by Matt Huynh.

27. On counting, see Judith Butler's *Precarious Life* (20–21) and *Frames of War* (xx–xxii). Butler plays on both meanings of counting, as in "determining a number" and as in "taking into account," in her discussion of which lives specifically count as lives. Some lives, such as that of a Palestinian boy in Gaza are "ungrievable" "because the assaulted and destroyed body . . . was already conceived as a pure instrument of war" (*Frames,* xxi–xxii). The ungrievability of a life naturally has consequences for the dead: "The matter is not a simple one for, if a life is not grievable, it is not quite a life; it does not qualify as a life and is not worth a note. It is already the unburied, if not the unburiable" (*Precarious,* 34).

28. Patterson defines "social death" as the situation of the enslaved in "one of the most extreme forms of the relation of domination, approaching the limits of total power from the viewpoint of the master, and of total powerlessness from the viewpoint of the slave" (*Slavery and Social Death,* 3). Also see JanMohamed, *Deathbound Subject,* 5–6.

29. "A soil manured with black blood from two hundred years of oppression and exploitation until it sprang with an incredible paradox of peaceful greenery and crimson flowers and sugar cane. . . . [T]he planting of men too: the yet intact bones and brains in which the old unsleeping blood that had vanished into the earth they trod still cried out for vengeance" (Faulkner, *Absalom, Absalom!,* 202). In Danticat's novel, "farming" equally refers to the production and exploitation of cane stalks and human bones: "travay tè pou zo, the farming of bones" (*Farming,* 55).

30. Personal visits to the Whitney Plantation in 2015 and 2016. See also the museum-plantation's official website: https://www.whitneyplantation.com/, accessed May 28, 2019.

31. "The ritual of degrade . . . harkens back to the Ibo, whose longed-for return to Africa was thwarted by white masters who desecrated the body so it could not travel" (Dayan, *Haiti, 261*).

32. See Andrew Buncome, "Louisiana Flooding," *Independent,* August 16, 2016, https://www.independent.co.uk/news/world/americas/louisiana-flooding-2016-coffins-floating-down-streets-a7193876.html, accessed May 28, 2019.

33. This in no way repeals the presence or value of religion in these cultural or aesthetic expressions, but simply indicates that a secular sacred is possible. In *Religion of the Field Negro,* Lloyd contends that "black secularism," is often funded by white institutions and supported by white supremacist ideology (4–5). Since, as Lloyd demonstrates, "black theology is social criticism" and

"social criticism is black theology" (5), uncoupling political action from theology weakens the political strength of black social criticism and political action.

34. "Dead blacks are part of normal life here. Dying in ship hulls, tossed into the Atlantic, hanging from trees, beaten, shot in churches, gunned down by the police or warehoused in prisons . . ." (Rankine, "The Condition of Black Life"). On the wide circulation of rituals and the "sacred life" within Black Lives Matter, see Lloyd's "MLK Day."

35. See, for instance, Johanna C. Kardux's *Monuments of the Black Atlantic.*

36. In his *Habeas Viscus,* Alexander G. Weheliye crucially argues that "since bare life and biopolitics discourse [in Foucault's and Agemben's writings] largely occludes race as a critical category of analysis . . . it cannot provide the methodological instruments for diagnosing the tight bonds between humanity and racializing assemblages in the modern era" (8; see also 5–9, and 38). Weheliye's book remediates this absence.

37. See "Beyond Competitive Memory," 1–7.

38. *New York Times,* October 2, 2014, caption: "A 4-year old, foreground, and another child thought to have Ebola lay amid bodily fluids at a hospital in Makeni, Sierra Leone."

39. Representing photographs of the dead in the United States is regulated by ethics rather than law. See the NPPA Code of Ethics (https://nppa.org/code-ethics). As a notable exception, President Bush in 1991 enforced a ban on publishing photographs of flag-draped US military coffins. President Obama lifted the ban in 2009. Journalists and readers respond differently to the publishing of corpses of US vs. non-US citizens. See for instance op-ed by Margaret Sullivan: "Was Photo of a Dead Ambassador Acceptable?" which questions where to draw the "fine line between good taste and important journalism." *New York Times,* September 12, 2012, https://publiceditor.blogs.nytimes.com/2012/09/12/was-photo-of-dead-ambassador-acceptable/?_r=0, accessed May 29 2019.

40. See Moten's "Blackness and Nothingness (Mysticism in the Flesh)," 143.

41. See Angelique Nixon's "Creating Space and Speaking Silence."

42. A cenotaph, from the Greek *kenos* (empty) and *taphos* (grave) is a funerary monument built in the memory of an individual or collective departed.

43. Consult Susan Cooksey et al.'s *Kongo across the Waters* for various photographs and discussions of Kongo-religion,African-derived, and creolized forms of funerary rites in Africa, the Caribbean, and the United States. See, for instance, "Kongo Inspiration in Contemporary Art," 395–409.

44. For a fictionalized account of the countless possibilities of customizing funeral objects such as coffins and urns, see St. Thomas Tiphanie Yanique's short story "The International Shop of Coffins," in which an artisan works from a creolized variety of coffins from India, Mexico, Ghana, and local Virgin Islands wood, to beautify each individual casket. His shop looks like "an art gallery. A place to stroll through with hands clasped behind the back" (*How to Escape,* 86).

45. *Merriam-Webster's,* "relay (*n.*)," http://www.merriam-webster.com/dictionaryrelay, accessed June 5, 2018.

46. See "Relinked (Relayed), Related," *Poetics,* 169–79).

47. "Tombs exist to honour the dead, but also to hide them in so far as they are dead, to conceal the corpses and ensure that death as such is no longer visible" (*Things Hidden,* 163).

48. For more on the "poisson-chambre," see my *Orphan Narratives,* 43–45.

49. Keats's epitaph, Rome, Protestant Cemetery.

50. See Joël Castonguay Bélanger, "L'Édification d'un tombeau poétique."

51. For ethnographic or theological descriptions of the ceremony of *manje-lèmò*—a regular offering of food to the dead in Haitian Vaudou practices—see Deren, *Divine Horsemen,* 209–212; Hurbon, *Les Mystères,* 93–94; and Métraux, *Voodoo,* 263–65.

52. On the "Nine Nights" ceremonies, see Hurston, *Tell My Horse,* 39; Roach, *Cities of the Dead,* 34; and Hume, *Passages,* 113–24. On the "second line," see Proctor Smith, *Mardi Gras,* 27.

53. "Haiti, dear Haiti, no matter and tested and remapped by disaster, is not, in itself, disaster" (Jenson, "The Writing of Disaster," 111). The Haitian Revolution, or any "slave revolution," for Trouillot, was "unthinkable even as it happened" (*Silencing,* 73), since it was associated with "ready-made categories" like barbary in Western discourse. "Said another way," adds Díaz, Haiti's nightmarish vulnerability has to be understood as part of a larger trend of global inequality" (Díaz, "Apocalypse," n.p.).

54. "Constellation [L. Constellatio *-con,* "together," and *stella,* "a star"]. A group of fixed stars to which a definite name has been given; an assemblage of splendors or excellences (a constellation of poetic genius)" (*Merriam-Webster's*).

55. See the "African Constellations Star Map," in *A Collection for the Curricula for the Starlab African Mythology Cylinder* at https://www.raritanval.edu/sites/default/files/aa_PDF%20Files/6.x%20Community%20Resources/6.4.5_SD.7.AfricanMythology.pdf, accessed May 28, 2019.

56. Slave Wrecks Project: https://nmaahc.si.edu/explore/initiatives/slave-wrecks-project-0, accessed May 28, 2019.

1. Relational Sacred

1. See Jean-Pol Madou's *De Mémoire d'arbres* and Toni Morrison's *Beloved.*

2. Article 14 of the 1685 Code Noir (Black code) instructs plantation owners to have their baptized slaves buried in cemeteries reserved to that effect, and their unbaptized slaves buried "at night, in an unspecified field near the place of death" (*Code noir,* 22).

3. Roach, speaking chiefly of New Orleans, contends that the European imposition of the segration of the dead and the living on the people they colonized constitutes a "revolutionary spatial paradigm" (*Cities,* 48).

4. See Richard Price's "Chasing Death's Left Hand," on Caribbean and maroon deaths. Price's scholarly piece itself becomes a performative ritual in its concluding words: "I recommend that we join Saamakas in clapping our hand rhythmically and saying, *gaán tangi tangi f'unu*—let us give great thanks to all of them" (241).

5. Manuel Norvat, in discussion with the author, March 2013.

6. When he became critically ill, Glissant asked to be repatriated from New York to Paris. The "Regional and General Council of Martinique" subsidized the costs. This event was cause for scandal in Martinican circles. See "Les Collectivités viennent au secours d'Édouard Glissant."

7. See "Martinique/Mississippi."

8. See "The Black Beach" in *Poetics,* 121–27.

9. See "Expanse and Filiation" in *Poetics,* 47–63.

10. See Thierry Nicolas's "A la poursuite du patrimoine."

11. See Glissant's *Sartorius* for a description of the monument (162–64). I will discuss the Anse Caffard shipwreck further in chapter 4 .

12. For images of the sculpture, see "Martinique. Mémorial Cap 110," on the official site of "Comité pour la mémoire de l'esclavage." http://www.esclavage-memoire.com/lieux-de-memoire/cap-110-memorial-de-l-anse-caffard-martinique-35.html, accessed June 4, 2019.

13. For a reading of Valère's Cap 110 as mausoleum, and for a discussion of the role of women in the event and their absence from the monument, see Erika Serrato's "Mémoire et Fraternité."

14. See *Poetics,* 146–47.

15. Randal C. Archibold, "Trying to Protect a Reef With an Otherworldly Diversion," *New York Times,* August 13, 2012, https://www.nytimes.com/2012/08/14/world/americas/in-cancun-trying-to-protect-reef-with-underwater-statues.html, accessed May 24, 2019.

16. *Acoma* was a review published in Martinique in 5 volumes under the auspices of Glissant and his *Institut Martiniquais d'Études* between 1971 and 1973.

17. See Scarboro's documentary and Donatien's article.

18. I have met Victor Anicet on several occasions since 2010. During my visit to Martinique in May 2012, we began discussing Glissant's grave in a dialogue that continued in a series of emails exchanged between Atlanta, Georgia, and Schoelcher, Martinique.

19. The same image, albeit in red on white, serves as logo for the Institut du Tout-Monde: http://tout-monde.com/, accessed June 4, 2019.

20. "It works in a spiral: from one circularity to the next, it encounters new spaces and does not transform them into either depths or conquests" (*Poetics,* 199). On the spiral, space, time, and narrative order in the related topic of Haitian literature, see Kaiama Glover's *Haiti Unbound.*

21. Doctoral Seminars, Louisiana State University, Baton Rouge, 1991–94. See my introduction to *Entours d'Édouard Glissant* (7).

22. See the famous example of Sethe's whip scars growing into a tree in Toni Morrison's *Beloved:* "Schoolteacher made one open up my back, and when it closed it made a tree. It grows there still" (19).

23. *France-Antilles,* February, 3, 2012.

24. "The West is not in the West. It is a project, not a place" (*Caribbean,* 2).

25. On the East Indian influence on Glissant's creolization, see my essay "Between Breadfruit and Masala." More generally, see Brinda Mehta's work on Indian contributions to Caribbean creolization in *Diasporic (Dis)locations.*

26. Asia is also prevalent in Glissant's poetic world model in his introduction to his anthology where he cites "grains of rice" and haikus (*La Terre,* 13).

27. Email correspondence with the author, March 2013.

28. Critics such as Peter Hallward and Nick Nesbitt have commented on Glissant's increasing "depolitization" in both his actions and in his writing (see Hallward's *Absolutely Postcolonial,* 105, and Nesbitt's *Voicing Memory,* 184). By way of contrast, Celia Britton argues that Glissant's late emphasis on sustainability in Martinique and on a view of "the world as made of cultures rather than nations" ("Globalization," 11) in a globalized world does not preclude political action.

29. See "Kongo Afterlife in Florida" in *Kongo across the Waters,* 308–9.

30. Email correspondence with the author, March 2013.

31. Email correspondence with the author, March 2013.

32. Cailler argues that Glissant's Catholic funeral is in conflict with his long-standing opposition to the "thought of oneness" and to an "absolute with a universal vocation, included on a religious level" ("Rêve sur les funérailles religieuses," 239–40).

33. Glissant's characterization of Derrida as championing monolingualism, monotheism, and teleology is problematic at best, in light of Derrida's questioning of these monolithic thoughts, as evidenced in his *Monolingualism of the Other* and, arguably, his entire oeuvre. The dialogue between Derrida and Glissant ends abruptly in the transcription in print. According to witnesses, one of the two thinkers left the room slamming the door.

34. For further philosophical reflection on entanglement in Glissant, see Drabinski's "Ethics of Entanglement" in *Levinas and the Postcolonial,* 129–63.

35. Louisiana State University, Baton Rouge, 1991–94.

36. See *Poetics,* 191–92.

37. Email correspondence with the author, March 2013.

38. The epitaph also provides the concluding sentence of Glissant's *Terre magnétique:* "When even the most stubborn of rocks tiredlessly repeats: nothing is for true, all is totally alive: yes. that's how people translate the enraged breath of the rock, yes, that's it, Ammy says: nothing is true, all is alive [rien n'est vrai, tout est vivant]" (118). It is also the title of Glissant's last published speech delivered in 2010 at la Maison des Amériques, Paris. On the biopolitical intention of the epitaph, see Corio's "The Living and the Poetic Intention."

39. On the strategies and techniques of the Martinican Creole storyteller, see Chamoiseau and Confiant, *Lettres créoles,* 43–83.

40. See *Dissemination,* 78.

41. See Samia Kassab-Charfi's analysis of Glissant's poems in her "Et l'une et l'autre face des choses."

42. In conversation with Lise Gauvin in *L'Imaginaire des langues,* Glissant explains "poétrie" as a word that refers "not to a distinct literary genre, but rather, to a mixture of narrative, theatrical dialogue, poetry, essay, etc." (60). While *poétrie* looks like a neologism, Glissant borrows it from early modern French, rescusitating it, so to speak, from the grave. François Rigolot notes that rhetoricians used *poétrie* in order to "define the essence" of *poésie* [poetry]" (50). As he adds, *poétrie* is the science of teaching "how to . . . invent fabulous things" (52). Glissant certainly plays with the fabulating function of *poétrie.*

43. Glissant provides his own lyrical translation of "Strange Fruit." This is the only text Glissant translates in his anthology, as if to tie it more closely to his own poetry.

44. Leupin, "L'appel du futur," 238.

45. Literary critic Diana Fuss reflects on the genre of the "corpse poem": "A poem quickens language while a corpse stills it. The fantastical coupling of 'corpse' and 'poem' denotes an extravagant rhetorical conceit, an impossible literary utterance . . . Giving voice to the voiceless cadaver, corpse poems bring language more fully in line with death" (*Dying Modern,* 44). Glissant's *poétrie,* oscillating between movement and stiffness, contain the same paradox that brings death and language closer.

46. Nesbitt appropriately calls this loss of the enslaved an "entombment of memory," *Voicing Memory,* 3.

47. See my *Orphan Narratives,* 40–48.

48. See "Errantry, Exile" in *Poetics,* 11–22.

49. See Souleymane Bachir Diagne on Senghor's philosophy (*African Art*). Glissant directly mentions the Senegalese poet and philosopher in *Philosophie:* "Senghor's elegies [are] offered as if on a slow boat on the almighty river of the African land" 134.

50. On the collapse of place in Glissant's and Faulkner's works, see my "Faulkner's Caribbean Topographies."

51. See Carine Mardorossian's "Poetics of Landscape," in which the author reads Glissant's ecological theories alongside with creolization.

52. See, for instance, "Performing Origins," 42–47.

53. My goal here is not to question the difficult relation between ecological consciousness and Christian theology that Bruno Latour provocatively tackles in his essay "Will Non-Humans Be Saved? An Argument in Eco-Theology." While provocative, Latour's demonstration rests on an understanding of religion as organized around Christian spirituality. Glissant's thought instead relies on religion as relation spreading outside of organized faith or theology.

54. See Jane Bennett's *Vibrant Matter:* "By 'vitality' I mean the capacity of things—edibles, commodities, storms, metals—not only to impede or block the will and designs of humans but also to act as quasi-agents or forces with trajectories, propensities, or tendencies of their own" (viii).

55. Helen Cooper, "Grim History Traced in Sunken Slave Ship Found Off South Africa," *New York Times,* May 31, 2015, https://www.nytimes.com/2015/06/01/world/africa/tortuous-history-traced-in-sunken-slave-ship-found-off-south-africa.html?smid=fb-share, accessed May 24, 2019.

56. Cooper, "Grim History."

57. Cooper, "Grim History."

58. Emily Jane Hopkins, "History under the Surface: The National Museum of American History and Cultures' Partnerships with the Arican Slave Wrecks Project," ClassRaceGender, March 27, 2014, https: classracegender.wordpress.com/2014/03/27/history-under-the-surface-the-national-museum-of-african-american-history-and-cultures-partnership-with-the-african-slave-wrecks-project/, accessed May 30, 2019.

59. "Through exhibits and collaborations, the NMAAHC continues to expose the untold stories of the African American experience and empowers a global community to explore these stories." Hopkins, "History under the Surface."

60. "As long as we are careful not to confuse religion with the sacred, it becomes possible to devise a secular political strategy for preventing environmental catastrophe that does not fall into the error of moralism, much less the horror of fascism" (Dupuy, *Mark of the Sacred,* 33). "So, Sacred Matters is about robust, sacred forms of religious life, experience, and community that are less about theology, and more about anthropology" (Laderman, *Sacred Matters,* xv).

61. See also Yountae, *Decolonial Abyss,* 90–119, on Glissant's "secular theology." Yount reads Glissant's abyss as an apophaticist site, "which posits the relation between the spiritual and the political in the middle passage" (91).

62. Anicet claims that transcendental vertical cosmogonies are ill-fitted to a Caribbean context in which Amerindian and African symbols find themselves stranded together. In Amerindian cosmogony, the ceramicist claims, symbols were turned toward the sky to mark the link with deities. In contrast, Anicet's creations have Taino god figures facing the viewer instead of the sky in what he calls an "ineluctable horizontal cosmogony": "When a people only has imported religions, we need to restitute religion by a gaze turned upon ourselves. We don't have any relation with the cosmos" (Anicet in Hachad and Loichot, "Victor Anicet", 172) The artist's view appears as a concretization of Glissant's preference of the expanse over filiation and transcendence (*Poétique,* 70).

63. Leupin defines Glissant's art of recomposition and religiosity as polytheism in the Heraclitan sense (*Édouard Glissant,* 94).

64. Leupin, "Édouard Glissant: Poésie et coupures épistémologiques," lecture, Department of French and Italian, Emory University, September 2014.

65. *Poétrie* is the subtitle of Glissant's *Le Monde incréé,* a hybrid of drama, poetry, and prose fiction.

66. "This double concealment reproduces the way in which cultural differentiation develops on the basis of the founding murder" (Girard, *Of Things Hidden,* 166).

67. I would like to thank scholar Franck Andrianarivo for educating me on this ritual, for sharing the poems by Rabearivelo on the topic, and for recounting his lived experience of the *Famadihana.*

68. Serres, similarly, questions the origin of Genesis as separation: "Deciding on markers and borders indeed appears to be a moment of origin; without such decisions, there is no oasis separate form the desert . . . no sacred or profane space, isolated from each other by priestly gesture, no definition enclosing a domain, and therefore no precise language on which to agree, nor any logic; and finally, no geometry" (Serres, *Natural Contract,* 51–52).

69. "I call *Poetics of Relation* this potential of the imaginary that leads us to conceive the ungraspable totality of such a World-Chaos, while it allows us to notice some detail of it, and in particular to sing our place, unfathomable and irreversible" (*Traité du Tout-Monde,* 22). See also the general public text that Glissant assigned his doctoral students, which was influential to his own understanding of chaos theory: *Des Rythmes au Chaos* (written by atom physicists Bergé, Pierre, Yves Pomeau, and Monique Dubois-Gance).

70. On Lorenz's theories, see James Gleick's *Chaos,* especially 11–31. "The butterfly effect was the reason. For small pieces of weather . . . any predictions deteriorate rapidly. Errors and uncertainties multiply, cascading upward through a chain of turbulent features, from dust devils and squalls up to continental eddies that only satellites can see" (20).

71. Lorenz's relationship between "aperiodicity and unpredictability," Gleick explains, is "a link between the unwillingness of the weather to repeat itself and the inability of forecasters to predict it" (Gleick, *Chaos,* 22).

72. In all, an estimated 5 million Africans—30% of all those transported—perished before they reached the Americas. Understanding Slavery Initiative, 2011, http://www.understandingslavery.com/, accessed May 30, 2019.

73. Biologist Eugene F. Stoermer coined the term "Anthropocene" in the early 1980s to refer to the geological impact of human activities on the planet Earth. Atmospheric chemist Paul Crutzen popularized the term with Stoermer in 2000 (see Monastersky's "Anthropocene"). For a full discussion of the term and debates surrounding it, see Menely and Oak Taylor's *Anthropocene Reading.*

74. Cathy Delpech-Hellsten, "Texte intégral de la conférence d'Édouard Glissant, 'Rien n'est Vrai, tout est vivant,'" Mondesfrancophones.com, November 25, 2013, https://mondesfrancophones.com/dossiers/edouard-glissant/conference-dedouard-glissant-rien-nest-vrai-tout-est-vivant/, accessed May 30, 2019.

75. Interview with Glissant, Rosa Moussaoui et Fernand Nouvet, *L'Humanité,* February 6, 2007.

2. Graves for Katrina

1. The musical tributes in the aftermath of Hurricane Katrina, including the Neville Brothers' song featured in David Simon and Eric Overmeyer's *Treme* (season 3, 2012) are too numerous to name. See John Swenson's *New Atlantis: Musicians Battle for the Survival of New Orleans* for an extensive discussion of the matter.

2. "According to Big Chief Donald Harrison Sr., the Mardi Gras Indians are a living culture of pride and resistance that developed in the African American communities of New Orleans over the course of more than 150 years. The once-simple feathered suits, the chants, and the elaborate dance rituals are said to date from the mid- to late 1800s, with some researchers contending that the tradition reaches back to the 1700s" (Kennedy, *Big Chief Harrison*, 11).

3. "Will the Circle Be Unbroken: Affects [*sic*] of Gangs," June 4, 2008, https://www.youtube.com/watch?v=Y0GgTmDLLFs&feature=kp, accessed May 30, 2019.

4. Neville Brothers, *Yellow Moon* (audio CD), A&M Records, October 1989.

5. See Ricoeur's *Temps et récit I*, 40.

6. Social anthropologist Wyatt MacGaffey provides an introduction to the aesthetics and history of Kongo *minkisi* (*nkisi*, sing.) in his "Meaning and Aesthetics in Kongo Art." Europeans reduced the sacred objects to "fetishes, a term embodying the conviction that minkisi were random collections of oddments endowed by their makers with imaginary powers." (*Kongo across the Waters*, 172).

7. My grandmother's pronouncement is serendipitously reminiscent of the lyrics of the classic jazz standard immortalized by Ella Fitzgerald, "Comes Love": "Comes a fire, then you know just what to do . . . Comes love, nothing can be done." The common unstoppable nature of love and water remains to be explored.

8. *Merriam-Webster*, "frame (v.)," http://www.merriam-webster.com/dictionaryframe, accessed June 5, 208.

9. If the rectangle is the dominant way of framing visually, the examples, among many others, of the Hebraic biblical scroll, the oval-shaped pendant portrait of a loved-one, tattooed calligraphy, or digital hypertexts defy rules of linearity.

10. See Naïma Hachad and Valérie Loichot's "Victor Anicet : Le pays-Martinique ou le bleu de la *Restitution*." For reproductions of Anicet's trays, see "Victor Anicet: *Restitution*," Aica Caraïbe de Sud, September 27, 2013, https://aica-sc.net/2013/09/27/victor-anicet-restitution/, accessed May 30, 2019.

11. Jake Adam York, "Medicine as Memory," *Southern Spaces*, January 26, 2012, https://southernspaces.org/2012/medicine-memory-radcliffe-bailey-atlantas-high-museum-art#sthash.JlK8FkMo.dpuf, accessed May 30, 2019.

12. For critical evaluations of the disproportionate destructive effect of Katrina on African Americans and on its historical connection with race-based

enslavement, see Katrina Jeremy Levitt and Matthew Whitaker's *Hurricane Katrina,* David Dante Troutt's *After the Storm,* and Keith Wailoo et al.'s *Katrina's Imprint.*

13. Julien in *Callaloo* interview: "Some things got ruined, but luckily I took my negatives with me. The photographs I left behind were ruined." Waters expressed a similar loss of material production during Katrina in our personal interview in Atlanta (June 19, 2014).

14. See chapter 1 on the relational sacred and chapter 4 on the ecological sacred.

15. Ghanain artist Papa Joe as well as Jamaican artist Ebony Patterson push the association between coffin and installation art one step further with, respectively, their "fantasy coffins" and "lavish coffins." See Charlotte Jansen, "The Fantastical Coffins of the Legendary Ghanaian Artist Paa Joe, " Artsy, June 26, 2017, https://www.artsy.net/article/artsy-editorial-legendary-artist-made-coffins-art, accessed May 30, 2019.

16. "Rectangulist" invokes the term "spiralist," a school of mostly Haitian writers and artists such as René Philoctète, Jean-Claude Fignolé, and Frankétienne, who put the spiral at the center of their creations. See Glover's *Haiti Unbound.*

17. See Thompson's essay "Minkisi and Dikenga" in *Kongo across the Waters, 377–84.*

18. "Creolization diffracts while métissage flattens . . . In short, [creolization is] a form of métissage, but with a result that goes further and that is unpredictable" (Glissant, "Métissage et créolisation," 50).

19. While Waters is not one of the photographers featured in the book of photographs and essays *Before (During) After Katrina* (essays by John Biguenet, Steven Maklansky, and Tony Lewis), like the twelve photographers featured in the book, Waters's visual reaction to Katrina fits the description of the photographers given in the preface of the book: "We saw it / We captured it / We are forever changed by it" (4).

20. For a selection of Waters's photographs of New Orleans street scenes and artists, see the 2018 collection devoted to his art, *Freedom's Dance,* edited and narrated by Karen Celestan.

21. See the slideshow at Eric Waters Photography, http://www.ericwatersphotography504.com/find_us/new-orleans-culture/, accessed May 30, 2019

22. Eric Waters Photography, "Clarients: A New Orleans Metaphor," http://www.ericwatersphotography504.com/find_us/clarinets-a-new-orleans-metaphor/, accessed May 30, 2019.

23. Cinque Hinks, "The Fine Line Between Meaningful Art and Disaster Porn," Creative Loafing, August 3, 2010, https://creativeloafing.com/content-168684-The-fine-line-between-meaningful-art-and-disaster-porn, accessed May 30, 2019.

24. Kevin Sipp, *Solemn Sounds of Silence: A Photographic Project of Reverence and Remembrance* (n.p.).

25. White is a jazz clarinetist, composer, and professor teaching African American music at Xavier University in New Orleans.

26. Cinque Hinks, "The Fine Line Between Meaningful Art and Disaster Porn."

27. Waters's individual pieces in the "Clarinet Series" are unnamed. Twenty-five of them, all 17 by 22 inches, are reproduced in Kevin Sipp's *Solemn Sounds of Silence.* For clarity's sake, I name each photograph to which I refer with its page number in *Solemn Sounds.* Seventeen pieces, some not included in Sipp's book, are available on the photographer's website: see Eric Waters Photography, "Clarinets—A New Orleans Metaphor.".

28. The photograph, not reproduced in Sipp, can be viewed as image 6/17 on the artist's website.

29. Personal conversation with Eric Waters, Atlanta, June 19, 2014.

30. *Minkisi* will be discussed further in the Bailey section.

31. The photograph can be viewed as image 4/17 on the artist's website: http://www.ericwatersphotography504.com/find_us/clarinets-a-new-orleans-metaphor/, accessed May 30, 2019.

32. The pieces are listed as images 6/17 and 10/17 on the artist's website, http://www.ericwatersphotography504.com/find_us/clarinets-a-new-orleans-metaphor/, accessed May 30, 2019.

33. For a glimpse of Julien's artistic evolution, see Biguenet, Maklansky, and Lewis, Tony, *Before,* 68–75.

34. For a history of spirit photography, see Martyn Jolly's *Faces of the Living Dead.*

35. "Reflections," silver gelatin, 2003.

36. The artist invited me to join him on one of his excavating trips in a second-hand warehouse in New Orleans's Faubourg Marigny. Once there, he bought an axe that was used to break open an attic roof, which he was planning to use in his new work on the shooting of Brown. The axe directly relates the racial violence of "Katrina" with "Ferguson."

37. Epaul Julien, personal conversation with the author, New Orleans, February 2015.

38. For a thorough discussion of the Katrina "X-codes," see Moye's fascinating discussion and digital exhibit, "Katrina + 5: An X-Code Exhibition."

39. See Moye's piece for an illustration of the Ezili heart.

40. See Thompson's "Preface" to *Radcliffe Bailey: Memory as Medicine,* 11–17.

41. The Art of the Quilt: http://artofthequilt.com/news.html, accessed May 30, 2019.

42. See Moye's "Lift Every Voice and Sing: The Quilts of Gwendolyn Ann Magee."

43. Monica Hesse, "Quilting Magazine Exposes Craft's Risque Underside."

44. On the role of men in the African American quilting tradition, also see Gladys-Marie Fry, *Man Made.*

45. For a fictional representation based on actual New Orleans citizens, see the character of Albert 'Big Chief" Lambreaux (played by Clarke Peters) in David Simon and Eric Overmeyer HBO series *Treme,* sewing his own costume (Episode 12). For a popular history of Mardi Gras Indians with gorgeous photographs, see Michael P. Smith's *Mardi Gras Indians.*

46. See Dominique Aurélia's essay "Une Esthétique de la résistance," which deciphers the secret meanings of colors, signs, and geometric structures in African American quilting.

47. Personal conversation with artist, New Orleans, May 2015.

48. On the coincidence of the quotidian and catastrophe in post-Katrina New Orleans, see also Thomas Neff's post-Katrina photographs: Jerry Atnip, "Thomas Neff—Katrina: Hanging Out and Holding On," South x Southeast, September 2012, https://www.buildsxsemagazine.com/2012/09/thomas-neff-katrina-hanging-holding/, accessed May 30, 2019.

49. See, for instance, plates 1 and 2 in Spiegelman, *In the Shadow,* n.p.

50. "Groensteen terms the process of creating a network of visual and semantic correspondences "tressage,' which means braiding or 'interlacing' (Kuhlman, 855).

51. I use the term "compositionist" in the sense with which Latour famously endowed it. Similar to Glissant's concept of creolization, Latour's compositionism "underlines that things have to be put together (Latin *componere,* Latin) while retaining their heterogeneity" ("An Attempt," 473–74). In addition, compositionism has clear roots in art, painting, music, theater dance" (474) and "carries with it the pungent but ecologically correct smell of 'compost,' itself due to the active 'de-composition' of many invisible agents'" (474). While Glissant's creolization is born out of slavery and the plantation system, Latour's compositionism embraces an ecological sense of the Anthropocene. However, as I show in chapters 1 and 4, slavery and creolization overlap partially with the Anthropocene and its worldwide dimensions.

52. In his analysis of shotgun houses in Port-au-Prince and New Orleans, architectural historian John Michael Vlach has suggested that the shotgun house was influenced by both Arawak and Yoruba dwelling styles (see "The Shotgun House," part 2, 65–69). Rick Lowe and David Brown's interdisciplinary collection *Row,* including experimental, architectural, literary, and historical essays on the shotgun house, with contributors including bell hooks and Mabel O. Wilson offers a wealth of visual and critical information.

53. "The New Orleans Shotgun House," Archi-Dinamica Architects LLC: Journal of Architecture, Design, and Construction, August 12, 2011, https://archidius.wordpress.com/2011/08/12/the-new-orleans-shotgun-house/, accessed May 30, 2019.

54. Art therapy is more directly used as cure for victims of trauma. See, for instance, the Katrina initiative from the American Art Therapy Association: http://www.katrinaexhibit.org/, accessed May 30, 2019.

55. See Wyatt MacGaffey's "Meaning and Aesthetics in Kongo Art," 175.

56. In a show largely devoted to disasters, the closing date of the exhibit, marking the tenth anniversary of the attacks on the Twin Towers and the Pentagon, is significant.

57. For a description of the thirty-seven mixed-media objects and installations included in the exhibit, see Thompson's *Radcliffe Bailey,* which reproduces the artist's works enriched with personal memorabilia and African art.

58. The *Kongo across the Waters* exhibit (Jimmy Carter Presidential Library Museum, Atlanta, Georgia, May 17–September 21, 2014), gathering more than 160 works, heavily focused on *minkisi,* giving a sense of the continuity between artistic and sacred practices across the Atlantic. The exhibit also included works by contemporary artists (including Bailey) from countries including Cuba, Haiti, the United States, and AngolaKongo across the Waters.

59. For examples of memory jars in the US South, see *Kongo across the Waters,* 350–51. On *pakè,* see "Vodou: Art and Cult from Haiti," Universes in Universe https://universes.art/en/specials/2010/vodou/tour/packages_bizangos/, accessed May 30, 2019.

60. See, for instance, *Notes From Elmina III,* 10–11.

61. See the 2002 "Uprooted," a three-page unfolding illustration, 24.

62. See, for instance, the 2000 piece "Jamaica," 44.

63. "As a teenager Mr. Bailey, who grew up in Hank Aaron's neighborhood in Atlanta, pursued his early love of baseball and played semi-pro for a year. He ultimately decided he was too small for his position as catcher and followed his mother's vision for him by enrolling at the Atlanta College of Art." Hilarie M. Sheets, "In the Picture: Atlanta, Africa, and the Past," *New York Times,* June 30, 2011, https://www.nytimes.com/2011/07/03/arts/design/high-museum-in-atlanta-shows-radcliffe-baileys-art.html, accessed May 24, 2019.

64. See, for instance, the sound emerging from the conch shell in *Windward Coast.*

65. See the collage series *Notes from Elmina.*

66. *Notes from Elmina 1,* 139; *Notes from Elmina II,* 86; *Notes from Elmina III,* 87.

67. Thompson identifies the statuettes respectively as a "Fang figure" (*Elmina II*) (84) and a Kuyu sculpture from Congo (Brazaville)" (*Elmina III,* 84).

68. See "Caribbean Man" (1; 11), and DeLoughrey's notion of "tidalectics," derived form Brathwaite's thought: "Tidalectics engages what Brathwaite calls an 'alter/native' historiography to linear models of colonial progress . . . drawing from a cyclical model, invoking the continual movement and rhythm of the ocean" (*Routes and Roots,* 2).

69. Jake Adam York, "Medicine as Memory," *Southern Spaces,* January 26, 2011, https://southernspaces.org/2012/medicine-memory-radcliffe-bailey-atlantas-high-museum-art#sthash.JlK8FkMo.dpuf, accessed May 30, 2019.

70. Radcliffe Bailey, "Radcliffe on . . . Notes from Elmina," interview at the McNay Art Museum, San Antonio, Texas, https://vimeo.com/45451373, accessed May 30, 2019.

71. "The thing is inseparable from a person perceiving it, and can never actually be in itself because it stands at the end of our gaze or at the terminus of a sensory exploration which invests it with humanity" (Maurice Merleau-Ponty quoted in Bishop, *Installation Art,* 50).

72. An important predecessor is New York–based African American artist David Hammons, who set up an installation made out of train tracks in 1989 (See Thompson, *Radcliffe Bailey,* 23). In his *Placebo,* exhibited at the Museum of Contemporary Art in Los Angeles in 1994, Cuban installation artist Felix Gonzalez-Torres filled up a room with gold-wrapped candy that visitors were invited to take (see Bishop, *Installation Art,* 113–15). The changing shape of the exhibit is similar to Bailey's *Windward Coast.* Bailey's installation is also reminiscent of Chinese artist and dissident Ai Wei Wei, who, almost simultaneously, exhibited his *Sunflower Seeds* installation at the Tate Modern in London (October 2010–May 2011). http://www.aiweiweiseeds.com/, accessed May 30, 2019.

73. See Fanon's *Black Skin, White Masks,* especially chapter 8, "By Way of Conclusion" (198–206), and Aimé Césaire's *Nègre je suis, nègre je resterai.*

74. See for instance, 50.

75. "Strictly speaking, the 'second line' is the mass of people who follow a traditional African-American parade in New Orleans. In common speech, however, when people refer to a 'second line,' they imply the whole event—generally a brass band or black Indian parade or a jazz funeral sponsored by any of the city's large number of traditional black social clubs and civic societies" (Michael Proctor Smith, *Mardi Gras,* 27).

3. Mami Wata the Formidable

1. For an excellent version of the song "La Petenera" by the Veracruz band Tlen Huicani's, see https://www.youtube.com/watch?v=kzlbr8TF7ko, accessed May 30, 2019.

2. "Lasirenn, one of Vodou's most important female deities, who, together with Agwe, lord of the sea, rules over the oceans" (Bellegarde-Smith and Michel, *Haitian Vodou,* 90). For a discussion of "Lasirèn" in the Rada Vaudou pantheon, with a special focus on Danticat's *Claire of the Sea Light,* see Roselyne Gérazime's "Lasirèn: Labalèn."

3. I explore the Haitian concepts of *Anba Dlo* and *Lot Bo Dlo* in chapter 4.

4. "At once beautiful, protective, and potentially deadly, the water spirit Mami Wata (Mother Water) is celebrated throughout much of Africa and the

African Atlantic worlds" (Drewal, "Mami Wata," 60–83). Drewal elaborates on the specific creolizing sources of Mami Wata in Africa, Europe, and India.

5. See Drewal on Mami Wata's hair, 64.

6. See Gwendolyn Dubois Shaw's *Seeing the Unspeakable,* Sander Gilman's "Confession of an Academic Pornographer," and Kevin Young's "Triangular Trade."

7. Thompson, *Radcliffe Bailey,* 101n18.

8. On the relationship between visual arts and writing in Walker, see Young, "Triangular Trade."

9. "I have cobbled together from the Metropolitan Museum of Arts Collection . . . and from some of my own work a narrative of fluid symbols in which that fluidity is figurative and sometimes literal" (9).

10. "All the historical paintings and my images and typewritten texts precede the recent hurricanes, tsunamis, and to some extent, the global concern about rising sea levels" (Walker, *After the Deluge,* front page).

11. In *Frames of War,* Butler explains that "the frame does not simply exhibit reality, but actively participates in a strategy of containment, selectively producing and enforcing what will count as reality" (xiii).

12. Excerpt from book cover, *After the Deluge,* n.p.

13. For Fanon, the "nègre" (i.e., a "negro" or the more violent racial slur) is the object constructed by the white gaze, not subjects in their lived experience (see *Black Skin, White Masks,* 89). Walker's stereotyped victims of slavery would also be, for Fanon, "des nègres."

14. Another type of framing may be at work here. Indeed, it is not clear whether the photographed subjects would be considered as white according to the US census categories (yet another type of arbitrary framing) or as Hispanic or other.

15. The lack of value given to black lives in the United States has been evident in the gratuitous executions of black men during the post-Katrina craze as well as in recent police murder of young black men and boys, from Michael Brown's shooting in Ferguson, Missouri, to the police murder by chokehold of Eric Garner in Staten Island, among many other examples. On the lack of value given to black lives, see Dayan, who defines those killed, tortured, or put in solitary confinement within the confines of legality as stuck in a "negative personhood" (*Law is a White Dog,* xii). Read Jesmyn Ward's memoir, *Men We Reaped.* On the gratuitous police and private militia killing of mostly black men during hurricane Katrina, consult "Criminal Justice Collapse: The Constitution after Hurricane Katrina," by legal scholars Brandon L. Garrett and Tania Tetlow. Bibler also comments on what A. C. Thompson from the *Nation* has called Katrina's "hidden race war" ("The Flood," 3–13).

16. See Terence Blanchard's "A Tale of God's Will: A Requiem for Katrina," Audio CD, Blue Note, August 2007 (also soundtrack to Lee's When the Levees Broke).

17. *Merriam-Webster,* "muck (n.)," http://www.merriam-webster.com /dictionarmuck, accessed June 5, 2018.

18. See Marcus Rediker's *Slave Ship:* "Sharks followed slavers across the Atlantic, feeding hungrily on the corpses of sailors and especially slaves" (2nd illustration page after p. 210).

19. See James's "The Property" in *Black Jacobins* (6–26); Patterson's *Slavery and Social Death;* JanMohamed's *Death-Bound Subject;* and Glissant's "Open Boat" in *Poetics of Relation* (5–9).

20. See Glissant's *Poetics of Relation* (6) and Sullivan's commentary on Duval Carrié's paintings (*Continental Shifts,* 9–36). "In "The Crossing" we also see Duval employing the image of the tree that seems to grow up almost miraculously from the depths of the boat" (24). The tree growing out of sites and bodies of torture is also reminiscent of the chokecherry tree growing on Sethe's scars in Toni Morrison's *Beloved* (24).

21. The Minstrel Show, http://chnm.gmu.edu/courses/jackson/minstrel /minstrel.html, accessed June 1, 2019.

22. On acts of censorship that led to the removal of Walker's work from public places and exhibitions, see Dubois Shaw, "Seeing," 8, and Gilman, "Confessions," 27–35 for a critical analysis of the question of pornography in scholarship and art.

23. See, for instance, Devery Anderson, http://www.emmetttillmurder.com (accessed September 23, 2014) and the controversy around Dana Schutz's painting of Emmett Till: "It's not acceptable for a white person to transmute Black suffering into profit and fun," says artist Hannah Black. Lorena Muñoz-Alonso, "Dana Schutz's Painting of Emmett Till at Whitney Biennial Sparks Protest," ArtNet News, March 21, 2017, https://news.artnet.com/art-world/dana-schutz-painting -emmett-till-whitney-biennial-protest-897929, accessed June 1, 2019.

24. The exhibit was curated in partnership between Emory University and the Martin Luther King Jr. Historic Site in 2002.

25. "*Without Sanctuary,* James Allen," Twin Palms: https://twinpalms.com /books-artists/without-sanctuary/, accessed June 4, 2019.

26. Paige Parvin, "Strange Fruit: Emory Takes a hard look at one of America's Deepest Sorrow," Emory Magazine, Summer 2002, https://www.emory.edu /EMORY_MAGAZINE/summer2002/without_sanctuary.html, accessed June 3, 2019.

27. See particularly "Flipping the Script" (1–16), in which Yancy describes the necessary process of making whiteness visible and marked, as an ethical and political response to the hyper visible and marked black body in the overdetermining white gaze that Fanon had evaluated in *Black Skin, White Masks.* "'Look, a White!' returns to white people the problem of whiteness. While I see it as a gift, I know that not all gifts are free of discomfort" (Yancy, 6).

28. For a striking discussion of representations of Ethel Freeman's body and its treatment in Lee's documentary, see Bernie Cook's "Do You Know What It

Means" in her *Flood of Images,* 135–42. See also Patricia Smith's dirge poem "Ethel's Sestina" in *Blood Dazzler,* 45–46.

29. "Oh, when the stars fall from the Sky . . . I want to be in that number / When the saints go marching in." For the full lyrics, see https://www.lyricsfreak.com/l/louis+armstrong/when+the+saints+go+marching+in_20085348.html, accessed June 1, 2019.

30. See Noliwe Rooks's "Black Women's Status Update," *Chronicle of Higher Education,* June 26, 2014, https://www.chronicle.com/article/Black-Womens-Status-Update/147351/, accessed June 1, 2019.

31. See my essay "Blood Sugar."

32. See Bishop, "Activated Spectatorship," in *Installation Art,* 102–27.

33. On shame as inflected by the "whiteness" or "blackness" of spectators of Walker's cut-out silhouettes, see Sharpe's *Monstrous Intimacies,* especially 156–57.

34. See Sigmund Freud, *On Metapsychology*, 88.

35. Aristotle, *Poetics,* 1449b.

36. See Aristotle: "Under the influence of sacred music we see these people, when they use tunes that violently arouse the soul, being thrown into a state as if they had received medicinal treatment and taken a purge" (*Politics,* 1342a).

37. On the art of contrast in Walker, see Roberta Smith, "Kara Walker."

38. See *Saturday Night Live*'s "The Day Beyoncé Became Black, " February 14, 2016, https://vimeo.com/155287084, accessed June 1, 2019.

39. Shantrelle Lewis, http://shantrelleplewis.com/?page_id=44, accessed June 1, 2019.

40. Shantrelle Lewis, "'Formation" Exploits New Orleans' Trauma," Slate, February 10, 2016, https://slate.com/human-interest/2016/02/beyonces-formation-exploits-new-orleans-trauma.html, accessed June 1, 2019.

41. "Our Favorite Songs and Videos Right Now: Beyoncé, Kanye West, and More," *Rolling Stone,* March 2, 2016, https://www.rollingstone.com/music/music-lists/our-favorite-songs-and-videos-right-now-beyonce-kanye-west-and-more-81913/beyonce-formation-28298/, accessed June 1, 2019.

42. Vera Lou Derid, "Qui est Melina Matsoukas, la réalisatrice du clip 'Formation' de Beyoncé?" *Les Inrockuptibles*, April 3, 2016, https://www.lesinrocks.com/2016/04/03/musique/musique/melina-matsoukas-realisatrice-clip-formation-de-beyonce/, accessed June 1, 2019.

43. See also Madhu Krishnan, who describes Mami Wata as a controller of wealth as a resistance to patriarchal structure in Igbo culture ("Mami Wata and the Occluded Feminine," 4).

44. "If you want to see where the video for 'Hold Up' was born, take a look at Goude's 2007 commercial for the perfume Covet, in which Sarah Jessica Parker, dressed in a ball gown, smashes a window to get at her favorite fragrance" (Als, "Beywatch," *New Yorker,* May 23, 2016, https://www.newyorker.com/magazine/2016/05/30/beyonces-lemonade, accessed June 1, 2019.

45. The quick montage intermingling real footage and fictional shots is frequently used in the aftermath of Katrina. See for instance the opening of the

HBO drama series *Treme*. While Spike Lee only uses documentary images, he also begins his *When the Levees Broke* with a fast montage.

46. The politics of reclaiming or misappropriation of the former sugar-cane exploitation, Madewood Plantation House in Napoleonville, Louisiana, is thick. Sofia Coppola used the same set in her 2017 film *The Beguiled*. See Elizabeth Stamp, "Here's What Sofia Coppola's New Film, *The Beguiled*, and Beyoncé Have in Common," *Architectural Digest*, June 23, 2017, https://www.architecturaldigest.com/story/heres-what-sofia-coppolas-new-film-the-beguiled-and-beyonce-have-in-common, accessed June 1, 2019.

47. "That B.E.A.T.," Abteen Bagheri, January 28, 2013, https://vimeo.com/58423297, accessed June 1, 2019.

48. While some have argued that Black's material was taken from the documentary without proper credit or remuneration, the French magazine *Les Inrockuptibles* cites Beyoncé as claiming that the director had received proper credit and remuneration and Matsoukas as tweeting her recognition of his influence in the video production (Derid, "Qui est Melina Matsoukas?"). Black tweets his frustration: "I guess it's flattering that people fuck with the things you've created but also frustrating when they wanna use it like it's theirs." Bagheri thanks Beyoncé and Matsoukas for the credit:

49. Derid, "Qui est Melina Matsoukas?"

50. Jessica Goodman "Getting in Line: Working Through Beyoncé's 'Formation,'" *Entertainment Weekly*, February 6, 2016, https://ew.com/article/2016/02/06/beyonce-formation-music-video-that-beat/, accessed June 1, 2019.

51. Sharpe demands "wake work," an act of resistance, mourning, and acknowledgment that refuses the state of non-being imposed on black humanity. Concretely, "how might we stay in the wake with and as those whom the state positions to die ungrievable deaths and live lives meant to me unlivable?" (*In the Wake*, 22).

52. See, especially, "Work, Family, and Black Women's Oppression," and "Mammies, Matriarchs, and Other Controlling Images" (51–74 and 76–105, respectively).

53. BeauSoleil official website: https://beausoleilmusic.com/#!beausoleil-bio/c1j40, accessed June 1, 2019.

54. "[A term] used to describe a person who has no style, taste, or class" (*Urban Dictionary*) https://www.urbandictionary.com/define.php?term=bamma, accessed June 1, 2019.

55. See Als: "Too often the works of black artists are conflated with the reality of their lives, rather than the grace of their imaginations: if you're black, you have to be 'authentic.'" Als, "Beywatch."

56. See Littlewood, *The Variations of Johanes Brahms*, 264.

57. John Caramanica, Wesley Morris, and Jenna Wortham, "Beyoncé in 'Formation,'" *New York Times*, February 6, 2016, https://www.nytimes.com/2016/02/07/arts/music/beyonce-formation-super-bowl-video.html, accessed May 27, 2019.

58. See Wendy Sifret's blog post on Messy Mya and his afterlife in Beyoncé's "Formation": "The inclusion of the sample doesn't only pay homage to a piece of local culture, but serves as a reminder that Messy's life and murder, and the following trial continue to represent the city's ongoing battle with crime and violence." https://i-d.vice.com/en_us/article/a3gq9g/the-story-of-messy-mya-the-tragic-voice-on-beyoncs-new-track, accessed June 1, 2019. See also Als's *"Beywatch,"* which reads the guest opening by Messy Mya as a manifestation of the consciousness of the devastation caused both by Katrina and racial discrimination in New Orleans.

59. Regina Bradley, "Getting in Line," Huffington Post, February 12, 2016, https://www.huffpost.com/entry/getting-in-line-working-t_b_9218736, accessed June 1, 2019.

60. For an extended reflection on the copresence of death and life in Vaudou-derived religions and practices, such as carnival traditions, see Donald J. Cosentino's *In Extremis,* which includes a section on New Orleans funeral "Bone Gangs" and the omnipresence of death in carnival. See, especially, Stephen C. Wehmeyer's "Playing Dead: The Northside Skull and Bone Gang" (143–59).

61. Regina Bradley, "Getting in Line," Red Clay Scholar, February 17, 2016, https://redclayscholarblog.wordpress.com/2016/02/07/getting-in-line-working-through-beyonces-formation/, accessed June 1, 2019.

62. Lasiwèn is one of many references to Afro-diasporic deities in *Lemonade.* See Kamaria Robert's "What Beyoncé Teaches Us about the African Diaspora in Lemonade."

63. See, for instance, the Indigo Arts Gallery website (https://indigoarts.com/tags/mermaids, accessed June 4, 2019) for visual references to Lasiwèn.

64. On Lasiwèn as Ezili's manifestation, see Deren's *Divine Horsemen,* 121–22.

65. "Oh: And this song is remarkably gay. She takes bounce music—which is pretty gay to start with—and repeats the word 'slay' in different ways. . . . 'Slay' is an amazing word here, and the choreography seizes on it. It's violent, obviously. But, in a gay context, it's also triumphant. . . . The video also features Big Freedia, the gay star of New Orleans bounce music, a call-and-response style of hip-hop" (Als, "Beywatch"). See also Tinsley's Beyoncé in Formation on Big freedia bringing "black LGBT life to millions of viewers" (142).

66. See O'Neill and Tinsley's "Beyonce's 'Formation' Is Activism for African Americans, and LGBTQ People." On Ezili's realm, water, as a privileged site of eroticism between women, see Tinsley's *Thiefing Sugar,* her essay "Black Atlantic, Queer Atlantic," and her *Ezili's Mirrors.*

67. Thinking "in terms of the oceanographic, the aquatic, and the liminal-watery-marginal border spaces," Solomon contends, allows for "certain stories," such as queer narratives, to "find nourishment and room to be told" ("Southernmost Currents," 12).

68. Tinsley crucially argues that Beyoncé's *Lemonade* transitions from black women "muscling through" water to women "becoming water": "But in this

triumphant finale, black women don't have to navigate water because they are water" (*Beyoncé,* 157).

69. See, for instance, the Baton Rouge flood of 2016, Richard Ashmore, "Worse than Hurricane Katrina," *Mirror,* August 6, 2016, https://www.mirror.co.uk/news/world-news/worse-hurricane-katrina-coffins-float-8637663, accessed June 1, 2019.

70. Caramanica, Morris, and Wartham, "Beyoncé in 'Formation.'"

71. "For the Texas Bama Femme: A Black Queer Femme-inist Reading of Beyoncé's *Lemonade,*" Tinsley, (Author/speaker) talk, Emory University, March 23, 2017. See also Tinsley's "Beyoncé Femme-inism" (*Beyoncé in Formation,* 7–14).

72. See *Leviticus* 15:19.

4. Drowned

1. DeLoughrey identifies a recent shift in oceanic studies from "a long-term concern with mobility across transoceanic surfaces to theorizing oceanic submersion, thus rendering vast oceanic space into ontological space" ("Submarine Futures," 32). This chapter shares a similar concern with oceanic subversion and ontological depth.

2. "The Unity is Submarine," *Contradictory Omens,* 64.

3. Duval Carrié, in his interview with Jenny Sharpe, relates that his installation on the Benin (Fon) coast made of antennae meant to guide the lost water spirits attempting to rejoin Africa from their Caribbean shores was mistaken for a sacred altar: "[The African artists] told me that [Dago the priest] finally took out his real fetishes . . . and when I asked them to explain, I realized they were talking about my sculptures. It was fabulous!" ("Punder and Play," 564)

4. The ancient rituals of burial at sea, civilian or military, have regained contemporary popularity. Read Kate Sweeney's "With the Fishes" (151–73), which ponders new forms of burials at sea such as those provided by the Eternal Reefs company that "mixes the cremated ashes of your loved one with a cement compound to create part of an artificial coral reef" (153). The submerged compounds strikingly resemble Taylor's sculptures: "Covered in algae and plant life and eroded some with the years, they look organic; beautiful and worn and almost ethereal in that way of organisms of the demersal deep" (161–62). The underwater cemetery of the Neptune Society, off the coast of Miami, like Taylor's installations, is designed "to attract fish and promote the growth of coral" (Foer, Joshua et al., *Atlas Obscura,* 342).

5. "In Varanasi the ashes and bones are thrown into the river straight away; the holiness of the city and the river makes elaborate procedures unnecessary" (Firth, *Dying,* 90). "The ashes of the cremated body are immersed in holy waters the same rivers that feed and irrigate paddy fields; the same water that cooks the rice and bathes the dead before cremation" (Narayanan, "Water, Wood, and Wisdom," 179).

6. For Barthes, the punctum in a photograph is "what pierces me like an arrow" (*Camera Lucida,* 48)

7. Brandon Griggs, "Photographer Describes 'Scream' of Migrant Boy's 'Silent Body'," CNN, September 3, 2015, https://www.cnn.com/2015/09/03/world/dead-migrant-boy-beach-photographer-nilufer-demir/, accessed June 2, 2019.

8. See Chimamanda Ngozi Adichie's "The Danger of a Single Story," TED Global, July 2009, https://www.ted.com/talks/chimamanda_adichie_the_danger_of_a_single_story, accessed June 2, 2019.

9. Brendan O'Neill. "Sharing a Photo of a Dead Syrian Child Isn't Compassionate, It's Narcissistic," *Spectator,* September 3, 2015.

10. "Sand Artist Sudarsan Pattnaik's Tribute to Aylan Kurdi," Catch News, September 4, 2015, http://www.catchnews.com/lite/sand-artist-sudarsan-pattnaik-s-tribute-to-aylan-kurdi-1441383236.html, accessed June 2, 2019.

11. Jay Akbar, "Touching or Creepy," *Daily Mail,* March 3, 2016, https://www.dailymail.co.uk/news/article-3475658/Artist-creates-moving-sculpture-tragic-migrant-child-Aylan-Kurdi-lying-dead-sand.html, accessed June 2, 2019.

12. Ratnam, Niru. "Ai Weiwei's Aylan Kurdi's Image," *Spectator,* February 1, 2016, https://blogs.spectator.co.uk/2016/02/ai-weiweis-aylan-kurdi-image-is-crude-thoughtless-and-egotistical/, accessed June 2, 2019.

13. Other artists who submerge their work include the French duo "Forlane 6" of Mathieu Goussin and Hortense Le Calvez (https://forlane6studio.com/about-forlane6/, accessed June 2, 2019) and Quebecois painter-ceramicist René Dérouin (http://www.renederouin.com/wp/wp-content/uploads/2013/11/migration-largage.pdf, accessed June 2, 2019). New Orleans native Michel Varisco photographs human subjects, plantlife, and engineered objects underwater to reflect on environmental vulnerability and regeneration in wetlands. Consult, for instance, her "Below Sea Level," "Fluid States," and "Shifting" series on her official website (https://www.michelvarisco.com/, accessed July 13, 2019).

14. For a visual and sonorous immersion near Manman Dlo and Yemeya, see the filmed diving expedition on Valère's website: https://www.laurentvalereartstudio.com/, accessed June 2, 2019.

15. MUSA, Museo Subacuático de Arte, "The Art of Conservation," https://musamexico.org/, accessed May 26 2019.

16. "Imagine, if you can," Glissant, *Poetics,* 5.

17. Jason deCaires Taylor, "Overview," https://www.underwatersculpture.com/about/overview/, accessed June 2, 2019. Tanya Shields also qualifies Taylor's project as touristic rather than ecological: "Taylor's sculptures are a tourist destination rather than a monument with which Grenadian people interact" (*Bodies and Bones,* 48).

18. African American designer Wayne James was more intentional than Taylor in his 1998 underwater installation. Through his Homewardbound Foundation, James commissioned a twelve-foot aluminium arch realized by seven metal artists from St. Croix. The monument, which was "lowered to the bottom of the ocean" in international waters off New York harbor, was meant as "a grave

marker on the world's largest, yet unmarked graveyard, the Atlantic Ocean's infamous Middle passage" (James in Kardux, *Monuments,* 89).

19. On the equivalence between the *anba dlo* and Guinen, see Deren: "Here is Guinée, Africa, the legendary place of racial origin. Here, on the Island Below the Sea, the loa have their permanent residence, their primal location" (*Divine Horsemen,* 36).

20. See Sutherland's "The Afterlife of Art," *Continental Shifts,* 81–87. Daagbo Hounon, supreme chief of Vaudou in Benin, tells Duval Carrié about his installation on the beach in Ouidah: "This is definitely not art. This is like heavy religion". To which the artist replies: "I'm no witchdoctor. I'm an artist'" (both quoted in Sutherland, 84).

21. "In Haitian Creole, when someone is said to be lòt bò dlo . . . it can either mean that they've traveled abroad or that they have died" (Danticat, *The Art of Death,* 22).

22. See Moyes's "Lift Every Voice and Sing: The Quilts of Gwendolyn Ann Magee", which includes a reproduction of the quilt: *Southern Spaces.* September 11, 2014, https://southernspaces.org/2014/lift-every-voice-and-sing-quilts-gwendolyn-ann-magee, accessed May 27, 2019

23. See, for instance, Edward J. Sullivan's gorgeous collection *Continental Shifts.*

24. Duval Carrié explains that he grew up with the Ambaglos from early childhood, when his "domestic workers and nannies" told him stories about the ambaglo realm where some of their acquaintances would sometimes travel and return with a ring or a diamond that would explain their new wealth. The ambaglo, the artist confessed, both "terrified and amused him" (Loichot, personal conversation with the artist, Little Haiti Cultural Complex, Miami, August 2017). Duval Carrié uses the spelling *ambaglo* to refer to the *anba dlo.*

25. Mixed media on plexiglass, 365 cm X 198 cm., reproduced in Sullivan, *Continental Shifts,* 165.

26. Duval Carrié, interview with Jenny Sharpe, "Plunder and Play," 563.

27. Loichot, personal conversation with the artist, Little Haiti Cultural Complex, Miami, August 2017.

28. Conversely, anthropologist Rachel Beauvoir-Dominique refutes the presence of *Vèvès* in the work and interprets the distance of the Queen as a failure to help migrants: "In Duval Carrié's case, the signs are not those sacred symbols. Thus the Reine des ambaglos . . . loses her identity, and in the process, the support she provides the migrants becomes rather dubious. The proliferation of signs and dots over the allegory of democracy serves only to hide the emptiness of what she represents" (54).

29. Ezili Danto, a "hardworking and fiercely protective mother," is recognizable by her dark skin, which contrasts with her rival Ezili Freda's light-skin (Cosentino, *Sacred Arts,* 300)

30. Loıchot, personal conversation with the artist, Little Haiti Cultural Complex, Miami, August 2017.

31. *Zong!,* back cover.

32. Frantz Zephirin, biography, iArtX, https://iartx.com/zephirin-frantz.html, accessed June 2, 2019.

33. For discussions of Zéphirin see Cosentino's *In Extremis,* 51–52, 184; and Russell's *Masterpieces of Haitian Art,* 173–74. Zéphirin's 2007 painting "The Resurrection of the Dead" was featured as cover art in the *New Yorker* in the immediate aftermath of the 2010 earthquake (January 25, 2010).

34. Many other paintings by Zéphirin feature sacred underwater beings. For examples of the Haitian artist's *anba dlo* related paintings, see samples of his works on the Haitian Art Company Website: http://www.haitian-art-co.com/artists/fzephirin.html, accessed June 19, 2019.

35. Water, like a dance or a dirge, by its progress and movement, reminds us of the performative function Roach theorizes as an essential element of collective mourning (*Cities of the Dead,* 50).

36. See Simone Schwarz-Bart, "Du Fond des casseroles," 175.

37. On the importance of roots as historical, memorial, and sacred conduits, see Mimi Sheller, who evokes a "history from below" and an arboreal vitality" performed by tree life (*Citizenship from Below,* 187 and 189).

38. "Guinea" here is to be understood as West Africa and the *anba dlo.*

39. Erol Josué, "Depi M Soti Lan Ginen," February 8, 2014, https://www.youtube.com/watch?v=h-Dw8oVnZ4g, accessed June 2, 2019.

40. Lyrics can be found on http://www.bookmanlit.com/depimsotilanginen.html, accessed June 2, 2019.

41. See Bennett's take: "By vitality' I mean the capacity of things—edibles, commodities, storms, metals—not only to impede or block the will and designs of humans but also to act as quasi-agents or forces with trajectories, propensities, or tendencies of their own" (*Vibrant Matters,* viii).

42. See the "Environment" rubric on Taylor's website: https://www.underwatersculpture.com/environment/artificial-reefs/?doing_wp_cron=1475588582.5318269729614257812500, accessed June 2, 2019.

43. On endangered sea species, see the National Oceanic and Atmospheric Administration (NOAA) website: https://www.noaa.gov/topic-tags/endangered-species, accessed, June 2, 2019.

44. "A nail or a blade was driven into the sculpture each time its force was invoked through ritual, thereby provoking the spirit into action." Art Institute of Chicago, http://www.artic.edu/aic/collections/artwork/151358, accessed June 2, 2019.

45. On *Quimbois* in Guadeloupe and Martinique, see Anny-Dominique Curtius's *Symbiose d'une mémoire,* 107–25.

46. "Underwater Sculptures Are Haunting," Macro Caribbean Living, https://www.macocaribbeanliving.com/create/underwater-sculptures-are-haunting/, accessed June 2, 2019.

47. “La Diablesse and Other Sweet Grenadian Dreams,” *The Romantic Traveller,* January 18, 2013, https://theromantictraveller.blog/2013/01/18/la-diablesse-and-other-sweet-grenadian-dreams/, accessed June 2, 2019.

48. See, for instance, André Eugène’s 2009 mixed-media sculpture of Gede Etwal and Jean Hérad Céleur’s 2012 metal and mixed-media Gede, reproduced in Donald Cosentino’s *In Extremis,* 56 and 59, respectively.

49. Throughout her work, Alaimo has emphasized the need to consider the Anthropocene as aquatic: “And while the geological origins of the term ‘anthropocene’ have sprawned dark terrestrial figurations of man and rock . . . the acifying seas, the liquid index of the anthropocene, are disregarded, even as billions of tiny shelled creatures will meet their end in a catastrophic dissolve, reverberating through the food webs of the ocean” (*Exposed,* 143).

50. “Underwater Sculptures Are Haunting.”

51. “Multidirectional Memory is not competitive” “[It is] subject to ongoing negotiation, cross-referencing, and borrowing . . . productive and not privative” (Rothberg, *Multidirectional Memory,* 3).

52. “Soul Amère: Exposition de peintures et installations,” Potomitan, http://www.potomitan.info/matinik/donatien-yssa.php#top, accessed June 2, 2019.

53. For a reproduction of *Soul amère,* see http://latribunedesantilles.net/v2/article/soul-amere-28-fevrier-23-mars-exposition-de-peintures-de-patricia-donatien-yssa, accessed June 19, 2019.

54. See Martha Ward’s *Voodoo Queen,* 22.

55. See Tristan Yvon’s *La Production d’Indigo.*

56. For a thorough discussion of *blès* in postslavery Caribbean societies, see Donatien, *L’Exorcisme,* 16–19.

57. Anicet also adopts this notion of *blès,* which he described during a conversation with cultural critic Naïma Hachad and myself as “a stain on the skin that represents symptomatically an ill body. When the skin is stained, the entire body seems ill” (“Victor Anicet,” 53).

58. *Merriam-Webster,* “blessing (n.),” http://www.merriam-webster.com/dictionaryblessing, accessed June 5, 2019.

59. DeLoughrey theorizes a similar present-past-future spectrum in water, which suggests the “collapse of linear time” (“Submarine Futures,” 36) and a continuum between species, which she terms a “multispecies ecology” (33). Coral constitutes a privileged example for the latter since the latter is especially present in coral since “the reef is an ecology, a zoophytalite (animal-plant-mineral)” (40).

60. Notably, Danticat’s title, *Dew Breaker,* is the English translation of “casseur de la rosée,” which, once translated, clearly evokes Jacques Roumain’s 1944 *Gouverneurs de la rosée, Masters of the Dew.* Roumain’s foundational Haitian novel was translated by his friend Langston Hughes, which reveals yet another Caribbean-United States connection. It is also a translation of the *Kreyòl choukèt laroze,* “soldiers and paramilitary men and women,” who, under the Duvalier regime, would “routinely take people to some of the country’s worst prisons and

torture chambers coming for them late at night or at dawn" (Danticat, *The Art of Death,* 99).

61. While still discreet in *The Dew Breaker,* Danticat's ecological concern becomes sharper in her latest texts. With her 2013 *Claire of the Sea Light,* published in the direct aftermath of the 2010 earthquake in Haiti, her writing decidedly takes an ecological turn.

62. Randal C. Archibold, "Trying to Protect a Reef With an Otherwordly Diversion," *New York Times,* August 13, 2012, https://www.nytimes.com/2012/08/14/world/americas/in-cancun-trying-to-protect-reef-with-underwater-statues.html, accessed May 25, 2019.

63. Jason deCaires Taylor, "Recent Works," https://www.underwatersculpture.com/works/recent/, accessed June 2, 2019.

64. See, for instance, "Night." https://www.underwatersculpture.com/works/recent/, accessed June 2, 2019.

65. Jason deCaires Taylor, https://www.underwatersculpture.com/about/overview/?doing_wp_cron=1559477503.7039160728454589843750, accessed June 2, 2019.

66. Burke et al., *Reefs at Risk Revisited,* 38.

67. Aristotle's Scala Nature, http://palaeos.com/systematics/greatchainofbeing/scala_naturae.html, accessed June 2, 2019.

68. "Their scale is enormous; the Indo-Pacific coral reef province . . . is the largest ecosystem on earth" (Sheppard, *Coral Reefs,* 2).

69. On Glissant's notion of the rhizome, which facilitates relation, creolization, and non-linear connections, see the chapter "Errantry and Exile" *Poetics of Relation* (11–22)

70. Spalding, Ravilious, and Green, *Reefs at Risk,* 205–45.

71. "Coolitude situates the 'Indian' presence in discourses and processes of creolization" (Pirbhai,"Recasting Jahaji-Bhain," i, 44). Like the word Negritude, it transforms an ethnic or racial slur ("Coolie," "Nègre") into a catalyst for aesthetic production and political action.

72. "Khal Torabully : . . . la coolitude n'est ni un pavé ni une pierre, mais un corail," Courrier des Afriques, August 2015, http://www.courrierdesafriques.net/2015/08/khal-torabully-la-coolitude-nest-ni-un-pave-ni-une-pierre-mais-un-corail, accessed June 2, 2019.

73. Material barriers have thus far prevented me from swimming in the underwater sites. It is still my intention to do so.

5. Stone Pillow and Bone Water

1. In a similar vein, Algerian writer Tahar Djaout's 1984 novel *Chercheur d'os* (*The Bone Seekers, 2018*) recounts the epic quest of a teenage boy looking for his brother's bones. However, once he finds his brother's skeleton, the young man, concludes that bones betray. His brother, "so uncommunicative in life thus became a laughing skeleton" (146). The narrator's disillusion for his personal

search turns into a harsh criticism of the memorial politics of the nation: "What a strange land! . . . People exhume [the dead] to see whether they can't get one more last little thing from them before reburying them even deeper where memory itself will fail to find them" (149).

2. Natasha Tretheway, Emory University commencement address, May 2017, https://www.youtube.com/watch?v=WdcYQx1OzHE&feature=youtu.be%29, accessed June 2, 2019.

3. Annie Ramos, "Child Refugees Scarred by War," CNN, November 11, 2015, https://www.cnn.com/2015/11/08/world/cnnphotos-syrian-children-refugees-sleeping/index.html, accessed June 2, 2019.

4. Trethewey's word clearly resonates with Kimberlé Crenshaw's concept of "intersectionality" featured in her 1991 "Mapping the Margins" and with its widespread antecedents and posterities in sociology, critical race theory, and gender and sexuality studies. The force of Trethewey's theory is expressed in the intransitive use of the verb, which indicates that identity simply intersects—or, rather, intersects in an immense and absolute way.

5. On the segregation of cemeteries in the US South, see Auslander's chapter "The Other Side of Paradise: Mythos and Memory in the Cemetery," in *The Accidental Slaveowner,* 128–50.

6. I use the first name "Natasha" without the author's last name when I refer to the self-poetic persona of the child staged in Trethewey's poems.

7. See my *Orphan Narratives,* "Faulkner's Crossroads," 117–56, for a discussion of Joe Christmas's "race" and name.

8. Jack White, "Wayfaring Stranger," April 16, 2013, https://www.youtube.com/watch?v=MwVLpsgAe8E, accessed June 2, 2019.

9. The jacket design of *Native Guard* is by Michaela Sullivan.

10. Paul Robeson, "Ol' Man River" (*Showboat,* 1936), https://www.youtube.com/watch?v=eh9WayN7R-s, accessed June 2, 2019.

11. Louisiana State University Press, 1998, from cover jacket.

12. Image 108 of Nathan W. Daniels Diary: Vol. I, 1861–64, Library of Congress, https://www.loc.gov/resource/mss84934.00101/?sp=108), accessed June 2, 2019.

13. The diary begins with many almost empty pages, with dates listed without written entries, to lists of names of men, to an increasingly denser, then multilayered writing, ending with handwritten inscriptions partly covered by collated photographs and newspaper clippings. Another story is there waiting to be told.

14. Francis E. Dumas, a light-skinned free black, was Daniel's major and likely close friend, as a portrait of the two men reproduced in the diary and in Weaver's indicates (see portrait in Weaver, *Thank God My Regiment,* 41). Dumas, like many French names born by black soldiers, were likely of Haitian origin. On that note, one may wonder if Major Dumas was related to the great French writer of Haitian ancestry and author of The Count of Monte-Christo Alexandre Dumas. More significantly, is Francis Dumas related to the writer's

father, Thomas-Alexandre Dumas Davy de la Pailleterie (1762–1806), a general in Revolutionary France, and the highest-ranking man of African descent ever in a European army? If not historically proven, the poetic link between military bravery and letters; Haiti and the United States is at least poetically imagined in Trethewey's work (see Reiss, *The Black Count,* 145 and 147).

15. "The Native Guards, like the later black regiments, needed the ultimate test of battle to prove their worth and equality as soldiers. Most whites doubted the abilities of black soldiers" (Weaver, *Thank God My Regiment,* 40)

16. See "The Quarrel with History," *Caribbean Discourse,* 61–65.

17. The expression echoes early twentieth-century Russian poet Marina Tsvetaeva, who identifies "Poets with History and Poets without History." However, this is where the congruence between Trethewey and Tsvetaena ends, since Tsvetaeva's "poets with history could be depicted graphically as an arrow shot into infinity" whereas "poets without history" adhere to the circle (*Art in the Light of Conscience,* 136). Trethewey, while she writes "poems of history," as I like to call them, seems to favor circular repetitions and echoes rather than teleology.

18. See Crosby, *Little Taste of Freedom,* 3.

19. Vicksburg Spring Pilgrimage: http://www.vicksburgpilgrimage.com/, accessed June 2, 2019.

20. See Erin Blakemore's "How Civil Rights Wade-Ins Desegregated Southern Beaches," History, July 21, 2017, https://www.history.com/news/how-civil-rights-wade-ins-desegregated-southern-beaches, accessed June 2, 2019.

21. Trethewey, writing "poems of history," demarks herself once more from Tsvetaeva's poets with history, who "simply don't turn round to themselves—no time for it, only onward!" (*Art in the Light of Conscience,* 137)

22. See summary of court case *Trethewey v. Dekalb County,* Georgia: https://www.leagle.com/decision/1987908662fsupp2461850, accessed June 2, 2019.

23. William Wordsworth, "I Wandered Lonely as a Cloud," Poetry Foundation. https://www.poetryfoundation.org/poems/45521/i-wandered-lonely-as-a-cloud, accessed June 3, 2019.

24. See Threthewey's poem "Imperatives for Carrying On in the Aftermath" in *Monument,* 1–2.

25. For an authoritative discussion of the Zong atrocity and its legal, historical, artistic, literary, and ethical ramifications, see Ian Baucom's *Specters of the Atlantic.* For a reading of the Zong as neo–slave narrative, see Stephanie Iasiello's: "Slavery and its Afterlives."

26. On the reconstructive potential of broken objects, see Cartwright's interpretation of turtle's "powers of shell-shaking reassembly" ("Confederacies of Undead Imagination," 15) uniting Afro-diasporic literatures from Nigeria, Cuba, Puerto Rico, Brazil, and Creole Louisiana in his *Sacral Grooves, Limbo Gateways* (204–8).

27. In maritime law, flotsam and jetsam refer to two types of debris: flotsam result from shipwreck or other unwanted causes. Jetsam are the debris from objects thrown voluntarily from the ship, for instance to lighten cargo. Jetsam can

be reclaimed, while flotsam cannot. See NOAA website: https://oceanservice.noaa.gov/facts/flotsam-jetsam.html, accessed June 2, 2019.

28. Corio complements Foucault's and Agamben's respective notions of "biopower" and "bare life" by emphasizing plantation slavery as a privileged example for these concepts: "Contrary to Foucault's suggestion that biopower was a western modern innovation, this study argues that the very need to produce and accumulate life was itself engendered in the Atlantic world by the assemblages of chattel slavery" (*Anagrams of Annihilation,* 332).

29. Philip in Saunders, "Defending the Dead," 75.

30. Cover by Joss Maclennan Design.

31. "Os" is also a homonym of the exclamation "O" of the ode and stupefaction. In addition, Moïse sees in the title "Os" and its anagrammatic rearrangement on the page a call for help: "In *Zong!,* the letters composing the French word 'os' [Bone(s)] are used to materialize the drowning page, as the poet recreates the slaves' S.O.S." "Grasping the Ungraspable," 28).

32. For a compelling regendering of captured Africans, read Kanor's novel *Humus,* which performs the narrative of fourteen captive girls and women who rebel against slavery by jumping into the water.

33. See James's *The Black Jacobins,* 6–12, and Glissant's *Poetics of Relation,* 5–9.

34. Baucom indeed argues that Turner, with his brushstroke, represents the unimaginable horror of the murder of the enslaved as an alternative to mathematical abstractions of the lives of enslaved humans: "Turner, that is, applies a smear of paint where the committee applies statistics" (*Specters of the Atlantic,* 275).

35. "Take two dried walnuts, two figs, and twenty leaves of rue; pound them all together, with the addition of a grain of salt; if a person takes this mixture fasting, he will be proof against all poisons for that day" (Pliny's *Naturalis Historia,* 77 AD, book 23, LXXVI, 149).

36. "The docility [of zombis] is total provided you never give them salt. If imprudently they are given a plate containing even a grain of salt the fog which cloaks their minds instantly clears away and they become conscious of their terrible servitude" (Métraux, *Voodoo,* 283). Danticat similarly indicates that zombies "can be liberated from their living death by eating salt" and that people in distress can be given salt "in their coffee . . . to help ward of the *sezisman,* 'the shock" (*Art of Death,* 140).

Epilogue

1. See DeLoughrey's "Revisiting Tidalectics."

2. "Study Puts Puerto Rico's Death Toll from Hurricane Maria near 5,000," Harris, Richard, NPR, "All Things Considered," May 29, 2018.

3. "Colonial powers have constructed the trope of the isolated island by mystifying the importance of the sea . . . thus rendering tropical island spaces as ahistorical and isolated" (DeLoughrey, "Revisiting," 98).

4. For a gut-wrenching homage to the Vietnamese refugees attempting to cross the Pacific, read and experience Matt Huynh's interactive graphic novel "The Boat": http://www.sbs.com.au/theboat/, accessed June 2, 2019. On water exiles in the Indian Ocean, see Mehta's *Diasporic Dislocations: Indo-Caribbean Women Writers Negotiate the Kala Pani,* and Bruno Jean-François's "De la thalassologie à la Relation."

5. "The Italian Navy rescued survivors of a shipwreck 20 miles north of Libya. After hundreds of men, women, and children drowned in 2013 off the islands of Sicily and Malta, the Italian government assigned its navy to help rescue refugees at sea, in a campaign called "Mare Nostrum." In 2014 alone, 170,081 people were rescued and taken to Italy. See James Estrin, "A Subtle Moment," *New York Times,* February 12, https://lens.blogs.nytimes.com/2015/02/12/a-subtle-moment-becomes-the-world-press-photo-of-the-year/?smprod=nytcore-ipad&smid=nytcore-ipad-share&_r=0, accessed June 2, 2019.

6. Consult UNHCR (L'Agence des Nations Unies pour les réfugiés), https://www.unhcr.org/fr/news/briefing/2018/7/5b3f8059a/baisse-arrivees-taux-accru-mortalite-mediterranee-hcr-appelle-intensifier.html; and Owen Bennett, "The Mass Cemetery of Europe," *Express,* April 2, 2014, https://www.express.co.uk/news/world/468214/Asylum-seekers-drowning-in-their-thousands-as-Mediterranean-becomes-Europe-s-cemetery, both accessed June 2, 2019.

7. Lanzarote Underwater Sculptures: see https://www.lanzaroteatlanticmuseum.com/about-underwater-sculptures, accessed June 2, 2019.

8. The Underwater Museum: see http://www.cactlanzarote.com/en/cact/the-underwater-museum-lanzarote-museo-atlantico/#1524487874772-4ac0cfff-6fc0, accessed June 2, 2019.

9. Museo Atlántico. Photographs of the sculptures can be found on the same site: http://www.cactlanzarote.com/en/cact/the-underwater-museum-lanzarote-museo-atlantico/#1524487874772-4ac0cfff-6fc0, accessed May 26, 2019.

10. BBC, "The Cultural Frontline," "The Underwater Museum," https://www.bbc.co.uk/programmes/p04q55mr/p04q5f6z, accessed June 2, 2019.

11. The scant representation of women on boats needs to be rectified. While Géricault includes only one dead woman in his geometrically organized human pile, one of the survivors of the historical frigate Méduse was a woman who published the narrative of her survival on the ship and, subsequently, on the Senegalese shore. Taylor as well includes one woman in "Raft of Lampedusa." *La Pirogue,* the 2012 film by Senegalese director Moussa Touré, similarly casts one woman amongst the thirty Senegalese migrants who attempt to reach Europe on a fishing boat. Kanor rectifies this accessory representation in her 2006 novel *Humus* by putting women and girls centerstage.

12. Jason deCaires Taylor, "New Underwater Museum in Lanzarote, Spain," 2016, https://us1.campaign-archive.com/?u=cc2635caea4cd7d13806fa608&id=24cc8e2724, accessed June 4, 2019.

13. Jason deCaires Taylor, "An Underwater Museum, Teeming With Life," TED Talk, January 22, 2016, https://www.youtube.com/watch?v=RWiI7AkDX-o, accessed June 19, 2019.

14. Lanzarote Atlantic Museum, https://www.lanzaroteatlanticmuseum.com/about-underwater-sculptures, accessed May 26, 2019.

15. Lanzarote Atlantic Museum.

16. Chamoiseau and Glissant, *Quand les murs tombent.*

Works Cited

Adams, Vincanne. *Markets of Sorrows, Labors of Faith: New Orleans in the Wake of Katrina*. Durham, NC: Duke UP, 2013.

Agamben, Giorgio. *Homo Sacer: Sovereign Power and Bare Life*. Stanford, CA: Stanford UP, 1998.

Alaimo, Stacy. *Exposed: Environmental Politics and Pleasures in Posthuman Times*. Minneapolis: U of Minnesota P, 2016.

Allen, James. *Without Sanctuary: Lynching Photography in America*. Sante Fe, NM: Twin Palms, 2003.

Allewaert, Monique. *Ariel's Ecology: Plantations, Personhood, and Colonialism in the American Tropics*. Minneapolis: U of Minnesota P, 2013.

Als, Hilton. "Beyoncé in 'Formation': Entertainer, Activist, Both?" *New York Times*, February 6, 2016.

———. "Beywatch: Beyoncé's Reformation." *New Yorker*, May 13, 2016.

Anicet, Victor. "De Martinique, Victor Anicet: la complicité dans la création."

Aristotle. *Poetics*. http://www.perseus.tufts.edu.

———. *Politics*. http://www.perseus.tufts.edu.

Aurélia, Dominique. "Une Esthétique de la résistance: L'Exemple du Quilt afro-américain." *Cercles: Revue Pluridisciplinaire du monde anglophone* 15, 2006, 120–34.

Auslander, Mark. *The Accidental Slaveowner: Revisiting a Myth of Race and Finding an American Family*. Athens: U of Georgia P, 2011.

Bachelard, Gaston. *L'Eau et les rêves*. Paris: Le Livre de Poche, 2014.

———. *Water and Dreams*. Trans. Edith R. Farrell. Dallas: Pegasus Foundation, 1994.

Barthes, Roland. *Camera Lucida: Reflections on Photography*. Trans. Richard Howard. New York: Hill & Wang, 2010.

———. *La Chambre claire: Note sur la photographie*. Paris: Cahiers du Cinéma, Gallimard, 1980.

Bassi, Ernesto. *An Aqueous Territory: Sailor Geographies and New Granada's Transimperial Caribbean World*. Durham, NC: Duke UP, 2017.

Baucom, Ian. *Specters of the Atlantic: Finance, Capital, Slavery, and the Philosophy of History.* Durham, NC: Duke UP, 2005.

Beauvoir-Dominique, Rachel. "Edouard Duval Carrié: The Vodou Pantheon." In Sullivan, *Continental Shifts,* 41–47.

Bélanger, Joël Castonguay. "L'Édification d'un tombeau poétique: du rituel au recueil." *Études françaises* 38 (3), 2002, 55–69.

Bellegarde-Smith, Patrick, and Claudine Michel. *Haitian Vodou: Spirit, Myth, and Reality.* Bloomington: Indiana UP, 2007.

Bennett, Jane. *Vibrant Matter: A Political Ecology of Things.* Durham, NC: Duke UP, 2010.

Bergé, Pierre, Yves Pomeau, and Monique Dubois-Gance. *Des Rythmes au Chaos.* Paris: Odile Jacob, 1994.

Berger, John. *Understanding a Photograph.* Ed. Geoff Dyer. New York: Aperture, 2013.

Beyoncé. "Formation (Explicit)." Music video. Posted December 9, 2016. https://www.youtube.com/watch?v=hrHqXI3wRvY. Accessed June 19, 2019.

Bibler, Michael. "The Flood Last Time: 'Muck' and the Uses of History in Kara Walker's 'Rumination' on Katrina." *Journal of American Studies* 44 (3), 2010, 503–16.

Biguenet, John, Steven Maklansky, and Dr. Tony Lewis. *Before (During) After Katrina: Louisiana Photographers's Visual Reactions to Hurricane Katrina.* New Orleans: UNO P, 2010.

Bishop, Claire. *Installation Art: A Critical History.* London: Tate, 2005.

Blanchard, Terrence. *A Tale of God's Will (A Requiem for Katrina).* CD. Blue Note Records, 2006.

Blanchot, Maurice. *The Writing of the Disaster.* Trans. Ann Smock. Lincoln: U of Nebraska P, 1995.

Blanco, Richard. *Directions to the Beach of the Dead.* Tucson: U of Arizona P, 2005.

———. *Matters of the Sea / Cosas del mar.* Trans. Ruth Behar. Pittsburgh: U of Pittsburgh P, 2015.

Blevins, Steven. *Living Cargo: How Black Britain Performs its Past.* Minneapolis: U of Minnesota P, 2016.

Borges, Jorge Luis. *The Book of Imaginary Beings.* Trans. Andrew Hurley. London: Penguin, 2005.

———. *Collected Fictions.* Trans. Andrew Hurley. New York: Viking, 1998.

Bradley, Regina. "Getting in Line: Working Through Beyoncé's Formation." Huffington Post, February 2, 2017. https://www.huffpost.com/entry/getting-in-line-working-t_b_9218736. Accessed May 27, 2019.

Brand, Dionne. *A Map to the Door of No Return: Notes to Belonging.* Toronto: Vintage Canada, 2001.

Brannon, Jean M, ed. *"The Negro Woman": Phillis Wheatley, Sojourner Truth, Harriet Tubman, Frances Ellen Watkins Harper, Ida B. Wells Barnett, Mary*

Church Terrell, Mary McLeod Bethune. https://media.smithsonianfolkways.org/liner_notes/folkways/FW05523.pdf. Accessed May 27, 2019.

Brathwaite, Kamau. *Black + Blues.* New York: New Directions, 1995.

———. "Caribbean Man in Space and Time." *Savacou* 11–12, 1975, 1–11.

Britton, Celia. "Globalization and Political Action in the Works of Edouard Glissant." *Small Axe* 30, November 2009, 1–11.

Brown, David, and Rick Lowe. *Row: Trajectories through the Shotgun House.* Houston: Rice U School of Architecture, 2004.

Brown, Kimberly Juanita. *The Repeating Body: Slavery's Visual Resonance in the Contemporary.* Durham, NC: Duke UP, 2015.

Brown, Vincent. *The Reaper's Garden: Death and Power in the World of Atlantic Slavery.* Cambridge, MA: Harvard UP, 2008.

Buffon. *Oeuvres.* Paris: Gallimard, Bibliothèque de la Pléiade, 2007.

Burke, Lauretta, K. Reytar, M. Spalding, and A. Perry. *Reefs at Risk Revisited.* Washington, DC: World Resources Institute, 2011.

Butler, Judith. *Frames of War: When Is Life Grievable?* New York: Verso, 2010.

———. *Precarious Life: The Powers of Mourning and Violence.* New York: Verso, 2004.

Cable, George Washington. *Old Creole Days.* Gretna, LA: Pelican, 2009, 121–47.

Cailler, Bernadette. "Rêves sur les funérailles religieuses d'Édouard Glissant." In Loichot, ed. *Entours,* 239–50.

Carbado, Devon W., and Cheryl L. Harris. "Loot or Find: Fact or Frame?" In *After the Storm: Black Intellectuals Explore the Meaning of Hurricane Katrina,* ed. David Dante Troutt, 87–110. New York: New P, 2007.

Cartwright, Keith. "Confederacies of Undead Imagination." In *Undead Souths: The Gothic and Beyond in Southern Imagination,* ed. Eric Gary Anderson, Taylor Hagood, and Daniel Cross Turner, 10–22. Baton Rouge: Louisiana State UP, 2015.

———. *Sacral Grooves, Limbo Gateways: Travels in Deep Southern Time, Circum Caribbean Space, and Afro-Creole Authority.* Athens: U of Georgia P, 2013.

Celestan, Karen (editor and narrator), and Eric Waters (photographer). *Freedom's Dance: Social, Aid, and Pleasure Clubs in New Orleans.* Baton Rouge: Louisiana State UP, 2018.

Césaire, Aimé. *Cahier d'un retour au pays natal.* Paris: Présence africaine, 1983.

———. *Nègre je suis, nègre je resterai: Entretiens avec Françoise Vergès.* Paris: Albin Michel, 2005.

———. *Notebook of a Return to the Native Land.* Trans. Clayton Eshleman and Annette Smith. Middletown, CT: Wesleyan UP, 2001.

Chamoiseau, Patrick. "'*L'arbre du voyageur commence à me parler,' hommage de Patrick Chamoiseau à Édouard Glissant.*" Mondes francophones, February 12, 2011. https://mondesfrancophones.com/espaces/creolisations/larbre-du-voyageur-commence-a-me-parler-hbommage-de-patrick-chamoiseau-a-edouard-glissant/. Accessed May 27, 2019.

———. "Caribbean Discourses: A Roundtable with Patrick Chamoiseau," Emory University, March 22, 2017. https://www.youtube.com/watch?v=WHXFxf-tK4U. Accessed June 19, 2019.

———. *Un Dimanche au cachot.* Paris: Gallimard, 2009.

———. *Frères migrants: Déclaration des poètes.* Paris: Seuil, 2017.

———. *La Matière de l'absence.* Paris: Seuil, 2016.

———. *When the Walls Fall: Is National Identity an Outlaw?* Trans. Jeffrey Landon Allen and Charly Verstraet. *Contemporary French and Francophone Studies* 22 (2), 2018, 259–70.

Chamoiseau, Patrick, and Raphaël Confiant. *Lettres créoles.* Paris: Gallimard, 1999.

Chamoiseau, Patrick, and Édouard Glissant. *Quand les murs tombent: l'identité nationale hors-la-loi?* Paris: Galaade, 2007.

Chen, C., J. MacLeod, and A. Neimanis. *Thinking with Water.* Montreal: McGill-Queen's UP, 2013.

Christophe, Marc. "Rainbow over Water: Haitian Art, Vodou Aesthetism, and Philosophy." in Bellegarde-Smith and Michel, *Haitian Vodou,* 84–102.

Le Code noir. Paris: L'Esprit frappeur, 1998.

Cohen, Jeffrey Jerome, ed. *Prismatic Ecologies.* Minneapolis: U of Minnesota P, 2014.

"Les Collectivités viennent au secours d'Édouard Glissant." DOMactu, September 9, 2019. http://www.domactu.com/actualite/109620101464971/martinique-les-collectivites-viennent-au-secours-d-edouard-glissant/. Accessed June 19, 2019.

Collins, Patricia Hill. *Black Feminist Thought: Knowledge, Consciousness, and the Politics of Empowerment.* New York: Routledge, 1991.

Cook, Bernie. *Flood of Images: Media, Memory, and Hurricane Katrina.* Austin: U of Texas P, 2015.

Cooksey, Susan, Robin Poynor, and Hein Vanhee. *Kongo across the Waters.* Gainesville: UP of Florida, 2013.

Cooper, Helene, "Grim History Traced in Sunken Slave Ship Found Off South Africa." *New York Times,* May 31, 2015. https://www.nytimes.com/2015/06/01/world/africa/tortuous-history-traced-in-sunken-slave-ship-found-off-south-africa.html?smid=fb-share. Accessed June 19, 2019.

Copeland, Huey. *Bound to Appear: Art, Slavery, and the Site of Blackness in Multicultural America.* Chicago: U of Chicago P, 2013.

Corbin, Jacques. *La Mer: terreur et fascination.* Paris: Bibliothèque nationale de France, 2011.

Corio, Alessandro. "*Anagrams of Annihilation*" *International Journal of Francophone Studies* 17 (3–4), 2014, 327–48.

———. "The Living and the Poetic Intention: Glissant's Biopolitics of Literature," *Callaloo* 36 (4), 2013, 916–30.

Cosentino, Donald J., ed. *In Extremis: Death and Life in 21st-Century Haitian Art.* Los Angeles: Fowler Museum at UCLA, 2012.

———. *Sacred Arts of Haitian Vodou.* Los Angeles: Fowler Museum at UCLA, 1995.

Crenshaw, Kimberlé. "Mapping the Margins: Intersectionality, Identity Politics, and Violence against Women of Color." *Stanford Law Review* 43 (6), 1991, 1241–99.

Crosby, Emilye. *Little Taste of Freedom: The Black Freedom Struggle in Claiborne County, Mississippi.* Chapel Hill: U of North Carolina P, 2006.

Curtius, Anny Dominique. *Symbioses d'une mémoire: Manifestations religieuses et littératures de la Caraïbe.* Paris: L'Harmattan, 2006.

Dal Lago, Alessandro. "Fluidi Feretri," "Cercueils fluides," "Watery Graves." *California Italian Studies* 1 (1), 2010, 1–12.

Daniels, Kyrah Malika. "Mirror Mausoleums, Mortuary Arts, and Haitian Religious Unexceptionalism." *Journal of the American Academy of Religion* 85 (4), 2017, 957–84.

———. "Ritual." In *Encyclopedia of Aesthetics.* 2nd ed. Ed. Michael Kelly, 400–404. Oxford: Oxford UP, 2014.

Danticat, Edwidge. *The Art of Death: Writing the Final Story.* Minneapolis: Graywolf, 2017.

———. *Claire of the Sea Light.* New York: Vintage, 2013.

———. *Create Dangerously: The Immigrant Artist at Work.* Princeton, NJ: Princeton UP, 2010.

———. *The Dew Breaker.* New York: Vintage, 2004.

———. *The Farming of Bones.* New York: Penguin, 1998.

———. *Krik? Krak!* New York: Soho, 1991.

Dash, J. Michael. "Martinique/Mississippi: Édouard Glissant and Relational Insularity." In *Look Away! The U.S. South in New World Studies,* ed. Jon Smith and Deborah Cohn, 94–109. Durham, NC: Duke UP, 2004.

———. "Ni réel, ni rêvé: Édouard Glissant—Poétique, peinture, paysage." *Littérature* 174, 2014, 33–40.

Dayan, Joan (Colin). *Haiti, History, and the Gods.* Berkeley: U of California P, 1995.

———. *The Law Is a White Dog: How Legal Rituals Make and Unmake Persons.* Princeton, NJ: Princeton UP, 2011.

DeLoughrey, Elizabeth M. "Heavy Waters: Waste and Atlantic Modernity." *PMLA* 125 (3), 2010, 703–12.

———. "Revisiting Tidalectics: Irma/José/Maria 2017." In *Tidalectics: Imagining an Oceanic Worldview Through Art and Science,* ed. Stefanie Hessler, 93–101. Cambridge, MA: MIT P, 2018.

———. *Routes and Roots: Navigating Caribbean and Pacific Island Literatures.* Honolulu: U of Hawai'i P, 2007.

———. "Submarine Futures of the Anthropocene." *Comparative Literature* 69 (1), 2017, 32–44.

Deren, Maya. *Divine Horsemen: The Living Gods of Haiti.* New York: McPherson, 2004.

Derrida, Jacques. *Dissemination.* Trans. Barbara Johnson. Chicago: U of Chicago P, 1981.

———. *Monolingualism of the Other: or, the Prosthesis of Origin.* Trans. Patrick Mensah. Stanford, CA: Stanford UP, 1998.

———. *Glas*. Paris: Éditions Galilée, 1974.

———. *Specters of Marx: The State of the Debt, the Work of Mourning, and the New International.* Trans. Peggy Kamuf. New York: Routledge, 2006.

Dessens, Nathalie. *From Saint-Domingue to New Orleans: Migrations and Influences.* Gainesville: UP of Florida, 2010.

Diagne, Souleymane Bachir. *African Art as Philosophy: Senghor, Bergson, and the Idea of Negritude.* London: Seagull, 2012.

Diawara, Manthia. "Radcliffe Bailey: One World Under the Groove." In Thompson, *Radcliffe Bailey,* 135–41.

Díaz, Junot. "Apocalypse: What Disasters Reveal." *Boston Review,* May 1, 2011.

Djaout, Tahar. *The Bone Seekers.* Trans. Marjolijn de Jager. New Orleans, LA: Diálogos, 2018

———. *Les Chercheurs d'os.* Paris: Seuil, 1984.

Donatien, Patricia. *Exorcisme de la blès: vaincre la souffrance dans* Autobiographie de ma mère *de Jamaica Kincaid.* Paris: Le Manuscrit, 2011.

———. "Fwomajé and Totem: The Beginnings and Consolidation of an Artistic Language in Martinique." *Small Axe* 30, November 2009, 115–27.

Drabinski, John. *Levinas and the Postcolonial: Race, Nation, Other.* Edinburgh: Edinburgh UP, 2011.

Drewal, Henry John. "Mami Wata: Arts for Water Spirits in Africa and Its Diasporas." *African Arts* 41 (2), 2008, 60–83.

Dubois, Laurent. *Haiti: The Aftershocks of History.* New York: Picador, 2012.

Dubois Shaw, Gwendolyn. *Seeing the Unspeakable: The Art of Kara Walker.* Durham, NC: Duke UP, 2004.

Dupuy, Jean-Pierre. *The Mark of the Sacred.* Stanford, CA: Stanford UP, 2013.

Du Tertre, Jean-Baptiste. *Histoire générale des isles.* Paris: Jacques Langlois, 1654.

Fanon, Frantz. *Black Skin, White Masks.* Trans. Richard Philcox. New York: Grove, 2008.

Faulkner, William. *Absalom, Absalom!* New York: Vintage, 1990.

———. *Light in August.* New York: Vintage, 1991.

Fennell, Christopher C. "Kongo and the Archeology of Early America." In *Kongo across the Waters,* ed. Cooksey et al., 229–37.

Firth, Shirley. *Dying, Death and Bereavement in a British Hindu Community.* Louvain, Belgium: Peeters, 1997.

Flores, Tatiana, and Stephens, Michelle A. *Relational Undercurrents: Contemporary Art of the Caribbean Archipelago.* Long Beach, CA: Museum of Latin American Art, 2017.

Foer, Joshua, Thuras, Dylan, and Morton, Ella. *Atlas Obscura.* New York: Workman, 2016.

Forbes, Jack D. *Columbus and Other Cannibals.* New York: Seven Stories, 2008.

Forde, Maarit, and Yanique Hume, eds. *Passages and Afterworlds: Anthropological Perspectives on Death in the Caribbean.* Durham, NC: Duke UP, 2018.

France Antilles. http://www.martinique.franceantilles.mobi/regions/departement/l-hommage-0302-2012-143289_32.php. Accessed August 2, 2012.

Freud, Sigmund. *On Metapsychology.* New York: Penguin, 1991.

Fry, Gladys-Marie. *Man Made: African American Men and Quilting Traditions.* Washington, DC: Anacostia Museum of African-American Life and Culture, 1998.

Fuchs, Richard. *An Unerring Fire: The Massacre at Fort Pillow.* Mechanicsburg, PA: Stackpole, 2002.

Fuss, Diana. *Dying Modern: A Meditation on Elegy.* Durham, NC: Duke UP, 2013.

Garrett, Brandon L., and Tania Tetlow. "Criminal Justice Collapse: The Constitution after Hurricane Katrina." *Duke Law Journal* 56, 2006, 127–78.

Gérazime, Roselyne. "Lasirèn: Labalèn. L'Abysse en migration dans Claire of the Sea Light." *Journal of Haitian Studies* 25 (1), 2019, 178–200.

Gilman, Sander. "Confession of an Academic Pornographer." In *Vergne, Kara* Walker, 27–35.

Gilroy, Paul. *The Black Atlantic: Modernity and Double-Consciousness.* Cambridge, MA: Harvard UP, 1995.

Girard, René. *La Violence et le sacré.* Paris: Grasset, 1996.

———. *Des choses cachées depuis la fondation du monde.* Paris: Grasset, 1978.

Gleick, James. *Chaos: Making a New Science.* New York: Viking, 1987.

Glissant, Édouard. *Caribbean Discourse.* Trans. J. Michael Dash. Charlottesville: U of Virginia P, 1989.

———. *La Case du Commandeur.* Paris: Seuil, 1981.

———. *La Cohée du Lamentin.* Paris: Gallimard, 2005.

———. *L'Imaginaire des langues: Entretiens avec Lise Gauvin (1991–2009).* Paris: Gallimard, 2010.

———. *Les Indes.* Paris: Seuil, 1965.

———. "Métissage et créolisation." In *Discours sur le métissage, identités métisses: en quête d'Ariel,* ed. Sylvie Kandé, 47–53. Paris: L'Harmattan, 1999.

———. *Le Monde incréé: Poétrie.* Paris: Gallimard, 2000

———. "La Pensée du tremblement." In *Annali: Fondazione Europea del disegno (Fondation Adami),* ed. Amelia Valtolina, 81–90. Milano: Bruno Mondadori, 2006.

———. *Philosophie de la Relation.* Paris: Gallimard, 2009.

———. *Poetics of Relation.* Trans. Betsy Wing. Ann Arbor: U of Michigan P, 1997.

———. *Sartorius: Le Roman des Batoutos.* Paris: Gallimard, 1999.

———. *Soleil de la conscience.* Paris: Gallimard, 1997.

———. *La Terre le feu l'eau et les vents: une anthologie de la poésie du Tout-Monde.* Paris: Galaade, 2010.

Glissant, Édouard, and Sylvie Séma. *La Terre magnétique: Les errances de Rapa Nui, l'île de Pâques*. Paris: Seuil, 2007.

Glissant, Sylvie. "Une vision prophétique du passé." Talk, delivered at Louisiane/Antilles: Un espace/temps partagé International Colloquium, Louisiana State University, Center for French and Francophone Studies, November 2016.

Glover, Kaiama. *Haiti Unbound: A Spiralist Challenge to the Postcolonial Canon*. Liverpool: Liverpool UP, 2010.

Grant, Ulysses S. *Personal Memoirs*. New York: Library of America, 1990.

Hachad, Naïma, and Valérie Loichot. "Victor Anicet: Martinique ou le bleu de la Restitution." *Small Axe: A Caribbean Platform for Criticism* 3, November 2012, 39–57.

Hallward, Peter. *Absolutely Postcolonial: Writing Between the Singular and the Specific*. Manchester: Manchester UP, 2001.

Handley, George. *Home Waters: A Year of Recompenses on the Provo River*. Salt Lake City: U of Utah P, 2011.

Hartman, Saidiya. "Venus in Two Acts." *Small Axe* 26, 2008, 1–14.

———. *Lose Your Mother: A Journey Along the Atlantic Slave Route*. New York: Farrar, Strauss & Giroux, 2007.

Harvey, John. *Photography and Spirit*. London: Reaktion, 2007.

Hegel, G. W. F. *On Art, Religion, Philosophy: Introductory Lectures on the Realm of Absolute Spirit*. Trans Bernard Bosanquet. New York: Harper Torchbooks, 1970.

Hesse, Monica. "Quilting Magazine Exposes Craft's Risque Underside." *Washington Post,* March 5, 2009. http://www.washingtonpost.com/wp-dyn/content/article/2009/03/04/AR2009030403994.html. Accessed June 19, 2019.

Hicks, Cinque. "The Fine Line Between Meaningful Art and Disaster Porn: Hurricane Katrina's Five-Year Anniversary Informs Three New Exhibits." *Creative Loafing,* August 3, 2010.

Holloway, Karla. *Passed On: African American Mourning Stories, A Memorial*. Durham, NC: Duke UP, 2002.

Hosseini, Khaled. *Sea Prayer*. Illus. Dan Williams. New York: Riverhead, 2018.

Hume, Yanique. "Death and the Performance of Social Space: Land, Kinship and Identity in the Jamaican Mortuary Cycle." In Forde and Hume, *Passages,* 109–38.

Hurbon, Laënnec. *Les Mystères du vaudou*. Paris: Gallimard, 1993.

Hurston, Zora Neale. *Tell My Horse: Voodoo and Life in Haiti and Jamaica*. New York: Harper Perennial, 2009.

———. *Their Eyes Were Watching God*. New York: Harper Perrenial, 2013.

Huynh, Matt. "The Boat." Screendriver, 2015.
https://screendiver.com/directory/the-boat-interactive-graphic-novel-matt-huynh/. Accessed May 27, 2019.

Iasiello, Stephanie. "Slavery and its Afterlives: Contemporary (Re)imaginings of the Zong Massacre." PhD diss., Emory U, 2018.

Institut du Tout-Monde. Official website. http://www.tout-monde.com. Accessed June 19, 2019.

JanMohamed, Abdul. *The Death-Bound-Subject: Richard Wright and the Archeology of Death.* Durham, NC: Duke UP, 2005.

James, C. L. R. *The Black Jacobins: Toussaint L'Ouverture and the San Dominguo Revolution.* 2nd ed., rev. New York: Vintage, 1989.

Jean-François, Bruno. "De la thalassologie à la Relation: la voix de Charlesia Alexis, entre mémoire, ressassement et lutte pour les droits humains." In *Îles/Elles: Résistances et revendications féminines dans les îles des Caraïbes et de l'océan Indien,* ed. Valérie Magdelaine-Andrianjafitrimo and Marc Arino, 137–52. Saint Denis, Réunion: K'A Editions, 2015.

Jenson, Deborah. "The Writing of Disaster in Haiti: Signifying Cataclysm from Slave Revolution to Earthquake." In *Haiti Rising: Haitian History, Culture, and the Earthquake of 2010,* 103–12. Mona, JA: U of the West Indies P, 2011.

Jolly, Martyn. *Faces of the Living Dead: The Belief in Spirit Photography.* London: British Library, 2006.

Jones, Lee, ed. .Foreword by Cornel West. *Making It on Broken Promises.* Sterling, VA: Stylus, 2002.

Jones, Meta Duewa. "Reframing Exposure: Natasha Trethewey's Forms of Enclosure." *EHL* 82, 2015, 407–29.

Julien, Epaul. "Interview with Wendell Gorden & Charles Henry Rowell." *Callaloo* 29 (4), 2006, 1147–48.

———. Epaul Julien Studio. https://epauljulien.com/. Accessed May 27, 2019.

Kanor, Fabienne. *Humus.* Paris: Gallimard, 2006.

———. "Le là d'où je viens." Multimedia performance. Emory U, February 9, 2017.

Kardux, Johanna C. "Monuments of the Black Atlantic: Slavery Memorials in the United States and the Netherlands." In *Blackening Europe: The African American Presence,* ed. Raphael-Hernandez, Heike, 87–105. New York: Routledge, 2004.

Kassab-Charfi, Samia. *"Et l'une et l'autre face des choses": La déconstruction poétique de l'Histoire dans* les Indes *et* le Sel noir *d'Édouard Glissant.* Paris: Champion, 2011.

Keller, Catherine. *Cloud of the Impossible: Negative Theology and Planetary Entanglement.* New York: Columbia UP, 2015.

Kennedy, Al. *Big Chief Harrison and the Mardi Gras Indians.* Gretna, LA: Pelican, 2013.

Kennedy, David. *Elegy: The New Critical Idiom.* New York: Routledge, 2017.

Khan, Almas. "Poetic Justice: Slavery, Law, and the (Anti-)Elegiac Form in M. NourbeSe Philip's Zong!" *Cambridge Journal of Postcolonial Inquiry* 2 (1), 2015, 5–32.

Krishnan, Madhu. "Mami Wata and the Occluded Feminine in Anglophone Nigerian-Igbo Literature." *Research in African Literatures* 43 (1), 2012, 1–18.

Kristeva, Julia. *Powers of Horror: An Essay on Abjection.* Trans Leon S. Roudiez. New York: Columbia UP, 1982.

Kuhlman, Martha. "The Traumatic Temporality of Art Spiegelman's *In the Shadow of No Towers.*" *Journal of Popular Culture* 40 (5), 2007, 849–966.

Laderman, Gary. *Sacred Matters: Celebrity Worship, Sexual Extsies, the Living Dead, and Other Signs of Religious Life in the United States.* New York: New P, 2009.

Latour, Bruno. "An Attempt at a 'Compositionist Manifesto.'" *New Literary History* 41, 2010, 471–90.

———. "Will Non-Humans Be Saved? An Argument on Ecotheology." *Journal of the Royal Anthropological Institute* 15, 2008, 459–75.

Lautréamont, le Comte de [Isodore Ducasse]. *The Songs of Maldoror.* Chicago: Solar, 2011.

Lee, Spike. *When the Levees Broke: A Requiem in Four Parts.* Documentary series. HBO Productions, 2006.

Leupin, Alexandre. "L'Appel du futur: sur les essais d'Edouard Glissant." In Loichot, ed., *Entours d'Édouard Glissant,* 225–38.

———. *Édouard Glissant Philosophe.* Paris: Hermann, 2016.

Levi, Primo. *If This Is a Man.* Montreal: Abacus, 2003.

Levitt, Katrina Jeremy, and Matthew Whitaker. *Hurricane Katrina: America's Unnatural Disaster.* Lincoln: U of Nebraska P, 2009.

Lewis, Simon L., and Mark A. Maslin. *The Human Planet: How We Created the Anthropocene.* New Haven, CT: Yale UP, 2018.

Liquid Blackness. Georgia State University, http://liquidblackness.com/. Accessed May 27, 2019.

Littlewood, Julian. *The Variations of Johanes Brahms.* London: Plumbago, 2004.

Lloyd, Vincent W. "MLK Day and the Emergence of the 'New Sacred Politics.'" Political Theology Network, January 16, 2017. https://politicaltheology.com/mlk-day-and-the-emergence-of-the-new-sacred-politics-vincent-lloyd/. Accessed June 17, 2019.

———. *Religion of the Field Negro: On Black Secularism and Black Theology.* New York: Fordham UP, 2018.

Loichot, Valérie. "Between Breadfruit and Masala." *Callaloo* 30 (1), 2007, 124–37.

———. "Faulkner's Caribbean Geographies in *Absalom, Absalom!*" In *Faulkner's Geographies: Faulkner and Yoknapatawpha.* ed. Jay Watson and Ann J. Abadie, 112–28. Jackson: UP of Mississippi, 2015.

———. "Kara Walker's Blood Sugar: *A Subtlety or the Marvelous Sugar Baby.*" *Southern Spaces,* July 8, 2014. http://southernspaces.org/2014/kara-walkers-blood-sugar-subtlety-or-marvelous-sugar-baby. Accessed June 25, 2019.

———. *Orphan Narratives: The Postplantation Literature of Faulkner, Glissant, Morrison, and Saint-John Perse.* Charlottesville: U of Virginia P, 2007.

———, ed. *Entours d'Édouard Glissant.* Lille: *Revue des Sciences humaines.* 309 (1) Spring 2013.

Lowe, John Wharton. *Calypso Magnolia: The Crosscurrents of Caribbean and Southern Literature.* Chapel Hill: U of North Carolina P, 2016.

MacGaffey, Wyatt. "Meaning and Aesthetics in Kongo Art." In Cooksey et al., *Kongo across the Waters,* 172–81.

Mackey, Nathaniel. "An Interview with Edward Kamau Brathwaite." *Hambone* 9, 1991, 42–59.

MacLoud, Janine. "Water and the Material Imagination: Reading the Sea of Memory Against the Flows of Capital." In Chen, MacLeod, and Neimanis, *Thinking with Water,* 40–60.

Madou, Jean-Pol. *Edouard Glissant: de mémoire d'arbres.* Amsterdam: Rodopi, 1996.

Mardorossian, Carine. "Poetics of Landscape: Édouard Glissant's Creolized Ecologies." *Callaloo* 36 (4), 2013, 983–94.

"Martinique: Mémorial Cap 110." "Comité pour la mémoire de l'esclavage." http://www.cnmhe.fr/spip.php?article806. Accessed June 17, 2019.

McCarthy, Cormac. *The Road.* New York: Vintage, 2006.

McCormick, Carlo, and Helen Scales. *The Underwater Museum: The Submerged Sculptures of Jason DeCaires Taylor.* San Francisco: Chronicle, 2014

McKay, Nellie. "An Interview with Toni Morrison." *Contemporary Literature* 24, 1983, 413–29.

Mehta, Brinda. *Diasporic (Dis)locations: Indo-Caribbean Women Writers Negotiate the "Kala Pani."* Kingston, JA: U of the West Indies P, 2004.

Menely, Tobias Jesse, and Jessie Oak Taylor. *Anthropocene Reading: Literary History in Geological Time.* University Park: Penn State UP, 2017.

Mentz, Steve. *At the Bottom of Shakespeare's Ocean.* New York: Continuum, 2009.

———. "Enter Anthropocene, Circa 1610." In Menely and Oak Taylor, *Anthropocene Reading,* 43–58.

———. *Shipwreck Modernity: Ecologies of Globalization, 1550–1719.* Minneapolis: U of Minnesota P, 2015.

Métraux, Alfred. *Voodoo in Haiti.* New York: Schocken, 1972.

Moïse, Myriam. "Grasping the Ungraspable in M. Philip NourbeSe Poetry." *Commonwealth* 33 (1) 2010, 23–32, 28.

Monastersky, Richard. "Anthropocene: The Human Age." *Nature,* March 11 2015. https://go.nature.com/2U5dc7b. Accessed June 17, 2019.

Morrison, Toni. *Beloved.* New York: Knopf, 1994.

Mosley, Walter. *Folding the Red into the Black: Or, Developing a Viable* Untopia *for Human Survival in the 21st Century.* New York: OR, 2016.

Morton, Timothy. *Hyperobjects: Philosophy and Ecology after the End of the World.* Minneapolis: U of Minnesota P, 2013.

Moten, Fred. "Blackness and Nothingness (Mysticism in the Flesh)." *South Atlantic Quarterly* 112 (4), 2013, 737–80.

———. *In the Break: The Aesthetics of the Black Radical Tradition.* Minneapolis: U of Minnesota P, 2003.

Mouawad, Wajdi. *Anima*. Paris: Leméac, Actes Sud, 2012.

Moussaoui, Rosa, and Fernand Nouvet. Interview with Edouard Glissant. *L'Humanité,* February 6, 2007.

Moyes, Dorothy. "Katrina + 5: An X-Code Exhibition." *Southern Spaces,* August 26, 2010. https://southernspaces.org/2010/katrina-5-x-code-exhibition. Accessed May 27, 2019.

———. "Lift Every Voice and Sing: The Quilts of Gwendolyn Ann Magee." *Southern Spaces,* September 11, 2014. https://southernspaces.org/2014/lift-every-voice-and-sing-quilts-gwendolyn-ann-magee. Accessed May 27, 2019.

Narayanan, Vasudha. "Water, Wood, and Wisdom: Ecological Perspectives from the Hindu Traditions." *Daedalus* 130 (4), 2001, 179.

Ndione, Abasse. *La Pirogue*. Directed by Moussa Touré. France and Senegal: Les Chauves-Souris and Astou Films, 2012.

Nesbitt, Nick. *Voicing Memory: History and Subjectivity in French Caribbean Literature*. Charlottesville: U of Virginia P, 2003.

Nicolas, Thierry. "A la poursuite du patrimoine." EchoGéo, July 9, 2009. https://journals.openedition.org/echogeo/11300. Accessed May 27, 2019.

Nixon, Angelique. "Creating Space and Speaking Silence in Black Women's Performance Art: The Body Power of Gabrielle Civil's 'Fugue—Dissolution, Accra." ARC, September 4, 2014. http://arcthemagazine.com/arc/2014/09/creating-space-and-speaking-silence-in-black-womens-performance-art/. Accessed May 27, 2019.

Nixon, Rob. *Slow Violence and the Environmentalism of the Poor.* Cambridge, MA: Harvard UP, 2011.

Noland, Carrie. "Edouard Glissant: A Poetics of the Entour." In *Poetry After Cultural Studies,* ed. Heidi R. Bean and Mike Chasar, 143–72. Iowa City: U of Iowa P, 2011.

Nora, Pierre. *Les lieux de mémoire*. Paris: Gallimard, 1984.

Norvat, Manuel. *Le Chant du divers: Introduction à la philopoétique d'Édouard Glissant*. Paris: L'Harmattan, 2015.

Noudelmann, François. "Glissant, le Déchiffreur." *Littérature* 154, 2009, 36–42.

———. "Edouard Glissant: 'Rien n'est vrai, tout est vivant.'" Interview with Édouard Glissant, March 2010, https://www.dailymotion.com/video/xcvrg8. Accessed May 27, 2019.

Le nouveau Petit Robert. Paris: Dictionnaires Le Robert, 1996.

Ollivier, Émile. *Mille eaux*. Paris: Gallimard, 1999.

O'Neill, Caitlin, and Omise'eke Natasha Tinsley. "Beyoncé's 'Formation' Is Activism for African Americans, Women, and LGBTQ People." *Time,* February 8, 2016.

Overmeyer, Eric, and Simon, David. *Treme*. HBO Productions, 2010–13.

Parham, Marisa. "Black Haunts in the Anthropocene." https://blackhaunts.mp285.com/. Accessed May 27, 2019.

Patterson, Orlando. *Slavery and Social Death: A Comparative Study.* Cambridge, MA: Harvard UP, 1982.

Philip, M. NourbeSe. *She Tries Her Tongue, Her Silence Softly Breaks.* Foreword by Eevie Shockley. Middletown, CT: Wesleyan UP, [1989] 2014.

———, and Setaey Adamu Boateng. *Zong!* Middletown, CT: Wesleyan UP, 2008.

Pirbhai, Mariam. "Recasting Jahaji-Bhain: Plantation History and the Indo-Caribbean Women's Novel in Trinidad, Guyana, and Martinique." In *Critical Perspectives on Indo-Caribbean Women's Literature,* ed. Joy Mahabit and Mariam Pirbhai, 27–47. New York: Routledge, 2013.

Polk, Patrick A. "Remember You Must Die! Gede Banners, Memento Mori, and the Fine Art of Facing Death." In Cosentino, *In Extremis,* 114–41.

Pourchez, Laurence and Isabelle Hidair. *Rites et constructions identitaires créoles.* Paris: Edition des Archives Contemporaines, 2013.

Price, Richard. "Chasing Death's Left Hand: Personal Encounters With Death and its Rituals in the Caribbean." In Forde and Hume, *Passages and Afterworlds,* 225–42.

———. *The Convict and the Colonel: A Story of Colonialism and Resistance in the Caribbean.* Boston: Beacon, 1998.

Proctor Smith, Michael. *Mardi Gras Indians.* Gretna, LA: Pelican, 1994.

Ramazani, Jahan. *Poetry of Mourning.* Chicago: U of Chicago P, 1994.

Rankine, Claudia. *Citizen: An American Lyric.* Minneapolis: Graywolf, 2014.

———. "The Condition of Black Life Is One of Mourning." *New York Times Magazine,* June 22, 2015.

Rediker, Marcus. *The Slave Ship: A Human History.* London: Penguin, 2007.

Reiss, Tom. *The Black Count: Glory, Revolution, Betrayal, and the Real Count of Monte Cristo.* New York: Crown, 2012.

Rice, Alan. *Radical Narratives of the Black Atlantic.* London: Continuum, 2003.

Ricoeur, Paul. *Temps et récit.* Vol. 1. Paris: Seuil, 1983.

Rigolot, François. *Poétique et onomastique: l'exemple de la Renaissance.* Geneva: Droz, 1977.

Rimbaud, Arthur. *Poèmes.* Paris: Livre de Poche, 1960.

Roach, Joseph. *Cities of the Dead: Circum-Atlantic Performance.* New York: Columbia UP, 1996.

Robert, Kamaria. "What Beyoncé Teaches Us about the African Diaspora in *Lemonade.*" PBS NewsHour, April 29, 2016. https://www.pbs.org/newshour/arts/what-beyonce-teaches-us-about-the-african-diaspora-in-lemonade. Accessed May 27, 2019.

Rolle, William. "Les Cimetières comme patrimoine: anthropologie visuelle des cimetières Martiniquais." Unpublished paper.

———. "Les Rituels mortuaires Martiniquais 'traditionnels' sont-ils encore opératoires? La catastrophe de Maracaibo." In *Rites et constructions identitaires créoles,* ed. Laurence Pourchez and Isabelle Hidair, 153–64. Paris: Editions des archives contemporaines, 2013.

Rose, Chris. *1 Dead in Attic.* New York: Simon & Schuster, 2005.

Rothberg, Michael. *Multidirectional Memory: Remembering the Holocaust in the Age of Decolonization.* Stanford, CA: Stanford UP, 2009.

Trouillot, Michel-Rolph. *Silencing the Past: Power and the Production of History.* Boston: Beacon, 1995.

Salas Rivera, Raquel. "el obrero se limita a producir el valor de su fuerza de trabajo." *The River Rail,* January 18 2018. https://brooklynrail.org/special/RIVER_RAIL/river-rail/el-obrero-se-limita-a-producir-el-valor-de-su-fuerza-de-trabajo. Accessed June 17, 2019.

Saloy, Mona Lisa. *Second Line Home: New Orleans Poems.* Kirksville, MO: Truman State UP, 2014.

Saunders, Patricia J. "Fugitive Dreams of Diaspora: Conversations with Saidiya Hartman." *Anthurium: A Caribbean Studies Journal* 6 (1), 2008, 1–16.

Scales, Helen. "From Polyp to Rampart: The Science of Reef Building and How Art Can Inspire a Sustainable Future." In *The Underwater Museum: The Submerged Sculptures of Jason DeCaires Taylor, ed.* Carlo McCormick and Helen Scales, 18–29. *San Francisco: Chronicle, 2014.*

Scarboro, Ann Armstrong. *Victor Anicet: céramiste et artiste martiniquais.* Full Duck Productions et Mosaic Media, 2008.

Schwarz-Bart, Simone, "Du Fond des casseroles." In *Nouvelles de Guadeloupe,* 78–81. Paris: Miniatures, 2009.

Serrato, Erika. "Mémoire et Fraternité: Remnants et Historical Misdirection." Unpublished paper delivered at the Modern Language Association Convention, Vancouver, 2015.

Serres, Michel. *Le Contrat naturel.* Paris: Flammarion, 1992.

———. *The Natural Contract.* Trans. Elizabeth MacArthur and William Paulson. Ann Arbor: U of Michigan P, 1995.

Sharpe, Christina. *Monstrous Intimacies: Making Post-Slavery Subjects.* Durham, NC: Duke UP, 2010.

———. *In the Wake: On Blackness and Being.* Durham, NC: Duke UP, 2016.

Sharpe, Jenny. "The Archive and Affective Memory in M. NourbeSe Philip's *Zong!*" *Interventions* 16 (4), 2014, 465–82.

———. "Plunder and Play: Edouard Duval Carrié's Artistic Vision." *Callaloo* 30 (2), 2007, 561–69.

Sheller, Mimi. *Citizenship From Below: Erotic Agency and Caribbean Freedom.* Durham, NC: Duke UP, 2012.

Sheppard, Charles. *Coral Reefs: A Very Short Introduction.* Oxford: Oxford UP, 2014.

Shields, Tanya. *Bodies and Bones: Feminist Rehearsal and Imagining Caribbean Belonging.* Charlottesville: U of Virginia P, 2014.

Shockley, Evie. "Going Overboard: African American Poetic Innovation and the Middle Passage." *Contemporary Literature* 52 (4), 2011, 791–817.

Sipp, Kevin. *Solemn Sounds of Silence: A Photographic Project of Reverence and Remembrance.* Photography by Eric Waters. Atlanta: Mason Murer Fine Art, 2010.

Slave Wrecks Project. National Museum of African American History and Culture, Smithsonian Institution. https://nmaahc.si.edu/explore/initiatives/slave-wrecks-project-0. Accessed May 27, 2019.

Smith, Michael P. *Mardi Gras Indians.* Gretna, LA: Pelican, 1994.

Smith, Patricia. *Blood Dazzler.* Minneapolis: Coffee House, 2008.

Smith, Roberta. "Kara Walker Makes Contrasts in Silhouettes in her own Met Show." *New York Times,* March 24, 2006. https://www.nytimes.com/2006/03/24/arts/design/kara-walker-makes-contrasts-in-silhouette-in-her-own-met-show.html. Accessed June 17, 2019.

Solomon, Eric. "Southernmost Currents: Liminal Narratives of the Florida Straits." PhD diss., Emory U, 2017.

Sontag, Susan. "The Imagination of Disaster." In *Against Interpretation and Other Essays,* 209–25. New York: Picador, 1966.

———. *On Photography.* New York: Farrar, Strauss & Giroux, 1977.

———. *Regarding the Pain of Others.* New York: Farrar, Strauss & Giroux, 2003.

Southwell Wahlman, Maud. *Signs and Symbols: African Images in African American Quilts.* Atlanta: Tinwood, 2001.

Spalding, James et al. *World Atlas of Coral Reefs.* Berkeley: U of California P and UNEP/WCMC, 2001.

Spiegelman, Art. *In the Shadow of No Towers.* New York: Pantheon, 2004.

Spillers, Hortense. *Black, White, and in Color: Essays on American Literature and Culture.* Chicago: U of Chicago P, 2003.

Stewart, Dianne. "Kumina: A Spiritual Vocabulary of Nationhood in Victorian Jamaica." In Tim Barringer and Wayne Modest, eds. *Victorian Jamaica,* ed. Tim Barringer and Wayne Modest, 602–21. Durham, NC: Duke UP, 2018.

Sublette, Ned. *The World That Made New Orleans: From Spanish Silver to Congo Square.* Chicago: Lawrence Hill, 2008.

Sullivan. Edward, Ed. *Continental Shifts: The Art of Édouard Duval Carrié.* Miami: American Art Corporation, 2007.

Sutherland, Peter. *The Afterlife of Art.* In Sullivan, *Continental Shifts,* 81–87.

Sweeney, Kate. *American Afterlife: Encounters in the Customs of Mourning.* Athens: U of Georgia P, 2014.

Swenson, John. *New Atlantis: Musicians Battle for the Survival of New Orleans.* Oxford: Oxford UP, 2011.

Taylor, Jason deCaires. Official website. https://www.underwatersculpture.com/. Accessed May 27, 2019.

———. "An Underwater Museum, Teeming With Life." TED Talk, January 22, 2016. https://www.youtube.com/watch?v=RWiI7AkDX-o. Accessed May 27, 2019.

Tinsley, Omise'eke Natasha. *Beyoncé in Formation: Remixing Black Feminism.* Austin: U of Texas P, 2018.

———. "Black Atlantic, Queer Atlantic: Queer Imagining of the Middle Passage." *GLQ: A Journal of Lesbian and Gay Studies* 14 (2–3), 2008, 191–215.

———. *Ezili's Mirrors: Imagining Black Queer Genders*. Durham, NC: Duke UP, 2018.

———. "For the Texas Bama Femme: A Black Queer Femme-inist Reading of Beyoncé's *Lemonade*." Talk, Kemp Malone Lecture Series, Emory U, March 23, 2017.

———. *Thiefing Sugar: Eroticism Between Women in Caribbean Literature*. Durham, NC: Duke UP, 2010.

Thompson, Carol. *Radcliffe Bailey: Memory as Medicine*. New York: Prestel: 2011.

———. "Minkisi and Dikenga in the Art of Radcliffe Bailey: Multiplied Exponentially." In Cooksey et al., *Kongo across the Waters*, 377–8.

Torabully, Khal. *Chair Corail, Fragments Coolies*. Paris: Ibis Rouge, 2000.

Trethewey, Natasha. *Beyond Katrina: A Meditation on the Mississippi Gulf Coast*. Athens: U of Georgia P, 2010.

———. Emory University Commencement Address. May 2017. https://www.youtube.com/watch?v=WdcYQx1OzHE&feature=youtu.be%29. Accessed June 17, 2019.

———. *Monument*. Boston: Houghton Mifflin Harcourt, 2018.

———. *Native Guard*. Boston: Mariner, 2007.

Troutt, David Dante, ed. *After the Storm: Black Intellectuals Explore the Meaning of Hurricane Katrina*. New York: New P, 2007.

Tsvetaeva, Marina. *Art in the Light of Conscience: Eight Essays on Poetry by Marina Tsvetaeva*. Trans. Angela Livingstone. Cambridge, MA: Harvard UP, 1992.

Vergne, Philippe, ed. *Kara Walker: My Complement, My Enemy, My Oppressor, My Love*. Minneapolis: Walker Art Center, 2007.

Vété-Congolo, Hanétha. "L'Acomat. Le Féal. Edouard Glissant." In Loichot, *Entours*, 251–56.

Vlach, John Michael. "The Shotgun House: An African Architectural Legacy: Part II." *Pioneer America* 8 (2), 1976, 57–70.

Wailoo, Keith et al. *Katrina's Imprint: Race and Vulnerability in America*. New Brunswick, NJ: Rutgers UP, 2010.

Walcott, Derek. *What the Twilight Says: Essays*. New York: Farrar, Straus & Giroux, 1998.

———. "Sea Is History." In *Collected Poems, 1948–1984*. New York: Farrar, Straus & Giroux, 1987.

Walker, Kara. *After the Deluge: A Visual Essay by Kara Walker*. New York: Rizzoli, 2007.

Ward, Jesmyn. *Men We Reaped: A Memoir*. New York: Bloomsbury, 2013.

———. *Salvage the Bones*. New York: Bloomsbury, 2011.

———. *Sing, Unburied, Sing*. New York: Scribner, 2017.

Ward, Martha. *Voodoo Queen: The Spirited Lives of Marie Laveau*. Jackson: UP of Mississippi , 2004.

Wardi, Anissa Janine. *Water and African American Memory: An Ecocritical Perspective*. Gainesville: UP of Florida, 2011.

Waters, Eric. "*Clarinets: A New Orleans Metaphor.*" http://www.ericwatersphotography504.com/find_us/clarinets-a-new-orleans-metaphor/. Accessed May 7, 2019.

Weaver, C. P., ed. *Thank God My Regiment an African One: The Civil War Diary of Colonel Nathan W. Daniels*. Baton Rouge: Louisiana State UP, 1998.

Webster's New World Dictionary of the English Language. Chicago: Consolidated, 1965.

Wehmmeyer, Stephen C. "Playing Dead: The Northside Skull and Bone Gang." In Cosentino, In Extremis, 143–59.

Woubshet, Dagwami. T*he Calendar of Loss: Race, Sexuality, and Mourning in the Early Era of AIDS*. Baltimore: Johns Hopkins UP, 2016

Wright, Charles. *Black Zodiac*. New York: Farrar, Strauss & Giroux, 1998.

Yaeger, Patricia. "Beasts of the Southern Wild and Dirty Ecology." *Southern Spaces,* February 13, 2013. https://southernspaces.org/2013/beasts-southern-wild-and-dirty-ecology. Accessed May 27, 2019.

———. "Circum-Atlantic Superabundance: Milk as World-Making in Alice Randall and Kara Walker." *American Literature* 78 (4), 2006, 769–98.

———. *Dirt and Desire: Reconstructing Southern Women's Writing, 1930–1990*. Chicago: U of Chicago P, 2000.

Yancy, George. *Look, a White! Philosophical Essays on Whiteness*. Philadelphia: Temple UP, 2012.

Yanique, Tiphanie. *How to Escape from a Leper Colony*. Minneapolis: Graywolf, 2010.

———. *The Land of Love and Drowning*. New York: Riverhead, 2015.

York, Jake Adam. "Medicine as Memory: Radcliffe Bailey at Atlanta's High Museum of Art." *Southern Spaces,* January 26, 2012. https://southernspaces.org/2012/medicine-memory-radcliffe-bailey-atlantas-high-museum-art. Accessed May 27, 2019.

Young, James E. *At Memory's Edge: After-Images of the Holocaust*. New Haven, CT: Yale UP: 2000.

———. "The Counter-Monument: Memory against itself in Germany Today." *Critical Inquiry* 18 (2) 1992, 267–96.

———. *The Texture of Memory: Holocaust Memorials and Meaning*. New Haven, CT: Yale UP, 1993.

Young, Kevin. "Triangular Trade: Coloring, Remarking, and Narrative in the Writings of Kara Walker." In Vergne, *Kara Walker,* 37–51.

Yusoff, Kathryn. *A Billion Black Anthropocenes or None*. Minneapolis: U of Minnesota P, 2018.

Yvon, Tristan. *La Production d'Indigo en Guadeloupe et Martinique*. Paris: Khartala, 2015.

Zeitlin, Benh. *Beasts of the Southern Wild*. DVD. New York: Cinereach Productions, 2012.

Index

Recent books in the series

New World Studies

Water Graves: The Art of the Unritual in the Greater Caribbean
Valérie Loichot

The Sacred Act of Reading: Spirituality, Performance, and Power in Afro-Diasporic Literature
Anne Margaret Castro

Caribbean Jewish Crossings: Literary History and Creative Practice
Sarah Phillips Casteel and Heidi Kaufman, editors

Mapping Hispaniola: Third Space in Dominican and Haitian Literature
Megan Jeanette Myers

Mourning El Dorado: Literature and Extractivism in the Contemporary American Tropics
Charlotte Rogers

Edwidge Danticat: The Haitian Diasporic Imaginary
Nadège T. Clitandre

Idle Talk, Deadly Talk: The Uses of Gossip in Caribbean Literature
Ana Rodríguez Navas

Crossing the Line: Early Creole Novels and Anglophone Caribbean Culture in the Age of Emancipation
Candace Ward

Staging Creolization: Women's Theater and Performance from the French Caribbean
Emily Sahakian

American Imperialism's Undead: The Occupation of Haiti and the Rise of Caribbean Anticolonialism
Raphael Dalleo

A Cultural History of Underdevelopment: Latin America in the U.S. Imagination
John Patrick Leary

The Spectre of Races: Latin American Anthropology and Literature between the Wars
Anke Birkenmaier